BURNING
POINT

"... And where we had thought to find an abomination, we shall find a god; where we had thought to slay another, we shall slay ourselves; where we had thought to travel outward, we shall come to the center of our own existence; where we had thought to be alone, we shall be with all the world."

Joseph Campbell
The Hero with a Thousand Faces

BURNING POINT

Dennis N. Hinkle

ALAMO SQUARE PRESS
New Mexico

Library of Congress Card Number: 00-102017

ISBN:1-886360-08-1

10 9 8 7 6 5 4 3 2 1

Acknowledgment

I wish to express my deepest gratitude for the love, kindness and wisdom of those many people who have facilitated my spiritual journey. All that I have written is true, except for names that have been changed to protect the privacy of several people. My name has not been changed.

This book would not exist had it not been for Bert Herrman and the encouragement of Peter Carroll and my friends, especially Dr. Gesine Schaffer and Bill Schaffer, Teresa Lauer, Dr. John Ensign, Lee Kaiser, Bill Wilhelm, and my sister, Judy. I give special thanks to my dear friends, Carl Jech, an ordained minister and graduate of the Harvard Divinity School, and Sharon Duerksen, a devout, loving, aware Christian who volunteered to type and edit this manuscript.

Finally, no words can adequately express my gratitude to Keith, David, Jack and, especially, Joyce. My thankfulness for Gary is boundless, and to him, this book is lovingly dedicated.

Chapter One

"The inability to love is the central problem, because that inability masks a certain terror, and that terror is terror of being touched. And if you can't be touched, you can't be changed. And if you can't be changed, you can't be alive."

James Baldwin

I'm glad to be home at last. I had an emotional day with my clients in private practice. I've been a clinical psychologist for many years; but, even after all the songs of people's souls I've heard, compassion still rips my guts. That white-haired old man today told me his "roommate," a man ten-years older than he, died two years ago. I asked him how long they'd been roommates. Forty-three years, he said. He carried a brown paper sack with him. In that sack were old photographs of him and his lover from the '40s. They served in the Navy in the South Pacific during World War II, Guadalcanal. He said he had recently found a single hair caught in the wood of the headboard of their bed, a hair from the head of his dead lifemate. He carefully opened a neatly folded envelope and showed it to me, and then he wept uncontrollably as he held that single hair in his trembling hand. Forty-three years of such love, and he was asking me to give him a reason to live.

He never says, "gay," "homosexual" or "queer," but whispers, "that way." When I mentioned this, he said with pain and bitterness, "My life has been entirely controlled by fear." The effects of fear are longer lasting and spread more widely than those of reward and pleasure. Fear, it seems, has the greater survival value. Tyrants understand and use our fear of alienation, pain, and death—as do parents and priests.

I was a member of the conforming, silent generation of the '50s. Silence was my shield, but never again. Lives are destroyed by silence, the soil that grows dysfunctional people, families, institutions, and societies—the fertilizing shit hidden deep in the toilets of our psyches because of fear. This book is a true record of my long struggle to become an authentic human being. Being human is not a birthright, but a considerable achievement, and oppression and fear are not limited to people of color, women and gays. In countless ways, everyone has been oppressed by others, and, in turn, oppresses. The essential horror of the Holocaust, that metaphor for our human condition, was the betrayal of humanity, yet we all betray the humanity of others. In India recently, I saw a group of old people starving to death. Their bones showed, like the victims of the Nazi death camps. They were begging for food. Their eyes were crazed, frantic, and pleading as they looked into mine. That evening, to the sensuous sounds of a sitar, I thought of them as handsome waiters served our ten-course dinner on silver trays.

I wish I could shout, cry, and scream away the pain of the memories of my past, but if this record of my struggle to become a real person can be of use for you, then I welcome the suffering of having to relive it all. I learned long ago that suffering is a master teacher of life. I spend my days helping people end their repressions, face their betrayals, fears and confusions, and learn the life-giving lessons of their sorrow.

My particular betrayal was of love, that most serious of betrayals, and that almost cost me my life. Gay people are not the only ones who must come out of their closets. This world is filled with billions of closeted human beings, conforming souls imprisoned by fear and ignorance. Look around. Perhaps glance in the mirror of your soul. We're really not very different, only the plots and circumstances of our human dramas vary. And our humanity is what it's all about—the destination and the path.

To understand my struggle to become a person, I must talk at length about my sexual love life, the psychology of it. Actually, I can hardly wait to talk about it. I've had my fill of the death-kissing erotophobia of my Puritan Christian culture. Sex, for me, is the life-force, and its moment of fusion is as close to divine revelation as we mortals come. (I've even talked to God on several occasions. His name was Gary, or was it Jack, or Keith?) Sex is what we are, not what we do. The Chinese call it the act of many significances. So for those who will attempt to dismiss this book as just a sex story, I hope that someday they will gain insight into themselves and end their harmful ignorance and indifference. That indifference is killing people. The primary purpose of my story is to add to the understanding of what we human beings are—that most important of questions. Our sexually passionate love is a central part of the descriptive answer.

Today's mail brought Father's Day cards from my three fine sons and a pile of birthday cards, both sentimental and humorous. In my sixth decade, birthday cards seem like friendly, gentle reminders of death. "Live today," "cherish the moment," "time eats you alive," they whisper. I kept tossing them aside and then picking them up again. How did this old man's body grow on me—a boy of 18? When I look in a mirror, I think I'm a guest at a bizarre costume party, and I didn't get to pick the costume.

That last client of mine today was 18. What a beautiful face he has. There he stands, vital, full of himself, bright and promising, at the brink of life—and scared shitless. "Go with the force, Luke!" I tried to tell him, "trust yourself; be yourself." I know he sees me as old as Obi Wan Kenobi, like a wise grandfather; but, from where I sit, I'm only his slightly older brother. He's off to college, his first time away from home. I understand him more deeply than he can imagine. His struggle to become a person is just beginning. I was like him once. Youth is so beautiful but blind. How vividly I remember my life at his age, a good place to begin even though I'm still feeling fear after all these years about telling the whole truth.

How long ago was it when I first left home at 18, like him, to begin my search for happiness? Was it that long ago? Yes, September of 1953, Purdue University. The Korean war was winding down, Eisenhower was president. The monster Joseph Stalin died. The TV era was just beginning, and I watched the Coronation of Elizabeth II on black and white TV. What a different world it was then, smaller, more provincial. People were kinder, but more naive. Honor, honesty, reputation, excellence, productivity, consideration for others, discipline, respect for authority, and conformity were important then, especially conformity. There was blatant racism and the McCarthy inquisition against commies and homos—a movement supported by the right wing. People conformed to strict rules of conduct and lived in fear of authority. My father was a good example of this.

Hard to believe in today's world, but in my freshman year at Purdue, there was a daring act of such adolescent rebellion that we believed it bordered on sedition. I still remember the adrenaline rush and the pounding of my teenage heart. It was a Saturday night in springtime. Some hot-blooded guys invaded a girls' dorm—the girls invited them—and stole a pair of pink underpants. Hundreds of us marched triumphantly behind this flapping golden fleece to the very residence of the president of the university, himself, where in frightened defiance of our university father we sang Purdue football songs and threw those pink panties right down on his front lawn! We, too, were sexual young men—at least we desperately wanted to be, and we wanted this old bull, who controlled the harem, to know this, but with the dignity and exalted power of his office, he wouldn't lower himself by acknowledging us, although his wife did peer out from behind the formal white curtains of a second-story window from time to time. So long ago...such a different world.

I remember my excitement as my mom, dad and my kid sister helped me carry my things into my dorm room in Cary Quadrangle. The quad was beautifully built in the Tudor style, and I felt as though I were going to Oxford or Cambridge instead of Purdue University in West Lafayette, Indiana. My last year in high school hadn't been good at all—the worst of my life, almost the end of my life—and I welcomed the instant status of being a university student. I didn't even mind wearing the silly green beanie with the yellow plastic propeller on top that freshmen had to wear for the first week, even though my father kept teasing me about it, "It makes you look like a pea-brained idiot, Denny!" I could hardly wait for my family to be gone. This was my first time on my own. I wanted my new life to begin. I was always beginning my life over again; but, I told myself, this time would be different. It would! "Gentlemen, gentlemen, off on a spree, doomed from here to eternity...baa...baa...baa." Was I a doomed black sheep, I wondered as our adolescent voices joined in this old college song. I knew I was different, painfully different, a fact I could only accept, but not understand.

I have such compassion for that young man I used to be. He was so hopeful...and so scared. He thought he was about to begin the heroic journey he called his life, to discover who he was and to find happiness. He didn't realize he'd been on his way since birth, and his journey would be very long and would take him to the center of his darkness before he would see the light.

He'd forgotten so much of his past because he didn't want to remember. Youth is a condition of nearsightedness in which, sadly, we can't see the sunlit patterns of the tapestries of our lives, nor how the warp and woof of one life is intricately interwoven with those of others to form the restless whole.

There were very few women in universities in those days, especially at Purdue, an engineering school. The sexes were strictly segregated. Dormitory hours were enforced. Most women in those days were virgins when they married and wanted to be, but there were the cherished practices of fantasy: necking, petting, and—if a guy was very lucky—heavy petting. Guys masturbated often but hid the guilty fact from one another; such was still the power of the authority of churches in those days. Life was formal and disciplined.

I made friends easily at Purdue. We were all excited, lonely and scared. It was odd seeing mostly guys on campus with their leather-sheathed slide rules hanging from their belts like the short swords of Samurai warriors. The relative absence of women reminded me of an old tune: "Ruben, Ruben, I been thinking, what a strange world this would be, if the men were all transported far beyond the Northern Sea!" That might not be so bad, I thought, not recognizing my fantasy as queer. I was simply happy to be away from home, with friends, and on my own at last.

My classes—chemistry, calculus, metallurgy, and that sort of thing—were completely boring, except for an English class taught by a white-haired professor. After reading one of my essays, he called me aside one day and told me I'd never be happy as an engineer. "You're too full of life, passion, and conflict, son. You should be a writer. You like people more than things. Think about it." His recognition of my passion and conflict made me positively paranoid, worrying if he knew that my conflict was about passion. I didn't even have the concept of a closet in those days. I lived in silence in a steel vault and didn't know it.

It was my father who told me that engineering was the smart way to go in those days. He came from terrible poverty in the hills of West Virginia. As a young man, he moved to Akron, Ohio to survive during the Great Depression. He pulled tires off the hot rubber molds of B.F. Goodrich and was grateful to have a job. Many years later, just before he retired from Goodrich, he was offered a vice presidency of the company. He lived his life in fear of poverty and saw engineering as a path for me to job security. Earning money was the purpose of his lonely life. For many years I avoided the financial and business sections of a newspaper.

I became close to three or four guys in my residence hall that freshman year and spent more time with them than I did with my school work. One of them, Charlie Benson, was muscular and handsome. He had chestnut brown eyes. I couldn't understand why he liked me so much, except for the fact he knew I admired him. Charlie became a hero in our hall. While he was showering one Sunday morning, some of the guys saw fresh fingernail scratches on each side of his powerful back. They knew that the night before, Charlie made his first trip to 212 Alabama Street—an address memorized by all freshmen, for there was the biggest and best whorehouse in town. Whole fraternities went there to initiate their virgin pledges into the love-life of men. When

Charlie explained his injuries by saying, "I guess the gal I was with got a little excited and carried away," his scratches instantly became chevrons of the highest honor bestowed on him by an acknowledged expert on male sexual performance. When he walked down the hall, guys would whisper, "That's Charlie Benson, the guy who's so good, he can drive even a whore crazy!"

Charlie wanted to take me to 212 Alabama Street. He said he'd get me fixed up with the same girl he was going to have. I joked that I'd get some disease for sure. He laughed and said I could go first. About 10:30 on a Friday night, and after a few illegal swigs of beer, Charlie and I—eager heroes—knocked on the infamous black door of this den of iniquity, yearning to penetrate the lower life forms inside with the magic swords of our young loins. The stylish madam, in her 50's, dressed in black and flashing long, cherry-red fingernails, ushered us into the large, red reception room where nervous young men waited in silence for their trial by vagina. Occasionally, a scantily clad young girl, looking tired, would come up to the next young man, force a smile, introduce herself, and lead him back into the maze. We studied his face as he took one last look at his buddies before his solitary descent into the warm wet darkness.

The madam came over to Charlie: "Lorraine isn't working tonight. I know you liked her. We've got a slow-moving fraternity in here tonight, and we're short on girls, so it's going to be at least an hour." Charlie looked annoyed, but I jumped at this chance to end my sexual apprehension with honor: "To hell with it, Charlie. It's not worth it. Let's go!" I had only had sex once with a woman, when I was 13. Having assembly-line sex with a stranger was beyond my capability or desire. The loneliness of it seemed unbearable. Besides, I only went there to be with Charlie and to have something to share with him.

Charlie knew I'd taken up oil painting. When we got back to the dorm, he asked to see what I'd done. He seemed impressed and asked me questions about myself. I asked him if it were really true that he had scratch marks across his back. He revealed himself, then poked me and laughed, "You just want to see me with my shirt off! I know your kind!" I got angry with him and protested his unfair characterization of me, but he just laughed and started wrestling with me. He shoved me down on my bunk, and we started to grapple in earnest, him laughing all the time. He pinned my shoulders down, and as I struggled to shove him away, my hands pressed against his powerful chest muscles. While looking at his smiling face, I suddenly relaxed my body and let my hands rest on his sides. I felt the expansions and contractions of his rib cage as he breathed. Neither of us moved; we just looked into each other's eyes. My heart began to pound with excitement. He was stronger than I. His expression at first was serious, then an impish grin, and he leaned forward and nuzzled my nose with his—an Eskimo kiss! He laughed, jumped off me, and said pensively as he stood at the door to leave, "You are different, Denny. You're weird. Do you know that?" We both knew what the threat was. I've lost many friends because of it. I told him he was the weird one. He avoided me after that. The charge of nonconformity in those days was very serious.

Actually, I became a clinical psychologist because of Charlie Benson—

well, partly because of him. I remember the particular evening well. I was trying to study, but the texts had no relevance to the issues of values, identity, and sexuality in my adolescent life. I faintly heard the sound of the Steinway grand piano in the lower lounge of our residence hall. Someone was playing Rachmaninoff. Welcoming the excuse, I went to the lounge and found Charlie playing. He stopped when I came in. I begged him to continue, and since we were alone, he finally relented. For the next hour, Charlie's soul concentrated itself into his powerful hands and agile fingers, and that Steinway sang with his emotions. I had never imagined that Charlie's body contained such sensitive and complex feelings. When he finished, our eyes locked in the intimacy of the moment. My heart was in my gaze and went out to him. He probably didn't play all that well, but he was my hero. "I see you understand music, too," he said.

I asked how he could study engineering with all those emotions inside him. He said he was just trying to be practical; he didn't think he could earn a living as a musician or composer, even though that was what he really wanted to do. I told him there had to be more to life than just keeping the body going; there just had to be. "What are you searching for, Denny?" he asked. I felt understood. That was rare for me. I believed I had experienced too much too soon in my life and that this special knowledge of mine made it difficult for others to understand me. I believed that for years. I was also afraid to be understood, especially then in my life, so I never explained anything to anyone about what I felt. I certainly couldn't consciously admit to myself that I wanted to worship Charlie's fantastic body and make love to him until I died of ecstasy or my dick dropped off. So I told Charlie truthfully that I didn't know what I was searching for. If I did, I said, I'd know where to begin to look for it. He smiled, cocked his head in his impish style, and asked if I had a favorite piece of music—one that really meant something to me. I told him he'd already played one of my favorites, one I had listened to often when I was in high school. He asked me not to tell him which one; he sat there thinking and searching my face. Then he laughed with the satisfaction of having suddenly solved a puzzle and played Ravel's *Pavane pour une Infante Defunte*, a composition of dignified sorrow. When I could no longer mask my feelings, I lowered my eyes, and I remember him saying, "I knew it! Did you know this piece is about someone who died—a princess! I used to play it after I broke up with my girl. I know what you're all about, kiddo! You need to get laid! You do!" It was shortly after this that Charlie took me to 212 Alabama Street, that McDonald's for the male libido, guaranteed to make every little Mac feel like a big Mac.

Later that evening, as I was trying to sleep, I kept remembering Charlie's expressions as he caressed that Steinway and my resonant feelings. Nothing is more complex, important, or fascinating than a human being, I thought. Suddenly, I felt a change taking place in me. I didn't recognize that it was motivated by my unconscious love and sexual desire for Charlie. I sat bolt upright in bed and was amazed to hear myself saying with certainty to my astonished roommate—a poor, frightened Bible thumper long lost in the putrid quagmire of religious fundamentalism, "John, I'm not going to study electrical engineering! I'm going to be a clinical psychologist!" I was resolved, and I committed myself to a life of intimacy and the boundless possibilities for knowledge of myself and others. As a psychologist, I could look long and deep into the secret places of others like Charlie and not risk having my own closet door opened. I could probe with my mind, but not be probed. The symbolic fucking is transparent now. So is the homophobic idol worship of the muscular heterosexual stud. Idol worship is often a sign of social oppression.

On the last day of my freshman year, as I sat in my room waiting for my ride home, Charlie Benson, who had avoided me for months, poked his handsome head into my room, smiled that ideal smile of his, and said, "Hey kiddo! You really are weird, you know!" Then he winked, laughed, and was gone forever—except from my soul. Charlie was a hero of mine at a time in life when I still needed and believed in heroes.

Charlie Benson was right about me. I did need to get laid—desperately, but not for the same reason as all the rest of sperm-brained guys on campus who wandered around with their aching balls and insistent hardons and who found some small measure of relief by quietly jerking off under their blankets at night so as not to wake their sleeping roommates, who were probably jerking off, too. It took skill to keep the metal bunks from squeaking too rhythmically and to hold your breath when you came instead of gasping and screaming in ecstasy the way you really wanted to. There was a guy in my calculus class who once figured out how many hundreds of gallons of semen all the young men of Purdue ejaculated in a typical school year, changing forever my view of my classmates. He came from Chicago, so he also figured out how many 55 gallon drums it would take to hold a year's supply from the males of that city. He used statistics from Kinsey's book on male sexuality. He probably made a good engineer.

The reason I needed to get laid was because of my special knowledge— my temptation. This special knowledge, my experience of too much too soon in my young life, made me feel lonely, vulnerable and alien. My shame and ultimate secret, my cross and curse, was that I had actually messed around with other males. I didn't think of myself as a pervert, fairy, pansy, queer, faggot, homo or—God forbid—a sissy, the ultimate male degradation and condemnation of the feminine. I knew I wasn't one of those. I was a man, maybe an unusual man, a young man, but a man. I would have hated anyone who said I wasn't, and I would have enjoyed their slow, agonizing death, or so it seemed at the time. I wasn't a pervert. I had been taught and I believed— as did most everyone—that perverts, fairies, queers were sick, ugly, insane, pathetic criminals. Their sins were so monstrous and animalistic that they were unspeakable and unprintable. Their actions were the abominations of inverted degenerates, irredeemable crimes against nature and God, perversions of the soul beyond understanding by all decent people. They were properly excluded from all benefits of civilized society and were universally held in contempt, for they were worse than murderers and were forever despised by all God-fearing Christians. They were depraved heretics who were not of our kind, and we put them in prisons and mental hospitals where they belonged. They were sometimes castrated in an attempt to cure them of their disease—although this seemed more like a punishment to me. Pretty heavy crap for a kid who'd messed around. No, I wasn't a pervert, and I was never going to be one. I was a regular guy who was going to get married after I graduated from college and could properly support a wife and children.

Women didn't put out in those days. They exchanged their virginity for a legally binding contract of financial support for themselves and their children. What were we to do? So, many of us hot-blooded members of the teenage testosterone tribe messed around a little with each other. I mean, normal, red-blooded young guys have to get their rocks off, so we helped each other out a little bit, sometimes. No harm done unless it became a habit or something like that. I mean, it was okay as long as you didn't get carried away or anything like that. If you just did it now and then and didn't really need to do it, it was okay. That's what I believed, what I had to believe.

What really bothered me was when guys called each other cocksuckers. That really got to me. Suck just one cock, even put part of it in your mouth just once, and you're a cocksucker for sure, and there isn't a damned thing you can ever do to change that fact for the whole rest of your damned life. That's why I wanted guys to do it to me, but I didn't want to return the favor. I did do it with a couple of guys, though—well, more than a couple. But I figured I didn't do it enough times to make me a real honest-to-god, died-in-the-wool, holy-communion-type cocksucker though, and I didn't get carried away, at least, not that much. We were just messing around. Anyway, at 18, I still had three more years to go before I had to live up to adult standards. Kids were expected to screw up now and then, and they could be forgiven, but not after they became 21.

Standards were strictly enforced then. In 1953, Senator Joe McCarthy, the great commie and homo hunter, was still on the loose. My high school and college years were darkened by the shadow of this grand inquisitor from the Midwest. His power grew like a cancer on the face of the nation as he developed a large and loyal following. Senator McCarthy cowed his opponents by sensational and highly-publicized personal attacks, usually unsubstantiated, while evading demands for tangible proof. Encouraged by many Republicans, he accused the Franklin D. Roosevelt and Harry S. Truman administrations of "20 years of treason." Ironically, literally under the senator's nose was Roy M. Cohn, his chief counsel, who was homosexual.

It wasn't until 1954, during the televised Army-McCarthy hearings, that I finally saw the Senator opposed. McCarthy, fighting to retain his ebbing credibility, made a particularly vicious attack on some poor soul. This so astonished the Counsel for the Army, Joseph Welsh, that he turned to the Senator and said, "Have you no sense of decency, sir?" I cried when I saw this, and I'm still grateful for his humanity. I like to cry. A day without emotion is like food without spice. My father used to tell me I was nothing but a goddamned cry-baby. He never cried; he was a lip-biter.

When the United States Senate voted in December 1954 to condemn McCarthy, 67 to 22, his influence declined sharply. But the vast support given to this demagogue struck terror in my heart. No one seemed to doubt that all homosexuals were degenerate criminals who deserved expulsion from the human community. No one questioned that. Even a communist was better than a fag in those days. I thought I was a decent guy, a regular guy, and so were my buddies—even the ones I messed around with. There was no way we could even think that we might be queers, sissies, perverts. Not us. Never! Homosexuals were unnatural insane criminals; everybody believed that. Cocksucker really bothered me, though. I worried about that a lot.

So Purdue University was to be the new chapter in my life, "a clean slate" my dad said. I remember my first day there, waiting for my new roommate and wondering what he would be like. I was relieved to be away from my parents and dreamed about my future. What I would become was entirely in my own, 18-year-old hands. I'm the captain of my ship, I thought, master of my destiny. It's easy to be idealistic when you don't know anything.

I didn't know anyone at Purdue, except a couple of guys from the high school in Dayton, Ohio, where I suffered my senior year, and David Rose from Richmond, Indiana, where I spent my sophomore and junior years. David was my best friend. We'd been classmates and amateur radio operators together. I practically lived over at David's house. David's mother, Ruth, was closer to me than my own mother. I really loved that woman. David had wanted me to room with him in the new X quad, but I picked a residence hall as far away from his as I could.

David Rose was tall and lean with an angular face, high cheek bones, light sand-colored hair, and blue-green eyes. He was shy and sensitive, but highly intelligent. His perfect complexion was as smooth and soft as a baby's butt. David and I first had sex together in our sophomore year in high school. I remember how his white skin would turn flaming pink with embarrassment whenever I stared at the astonishing length of his erect penis. I told him we should send a picture of it to *Ripley's Believe It Or Not*, but he thought I was obscene and unfeeling. But now, with this clean slate at Purdue, I was determined that our messing around with each other was going to stop forever; it simply had to.

David said he loved me. Whenever he said that, I said nothing. I thought he was weak. Real men need to get their nuts off, I believed, but they certainly didn't love other men—or much else, for that matter. Love makes you vulnerable and weak; real men are strong and independent, they control relationships that way; that's what I believed. Nothing wrong, though, with letting your best buddy help you out now and then. Besides, the severe penalties attached to those criminal acts made the risks even more exciting and rebellious for us; it proved the intensity of your fuck buddy's need and forged a lasting bond of sperm between us degenerate brothers of guilt and shame, as we violated the ancient taboo against sex with your own kind. Heavy stuff for us lonely teenagers, who were supposed to be thinking about differential calculus and the theory of chemical bonding and writing letters home to our proud mothers.

As I sat alone in my room that first night at Purdue, I felt waves of loneliness. There was a knock at my door, and I opened it with excitement. There stood David, smiling shyly. I felt some apprehension and resentment, but I invited him in. Within 20 minutes, we were squeezed in my squeaking, metal bunk bed, naked, and I let him get me off. I didn't do anything for him. I didn't even touch him, because I was annoyed with him for what we were doing on our first day at Purdue, but he wanted to stay the night anyway, and I let him. He slept with his arms around me. The next day, I was in total despair, because I had been so weak willed. "You have no will power, no discipline! Life is going to cut you down to size!" my father often told me. I feared he might be right.

I tried to avoid David after that. Each day I struggled against my sexuality. Defensively, I absorbed myself in the intellectual life of the university. I attended lectures ranging from Neo-Thomistic philosophy, Celtic symbolism, and mathematical manifolds to the theories of nuclear electron spin—anything that would focus my attention elsewhere. The more I suppressed my impulses, the more intense were my relapses and the darker the despair that followed.

Down the hall from David's room were two roommates I often spoke with when I visited David. They were exceptionally handsome athletes, and I admired the warmth and closeness of their friendship. One weekend, when David's bumpkin roommate was gone, David talked me into staying the weekend with him. I mentioned that I hadn't seen the two young men recently. Quite unconcerned, David said they had been expelled from the university. A dorm counselor had walked into their room unannounced one afternoon and caught the poor luckless souls, to use the coy legal phrase, "in flagrante delicto," which literally means "while the crime is blazing." They were immediately expelled for the felony of sexual love. David said their university transcripts were stamped "HOMOSEXUAL," assuring they would never again be admitted to any institution of higher learning. There were others who met this swift fate; one couple was from my own residence hall. I knew them both. These expulsions terrified me, and I began to worry in a paranoid way that our rooms were electronically bugged by university officials. When I shared these fears with David, he just laughed and said it was too late to worry about that after all the noise we made.

(Even today, this love is still a crime in almost half the states of this land of liberty, and those laws, by one vote, were reaffirmed in 1986 (Bowers v. Hardwick) as constitutional by our Supreme Court. The conservative justices linked law to religion by citing the ancient Judeo-Christian historical tradition of contempt for homosexuality as their justification. Did these justices not realize that such an argument could also be used to support racism, bigotry, the continued suppression of women and minorities, and all of our other traditional forms of injustice?)

Soon after this, I learned that an undergraduate and a graduate student in my quadrangle had been caught together while they were "blazing" and were expelled—their careers ruined forever. David told me about another student who had been caught in his dorm. The young man had misread the warmth and friendliness of one of his best buddies and made a pass; his best buddy turned him in. I panicked and told David we should deny everything if we were ever accused of loving one another. (People thought of sex as an act of love in those days.) We solemnly promised never to reveal the truth no matter what the consequences. I told David that if we didn't stop our relationship, we'd both wind up as homosexuals living our lives in solitary prison cells. I warned him over and over about the terrible, lifelong consequences and begged him to stop. I told him he ought to try sex with a woman, and I mentioned 212 Alabama Street. I remember him crying out, "I'd rather give up sex than do it with a stranger! How can you suggest I go to a whore? Don't you know it isn't sex I really want? Don't you know that by now? Don't you understand me? Love is what I want, Denny! It's not the sex! It's the love! Okay, we can stop the sex forever—I don't care, but don't stop seeing me! I couldn't stand that." I was moved but frightened by his caring for me. I told him I wouldn't end our friendship, but I didn't want us to be together so often; because, when I was around him, I couldn't stop thinking about sex. He laughed and said I couldn't stop thinking about sex even when he wasn't around—which was true. He asked if we could do it just one last time. I wanted to, but I said no. I'll never forget the look on David's face—I'd hurt him, and he was now afraid of the loss of his first love.

When I returned from David's that Sunday afternoon, my dorm counselor called me into his room to find out where I'd been. I was terrified. My roommate had become worried about me when I hadn't returned Friday or Saturday nights and reported me missing, but not much came of it.

The two counselors in my residence hall were doctoral students in clinical psychology. I spent hours listening to them talk about psychology and psychotherapy. I asked so many questions that one, in exasperation, gave me a gift of two books to read: Essays on Man by Ernst Cassier and the Modern Library edition of The Basic Writings of Sigmund Freud. Those books—I still have them—changed my life. I'd never read anything that excited my imagination as much as those books. I skipped classes to finish them.

Psychoanalysis was the rage in the '50s, very in. Freud's concept of the unconscious mind and his descriptions of the defensive strategies of repression and denial revealed a fantastic realm of reality deep within me. These powerful concepts made intuitive sense. Here, I hoped, was the key to understanding my problem—my participation in criminal sexual acts. I knew I was weird, because I couldn't figure out why most people condemned these passions. I couldn't see the harm, only the joy. So I began to suspect that I might have an unconscious tendency toward...perversion. If that were true, I thought, I would kill myself, because I wouldn't live as a criminal. That was the reality of the '50s. And over four decades later, many men still choose suicide rather than face what they mistakenly believe is the fate of a cocksucking queer.

I lived and breathed psychoanalysis as if my survival depended on it. It was the beginning of the ultimate adventure of understanding what we are. Oral, anal, phallic, and genital stages of psychosexual development, sex and aggression, Eros and Thanatos, wanting to fuck your mother but fearing your daddy would rip your balls off—exciting food for my teenage mind.

Once, pretending only an academic interest, I dared to ask the dorm counselor how Freud explained homosexuality. I knew by his sudden smile that I hadn't conned him, but I kept my mask firmly in place as he spoke about an arrested development caused by an unresolved Oedipus complex. It was true that, from an early age, I hadn't wanted to identify with my father, but the thought of wanting to have sex with my mother just made me want to laugh! The dorm counselor admitted, though, that Freud's explanation for homosexuality was inadequate. Freud, he said, once wrote a letter to the mother of a homosexual son to tell her that homosexuality was not a pathology and was nothing to be ashamed of. The counselor, smiling at me again, added that most men have homosexual feelings and that, when he was in the Army, he knew many men who acted on those feelings. He indicated he'd been tempted himself and asked if I had ever been troubled by those feelings. He seemed so friendly, and I wanted to talk, but I panicked. I believed he was leading me on, trying to get me to admit what he suspected. That was why he wanted to know where I'd spent the weekend. He even asked me about girl friends and whether I'd ever had sex with a woman. That sly bastard, I thought. If I admitted even one thing to him, I believed I'd be kicked out of Purdue, finished forever, maybe even sent to jail. He told me he'd even been tempted, himself, but I suspected he'd do anything to trap me. I worried that McCarthy probably has informers at Purdue! In that era, it was an advantage to be paranoid.

The counselor continued in his friendly style and said my roommate told him I rarely studied. I was slowly flunking out, but I was damned good at denial and lived, like most people, in a rose-colored world of optimistic illusions. He had looked at my paintings. The psychology of art was a special interest of his. I suspected he probably even searched my desk. He believed one of my paintings indicated I was depressed and in conflict about something. He insisted I go to the University Psychology Clinic at least once. There, I would see a doctoral student who would be supervised by the clinical psychology faculty. I agreed to do this to get him off my back. Part of me was curious about psychologists anyway, and part of me was screaming for someone to save me from myself.

I was very nervous about going to the psychology clinic. If anybody saw me go in, they'd think for sure I was fruitcake crazy. The clinic was in the basement of an old, brick building. I watched the entrance until nobody was around and darted in. Four or five other guys were waiting, one was from my dorm. He waved, smiled and continued reading his book. He was a guy I was attracted to; since I knew he wasn't crazy, I began to relax. Soon, an attractive woman of about 30 with warm, searching, brown eyes introduced herself to me as Miss Evans and escorted me back to her small, plainly furnished office. She had light-brown hair and wore a tan, fashionably tailored suit that accented her tall, slender figure. Her office was cramped, so we sat quite close together facing one another in comfortable, overstuffed chairs. My legs kept bumping hers.

I remember our session vividly. I can't recall the dialogue exactly, but our first meeting was like this:

"Aren't you a doctor—and where's the couch I'm supposed to lie on?" I asked.

"Well, I'm almost a Ph.D., a doctor, the good kind—not the medical kind.

We no longer use couches. We think this seating arrangement is more congenial. Are you comfortable?" She noticed I was carefully looking around the
room. "Is there something you're looking for?" I didn't reply. "I sense you're
not feeling at ease right now. Is there something I can do to make you feel
more at ease with me?"

In a flash, this thought hammered through my mind: Yes! Take off your
fine, expensive clothes and show me how to fuck so good I'll scream for
more. Make it feel so good I'll want to die for it! That's my problem, you
silly prig—and you can solve it! Make me love your tits! To hell with my
childhood and all that crap! You don't have to say a word—just fuck like your
life depends on it. You can cure me real quick. I bet I'd only have to shoot a
half dozen hot wads into you and I'd be cured forever! I'll never tell anybody
what happens in here. Don't you know that?

I felt that I was beginning to go crazy right in front of her. "Are we alone
in here?" I asked.

"Do you see others here?" She looked suddenly concerned, probably
thinking I was hallucinating. I explained that I meant would others be listening to us, would they know what we were doing?

"Well, I was going to come to that. What you say in here is kept in
complete confidence. I would like, however, your permission to record our
sessions, so I can go over them with my supervisor. That would help me to
help you more effectively. Each of the sessions will then be erased. May I
have your permission to do that?"

I told her absolutely not. I suspected the university officials might be
trying to get the goods on me. I told her I wouldn't say another word if anyone knew what we talked about. She seemed hurt. "Is there something about
me that makes you not trust me? Did I do something, or do I remind you of
someone you've known?"

I told her I trusted her, but I just didn't want anything to be used against
me, that was all. I said she reminded me of my Aunt Julia,

"I'll try very hard to understand you accurately, Denny. How did you feel
about your Aunt Julia?"

When I said I liked my aunt a lot, she said, "I'm glad. I hope you and I
can come to feel that way about each other. Since you don't want me to
record our sessions, I'll need to take notes as we talk." When she mentioned
notes, I became paranoid again and told her I didn't want anything written
down, because I didn't want anything to be used against me.

"Used against you? Can you tell me a little more about that?" she asked.

Be careful, I thought. These psychologists are damned clever. They've
been trained to be. Watch out for her!

By the end of the session, she was exasperated. "Denny, you obviously
need time to decide if you want to trust me or not. I gave you my word that
what you say will be kept in strict confidence. Only one faculty member will
supervise me, and he is bound to complete confidentiality. I hope you'll choose
to trust me; I would like working with you. I'll schedule this time for you next
week. If you don't show up, I'll feel sad, but I'll understand why. Good-bye
now." Miss Evans held out her hand to shake mine, normally such a simple

thing, but I hesitated, fearing contact. I felt the warmth of her hand in mine; I wanted to press it into my crotch and make her groan with desire, but I knew that would never happen.

The dorm counselor stopped by my room later and asked what I thought of Miss Evans and said she was a highly-skilled therapist, well regarded by the faculty. He said he had recommended that I see a female therapist, but his reasons for this were vague, so I became even more suspicious of him. He sensed this and was uncomfortable. He asked if I would continue to see Miss Evans. I told him I hadn't decided.

I believed that therapy was too risky for me. If anything got out about my sexual tendencies, I'd be expelled from the university, yet I was tempted because of my discovery of psychoanalysis. I was curious about repression in my own life, so I began a daily exercise I called "thinking the unthinkable." I forced myself to concentrate on and to visualize everything I wanted to avoid imagining, every repulsive topic, crime, horror, inhumanity. I argued against my deepest beliefs and highest values until I could hardly bear the conflict and tension I was creating. After several weeks of this, I gained access to some of the subterranean realms of my mind. I was stunned by their magnitude and complexity. Like my dreams, terrifying symbolic visual images that moved and changed could now easily flood my consciousness, but along with the bizarre and grotesque came images of luminosity and beauty. I couldn't understand the personal significance of these images, but my emotions flowed from horror to euphoria as I uncovered the dualities of my mind.

I learned that what I most wanted to avoid thinking about were the Nazi atrocities. Images from atrocity films I saw in high school kept flashing into consciousness and vanishing just as quickly. The pain of them was too much; indicating there was something significant about them I didn't want to know. Repulsion often conceals attraction and truth. When I realized that, I went to the Purdue library and forced myself to read everything available about the Holocaust. I was determined to know the unthinkable, to know myself. What disturbed me most were not the pictures of mutilated bodies, the gas ovens, the piles of dead children, or lamp shades made of tattooed human flesh, but the photographs of the faces of the German officers and guards—the oppressors. They were just ordinary, unthinking, conforming people who didn't question authority. They did what they were told to do—just as we were expected to do. Some of them were even handsome and attractive to me, especially in their Nazi butch drag. Both of my grandfathers were of German descent, and some of the people in the photographs, persecutors and prey, could have been my relatives. The other half of my bloodline was English, so I thought I was a half-breed of the good guys and the bad guys. This seemed fitting.

As I descended deeper into this horror, I became aware of a part of me that was fascinated by descriptions of human torture. I had to accept even this truth about myself if I were to be true to my mission. Even the obscene medical experiments of the monstrous Dr. Josef Mengele aroused my desire to know, and I remembered a toad I'd killed and dissected as a child. What I most wanted to understand about all of this were the experiences of the people who were tortured. I had to know why they wanted to live. I wondered how they could be made so utterly helpless, so devoured by fear and pain, so degraded, objectified, and violated and still retain the desire for life. How could they ever love again? Why did they want to live? In some strange but fitting way that I didn't understand then, I identified with them. What did I have to live for? I had not a clue.

I discovered I had an interest in the experiences of the torturer as well. I imagined myself as the SS commandant of my dorm, with the absolute power of life or death. My uniformed henchmen would drag Charlie Benson, struggling, into the torture chamber, strip him naked, and strap him spread-eagle on a rack. I would watch his terror as he realized his complete dependence on me for his life, and I sensed the potential for enormous intimacy between the torturer and his captive. It seemed to me that causing intense pain in another was not unrelated to causing powerful sexual sensations in them. What was in common was the ability to alter their consciousness with either pain or pleasure—the power to make them feel at least something. The opposite of this was alienation, the indifference of others to my existence, the lonely non-acknowledgment of my being. I wanted to know how to make people respond to me and end my alienation.

My curiosity about torture and the Holocaust was an attempt to understand myself. I began to feel overwhelmed by all that was opening up in me, so I decided to return to psychotherapy. To protect myself, I would talk about everything except sexuality.

Miss Evans was glad I returned. She said I was the most interesting person she'd been assigned to work with, and it pleased me that I interested her. When I told her about my days in the library reading about Nazi atrocities, she looked distressed. She said she wanted to give me a number of psychological tests: an IQ test, the Rorschach inkblot test, and perhaps others. I was afraid about what the Rorschach test could reveal, so I went to the library. I learned that the subject projects his personality unknowingly by the responses he gives to each of the ten cards. There were complex scoring systems for the Rorschach responses, making it seem like a mental x-ray machine. I became frightened until I realized that if I communicated my sexual conflicts to Miss Evans indirectly through this inkblot test, I would still be safe, because I wouldn't be admitting directly to anything. I could let her know what concerned me without being in any legal jeopardy. When I realized this, I could hardly wait to take her test.

Typically, it takes less than an hour to respond to the Rorschach cards. I took five hours, and poor Miss Evans could hardly write fast enough to keep up with me; she was not pleased. I was indirectly pouring my heart out to her with allusion and symbolism. I gave many examples of each of the categories of responses I'd read about. I was trying to impress her with my intelligence so she would like me and maybe have sex with me. At one point, I wanted her to know how sad I was, so I said of a small red spot on one of the cards, "This is the sound of a sad passage in Tchaikovsky's *Pathetique* symphony; it's like spilled blood." To another card, I said, "This wide part down here represents birth and the happiness of childhood. Here, where it narrows, is where adolescence begins and where the child becomes unhappy for years, but if he can survive all this, then, up here, it opens out again into adulthood, and he can be normal and free and happy. But first he has to make it through adolescence. He doesn't know how to grow up here, but he wants to, he has to, but he can't do it by himself. Up here at the very top is death. It's the same as at the bottom here before birth." When I said this, she was visibly moved. I was glad I was getting through.

I saw many things on the cards I was too embarrassed to tell Miss Evans about: penises, vaginas, breasts, two men dancing together wearing bras, a towering, monstrous giant with a tiny head and a huge penis the size of his legs (psychologists call this the father card), and one whole card that looked like a strange sort of penis deep inside a long thin vagina.

At the end of the test, Miss Evans asked, "Denny, people often see things in these cards that they don't want to mention. Did you see anything you hesitated to mention to me?"

"...Yes." I was suspicious and on guard as usual.

"Sometimes they have to do with sexuality. Was it that way for you?"

She's on to me, I thought. "I'm not going to tell you, and I'm never going to talk about that topic. I'll talk about anything else, but don't get into that one with me."

"Oh, I see. I meant no harm. I'm sorry." She looked troubled and confused. "I'll have your test results next week. It's been a long day for us, hasn't it? I'll bet you've missed dinner now. One thing before you go, Denny, I really do want you to know you can trust me. See you next week."

How did she know I saw those sex organs, I wondered. How did she know? I've got to be careful with her, I thought. She's very intelligent. She down plays it very cleverly.

Every day as I waited forever for my next appointment, I imagined Miss Evans pouring over my test results. It was good to imagine that someone of her status was interested in me. I arrived early for my appointment. Miss Evans had gone over the test results with her supervisor and the director of the clinic, Dr. Hadley. The IQ test indicated I was definitely not mentally retarded. Miss Evans said, "We believe your scores would be higher if it weren't for the psychological conflicts you're experiencing. I wish I'd done as well on my IQ test." I knew my dad would never believe these results, but I was relieved to know that he was wrong about my being an idiot. Maybe I could make something of myself, I thought, but her comment about psychological conflicts frightened me. What did she know?

I asked what psychological conflicts she was talking about, because I didn't really believe I was having any serious conflicts. This denial helped me preserve what little self-esteem I was clinging to. I remember her exact words: "Denny, I hate to be the messenger carrying bad news. Please, don't be angry with me for the message I must bring, but the Rorschach indicates you are suffering from some potentially very serious psychological problems. Dr. Hadley went over your Rorschach and wants to contact your parents today. He wants to talk with them as soon as they can come to Purdue. He said he never saw a Rorschach like yours, and he wants to talk with them about getting help for you before things become worse."

"Very serious psychological problems? Things getting worse? What are you talking about? I don't have any serious problems!"

"Well, maybe not right now, but there is a potential, unless we remove some of the stress and conflict from your life. Your parents need to be informed. We need their permission."

"Permission to do what? Are you planning to have me hospitalized? Is that what all this is about? Is it?"

"No, no, Denny. Nothing like that! I promise! It's just that, if you don't get the relief you need, you might have to be hospitalized. I know you were crying out to me for help on your test, and I heard you. I want to help you in every way I can. I really do, Denny."

I thought—suppressing the strong desire to yell this at her—then slip off that tight skirt of yours and make me normal! That's my only problem! I could feel my throat muscles quivering with the effort it took to remain solitary. While trying to appear calm, I asked her what else the test showed.

"Well, Dr. Hadley was quite concerned. He'd never seen a test that long or with as many different kinds of responses.

We talked about my feelings about my parents coming to see Dr. Hadley. She didn't want me to talk about my therapy with them, and she wanted to see me immediately after they left. She gave me some telephone numbers where she could be reached night or day and told me to call her any time I needed to talk. I was pleased by her concern for me but worried.

As I walked back to my dorm, the emotional impact of what Miss Evans said began to sink in—"very serious psychological problems...hospitalization." What else would I have to endure? I was not only afraid that my worst fears might be true—that I might just be a crazy pervert after all, but that I would go completely insane. I was to be severely punished for a crime I couldn't understand—like the victims of the Holocaust. I was to be tortured, too, but why was I singled out? Why was I different? What had I done?

Just then, on the other side of a tall, wire mesh fence separating me from them, I saw two healthy, athletic young men my age joyously playing catch with a softball on an open grassy field. Their laughter and happiness made me ache inside, and I stopped to watch them and became motionless with envy. They knew something vital I needed to understand. Their faces expressed the spontaneous, timeless joy that only youth can know, and their brisk movements had the grace of a dance. The tossing of the ball was a way of affecting one another, a way to make the other acknowledge and respond to one's existence. I was watching a sacred ritual of mutual affirmation, and I suddenly understood the point of it! I'm here, and you're here; I'm affecting you, and you're affecting me, and I'm glad we're both here! We're both a part of something now, you and I! This was holy communion in an ordinary game of catch. That was the point of it. They're just normal guys, I thought. Why can't I be happy just tossing a ball like them? Why can't that be enough for me, I wanted to know. How did they escape my fate?

Just then, one of the glowing youths noticed me looking through the wire mesh fence at him. I just wanted to understand. He yelled, "What are you looking at? Do you like what you see?" He posed like a poster girl, then rubbed his crotch, and yelled "Faggot!" They left together, laughing. I had never been called that before or any name like that.

I skipped classes that afternoon and sat in my room for hours, replaying the images of the two healthy college boys tossing that ball. Each time it was as if a beautiful, sunlit crystalline sculpture—that youth and my soul—was suddenly shattered—struck by the savage blow of a steel hammer...FAGGOT! My roommate became worried about how depressed I was and asked the dorm counselor to see me. The counselor asked if I was upset by my sessions with Miss Evans. I said I wasn't. He asked what was bothering me. How could I tell him it was the memory of two students tossing a ball on a beautiful open field of green in the warmth of the sun? Or that the beautifully sculptured athlete had seen into my soul with a mere glance?

My parents came to the university several days later. As usual, my father was annoyed at the inconvenience I was causing him. He was angry that I was so weak-willed that I needed to lean on a psychologist—and a female one at that, he said. Hard work and discipline was what I needed, he said, and if I didn't stop reading all those psychology and philosophy books, I'd wind up being a "weak-kneed sissy intellectual," which was the most disgusting thing he could imagine.

They talked with Dr. Hadley for an hour and a half longer than scheduled. I was worried. Miss Evans waited with me. When my parents finished their conference, their behavior was strangely different. My mother had been crying, and she came and hugged me, still crying. My father looked away to calm his emotions. He kept repeating, "Son, don't worry about a thing. I'll pay for everything. Just do what you need to do to get well. We're not going to put any more pressure on you about anything. Dr. Hadley told us not to ask you anything about your therapy; that's fine with me, but if you want to talk, I'll listen. Of course, I'd like to know our money isn't just being wasted. Psychologists aren't cheap, but don't you worry about that!" My parents had never been so considerate; this worried me. What did he mean by "get well," I wondered.

I walked my parents to their car. I remember my mother saying, "Oh Denny! Do take care of yourself! Don't skip any of your psychology sessions; I don't want you to have to be hospitalized! I don't know if I could ever visit you in one of those places!" I was hurt that she would hesitate to visit me in a hospital.

Alarmed, I demanded to know what Dr. Hadley said to them. With a look of fear and pity in her eyes, my mother said, "Oh, Denny! He said we shouldn't tell you anything he said, but I think you have a right to know. He's worried you might have a mental breakdown—a paranoid schizophrenic break with reality, he called it. I don't know what all that means, but you won't do that, will you? He was upset about that test you took. Don't tell him I told you; he'd be angry with me. I think you need to know the truth though."

My father scowled, "God damn it, Donna! I knew you couldn't keep your fat blabbing mouth shut for five minutes! You just had to tell him, didn't you? Now you're just going to get the boy all confused. Get in the car!"

Miss Evans was waiting for me in her office. "Well, what was it like to be with your parents, Denny?"

"Miss Evans, what is a paranoid schizophrenic?"

Her face contorted in shock and anger. "You wait right here!" She rushed down the hall to Dr. Hadley's office. When she returned a few minutes later, she was calmer. "Dr. Hadley will be calling your parents as soon as they return home. We both agree it would be best for your therapy if you stopped all contact with your parents for awhile. He is going to insist that they do this for you. You don't need any more stress from them. Now just forget about anything they might have said; I don't think either of them is very good at listening to people, and Dr. Hadley probably spoke over their heads. He does that sometimes." I knew she wouldn't answer my question; she was too kind to do that.

Back at the dorm, alone, stunned and staggering, with those dreaded words hammering into my brain, I asked, "My God, must I suffer insanity, too? Have you condemned me? Is my sin so great? Am I evil? Is that it? Is there to be no mercy? I just want to live, that's all I ask! Just let me live! A simple life, even for a little while. Please! I beg you!"

But, as I begged for mercy from an imagined father figure, the memory of a spring weekend the year before came seeping back into my mind like a silent fog of poisoned nerve gas. Oh God, not that, I cried out. You wouldn't want me to do that! You couldn't be that grotesque! Would you, God?

That weekend had been in the spring of my senior year when I was 17. We had moved to Dayton that year, and I couldn't break into any of the well-established cliques at the snobbish, upper-middle-class high school. Many of my classmates had been accepted to Ivy League schools, and I didn't even know what an Ivy League school was. I was extremely lonely that year and often thought, they must know I'm here, they don't bump into me in the halls, they must know.

There was a serious question about my graduating from high school because of my grades. A well-meaning but inept school counselor called me in and gave me several paper-and-pencil tests—an adjustment inventory and an IQ test. Since I had been quite depressed and lonely that year, I wasn't interested in taking her tests. A week later, she called my parents to the school. That evening, they ordered me into the living room and raged at me for over an hour. I'd never seen them so angry and in such complete agreement. I could never forget what was said. It went something like this:

"That fat bitch said your test results showed you had a poor family life! How could you betray us like that? Your own parents! How could you tell those lies about us? What kind of person are you, anyway?" bellowed my father.

"After all we've done for you, Denny, all these years," cried my mother, "and you think you can just turn your back on us and betray family confidences to complete strangers! How dare you talk about our family affairs behind our backs! What gives you the right to reveal our private lives? Where is your loyalty? What in the world did we ever do to you to make you hate us so much?"

"I just answered the questions on the tests she gave me," I mumbled. "I didn't think I was betraying anything. I just answered the questions. I didn't tell her I had a bad family life." I had violated the sacred no-speak rule of dysfunctional families.

"Well, you must have lied when you answered the test questions then! How dare you say to anyone that you have a bad home life? You ungrateful bastard, you! Maybe I should kick your ass out of here and make you earn your own living Then you'd come crawling back to me on your belly like a snake and beg me—your own father!—to take you back. I'd sooner stomp your forked-tongued head in! The worst mistake I ever made was siring you! You disgust me!"

"Denny, even if you answered those questions truthfully, didn't you stop to think that the counselor would tell other people about what you said? Didn't you even bother to think about that? Didn't you even care that all of our dirty linen was going to get aired all over town? What are the neighbors going to think about me as a mother every time they see me? I don't know how I can even go shopping now, and it's all your fault! I know we've got family problems, but didn't you even once think about me? Why did you think it was okay to throw our private dirt around? Answer me when I speak to you!" My mother's face was red with rage.

I said I was sorry; I didn't know. I just did what she asked me to. She said she wanted to help me. I didn't know I was telling her things I shouldn't.

"You answered true to questions that said my family doesn't talk much and I'm unhappy with my life at home. She showed them to me! Why do you lie like that?" snapped my father.

I said I didn't lie and that we didn't talk. I said I wasn't happy at home or anywhere. I wasn't happy at all, and I told them I had told her that.

"Well, you poor, ungrateful, self-pitying, sniveling son-of-a-bitch, you!" yelled my father. "You don't even know what unhappiness means! My father died when I was 12, and I had to be a man then—something you'll never understand! Nobody ever made it easy for me! Me and my brothers had to go to work to support my mother. Then we had to survive the Depression years. Bankers were selling apples on street corners then! I've kept your belly full from the day you were born, but I knew what it was to go hungry! I pulled tires off the molds in the rubber factories, and I was damn grateful I had a job for any pay! And you have the guts to criticize us about anything? Well, you'll get yours! The world will knock you down to size! You think you're so damned smart? That counselor told us your IQ is 90—below average! I've thought that all along; you might have fooled your mother, but not me! I can see right through you! The counselor said college was out of the question for you. You couldn't get admitted! You haven't got the brains! She said we should have sent you to a vocational school. She asked if you were interested in fixing cars, and I told her you weren't interested in a damned thing! Well, you're not going to sponge off me the rest of your miserable life! I don't care what your mother says, you can go live like a bum in the gutter for all I care! A bum! Now, get out of my sight before I turn your ugly face inside out! Get out of here!"

I still feel the pain of my father's disgust. I know that he was responding to specific circumstances and punishing certain behaviors of mine, but at the time it felt like he hated me—mind, body, and soul. I stayed in my room most of that week, except when I went to school. I got up to eat at night after they went to bed. I had nobody I could talk to. I had always thought I would go to college, but I began to believe my future was gone, and I had no one.

A short time later, when I was downtown in Dayton, I saw an ulcerated unshaven alcoholic shuffling along a back street with a bottle of wine in a paper bag. He had long, stringy, dirt-matted hair, and he was loudly cursing the demons of his brain. I was transfixed. Through his drunkenness, he saw me looking at him. He shuffled over and held out his green jug to me. He smelled of urine and rancid vomit. His grimy hand had long, dirty, broken fingernails, and he reached out with it and stroked my face. I couldn't move, because reality was screaming at me. As he looked at me quizzically, I recognized in him what I feared I would become. I wondered if I would sink so low in life that one day I would value the attention of even one such as he. Here, touching my cheek, was the curse of my father! "You can go live like a bum in the gutter for all I care!" As the pathetic old wino shuffled on, I began to cry uncontrollably for him...and for me. Something vital broke and gave way in me. It was hope.

When I got home, I found a terse note from my mother. They had gone away for the weekend and had taken my sister Judy with them. They would be home Sunday night. By late Saturday evening, my depression was far worse than anything I'd ever experienced. I had to talk to somebody who cared I was alive. I tried to call Ruth, David's mother, but nobody answered. I worried that my father would be angry at me for making a long-distance phone call to Richmond where they lived.

I went down to our basement and sat on the cool concrete floor. I remembered my father beating me with his leather belt in a dark cellar like this one. He'd been skinning rabbits. I was six, then. I talked back to him. He shoved me down the cellar steps, forced me to undress, and then he flogged me. I was naked, writhing, and screaming, trying to escape his lashes. I said anything he wanted to hear to get him to stop the pain. When it was finally over, he left me alone in the stench of that dark cellar. I remembered feeling the coolness of the concrete floor on my throbbing, welted skin and watching the gutted rabbits my father had just stripped and cleaned. They were hanging from wires suspended from the beams, swinging back and forth by their necks. I was like them.

When the pain of this old memory faded from my consciousness, I loaded my rifle—the one my father had given me when I was 12 as an acknowledgment of my passage to puberty and a symbol of manhood. I pressed the end of the cool, blued-steel barrel against the center of my forehead. I clicked off the safety and put my thumb on the trigger. The feeling of the cold circle of steel on my forehead relieved me. I remember thinking, this is where the bullet will enter me. I'm not helpless anymore. I can escape my future. I can end this. All it takes is just a little more pressure on this hair trigger. I wonder how long I'll stay conscious? I'll probably feel a bad pain as the bullet rips through my skin and cracks through my skull bone. It'll probably last a second or two. I can take that! Will the bullet have enough force to go through the back of my skull? Sure it will—the way it easily goes through all those boards. Skull bones can't be harder than that. I'll probably feel pain in the back of my head when the bullet goes out...then it will all be over. I won't even see blackness...I'll just be nothing...nothing at all.

I put more pressure on the trigger and felt it move. I imagined my mother's screams of horror as she runs down the basement steps toward my bloody body. I could see my father standing behind her as she sobs and holds my cold body in her arms. He would have a slight smile on his face—a problem solved for him. Then the police would come, and my father would act sad. "I don't know what got into the boy. He always was a little unbalanced in the head; sort of queer," he'd say. My mother would be crying, and my kid sister Judy would cry, too, but she'd be out playing with her friends the next day. Nobody at school would care. They'd say, "I always thought he was a bit weird; he didn't really fit in; he wasn't like us."

Who cares about me? No one! The trigger moved again. I wondered how much farther it would go. The sadness was becoming intense. I tried to think about what I would be leaving and losing. Not much, it seemed. Everything in my consciousness was becoming darkness as I was about to die. "Oh, God!" I uttered, as if beginning a prayer, the trigger moving. Then I remembered, "And God created man in his own image; man is created in the image of God." Yes, the image of God could save me! Just then, the grotesque and quizzical face of that pathetic, sodden, ulcerating wino flooded my consciousness, laughing at me! "Oh...my God!" I cried out in complete revulsion and pressed the trigger full force! The explosion was deafening. The whining bullet ricocheted around the basement...then, total silence. I knew I had deflected the weapon at the critical moment because somehow I still wanted to live, but I also knew I had condemned myself to the pain of my life. In the anguish of this awareness, I began to sob, and then I cried and cried until there was nothing left—nothing. I felt there was no one...and there never would be for me...and that would have to do.

That had happened only the year before, when I was 17. With the deadly fog of that memory filling me, I realized that my hope for a new beginning at Purdue, my second chance, was disintegrating into a greater horror than I had ever imagined possible. Was this wrathful God, the Father, I wondered, so disgusted with me that, with the laughter of an old sadist, he was giving me the choice between insanity and suicide? Why me? What had I done? "What was my sin?" I asked—as if I didn't know. "Doomed from here to eternity...baa...baa...baa!" I sang as I wept at the brink.

Chapter Two

It's difficult to understand another human being, to really understand. That takes a long time. When you do, you change, and compassion develops. With compassion, understanding deepens. To know another is to understand their invisible world, the hidden world of abstraction and symbolism. The myths of our nationalities, cultures, religions, and selves are of this invisible world, and we are often willing to kill and die for such abstractions.

The young man I was at Purdue both believed and didn't believe in the mythological world of religious superstition and tradition. He was a person of powerful contradictions—a normal guy who was a pervert. His contradictions were the source of his creative energy. At 16, he realized that truth is often hidden in paradox and contradiction—as when he saw this world as time's holy slaughterhouse, a paradise of emptiness. So in the loneliness of his crisis, he called out to his God—a sadistic God, not unlike his father—for mercy. The vast power of his invisible world was unknown to him. Even his history was inaccessible. He couldn't remember it, because he wouldn't grieve the pain of his past. I remember it all now, of course—every single year of it, but that took a long time. It was not without its price for me and others. As a youth, I couldn't verbalize what I experienced and that confused and isolated me; but, now as I look back, I understand and can tell the human truth. The major themes of my life developed early in my repressed history.

Our significant memories are vital clues to the mysteries of what we are. Some psychotherapists believe our earliest childhood memories are recalled because they are fitting metaphors for our present construction of the dramatic themes of our lives. Others believe they are recalled because they, in fact, were the events that structured our lives. Both are often correct, but in my case, the latter applies. I recall my earliest memory as if it were yesterday.

It's the middle of the night. I'm three or four years old. The sounds of sobbing have awakened me—cries in the hallway outside my bedroom door. In my blue flannel sleepers, I stumble out of my bedroom and see my mother crying, lying on a brown stretcher being carried down the hall by two dark-haired men wearing white uniforms. She tries to reach out to me. My worried father says sternly, "She's all right. Go back to sleep!" I feel frightened, excluded, and prevented by my father from comforting my mother.

I still don't know what happened in the dark of that night; my parents have always nervously claimed they don't recall it, but I can still hear my mother moaning helplessly there in the vividness of my memory. What was significant was that I was lied to by my father and prevented by him from helping my mother. None of us were truthful in my family. We never talked about anything personal, especially my father. In fact, we rarely talked at all.

When I was four, my father built a house in the country near Akron, Ohio. My next most significant memory was of one day when my mother and I drove over to pick my father up at the end of a hard day's work on the new house. I remember that he was tired and covered with sweat. She asked him to drive home, but he said he was too tired. She complained that she, too, had worked all day, and she wanted him to drive. From the back seat of the old blue Ford, I saw his face contort with frustration and anger as he yelled at her, "No, God damn it, you're going to drive! Now, don't argue with me!" His eyes were vigilant for the slightest sign of provocation from her, and his powerful arm muscles were tensed and poised. In that instant, my mother and father were transformed for me, because I saw for the first time the cowering fear in my mother's submissive face, and I realized that my father controlled us both—utterly. I knew we both feared him and were at his mercy. With fear, I realized she couldn't protect me from him; I had to do that for myself. I didn't like my father, and I knew in that instant I didn't want to be like him— not ever. Later, I told my mother this. She laughed and said, "Good, but all you men are just alike anyway." I believe that, soon after this, he became aware of my new attitude toward him—my mother would have delighted in telling him—felt rejected, and eventually became indifferent to me. Much later in my life, my father's indifference would come back to me in an incredible way—a life-saving gift from the gods.

I remember thinking at the time that, even though I didn't want to be like my father, I was glad I was a boy, not a girl. Even at four, I was already understanding the advantages of being a male in this male-dominated culture. Sexism, the pinks versus the blues, played a major role in my life, as it does for everyone. I was even more convinced of my male advantage when my sister was born later that year. I remember the day my mother made me wait with my eyes closed while she brought me "a very wonderful present!" Her voice had that exaggerated sing-songy sweetness about it—the clue that I was being conned. I opened my eyes, and there was this pudgy-faced, wrinkled baby—like a big doll—wrapped in a pink blanket. "Look, Denny, here is your new little sister!" my mother squealed. I stared blankly. I'd expected a nice toy, not an oversized Kewpie doll. "Take it back!" I said. Hoping to interest me, Mom peeled the pink package further until my sister was revealed, naked. Having never seen female genitals, I asked, "What's that?"

"It's her weewee-er, her little bun."

"Isn't it finished yet?"

"Yes, that's the way it is with girls."

"How does she go peepee?"

"She can, but not as easily as boys."

I remember feeling sorry for my baby sister. She had a deformity, a sort of deficiency that she couldn't help, but as long as she could peepee, as messy as it seemed it would be, I reasoned she could get by with her handicap. I was glad I was a boy, and I was proud that I was better. "Do you have a bun like hers?" I asked.

"Well, yes," admitted my embarrassed mother.

I was very proud of my male status—cocky. This theme of status and power was another major dimension of my life. Sexism is rooted in power.

During my fifth year, WPA workers repaired the streets near our home, and I spent days watching and listening to them. They liked me, and I begged them to teach me their wonderful profanities. I wanted to learn to swear, because its effect on adults was spectacular, and this gave me a sense of power. That was important for me then, because I had so little of it. I delighted in short-circuiting my aunt and mother. I also went around to the neighbors and tried out my new powers. They protested to my mother, who chased me around the house, caught me, pinned me to the ground, and crammed a bar of Fels Naptha soap in my mouth. "This will clean out that damned filthy mouth of yours! Eat it! You're just like your father!" This comparison angered and pleased me. When I got close enough to the back door, I yelled the most vile curses I knew at her. The chase was on, but she started to laugh so hard that I easily escaped. That evening, I overheard her tell my father what I had said, and he laughed, too.

At kindergarten, teachers tried to socialize me. My pint bottle of warm milk had to be drunk to the last disgusting sip—cream and all. I was to take naps when I wasn't tired; eyes were not to be opened until nap time was over. It was a matter of power. My protests were met with implacability, so I resorted to the magical force of WPA profanities. I was promptly expelled from public kindergarten. After this, my mother packed me a sack lunch each morning and told me not to come home until the sun had gone behind the tops of the trees to the west of us. She meant it, and I knew it. Many afternoons I sat on the side of a gravel road near our home waiting for the sun to touch the tops of those special trees. The pain of that daily exile forced me to discover the wonders of the natural world and, above all, to rely on myself.

I often tried to win my mother's love. Several miles from our house was a drug store. I took the coins from my piggy bank and set off one morning for the store. I asked the woman behind the counter what would be a nice present for my mother. After counting my coins, she said I could buy a bottle of Prince Matchabelli perfume, but I needed 12 more cents. I couldn't understand why a prince would waste his time making perfume, but I hiked home, begged mother for 12 cents, trudged back to the store, and then walked home again. I gave her my gift. She opened it, looked puzzled, and said, "Why did you buy me this? I don't even like this kind of perfume. You wasted your money."

Several days later, I found the largest trapdoor spider I'd ever seen. It, too, was a source of power—adults feared spiders. I put it in a large glass jar. My mother was taking a nap on a lawn chair in the back yard. I opened the jar, held it just above her face, and woke her up.

My constant companion during those days was a wonderful russet-colored Shetland sheepdog named Skipper. Joy was his nature, and I swear he smiled even when he was sleeping. Together, we penetrated the magic forests and fields surrounding my home, and together we waited beside the dusty gravel road for the sun to touch the tops of the trees to the west. I felt loved by my dog, and I often hugged him. No one else ever licked me, or sniffed my crotch with such interest.

We also had a cat. One day, our tabby cat died, and I was introduced to life's great theme, attachment and loss. Mother put the cat's stiff body into a velvet-lined wicker sewing basket, and we gave her a proper burial. Mom insisted I say good-bye to the dead cat. I protested the cat couldn't hear me anymore, but from my mother's stern expression, I knew my objections were useless. She insisted that our kitty was now happily eating catnip in cat heaven. Suspiciously, I asked if there were dogs in cat heaven, and she said no, they had their own heaven just like us. I didn't believe her. Early one morning months later, knowing I shouldn't, I dug up the wicker basket, opened the lid, and saw the cat's stinking body animated with wriggling maggots. When I told my mother how I knew our cat was definitely not in cat heaven, she looked disgusted but said nothing. In these vital lessons of childhood, I was learning about love, loss, pretence and power.

Across the street from my house was a large field, part of the farm belonging to crotchety Old Man McClures. Mother bought vegetables and awful tasting duck eggs from him. Behind the field was a forest that extended for miles. I spent my exiled days there and knew its secret places, hidden meadows and swinging vines. I was king of its trees, conquering their heights and surveying my kingdom. Once, deep in the forest, I found what I often searched for, what my parents had warned me about. There, standing alone in the sunlight, ringed by respectfully distant trillium, was a small poisonous messenger of Death, the lethal death's angel mushroom. In its tender white body was concentrated the greatest power I knew. Power fascinated me.

My mother and father were terrified by death, which I believed was controlled by a nasty old man with a scythe. Even Old Man McClures warned me about the poison sumac swamp near the forest. A beautiful white horse of his got stuck in the quicksand there, and death got it. If you listened carefully before a storm, he told me, you could sometimes hear the cries of that great white stallion as he was sucked down to death. He whispered that he once even heard the cries of several men and a boy my age who had died there. The men had tried to save the boy, who had been foolish enough to go into the poison sumac swamp. I didn't understand why he winked at my mother and why she laughed, but the dark, twisted branches of the sumac now held the excitement and terror of the power of death. I wondered if the sumac and the death's angel mushroom communicated. Were they aware of me? Did they know I was already planning to hear the death cries of the foolish boy, the men and the magnificent white stallion?

I surveyed the swamp from every side for days, and when the storm clouds came, I entered it. As I came close to the twisted sumac, they seemed to scream at my presence like the trees in a Disney film I'd seen, but they couldn't move; I could. Were they calling to the death's angel mushroom? He couldn't move, either. (I thought of death as a male force; my father was a hunter.) I probed the muck with a long pole to find the quicksand. I was alive with the excitement and exaltation of the power and terror of death! At any moment, that great stallion, carrying the men and the boy on his back, would come thundering out from behind the twisted branches, hooves splashing, nostrils flaring; and his blazing, enraged eyes would stare into mine, and I would smell his hot breath! I had invaded the realm of Death, himself! After I sloshed around in the muck for several hours, the magic waned, the territory had been won and was mine alone, and I, the muddy little hero, headed triumphantly home to confidently confront...my mother. This was an early rehearsal for my life—a metaphor, the hero conquering his fears—the fear of male power, his father's power.

On my way home, I found a decaying farm wagon in a field. It had a buckboard, metal-rimmed wheels, and badly-rusted brake levers. Bits of faded-blue paint could still be seen on the decaying wooden sides. It fascinated me, and I often returned to it. What intrigued me most was the place where the metal rims of the wheels were disintegrating into the ground. The wagon was becoming rusty earth; it was disappearing. Someday, I thought, it would all be dirt. I showed it to my parents, and they said it was over 100 years old. I asked where the people were who used it, and my father said they were all dead and had been for a long time. I often imagined those farm people when I sat on the wagon. More often, I would touch the wagon and think, I can touch the wagon now, but it's going away, and someday it will all be gone. I was beginning to understand that death touches everything, nothing escapes. Visiting the old wagon made me sad, but I couldn't resist checking those rusty rims and touching with my fingers the process of time.

(I'm reminded of the time when my oldest son, Nathan, was about four years old. It was a hot summer day, and he came running to me holding his favorite box turtle, George.

"Daddy! I can't make George wake up!" He stood there frantically shaking his pet turtle, and George's head flopped pathetically against his shell.

"George is dead, Nathan."

"What's dead mean?"

"It means George won't do anything anymore. He won't experience anything or feel anything ever again."

"What will happen to him?"

"He will slowly fall apart and eventually blend into the earth. Everything dies, Nathan."

"Daddy, do trees die?"

"Yes."

"Does the grass die?"

"Yes, Nathan, everything dies."

"Do mountains die?"

"Well, yes, in a way they do. They get worn down and disappear, but it takes a very long time.

"...Do mommies and daddies die?"

"Yes, my son, they do, and we will, too."

Nathan grew silent for a long time, then hesitantly asked, "Daddy...do little boys die?"

"Yes, they do, but usually not until they've grown up and become very old men."

"Daddy, when little boys die, does that mean they can't play anymore?"

"Yes, my son. Everything dies, but you have nothing to fear when death comes—nothing at all.")

I learned another lesson about the perpetual rhythm of attachment and loss in life when a mad dog came into our neighborhood. It was large, black, and growling. Foam dripped from its mouth as the dog ran around wildly attacking everything. My mother screamed, "Rabid dog! Rabid dog! Run, Denny!" It attacked my dog. Skipper howled in pain and was covered with blood and foam. His testicles had been bitten off. When my mother returned from the vet, she hugged me and smiled in the same way she had when she brought my sister home from the hospital, so I knew the news wasn't good. She said the vet couldn't help Skipper. He put him to sleep, so my dog wouldn't feel any more pain.

"When will he wake up?"

"Well, he won't wake up, Denny."

"Is he dead?"

"No, not exactly. Skipper is playing in the heaven for dogs now. He's happy now."

"Will he come back?"

"No, he won't."

"Not ever?"

"No. Not ever."

"Will he miss me?"

"Well, yes, but he is happy where he is."

"You liar! Skipper is dead! My dog is dead! Skipper is gone!" I knew my mother was lying, because I knew Skipper couldn't be happy without me. (I have two Shetland Sheep dogs now.)

Some time later, I saw a fat caterpillar attach itself with a silken sling to the branch of a rhododendron bush. I spent hours watching it become a chrysalis. My parents told me that it would become a beautiful butterfly someday. I was incredulous, since it hung there unchanging, seemingly forever. Eventually, the day came when its hard case did begin to change, and I was absorbed in the magic that followed for hours. I saw a black swallowtail butterfly come from where the caterpillar had been, dry itself and fly away. This was like the changing wagon wheel rims, only different—wonderfully different. Suddenly, the world seemed filled with endless varieties of these amazing creatures of exquisite beauty. They danced in graceful silence across the acres of swaying goldenrod and Queen Anne's lace near my house. I collected every species I could find and mounted hundreds in cigar boxes, but my enthusiasm for these flying jewels irritated my father. My budding aesthetic interest embarrassed him, and he made it clear that he didn't like having a butterfly-collecting son. My mother was delighted, though, and kept me supplied with boxes from the drugstore.

I couldn't understand why my father so strongly disapproved of something that brought me such happiness, but when I asked him, he didn't give me an answer. This wasn't unusual. Throughout my life, my father hardly ever revealed his feelings and motives and never spoke of his past or personal life. Because of this, he remained an enigma for me; as he was for my mother.

We eventually stopped trying to understand him.

In the house next to ours was a family who kept very much to themselves. They had a daughter I rarely saw. I thought she probably didn't like little boys. During the summer when I turned six, Sheila, who was 13, seduced me. "Do you want to have a lot of fun?" she asked me one day. She got an old car tire to sit in, took me to a secluded spot behind her garage, and insisted that we both undress. She lay down and showed me how she wanted me to stimulate her with my hand. I did what she wanted for a short time and then stopped. It seemed purposeless. This annoyed her. "You have to do it for a long, long time!" she insisted. After too long a time, she began to groan and moan. "What's wrong?" I asked. "Nothing! Go faster!" She thrashed around, bounced up and down, gasping and moaning, then laughed and said, "Stop! Enough!" She closed her eyes and relaxed. I asked if she was going to go to sleep; she smiled, opened her eyes, and said, "No...Wasn't that great fun?" When I said no, she looked annoyed, got up, rolled her tire back into the garage, and went into her house. I was puzzled why she made all those sounds and moved around the way she had. Sheila tried to get me to "have a good time" several more times that summer, but I refused. It seemed so pointless.

My father took an interest in me shortly after our confrontation about real boys and butterflies. He would teach me the ways of the male tribe. One weekend, he let me go horseback riding with him and his brothers. They took me to a nearby stable and showed me the horses. These magnificent animals towered above me and pawed the ground in a way that threatened and excited me, power again. I remembered the great white stallion of the sumac swamp and felt a rush of fear; I thought they might be his relatives, and I was worried that they might know about me! I personified almost everything at that age— birds, trees, clouds, even houses—the windows were eyes. It was an exciting world.

My father and his brothers selected fast, high-strung mounts for them-selves. My horse, they assured me, was a gentle old nag, and I had nothing to be afraid of. My father lifted me to the towering heights of the horse's saddle. My legs were much too short to reach the stirrups, so he told me to hang on to the saddle with both hands. "Hang on for dear life!" he said with a laugh and a look of mischief in his eyes. "Don't go fast!" I pleaded. "Oh, we won't go too fast. Just keep up with us," he said grinning.

We headed out along the bridle path. I calmed down and began to enjoy controlling such a powerful animal. When my horse went too slow, my father would say, "Kick him in the ribs, kick him hard!" I didn't like the idea of hurting such a fine creature, so I gently nudged him. This annoyed my father. "Quit acting like a sissy! Do you want to be a momma's boy?" When we reached a long dirt road, my father barked, "Hold on for dear life! Both hands!" He dug his heels into his horse's sides, slashed its flank with his whip, and he and his brothers were off at full gallop with my horse racing just behind. I was bounced from a sitting position to a horizontal one, and the ground was a blur far beneath me. I knew if I lost my grip on the saddle, I'd fall. Eventu-ally, my father dropped back and brought my horse to a halt. "What's the matter? Can't you keep up with us?" I was too flooded with emotion to speak. "What's the matter? Cat got your tongue?" I said nothing. I knew I wasn't what my father wanted me to be. This would remain true throughout our lives, a heavy burden for a young man, a sad loss for us both.

Another weekend, my father announced, "I'm taking you hunting today. You're old enough now." I was pleased that he wanted to do something with me, because he was usually asleep on the living room couch while my mother read books—a dozen a week, always murder mysteries. He had an old, double-barreled, 12-gauge shotgun, handed down from his family—West Virginia hill people. He took me to a field and explained about guns and safety. Finally, he said I could shoot the gun by myself. I was excited, because guns were very powerful and power fascinated me. He told me where to point it, but I could hardly lift it up with my short arms. He smiled like he was up to something and told me I should be sure to pull both triggers at exactly the same time, and I did. There was a deafening boom, white smoke belched from both barrels, and then I saw blue sky rolling into view as I was knocked backward to the ground, my shoulder aching. My father roared with laughter, saying it was the funniest thing he'd ever seen. Real men are tough and take it.

Later that day, after he had shot four or five rabbits, suddenly, just in front of us, a male ring-necked pheasant rocketed skyward in a flight for its life. It was so beautiful that I hoped my father would miss. Higher it rose toward blue freedom, then the slow and deliberate aim, the explosion, and the frozen moment of death before the fall. "Get it, Denny! Get it, now!" he ordered. I ran and knelt down beside it. That pheasant was the most beautiful thing I'd ever seen. What I remember most was its dead eyes looking at me. "Hurry up, Denny! It's just a bird!" yelled my father. I didn't believe him.

Whenever my father went hunting, he made me clean the rabbits. He went down into the starkly lit basement, attached wires to the ceiling beams, and hung each of the animals by the neck from a wire. When he finished, he would call me down into that shadowed place. My job was to make the rabbits naked by peeling off their skins, then I had to cut out their insides. No matter what my parents threatened, I would never eat any of them. My rebellion greatly angered my father. He shouted, "I'll teach you to back-talk your father! I'll teach you a lesson you'll never forget!" That was when he shoved me down the cellar steps, made me undress, and flogged me with that leather belt of his. I never did forget his lesson: I was absolutely of no value to him.

During that sixth summer, I had my tonsils removed. The operation was done in a doctor's office. I asked him to save my tonsils so I could see them. I was given ether and remember seeing purple and white concentric rings as I was going under. When I awoke, they told me I kicked the nurse, who was pregnant, in the stomach and accused her of stealing my pet rabbits. I asked to see the tonsils but was disappointed that they were just a couple of pieces of meat instead of the bones I'd imagined. My mother brought me home and let me sleep in their bed. When my father got home that evening, he came upstairs and sat on the bed next to me. I was surprised and very pleased. He was concerned about me. "How are you doing, you little son-of-a-gun?" he asked. When my father admired someone, he would say they were a "high caliber" person. If they were powerful, they were a "big gun." For my father, as for many people, masculinity was the power to dominate and control, not the power to create and love. I couldn't figure out what guns had to do with people, but I knew his calling me a son-of-a-gun was some sort of compliment, and I liked it. He'd brought me some presents. I was amazed. He, himself, stopped to buy me presents! The first was a wooden pop gun, the second, a water pistol. We had fun with the water pistol that evening, but soon, too soon, he was back to sleeping on the living room couch in the evenings while mother read her murder mysteries.

At the end of summer, my mother dressed me in new clothes and shoes and said I was going to school that day, first grade. She said if I used any swear words at school, the teacher would tell her, and then, "Your father will beat you within an inch of your life!" I'd had a dream of Gargantua, the famous gorilla, chasing me through a jungle. I was running at full speed, then he broke through the trees and was catching up with me. I could see him, huge and horrible. Instead of a gorilla's head, his head was that of my father! I woke up screaming just before he caught me. Yes, I did believe my mother's warning about the wrath of my father. But I longed for his acceptance.

I'd never seen as many kids as I did that first day at Fairlawn Elementary School. Some bigger boys were playing baseball. When I started to go over to them, several of my new friends called me back. They told me the big guys were eighth graders, "Eighth graders run the school. They like to beat up on first graders. Stay away from them!" Males were always the dangerous ones, never females.

My first grade teacher was Miss Klaus. She was tall and thin, and plainly dressed; her gray hair was pulled back severely into a tight bun. She reminded me of the Wicked Witch in *The Wizard of Oz*. She let us know that we'd better do what she wanted, or else. The "or else" was the principal and his large paddle with the holes in it that was said to make even the eighth grade boys cry. I was afraid every time I hurried past that entrance to the unknown terror labeled "PRINCIPAL'S OFFICE." I never saw beyond this door, but someone else did on the very first day of school. One of the boys talked back to Miss Klaus. She spoke sharply to him several times, but he continued. Slowly, with a tired expression, she walked over to him and grabbed his arm. He fought back. She got a good grip on his foot and dragged him screaming on his back down the long hall to the principal's office. We all watched from the doorway as into the dreaded office they went. She came out a short time later, but he never came back to our class. One boy said he probably ran away. Another boy said, "No! The principal murdered him!" I realized that my world was filled with powerful authority figures like my father.

My mother often asked me about the girls in my class and wondered if I had any favorites. She wanted to know all of their names. She said I was a handsome boy, and I would be a "lady's man, a lady killer" when I grew up. In those days, a man was either a man's man, a lady's man, or a sissy—a no man. It was better to be a man's man than a lady's man, because women had little power. A male contaminated by femininity, a sissy, was simply not an acceptable life form in those warrior days of World War II. The "lady killer" part of it expressed my mother's generally negative view of men and of my father in particular. My mother was pleased when I told her several girls had invited me to their houses after school.

One of these, Marjorie Windows, invited my friend, Ted Lewis, and me over one day. Ted had a beautiful pair of hand-tooled cowboy boots he wore to school every day. All of the boys admired them and wished their dads were as rich as Ted's must have been. Marjorie was pleased when we stopped by her house. "Do you guys want me to get some of my dolls for you?"

"No." I said. "Boys don't play with dolls."

"I know! Let's have a tea party with my new tea set!" she offered.

"No! Haven't you got anything fun for boys to do?" asked Ted.

She thought awhile and then said, "I know! Let's fuck!"

"What's fuck?" we asked.

"Fuck is when a Daddy puts his wiener in the Mommy and gives her a baby."

"Is it fun?"

"I guess so. My Mom and Dad like to do it." We hesitantly agreed, but only if it was going to be fun.

She took us to a large field near her house, where she undressed and lay down on the grass. She looked just like my sister, only bigger, and I had the same feeling that she was missing something, too. Marjorie told us to get undressed, but I was afraid we might get caught being naked. When Ted began to undress, I felt excitement and wanted to see him. I'd never seen another boy naked before. Neither had Ted. He said I had to get undressed, too, or he would stop. We laughed as we matched item for item until we had only our underpants on. I said he had to go first, and he did. His looked just like mine. He came over and took a close look at mine and touched it, and I touched his. We laughed with the pleasure of our nakedness and similarity. Annoyed, Marjorie demanded, "Hey, what about me? Aren't you going to fuck me?" She told me to lie on top of her and stick it in. I got on top of her, then asked where I was supposed to put it. I certainly didn't have an erection and didn't even know what one was. She said, "I don't know. There's supposed to be a hole down there somewhere." It all seemed dumb to me, like that time with Sheila, the girl next door. Then she had Ted try it, and they both seemed puzzled about what was supposed to happen. He got off of her and came over to me. Innocently, I asked if he wanted me to try to fuck him, and he laughed and lay on the grass like Marjorie. She said we were both silly and told us boys weren't supposed to fuck boys, just girls. But I wanted to touch Ted and lie down on him. I liked him and wanted to be close to him. He knew I was about to, so he jumped up laughing and started a game of chase. I felt hurt. Just then, Marjorie's mother called. We dressed quickly and left. I liked seeing my friend Ted in the brilliant sunlight, standing naked in his tooled leather cowboy boots, smiling at me. His body was like mine. He was like me. Marjorie was different. The process of male bonding and preference had begun.

School strengthened my curiosity about people and the world I lived in. I was filled with questions. Why can't we fly like the birds? Where does the sun go at night? Where does the world end? How many people are there? What's inside the earth? Why aren't snakes warm? How do caterpillars become butterflies? "Go ask your father," my mother answered, repeatedly. When my father told me the earth was round, I was amazed. "Why don't the Chinese on the bottom of the earth fall off?" He said something about ants not falling off a balloon, and I said ants held on with their feet, but people didn't. He didn't know, but he said mine were good questions. Several days later, he brought me two highly-illustrated science books for boys. He said he wasn't smart enough to answer all my questions but hoped the science books would help. I was emotional about his admitting that he couldn't do something and that he wanted to help me. I carried those books with me wherever I went. They were filled with wonder, but most of all, they were a gift from my father.

My dad bought me an old, red bicycle to ride to school when I was in the second grade. The school was three or four miles away. The bike was too big for me, so my dad put thick wooden blocks on the pedals. One day after school, I went out to the bike rack and found all the air had been let out of my tires. Some eighth grade boys were standing nearby, laughing. Then I noticed the tires on all of the bikes were flat. I had to push that heavy bike with its flattened thick balloon tires all those miles home. As I did, I remembered the laughter of those smirking boys. I hated them for the helplessness they made me feel. And I hated them for the easy closeness they shared. I couldn't understand why they wanted to be so cruel, or why they enjoyed it. I knew I wasn't like them, and I didn't want to be. I was different. They knew that, too, and they laughed at me.

My second grade teacher was Mrs. Robinson, a kind and friendly woman, who looked like my grandmother. From her, I learned penmanship and patriotism. Every morning we pledged our allegiance—whatever that was—to the flag, then turned toward the windows with the view of our black asphalt playground and sang *America the Beautiful*, with its "purple mountains' majesty and amber waves of grain." I'd never seen a mountain and was confused about what grain had to do with the ocean, but dear Mrs. Robinson always seemed to be emotional after leading us in this fine song. Several times I saw tears in her eyes. I liked her. It was World War II, but we hardly knew it. I suppose that's why she cried when we sang that song.

There were no kids near my home, and I missed my friends at school. I was lonely at home and began to explore deeper into the large forest near my house. Early one morning in the heart of this forest, I heard a branch crack. A bear, I thought! I hid behind a bush and waited. Leaves and twigs were snapping beneath its feet, then all sound stopped. I waited for what seemed to be hours, although it was probably only minutes. Quietly, I inched up to the crest of the hill where I'd last heard the sounds. I looked over, and there, below, I saw a boy; he seemed to be asleep. He was about 14—maybe an eighth grader. I shuddered, because I feared eighth graders. He had curly blond hair and a very pretty face, and he wore a torn tee shirt several sizes too big for him. I watched him for a long time. Nothing moved except his chest. I tossed a small twig at him. No response. Maybe he's sick, I thought. I crept down to him and watched him breathe, then I reached out and touched his arm. Suddenly, he exploded with yells; and, in an instant, I was pinned to the ground! He sat on my chest, laughing. He said he'd been following me for at least an hour, and I never even knew he was there. "Now, I'm going to tie you up and cook you in a cannibal pot!" he growled. We wrestled down the hill. "They'll never ever find your bones this far in the forest!" he shouted, and we began to laugh. He started tickling me, so I yanked on his tee shirt, accidentally ripping the shoulder out. "Now you're in for it, kid!" he warned. He grabbed my tee shirt, pulled it off forcefully, and threw it high into a tree. He smiled, said his name was Peter, and asked my name. He told me he was in the eighth grade, and I told him about the eighth graders and the bicycle tires. He said not all eighth graders were that way, after all, he just ate kids he found in the forest! I told him I was in the second grade, and he said I was very lucky I wasn't a first grader. I really liked him and was pleased that he seemed to like me. He said he knew every part of the forest and offered to show me some of his favorite places, especially the cliff with the swinging vines he'd cut, just like in the Tarzan movies. He confided he wanted to be like Tarzan.

When we came to the vine cliff, he demonstrated his skill at traveling by vines. He was agile and graceful, and I admired him. I felt excitement whenever he smiled at me. His adolescent body fascinated me, and I was aware of wanting to touch him, to explore his muscles, but I didn't, because my parents were not people who touched. They often told me to keep my hands to myself. (My grandfather was the only person I remember who ever touched me. When I was small, he liked to hug me, tickle me, and hold me on his lap while he told me stories. One time I felt a long, thick, hard thing in his pants. I grabbed it and asked him what it was. He was embarrassed and nervously said that it was a pipe stem, but I didn't believe him, because it was too thick and felt like rubber. I realized only as I was writing about this that I had actually felt the erect cock that had conceived my mother—one of life's more unusual gratuities.)

When we were resting, Peter—I thought of him as a young Tarzan—told me about his family; his was not a happy home. He was the youngest of four boys, and his brothers often beat him up. His father drank and his mother was dead. He listened to the stories about my family and said I was very lucky. With a rush of excitement, I said I'd ask my parents if he could come and live with me in our home. He looked sad and said it wouldn't work. Although he'd like to, he said his father would never let him go. He seemed to accept and care about me. He listened to me, and that was new and wonderful. Several times he said that he ought to be getting home before his father came back, but I did everything I could to keep him with me. When the forest began to darken ominously with the setting of the sun, he said he was really in for it, because his dad would already be home. He walked rapidly, and I followed him until we came to the path leading to my home. He put his hands on my shoulders, "I like you, Denny. Lucky you're a second grader! Bye now." I asked if I'd see him again. "Maybe. I come to the vine cliff a lot."

I went many times to Peter's vine cliff and waited. I imagined him swinging with that graceful freedom of his. I planned what we could do together when he returned. I missed him so much as I waited that I pretended to talk with him, but he never came. I told my mother about him; she knew where his family lived but warned me to stay away. His father was dangerous; he'd been in prison. Even so, I found Peter's house and often watched for him but never saw him. I was too afraid of his father to go to the door. There was this nature boy, a very strange enchanted boy, and I never saw him again—attachment and loss. But as a mysterious symbol of beauty, power, and acceptance, he continued to live as part of me. I was seven when Peter became my first idol, my first hint of love. Half a century later, I'm still attracted to males who look like Peter, and Nat King Cole singing *Nature Boy* fills me with a beautiful sadness.

My third grade teacher was a glamorous woman in her early 30's. She wore makeup, perfume, bright jewelry, and colorful, form-hugging skirts and blouses. She was the prettiest woman I'd ever seen. I liked to study the curves of her body that were so well outlined by her tight clothing. When she smiled at me, I felt embarrassed, because I thought she knew I was imagining her naked body and felt complimented by my interest. Every once in awhile, she would give me a hug—she did that with all of the boys—and when she did, I would be flooded with the musical tinkling of her bracelets, necklaces, and earrings and the wonderfully rich spiciness of her perfume. She looked like those rich and beautiful people I'd seen in *Life* magazine. I couldn't understand why such a pretty woman had to work; pretty women could easily get married, so I imagined that her husband had been killed in the war or something; I felt sad for her when I thought about that. But she seemed to be happy, and I was awed and excited by her.

I discovered the wonder of books and their new realities in her class. The one I liked best was called *Wagon Wheels*. It was about the western migration, mountain men, Indians, pioneers, and all sorts of exciting things. It was like my grandfather's tales of his voyages to the Arctic and the South Seas, of bare-breasted women of India he whispered to me about, of giant railroad trains and Ol' Dan McGinty, and of wild savages and vicious tigers. It wasn't until I was 12 that my mother told me all of his stories had been lies—yet another lesson in the rich weavings of attachment and loss in the fabric of my life.

We moved often during my upbringing. These moves strengthened my self-reliance and my loneliness. When my father was appointed manager of a munitions plant in Texarkana, Texas, we moved there from Ohio. My parents didn't like the town. It was the first time I'd seen "darkies." When my father put me beside an elderly black man on a cotton wagon to take my picture, I suddenly realized the old man was afraid of us. Segregation was all around us, but I was just beginning to see it. One evening, when I was downtown with my parents, I saw a car load of potbellied white men racing around the corner onto the main street. As the car passed in front of me, I saw a rope tied to the back bumper. The other end was tied around the neck of a black man— mercifully dead. My father told me the man had been tortured by those "good ol' boys." He wouldn't tell me what they did to the man, but I heard him tell my mother. He said they pulled his penis and testicles off...with pliers. My parents were greatly agitated after this. My father protested to various officials but was told by the town mayor, "If you Northerners don't like it here in the South, y'all should go back where y'all come from." I was very proud of my father for taking on the city officials. We left within the year.

The small group of families from the North who had come to run the munitions plant stayed to themselves. The Southerners resented us, so I was very lonely that year. I began to sleep walk and remember my father waking me up in our neighbor's yard one night. "What the hell do you think you're doing?" he barked with fear and anger.

There was a Southern boy living next door to us who had a pet squirrel. I liked the boy and tried to be friends with him, but his mother kept calling him in whenever I was around. As usual, my mother asked about the girls at school I liked, and she hired a taxi several times to take me over to one of their houses. I felt important and rich riding in a taxi, but I was still very lonely.

I became so seriously depressed that my parents were concerned about me. I didn't know what was wrong. I just sat around and did nothing. I was extremely lonely, and my cold family was hardly a resource. My mother became so worried that she had me spend a few days with an intelligent, well-educated friend of hers—a teacher. She talked with me for hours, trying to get me to do things. I wasn't interested. One day, she had me lie on the sofa. She covered me with a blanket and said she was going to play some music for me on her phonograph. It was Stravinsky's *Firebird Suite*. I was to listen for the firebird. The very idea of a firebird excited me. I wanted to see a picture of it, but there wasn't one on the album. When the music began, I came to life. Never had I heard anything as wondrous and complex. In my imagination, I could feel the heat from those feathers of flames. Again and again I had her play it. Neither of my parents were interested in music; it didn't exist for them. That day, with the bird of fire soaring in the sky above Texarkana, Texas, I entered the kingdom of music, one of the great realms that has enabled me to live.

Other than the magic of the firebird, my most significant memory from this year in Texas is about kites. I was still very lonely, so one weekend my parents took me to a nearby park. Many families were there that spring day, hundreds of people of all ages happily being together. Their happiness made me feel even more alienated. I was an outsider, and I didn't know how to get in—another theme of my life. I walked around looking at the ground, watching pairs of feet going to and fro. My father became excited and said, "Denny, lift your head up! Look over there! Look to the sky!" There against the brilliant blue, dancing with the graceful delight of a ballet, were hundreds of dazzling kites. The very townspeople who had cheered the death of a black man now celebrated the sheer delights of the arabesques of kites. I was grateful that these adults had created this beauty. It was as though they were giving me a gift to cheer me up, but I knew they didn't even know I was there. Against the background of my loneliness, the astonishing beauty of these kites of grace gave me a sudden hopeful feeling that perhaps I could value this world.

When the year in Texarkana was up, we moved north to Chiahoga Falls, Ohio, where my father continued his rise through the ranks of the B.F. Goodrich

Company. My fifth-grade year was as lonely and uneventful as my fourth. Baseball and football were popular, but I didn't know how to play. Ironically, my father was a college football star; his athletic scholarship made college possible for him. I asked him to teach me, but he said he didn't have the time. He did buy me a set of football shoulder pads, though, but since I didn't even know the rules of the game, I sold them to a neighborhood boy who coveted them. My father's reaction went beyond anger—in anger there is still hope for change—to contemptuous resignation, an attitude he never abandoned. I was not like him, and because of this, I was disgusting in the eyes of my own father. My mother understood my anguish. Privately, in her own way, she expressed compassion, but we both understood that she could not openly oppose him. One does not bite the hand that feeds.

There was a hero in our neighborhood, an athlete. He was tall, powerfully built, and very handsome—one of the bronzed gods of high school. What I remember most about Tom was his gentle, shy friendliness. He seemed to like me, and for this I was grateful, even honored. My mother talked about what a beautiful young man he was, with his wavy hair, his dark brown eyes, his large hands, his perfect lips. She said he looked like he was created by Michelangelo. I remember how shy and embarrassed she was whenever Tom came over. My father was even animated around him and, with unusual familiarity, shared with Tom his finest hours of football glory on the college fields of praise. "Fine young man, that Tom! Top caliber! You ought to spend more time with him, Denny," he advised. I knew exactly and painfully what he meant; Tom was the kind of son he wanted, a jock.

One day, I went over to the house of a boy my age and heard him screaming and crying. His mother was beating his bare bottom with a broom stick. Parents often beat their kids in those days; being God-fearing was considered a virtue. I told Tom what I'd seen, and the boy never forgave me. He said I was a liar and that he was going to get even with me. He harassed me for weeks. Tom said I shouldn't avoid a fight with him, but I didn't think I could control myself if I got into a fight. When I told Tom this, he said I was just afraid. A short time later, Tom told the boy to ambush me in a field on my way home from school. As I passed by, the boy leaped from behind a bush and knocked me to the ground. Something exploded inside of me, a combination of survival, vengeance and buried anger from my past. The next thing I was aware of was the sight of the boy's pretty face covered with blood. My hands were around his neck pounding his head into the ground while my thumbs forced his voice box into his throat. These actions seemed to be those of my hands, not me. Tom dragged me away from the terrified boy, and as if waking up, I became rational. "I'm sorry Denny, I didn't understand when you warned me," Tom said, still shaken. The boy missed several days of school and returned cut and bruised. He avoided me completely. When my father heard about the fight from the boy's angry parents, he said it was too bad I hadn't knocked the kid's front teeth out. He was proud of me! I told the boy I was very sorry I'd hurt him. He said he worried about what Tom would think of him if he knew his mother still spanked him and asked me to tell Tom I'd lied. But I didn't. Why should one deceive and betray his shy and friendly god?

Chapter Three

The year I turned 12, my father was transferred to Kirkwood, Missouri. It was a long, hot trip from Ohio, and my pet blue racer snake that was riding in the car trunk didn't make it.

Kirkwood altered the course of my life. It is my holy ground. It was a friendly, safe community. No one locked their doors. Visitors were always welcomed. (This was before TV replaced human interaction.) Most evenings, neighbors usually gossiped while kids played. Misbehavior was corrected by any adult who saw it, and everyone had a reputation.

The divorced woman next door to us was often visited by a young handsome priest from a nearby seminary in the afternoons. She said she was taking religious instruction from him, but the married women of the neighborhood were threatened by her and snubbed her. I understood how lonely she was. I always spoke to her, but my mother wouldn't.

We played too much baseball in the sixth grade. Although I didn't know it until I was 16, I was born with an eye condition that allows me to see with only one eye at a time. The sizes of the images from each eye are too different for visual fusion to occur, minimizing depth perception. I was so bad at catching and batting that I was relegated to right field, my Siberia—the gulag of sixth grade. There was nothing I could do but endure it. I counted dandelions. One day, I saw a boy who was playing catcher get hit full force on the side of his head with a bat. He was hospitalized with a fractured skull. Baseball stopped for that year, and I was glad to see it end. It all seemed so pointless.

At least I had nature, and my curiosity about it reached such a point that one day I decided I had to know what was inside of a toad. I found a particularly large one. I knew I shouldn't harm it, but the temptation was too strong. I decided that sacrificing just this one toad and never doing it again wouldn't be totally unforgivable. I used a razor blade. When I got to the heart, it was still beating. I cut it out, and it continued to beat. I felt awful, but I had to know what was inside the heart. I was a murderer of toads, but I still wanted to know. The eyes of toads still induce guilt.

. . .

These memories of significant episodes from my childhood are important, because it is against this background that the most crucial transformation of my life is to be understood. These seemingly unrelated episodes of meaning are interlocking parts of the seamless whole. The specific events of my new birth in Kirkwood were totally hidden in layers of repression when I was at Purdue. They were the keys I dared not find. Rarely, occasionally if we are very fortunate, events occur that transform our fragmented and superficial awareness into wholeness. These moments of heightened comprehension have the quality of holiness; they are the ultimately sensible moments of human existence by which we understand what we are. Through them we know the ground of our humanness. These moments become sacred symbols on the altars of our souls. In the spring of my 11th year, I was transformed by such a revelation, for which I am forever grateful.

In our back yard, suspended beneath old cherry trees, was a large orange hammock with white fringe, imported from Honduras. I was impressed that it was from a foreign country. One gentle spring afternoon when the cherry trees were in full bloom, I fell asleep in that hammock listening to the soft hum of bees in the clusters of white cherry blossoms above. Suddenly, the hammock moved, and I felt something touch my chest. I opened my eyes and saw a hand. I followed the extended arm to the shoulder, across the white tee-shirted chest to the neck, and then up to the startling face. Sitting on the hammock beside me was a boy a few years older than I, but there was something about him that made him seem much more mature. His head was crowned with graceful blond curls that were backlit by the sun, framing his face in a golden glow. Behind him was a profusion of white cherry blossoms against the brilliant blue of a perfectly clear sky. The immediate emotional impact of his face was visceral, intense, and permanent. Even five decades later, I can vividly see this scene by merely closing my eyes. My impression of that extraordinary person was of radiant beauty expressing joy, acceptance, openness, trust and warmth. His eyes were the smiling eyes of youth, the kind with the permanent smile lines along the lower lids, and these eyes mirrored the blue of the sky. His light, delicate, perfect skin and the shape of his amazing face gave him the mysterious beauty of androgyny. This astonishingly beautiful portrait was to become the master icon in the shrine of my soul, for this youth would become a symbol of the highest values I would have the ability to comprehend. This immediate transforming image would itself make my life possible. In that instant, the holy time of my life began.

"Hi! You're the new boy! I'm Keith, Keith Amadeus. What's your name?" he asked. His voice was filled with playful warmth, but I was too overwhelmed with his image to be able to reply. His face clouded over, and then, like the sun shining through, he smiled and asked, "Can't you talk?" Still I couldn't reply. "Are you mad I woke you up?"

I managed to blurt out my name and that I wasn't angry before the warmth of his smile played my emotions again, leaving me speechless. He was astonishing. His hand still rested on my chest, and his relaxed touch communicated an acceptance I hadn't known in my life. I felt a sudden sadness when Keith made an expressive gesture, ending the accepting contact. His eyes, however, maintained it. It was mostly the ease with which he accepted me that was astonishing—the rest was his beauty.

He was interested in the hammock, so I asked if he wanted to try it. I started to get out, but he stopped me, saying both of us would fit. When I moved over to give him more room, he laughed and said, "Don't you like me next to you?"

"You're very friendly, aren't you?" I observed.

"Yes! Everybody says that about me!" He asked where I was from, what

I liked to do, and about my family. He was full of questions, and finally, he began to talk about himself. I asked why I never saw him at school. He told me he was in the seventh grade, in junior high. He said I'd be going there next year, and we could go together. This pleased me. I was a little worried that he wouldn't want to relate to me, because I was still in grade school.

Keith told me, down-playing his pride, that he was the captain of a local baseball team, and his brother, who was 17, was a baseball star in high school. Keith invited me to watch him play, but I hesitated, because I didn't want him to know how poor a ball player I was. He sensed my hesitation and acknowledged that the game did get awfully boring at times. I agreed, a pretense to cover my real reason for hesitating.

When Keith talked about his parents, a sadness and confusion crept over him. He told me he didn't get along very well with them, and they sometimes hit him. I told him about my father beating me and he understood; he'd been punished with a belt, too. He remained silent and within himself for a few moments, then suddenly jumped up from the hammock, laughed, and pulling my arm, said, "Come on! I want to see your house. Show me your room!" And off we went into the incredible adventure of discovering one another. That process of discovery would develop into compassion, love, betrayal and, eventually, transcendent love. It was one of the most psychologically significant relationships of my life, but because of my repression, that lost, frightened young man I was at Purdue couldn't even remember Keith—for a good reason, survival.

Keith was popular, and friendship for him was an effortless thing. But, as our relationship grew, we spent less time with his friends and more time by ourselves creating the imaginative adventures of youthful heroes as we explored our world together. There were the fallen remains of an old stately home off by itself in a meadow. Its huge stone cellar was a perfect place for us to set off fireworks and gasoline bombs. There were stone ledges beside a forest stream where deadly copperhead snakes sunned themselves. A well-aimed stone thrown from daring safety would send them into the darkness from which they came. What a wondrous place of evil!

One evening, just at dusk—the kind of summer evening that draws adolescent males as light does to moths—Keith and I were playing tag with an older boy. Phil was about 15, tall and large. Keith could just outrun him and this frustrated Phil. The challenge was given and the chase was on, over fences, around trees, behind garages they streaked, Keith issuing challenges with taunting laughter and Phil responding. With a final effort, Phil lunged full force to tackle Keith. He caught a fleeing foot, and down they went. In an instant, Phil had Keith pinned beneath him. Keith's laughter was like a summer song, which Phil began to echo with his own. He tickled Keith, and the songs of their happiness greeted the stars.

After a while, Phil grew quiet and just looked at Keith. Keith was puzzled, and became silent, then Phil said, "I'm going to put my hand inside your pants and touch you!" "Bet you can't!" Keith shouted. With peals of laughter, they struggled, wiggled, and rolled around. Phil managed to loosen Keith's black leather belt and jerked it off; but, just as he shoved his hand under Keith's

Levi's, Keith twisted free, jumped up, and ran over to me. He was flushed and still laughing; but, as Phil started to walk over to us, Keith challenged, "You come one step closer and Denny and I'll pull all your clothes off and rip it off! Won't we, Denny?" Phil checked the strength of the alliance with a glance toward me, and it was over.

That night, I wasn't able to go to sleep. I kept seeing this image of Phil with his hand inside Keith's pants. I wondered what it would feel like to do that and what Keith looked like. He seemed to enjoy what Phil did. I could still hear his laughter in my mind. Did he want Phil to do that, I wondered. I couldn't understand why I kept getting erections, or even what they were. I worried that they were a symptom of some strange illness. When I did sleep, I had several dreams about Keith, and each time I woke up, the symptom had returned. In one dream, he was smiling and walking toward me, but the front of his Levi's was missing; I could see what I imagined he looked like. I had no knowledge of sex other than it was what parents did to make babies, and that had been learned in the first grade from Marjorie Windows. The topic was simply never discussed in those highly repressed days in which even the Kinsey report on male sexuality caused a front page national furor and was condemned from the floor of the U.S. Senate.

I felt a confusing excitement whenever Keith came over during the next few days. Keith sensed my mood and asked about it. I denied any change, but Keith was convinced something was different. "Tell me what you think!" he demanded.

"Okay! Maybe something is different, but I don't know what it is!" I replied, honestly. He studied my face and was silent and serious. Whenever he did this, he seemed beyond his age, and I felt uncomfortable. Cautiously, he asked, "Phil and me the other night, did that bother you, Denny?" I looked away; it fit.

"Did you want him to touch you?" I asked.

"Not really. I didn't care...maybe I did! Did it bother you?" he asked. I assured him it didn't and said I'd wanted to do what Phil had done. Keith seemed to relax then, and I told him I'd dreamed about him. He looked delighted. "About me?"

"Yes, you!" I was embarrassed when I told him about my dream with the front of his Levi's missing, but he just laughed and glanced down at his fly. Then he laughed again. I asked him why he'd looked at his fly. He blushed, and when I pointed out that his face had turned pink, he reached out and pinched my nose, and we both laughed.

Keith looked at me questioningly and became thoughtful. He seemed beyond me. For an instant, I felt alone again. Then he grabbed my hand and told me to come with him. His hands were always warm when he touched me. I felt puzzled as we walked along, but he was my friend, my best friend ever, and I trusted him completely.

He took me to a house in the neighborhood that was under construction. The workman had gone for the day. He motioned me into the finished garage and closed the side door behind us. Brilliant sunlight came through the single window on one side of the darkened garage and formed a large shaft of dazzling light like a spotlight. The window looked out on fruit trees in the vacant lot next door. I remember the refreshing coolness of the garage in contrast to the heat of that summer day. The room was filled with the clean smell of pine studding and fresh concrete. Low stacks of lumber were piled along the wall beneath the window. Keith smiled at me and, like a graceful gesture in a ballet, pulled off his white tee shirt. He came and took off mine. He smiled again and hugged me before taking off his shoes, socks, and jeans—and then mine. Our matching white shorts remained as the last sign of our society. My heart was pounding with curiosity, fascination, embarrassment, excitement, and fear. "Someone will see us!" I whispered. My fear concerned public nakedness, not sexuality, for I had no knowledge of sex.

"No one will see us," Keith said calmly, smiling in gentle reassurance.

He put our clothes together in a pile—I liked it that he had put them together—then he turned toward me. He took a single step forward, stopped, then looked at me with that look of strange maturity. He took another step toward me. Keith now stood in the center of the patch of sunlight on the floor and was dazzlingly brilliant against the surrounding blackness of the background. Then, like motions in a noble Balinese dance, with swift, natural grace, Keith freed himself from his Jockey shorts and motioned for me to do the same. He stood there like a perfectly-conceived classical Greek statue in a relaxed pose waiting for me, except that his erection was pointing straight up along the midline of his fine body, almost touching the smooth skin of his abdomen. I was utterly awed by the incredible beauty of the whole configuration that was Keith Amadeus! I noticed his erection, but it was merely part of the whole that was Keith—my very best friend ever. His astonishing skin was of uniform smooth flawlessness, accented by graceful veins flowing underneath. Every part of him was beautiful—the position and shape of his feet, the structure of his hands, the ripples within the triangle formed by his breasts and belly button, his blond pubic hair and the two lines running from there to the top of each hip, the graceful curve of his buttocks, the sinuous lines everywhere outlining the shape he was. His shoulders and neck were a perfect pedestal for the display of the magnificence of his face and head, which was crowned and framed by thick ringlets of curls glowing like gold in the sunlight. Contrasting with this golden glow was the vivid, sky-blue of his eyes looking at me. I noticed how at ease and gentle he seemed. I thought, Keith trusts me; he really does. He really likes me; I don't know why he does, but I'm glad.

I didn't know what to do. Keith smiled and, with a graceful gesture of his hand, motioned for me to come to him. I hesitated a moment, because I was still awed by his beauty...then I took off my shorts, and we stood there as we are, as we are in nature, freed from the confines of our society, bound together in the rebellion of our nakedness, revealed to one another. I felt we had opened a door that had always been there and crossed over into a new world that would be entirely of our own making—Keith and I. The emotional rush of my newly claimed freedom actually made the world seem to wobble for several moments.

He looked at me—at my erection—and said, "I see you like me, too!"

There was a look of radiant happiness and joy in his eyes. We embraced in that shaft of sunlight; his skin was so very warm. I began to tremble all over with sensations and emotions that were fine and new. He whispered into my ear, "You've never done this before?" The warmth of his breath caused waves of tingling up and down my entire body.

"No," I said, shaking uncontrollably with sexual feelings.

He told me to relax and said he would show me some things I'd really like. "Touch me now, Denny—touch me there!" As he said this, I felt the warmth of his fingers and palm embracing my hardness. And when I touched him, I discovered how firm and hot as a fever he was. He led me to a neatly piled stack of pine lumber—I remember the fresh pine scent—where we could lie down together on a painter's new, canvas drop cloth. We lay down, and Keith began to explore my body with his gentle hands, and I followed his lead. It was all so new and free! I was knowing him through my hands and skin! He touched my eyelids, face, and lips with his searching warm fingers and then explored me with large sections of his skin and muscles, and then with his lips and tongue, and his smooth warm penis, which he rubbed all over me.

What happened inside of me was a series of impressions—images, sounds, sensations, sights, movements, feelings, the many curves of his body, colors, the slightly sweet fragrance and wet glistening of his skin—all of it blending together like a collage. Heat, motions of our muscles, softness, hardness, urgencies, breathing, the palms and fingers of my hands aching for ever more knowledge of him, feeling his response, touching and being touched, receiving and seeking information, all of it changing and becoming more intense. Then, suddenly, he took me deep inside his warm, questing mouth, causing a profound shift of my consciousness. All of these changing images and growing sensations were running together and taking on a life of their own. I was momentarily frightened. I opened my eyes and looked at Keith and thought, I trust him, he wouldn't hurt me, he's my best friend, he knows what this is all about. I relaxed and became tidal waves of sensations and wondrous new feelings. It was as if I were expanding out and upward into the universe! The sense of myself disappeared, and then even the sense of Keith! There was no longer the distinction between inner and outer—it was all fusing together; there was only the groaning and surging of this swirling massive sea of the senses! I looked down at the array of Keith's blond curls between my thighs and—overwhelmed—reached down and ran my fingers through those magical golden locks. Their texture and color flooded me with emotions and, as I said his name, there occurred an ecstatic convulsion of everything that was! And another! And again, and again! Some time passed, and slowly the sense of Keith returned and finally of myself. When we were separate again, I was in a new reality. I flooded with gratitude for him and held him close, and he held me.

When I could talk again, I asked what had happened to me. "Denny, your toes curled! I saw them! It's the very best when they do that! They don't always do that, but you got the very best on your first time!" I didn't understand about the warm, white splotches of something that had jetted from Keith onto my chest and hair. He smiled, amused that I was confused, and patiently explained all he knew about sex, telling me the names and answering all my questions.

"Have you done it often?" I asked, not really wanting to hear what I expected. He told me he and his brother had been doing it for a year or so but added that it wasn't as good with him as it had been with me, because we were best friends.

"Yes, Denny, we're best friends now for sure. Get dressed before I get excited again!"

Keith and I understood the prohibition against nakedness, but it didn't occur to us that what we had just experienced together could be objected to by any sane person. Such was our innocence. We had not yet faced the sanctified hate of so-called Christians, marching as to war—against us. I was almost 12; he was going on 14. My first experience was not typical, but neither was Keith. Because of him, friendship, sexuality, and love would always be joined in my mind. For many people, the erotophobes, sexuality is separate—a biological necessity, a mere animal function, like a pleasurable crap.

During the next two years, Keith and I were inseparable. We made love often and everywhere: an attic, a bath tub, a movie theater, cars, anyone's yard at night, a pond, beautiful places we knew in the forest, and on a hilltop overlooking the valley during a summer thunder storm. Best of all was when Keith stayed overnight with me. We talked, made love, talked some more, fell asleep in each other's arms, and woke one another to make love again. When Keith couldn't stay over, there were times when, with the first showing of the sun, I would awaken to a tap, tap, tap of small pebbles hitting my second-story bedroom window. There below would be Keith, smiling and waiting. I'd unlock the back door and into my bed he would come. Is it possible that we could ever know again such innocent trust and such complete acceptance? Adam and Steve in paradise, before their fall from grace, before we had eaten of the forbidden fruit of the knowledge of Judeo-Christian good and evil, before we hid ourselves in our closets of silent shame, before we starved and died.

. . .

My mother was always pleased to see Keith. She made him pose for drawings even though this embarrassed him. "He has the head of an angel!" she would exclaim. He would wink at me during these posing sessions.

My father was often away from home on business trips. He did, however, buy me a rifle for my 12th birthday. It was a Remington .22, and I stayed up all night taking it apart and looking at it in wonder. It wasn't that I wanted a rifle, the rifle was a valued symbol of my father's trust in me and an instrument of power. It was an unexpected acknowledgment by my father of my entry into manhood, of my early puberty. I was a "big gun," and I could shoot for real.

Shortly after I got my rifle, my mother came up to my bedroom, something she rarely did. She looked disdainfully at the practicality of my room's disarray and said we were going to have a talk about the facts of life. She had a book with her, *Growing Up for Teens*, I believe. It wasn't a conversation I

was ever likely to forget. Here is a fairly accurate reconstruction of part of it:
"You mean about the birds and bees?" I asked suspiciously.

"Well, not just that, Denny, but about why your body has changed and about taking care of yourself—diseases, marriage, and all sorts of interesting things." The phony sweetness of her voice gave her away.

"I know all about it! Keith told me everything!"

"Well, I'm glad he did, but we're going to have a talk anyway!" She looked irritated.

"Why doesn't Dad talk to me about these things?"

"Well, your father isn't comfortable talking about these things; besides, he doesn't have much time anymore—for anything. It's difficult for me, too, so you don't have to make it harder for me, Denny."

"I'm not!"

"You are! Now listen to me. We're going to have a nice talk."

"I already know all about it!"

"You don't! You're still wet behind the ears."

"I'm not!"

"Stop acting like a callow youth!"

I didn't know what "callow" was, and I wasn't about to ask. I shrugged with resignation after studying her face. What followed was an embarrassed presentation of male and female anatomy, with medical nomenclature, a full-page picture of a gang of sperm raping an egg, condoms, and more diseases than I could remember. The colored picture of ulcerating canker sores on a pathetic penis was immediately followed by an increase in the dulcet tones of Mom's voice saying, "But in spite of all these problems, sex between a husband and wife can be an uplifting expression of their love; at least, that's the way it's supposed to be."

"Is that the way it is for you and Dad?"

"Well, sometimes. It was once. You're not supposed to ask people about their private affairs, Denny!"

"Do only married people have sex?"

"Well, people should only behave that way if they are married."

"Why?"

"Because, Denny, the man and woman want to give each other a gift, the gift of virginity, when they get married. You wouldn't want to get used merchandise, would you?"

"But then they wouldn't know what they were doing!"

"They learn! Just remember, you're not to do it until you're married."

"Well, why are you telling me now? I'm only 12."

"If you don't shut that smart mouth of yours, I'm going to slap it." (Mom was a face-slapper.) "Now listen! We're almost through, Denny." (She'd already told me about raping women, pregnancy, molesting children, and those diseases.) "Now there is one more thing: perverts. You must never, ever become a pervert! They are the worst people that live. People hate them."

"Are they worse than murderers?"

"Well, yes...no...yes, they are! Denny, you must never, under any circumstance, become one of them!"

"What do they do, tell me!" I implored. This wasn't going to be boring after all, I thought.

"Well, I hate to even think about it, but perverts are men, if you could even call them that, that do things with boys or even other men."

"What things? Tell me!"

"Horrible things! Sexual things! Things too terrible to even think about. They don't even try to control that animal part all you men have. They do disgusting things, and when they're caught, they're put in prisons and mental hospitals where they belong. They can't earn a living, because nobody would ever want to hire one. Well, that's all I had to say. Remember, in marriage a man can express his love and respect for his wife sexually in a way that's beautiful and holy. He can choose not to act like an animal if he wants to. Now, I want you to remember that when you get married. Someday your wife will thank me for talking to you this way."

"How do you know? You don't even know who she'll be!"

"Oh, you're just impossible, Denny! You're as hardheaded as your father! All you men are just alike!"

I was relieved when she left. I'm not an animal, I thought. She'd said a pervert was a man. Since Keith and I were boys, I reasoned we couldn't be perverts, but I felt the birth of a new discomfort. I knew that nakedness was not allowed, but it hadn't occurred to me until this talk that lovemaking with the same sex could be objected to—it was the love that dare not speak its name, after all, and I was unnerved by the extent of society's and my mother's condemnation of what seemed to me to be so harmless, so pleasurable and wondrous, and so completely meaningful. I especially wanted to know what perverts did that she wouldn't talk about, that really interested me. I decided to ask Keith. He would know. But when I asked him, he said he'd never heard of a pervert. "Is it like a convert?" he asked.

Outside our town was a public swimming pool that became another place of revelation for me—one of my holy places. Keith and I hitchhiked there often. The pool was surrounded by a beautiful forest. It was a special place for Keith and me. We were best friends and were very happy there in the warmth of that summer. The old man who handed out towels in the locker room liked us. He always made us talk with him before he would give us our towels. "You're a couple of fine looking boys and such good friends!" he'd say.

I remember watching Keith on the diving boards one sleepy afternoon. Keith climbed to the high dive, paused at the end of the board, looked around, saw me, waved, and called my name—I felt self-conscious—and then leaped gracefully skyward, completed a perfect jack knife, and disappeared with hardly a ripple on the surface of the water. His laughing face, ringed with wet golden curls, appeared at the side of the pool next to me. "Did you see that? Did you see me, Denny?" he asked with pride. As he got out of the pool and walked toward me, I felt the familiar surge of warm emotions again. He stood there tanned and relaxed, dazzlingly bright in the light of the noon sun and framed by the blue of the sky. He moved slightly, and a drop of water on his bronzed shoulder caught the sun's light and blazed like a diamond. Slowly, it meandered down his body as if in a caress. As I watched this glinting rainbow drop descend across his smooth tanned skin, I suddenly understood what he was feeling where it touched him; I felt the flow of what Keith was feeling! He moved his fingers to that drop, indicating his awareness of it. The revelation of this moment for me was the realization of the inner reality of another person. I suddenly understood the experiencing of another, and with this realization, the boundaries of separation disappeared. There was no loneliness, only oneness. I believe it was the beauty of this moment of empathy that led to my eventual decision to be a psychologist. My friend at Purdue, Charlie Benson, completed the process that began with Keith.

My ability to comprehend Keith as a person in this empathic way was essential for compassion to develop within me. With compassion, the ability to love and to act justly became possible. Comprehension causes this compassion, and it is compassion that is the ultimately wise human response to life itself. Without it, we can have no hope of becoming fully human, and without our humanity, we are completely lost to the darkness. The rainbow refraction of the light of the sun in that particular drop of water on the body of one I loved is forever the symbol of the enlightenment that makes my humanity possible. Comprehension increases compassion, and compassion increases our comprehension of people as they are.

As Keith walked toward me, I experienced the flow of his muscles and the sensations of his skin. I was astonished by this new dimension of intimacy with him. He saw the intensity with which I was viewing him, and he blushed and quickly lay down beside me. "The way you're looking at me is making me hard! If you don't stop, everybody will see me!"

"Stay rolled over on your stomach, nobody will see you!"

"Tell me what you were seeing, Denny! Tell me what you see!" Keith said this to me many times during the course of our relationship. It seemed to be one of his major interests in me. We talked endlessly, but at that age, all I could verbalize to him was the beauty of that water drop on his skin and how I suddenly knew what he felt when it moved over his body. "I like the way you see things, Denny! Tell me some more!"

The next spring, at that same pool, while we were there, and saw it all, our friend, Tom Bell...drowned. He was 14. The pool that had taught me so much with a water drop, now with its final lesson of death, tried to teach me about life, but I was eternal and invincible in that cherry-blossomed spring of my life. Decades would pass before I understood that the whole of which I am a part, this cosmos, is itself the process of creation and destruction.

Keith and I didn't say much about Tom's death for several weeks. We didn't know how to cope with the fact. When we did talk, it was stumbling and confused. We admitted we'd both imagined the other dead at the bottom of the pool. Keith resorted to humor. "Here's what I'd look like!" Sprawling out on the ground, he did his best rendition of looking really dead. When it was no longer funny, I told him, "You can stop now!" There was no movement. "Stop, Keith! Stop it!" Still nothing. Imagining him dead was quickly not becoming a choice. "Get up! God damn it, Keith! Get up now!" One of his eyes slowly opened, looked at me, winked, then slowly closed. "If you don't get up right now, Keith Amadeus, I know what to do to get you up damn quick!" I didn't know what to do, but I told him that. He got up laughing, and it was as if he had come back from the dead.

"Don't you like me dead?" he teased.

"I like you warm," I replied seriously.

Exploding with laughter, he retorted, "I like me hot and hard! Wanna see my skull?" He pulled the skin back from around his eyes and clacked his grinning jaws. That action now seems like a terse metaphor for the human condition. This living image of Keith's skull entered my being, and like a proud and noble prince, cloaked itself in the richest weavings of meaning, significance, darkness, and power. This Prince of Death drew to himself, as in a lover's embrace, his compliment—that first sun-touched portrait of Keith. For a terrifying instant, I imagined life without Keith, but the torment of that idea caused me to hurl it back into the appalling darkness from which it came. One's first love is unlike all others, because we do not anticipate its end.

. . .

Because of our intense friendship, Keith and I lived life at an accelerated pace. We knew the wonder of a great winter ice storm, which transformed our world into a magical crystal kingdom. We explored the earth's insides in deep, limestone caves; slept in her green, moist forests in jungle hammocks; got sick smoking Prince Albert pipe tobacco and once tried to race our sperm on a microscope slide. We ventured into the inner city of St. Louis where Keith, wearing dark sunglasses and using his deepest voice, bought two tickets to the Gaiety Burlesque Theater. The man in the ticket booth was laughing but gave him the tickets anyway. Inside were mostly disheveled, lonely men in threadbare coats. Many sat with newspapers across their laps. The comedians were met with little enthusiasm from this newspapered audience and mostly incomprehension from us. We decided afterwards that the most interesting part had been the synchronized breast-tassel-twirling talent of the painted ladies. Bored, we were; erotic, they were not.

Sometime later, Keith's brother told him about an older girl of about 19 named Sunny, who "did it" with him and other guys. Keith wanted us to try it. She'd seen Keith and was attracted to him, or so Keith's brother said. Keith, however, was nervous about it and made me promise that I would go first. His brother told him that "whore" in Spanish was "puta," so Sunny became known as the puta girl. One, after all, did not "do it" with respectable women—such as the Virgin Mary and, of course, our own mothers, who endured it only to conceive beloved sons like ourselves—or so it seemed in the black and white world of our youth.

After about two hours of inane conversation with Sunny, fragmented by bursts of nervous laughter and punctuated with "puta," she became suspicious and asked what we were up to. Keith told her what his brother had said. She replied, "That kiss-and-tell son-of-a-bitch will never touch me again! Sure, I'll do it with you guys. I'm sure his virgin kid brother would be better than him any day! You can tell him I said that, too! Did you guys bring rubbers, or are you going to use mine? Who's first?"

The experience with Sunny was a task-oriented performance, something like learning how to drive. You know what's expected, but you haven't done it, and it's important for a teenage male to do it. It was a situation of having to acquire competence while being watched. The competence in question was the ability to successfully masturbate using only the unfamiliar vagina of a stranger who judged you. I had trouble with the condom, since I'd unrolled it first. Sunny laughed and showed me the easy way with a new one. I concentrated and began.

"Say you love me, Denny!"

"I don't."

"Say it anyhow! Say it now!"

"I like you."

"Say it like you really mean it!"

"Don't talk." Eventually, I got enough stimulation, and it was over. I was no longer a virgin, and I could leave this rite of passage with dubious honor—and relief. Later, I worried I might be a father; I hadn't checked for leaks. I was 13. On my way out, I whispered to Keith not to unroll the rubber first. (Had this harmless interaction happened in today's climate of sexual hysteria, Sunny would be charged with felony child molestation!)

"How was it?" I asked him on our way home.

"Okay. It was okay."

"Did you do it?"

"Yes."

"That's all?"

"I did it, but it wasn't as good as us." I remember he reached out for my hand, and we walked home holding hands as we often did. Boys weren't self-conscious about being affectionate in those innocent days, and most people didn't pay attention to it. Those who did—older women, mostly—would smile with pleasure at seeing how much we liked one another. A few men would frown and look away. Once, I asked Keith about a man who looked at us this way; I didn't understand. Keith said, "I guess he feels bad he isn't best friends like us." I've always remembered that.

Keith and I were in the school orchestra together. He played the trombone and trumpet, and I played the clarinet. The conductor used both a baton and a deadly accurate water pistol to teach us. One day, he announced a field trip to Keil Auditorium in St. Louis to hear the symphony. As I sat in the darkening auditorium next to Keith, I remembered the excitement of the *Firebird Suite* I'd heard in Texarkana. I'd never seen a symphony orchestra perform before. The musicians finished tuning up; there were a few moments of complete silence, and then the conductor's baton was raised. I knew what would follow would be beautiful, and I was tingling in suspense. There was a slight upward arc of the baton tip, and then the downward stroke signaling the shattering of silence. Enveloping me was the wondrous movement of sound, and I was flooded with the tactile sensations of overwhelming beauty. These increased so much that I closed my eyes to limit my awareness of the musicians, but as I did, I was no longer distracted, and the music possessed me completely. I put my hand to my throat and pressed in to contain sobs that pushed to get out. I believe we cry for happiness; because, at the moment of fulfillment, we can also then experience the opposite, the sorrow and grief of emptiness, the absence of what is of worth. To know what is, is also to know what is not. Keith put his hand on my arm and asked if I was all right. I nodded yes, and he smiled.

The emotional impact of the beauty of that music was so great that for weeks afterward I begged my parents daily to buy a phonograph. They relented, and Keith and I spent many afternoons listening to music. I preferred classical to popular music, because my emotions were complex and didn't follow a simple rhythmic dance beat. The first two albums I bought were the Grieg and Tchaikovsky piano concertos. They expressed what Keith and I felt together, and they bring back so many memories of him.

Memories of Keith saved me from my seventh grade teacher, Mrs. Craig, a thoroughly unpleasant woman. She once had us write an essay on whether we should be completely honest or not. I took the position that, while honesty was generally good policy, it, nevertheless, depended on the specific situation. I argued it would be justifiable to lie to the enemy in time of war if doing so would save lives. This budding heresy of situational ethics in a young mind in her charge was not tolerated by this self-righteous religious bigot. After praising the class on their fine moral character, she hissed, "But there is one among you, only one, who is so depraved of moral character that he does not believe in complete honesty. He is like a Judas among us. And he is sitting...there!" When she pointed her crooked finger at me, everyone turned and stared in confusion, fear, or revulsion. Her face was frozen in the patronizing pose of virtue vanquishing vice. I felt cast out and heavy with humiliation. In order to endure, I remembered Keith. Like a prayer, I said to myself, "I have a friend. I have a friend. I have a friend." This was the first time I evoked the image of Keith to save myself; it would hardly be the last. Eventually, the class was over. Peter Brederhoff, a boy I greatly admired, smiled sadly at me and lowered his eyes in compassion. This image of Keith would become the central organizing symbol of my psychological life, of what I am.

About this time, Keith began to plan our future together. He wanted us to move out West, buy some land, start a sheep ranch, and live happily ever after. He was committed and insistent. I was moved by this, but parental projections of my future always included, "When you get married...When you have your children."

"Can we do that?" I asked him.

"We can do anything we want to do!" he answered with a touch of irritation. How moving this memory is for me now. What little faith I have, I've always gotten from the faith of others. Isn't this true for almost everyone?

Keith got books from the library on farming, sheep and cattle, and the wild West, and we made lists of things we'd need. We learned the names of every car that passed by our little corner of the universe; for us, they were the chariots of freedom. The one we most wanted was a jeep. A neighbor owned one, and we would sit in it by the hour dreaming our future together. "Won't we get lonely on a ranch out West by ourselves?" I once asked him. Keith grinned at the novelty of the idea, and then said confidently and simply, "No!"

One evening, we were walking over to the pond at St. Joseph's Seminary as we often did. Young seminarians in their long black cassocks were strolling two by two reading prayer books. Earlier that day, I'd seen myself in a mirror. I was surprised at my changed appearance; I was deeply tanned and no longer as boyish. I looked more like young males I'd seen in magazine ads. When I talked to Keith about this, he told me to stand still. With exaggerated concentration, he slowly walked around me and looked me over, smiling. It was a setup for sure. "Well," he said, "you do look good!" Then, grinning and readying himself for the inevitable chase, he added, "But you're not nearly as good-looking as me!" When I finally caught him, both of us panting, he pointed to the pairs of young seminarians and asked seriously, "Do you think they do it together?" Later that night, fresh from swimming in shimmering moonlight, we lay on the grassy banks of St. Joseph's pond. To the sounds of sacred chanting from the young seminarians, we made love like naked pagans celebrating the summer solstice.

The next week, Keith learned that his family was planning to go on a three-week vacation—out West. Keith tried to talk them into taking me along, but they didn't have enough room. He said if I couldn't go, then he wouldn't go. I arranged to have him stay with us, but his father said no, and that was that. Keith consoled himself with the thought that at least he could look for a place for us to live when we moved West.

The week before Keith and his family were to leave, my father went on a business trip. My mother insisted I stay home with her to "take care" of her and my sister—whatever that meant. "You've got to be the man of the family now, Denny. I'm here all alone again." I managed to stay with her for three-and-a-half days without seeing Keith. He was getting depressed, and I was getting angrier, yet she insisted I not leave. I pleaded that Keith would soon be leaving for three whole weeks and that I only wanted to spend a few hours with him, but she refused. I told her she was being selfish. She got angry, and so did I. We yelled at each other. I told her enough was enough, and I was going to see Keith; I would be back later that evening. "Over my dead body!" she shrieked. She came over and slapped my face full force. My left ear ached and rang; she meant to hurt me. I became deliberate, and with all of my strength and anger, I smashed my fist deep into her stomach sending her crashing to the floor, breathless. "You'll never hit me again," I said and left for Keith's, her screams following me, "Just wait 'til I tell your father! Just wait 'til he comes home! I'll have him beat you senseless! You'll wish you'd never been born! You'll pay! You'll pay for this!"

Keith and I talked about this crisis and planned. He explained the situation to his mother and asked if I could live with them. She seemed amused but reassured us that my mother and I would make up. Later, after Keith's mother sent him to bed, he climbed out his bedroom window, as he often did, and we spent the night under the stars on a hilltop talking and holding each other. I was frightened about my father's returning. We decided that if he hurt me, Keith and I would run away to Florida to live with my aunt and uncle in Miami. My aunt Julia and uncle Johnny had lived in Africa for several years. Johnny had even killed a python, making him a hero for us. Keith asked many questions about them, then said he almost hoped my father would hit me, because we could go to Florida sooner than we could go out West. We decided to hitchhike to Miami and agreed not to tell our parents where we were. The more we talked, the better our plans seemed. When we anticipated all we could, Keith became happily resolved, "Denny, we can be together! We can live together, soon, just the two of us!" The rising sun found us asleep, clinging.

On the day Keith left for the West, he again tried to convince his parents to take me along, but there was no room for me. Just as they were leaving, Keith whispered to me that he'd gone back into the house and unlocked his bedroom window for me. He told me I could hide in his house if I needed to, and when he got back, we could go to Florida. He said he'd think about me, and he'd find a place for us out West. He wanted me to sleep in his bed if I stayed in his house. He told me not to mess around with other guys. Then he was gone.

The truth is that a great many adolescent males "do it" together. Research indicates between one-third to one-half of all white males have had at least one same-sex experience. Homophobia couldn't exist with such intensity if we didn't all have the biological capacity for such straightforward delight and pleasure. This new-found sexual capacity was readily shared by us as was any other new joy. After the initial novelty, it became a kind of affectionate nuzzling between friends. After all, we had no television to stupefy us into passivity. Open displays of affection between males were far more accepted then, since the topic of homosexuality was unspeakable in those days. I did have sex with others while Keith was away. It was different. It was good. Novelty excites. But most of all, it lessened the ache inside me for him; I closed my eyes and remembered him.

I was tense the day my father was due home, but my mother, who wouldn't speak to me after our fight or prepare a meal for me, was excited and even cleaned the house. When we heard the sound of his car in the driveway, I went to my room, locked the door, and put my rifle beside me. Just as my father reached the front door, my mother started screaming and sobbing. I remember every detail of that scene, because fear imprints such things in memory. When my father rushed in yelling, "Donna, Donna! My God, Donna, what's wrong?" I could hear her thrashing around on the floor, wailing. With the practiced skill of an old hysteric, she heightened the theatrical drama by not responding to his inquires. I knew what she was doing, and I knew this was going to be her best performance yet. I also knew that she knew I was listening to every word; she was playing to me, too.

"My God, save me Rube! Save me!"

"Donna, save you from what?"

"Save me! Please save me!"

"Donna. Get a hold of yourself! Stop this!"

"Oh, my God! It was so awful!"

"Stop it, Donna!"

"You don't know how terrible! I can never tell you!"

"God damn it, Donna. Talk to me!"

"Oh Rube, I can't bear to think of it!"

"My God! Was it a man, Donna? Was there a man?"

"Oh, no! Much worse!"

"Tell me! Is someone dead?"

"I can't bear to hurt you. If I told you, you'd be crushed with grief for the rest of your life! I'll hold the pain inside of me to spare you, Rube!"

"If you don't tell me, I'm going to shake you, Donna!"

"Your son!"

"What about him? Is he okay?"

"He tried to...tried to...kill me! Your son tried to kill me! Your son tried to murder his own mother!"

"Now calm down, Donna, and tell me exactly what happened. Get a hold of yourself!"

They talked softly after that. I could only catch occasional phrases and words, but I knew she had overplayed it this time. Dad was no fool. After about half an hour, he called me and told me to come down. As I walked down the stairs, I ran through my plans again. I would sit out of his reach in the chair near the front door. At the first sign of trouble, I'd bolt out the door and head south to fool him and circle back to Keith's at night. I wondered if Keith had left enough food; I could get my friends to bring me some. "I'm not going to hurt you," my father said reassuringly. "Now, tell me what happened, Denny."

"Rube, I've already told you what happened! Why are you asking him? He'll just lie!" my mother whined.

"Donna, every story has two sides. Now be quiet and let the boy talk."

"How dare you tell me to be quiet! How dare you! I'm your wife! Who do you think you are?"

"I said be quiet and I mean it. Now, be quiet!"

I described exactly what happened. He asked my mother if it were true that she hadn't allowed me out of the house and if she had slapped me. She was evasive but eventually owned up to it. My father, like a wise judge, paused and grew silent before pronouncing his verdict: "Denny, it was entirely wrong for you to hit your mother. You are never, ever to do that again, or you'll answer to me personally! This woman is my wife and your mother! She gave birth to you! Now apologize to her."

"I'm sorry I hit you, Mom."

"Make him say it like he really means it, Rube!"

"Donna, he said he was sorry. That's enough! Donna, it was also wrong for you to keep him from his friends, and you shouldn't have slapped him. He's not a little boy anymore. He's a young man now, and you should respect him as a man. He can see his friends when he wants to. Now, let's hear no more of this." Thus spoke my father. I was amazed by his regard for me; the entire world suddenly seemed friendlier.

That night, when I went to the dinner table, there was no place set for me. This angered my father. "Set my son his place at my dinner table, Donna! Quit acting like a petulant child! Now, don't ever do anything like that again!" With seething submissiveness, she brought me a plate. When I noticed my meat portion was all fat and gristle, I looked up to see her smiling revengefully at me. It was a game, a triangle, a lover's quarrel, except I didn't love her. My father wanted her love, she wanted mine, and I wanted his. I had only to bring my father's attention to my plate for her to lose the round, but out of pity for her powerlessness, I said nothing. My father talked about some property in a town called Glendale where he was going to build a house. Mother said little. I thought about the West.

We made peace, and each morning, I asked my mother how many more days it would be until Keith came home. "One less than yesterday, Denny!" was always her reply. When the day arrived, I went to his house before breakfast. I'd often walked past it during those endless three weeks. Once at night, I'd gone through the window into his bedroom and lay on his bed, but it made me feel worse, so I just walked by the house hoping his family might return early. No car was there. "They probably won't get home until late, Denny. I'm sure Keith will come over as soon as he gets home. Thinking about it will just make it seem longer for you," counseled my mother. Keith didn't return that day.

"What if they had a car accident? Maybe Keith is in a hospital somewhere! Why aren't they back, Mom?"

"Denny, I'm sure they just got delayed somewhere. Maybe they decided to take a few extra days. Everything will be all right. Keith is fine. Just be patient for awhile."

"Nobody would know to call us if anything happened!"

"Denny, just be patient! ...Did Keith have any relatives around here?"

"No! That's why we'd never know!"

"He's all right, I tell you! Don't his grandparents live around here?"

"No! No! No!"

"Calm down, Denny."

"He's dead! Keith's dead! And I'll never know!"

"Stop it! You're just hurting yourself! Go over and see if they're back yet. And let me know right away if they are!" They still didn't return.

On the following afternoon, the neighbor next to Keith's signaled for me. "Keith's parents called us last night, Denny, there's been some trouble."

"Is it Keith?"

"Yes, they had to take him to the hospital."

"Why?"

"Well, he was climbing some rocks and slipped. He fell and broke his arm. It's in a cast now, but he's all right. They'll be home this evening."

The sky was being painted with the brilliant colors of a setting sun when I saw the dusty car in their driveway. Keith's mother was just entering the front door. She saw me, waved, and called into the house, "Keith! Denny's here!" From deep inside the house I heard it: "Denny! Denny! Denny!" Then Keith was rushing down the walk, eager, joyous, vital, wounded, looking more beautiful than ever, his face coming closer, flooding my universe with "Denny! Denny! Denny!"—sounds that would affirm my existence to the ends of all time. His immediate knowledge of the void, of absence, was shown by his tears wetting my face in holy communion. His kind mother, arms folded, sighed and smiled with contentment in the knowledge of her son's joy.

Chapter Four

That summer, my father decided I was old enough to work, so at 14 I got a job in the produce department of a grocery store lugging sacks of potatoes, trimming cabbages, stocking shelves and looking busy. Keith, who was also saving his allowance and doing odd jobs, was excited about our new income. In an old cigar box wrapped with green rubber bands that he kept under his bed, we pooled our fortune, 27 dollars, for our new life in the West.

The humid heat of that Missouri summer became oppressive. Like the dogs in our neighborhood, Keith and I sat in the shade and waited for the relief of nightfall. He'd found a place for us in the West, and he described that ranch in dream-filled detail. That place became larger and more beautiful with each day's telling—cool valleys, canyons, streams, clear lakes and gentle deer walked upon our mountainsides. When I mentioned a new discrepancy in his wishful recall, he'd say, "Who went West? Me! Who saw it? Me! Did you? No! Besides, there are places just like that out there somewhere. I know it!" His was a living faith; mine, a doubting hope.

One evening at dinner, my father broke his usual silence and said I'd better get rid of my pets and get my things packed, because our new house in Glendale would be finished sooner than he'd thought. The movers were coming the following weekend. I rushed over to Keith's house and told him, but Keith just said the house couldn't be finished that soon and kept on talking about how we could get more money for our life in the West. As it began to sink in to him, he asked if I found out if he could live with us. My parents said no, and my father just laughed at the idea and said I'd have plenty of new friends in Glendale. We talked about running away to Florida to live with my aunt and uncle, but I told him I didn't think it would work; they would have to tell my parents. He became angry with me and said I could do anything I wanted to do, attributing a power to me that I didn't have in order to create the illusion of control, and thus hope, in the essential arbitrariness of our fate. He even accused me of wanting to go to Glendale and said our neighborhood wasn't good enough for my stuck-up father and that maybe the people in Kirkwood weren't good enough for me. I begged him to stop, but he was hurt and angry. I remember he said, "Go live in your fancy new house! If that's what you want, then go. I don't care! I won't even know you're gone. I won't even think about you. See if I care. Just go!" I told him over and over that I didn't want to leave him, but I had no choice. I kept telling him we could talk on the telephone and maybe live together during the summers, but he was very angry and wouldn't listen. Keith refused to see me for three days.

When I heard that a dangerous thunderstorm was headed our way, I went to Keith's house and dragged him from his bedroom. I wanted us to watch the storm come in from the hilltop where the water tower was. His mother told me he'd just been staying in his room and not even going to his team's baseball games. She'd take dinner in to him, but he wouldn't eat. She was glad I was getting him to do something, but she was sorry I was leaving the neighborhood. She said she was pleased I'd asked Keith if I could live with them and said she'd be happy to have a son like me, but she reminded me that my mother loved me, too. I wasn't sure about that. She said Mr. Amadeus wasn't any easier to get along with than my father.

Keith and I hiked to the top of the hill overlooking our valley. The light was eerie with a greenish-yellow cast. In the west, we saw a long line of towering white clouds rolling on a layer of blackness. The radio had warned of tornadoes. Keith agreed to come with me only when I told him about them. We wanted them. "Maybe they'll hit Glendale," he said bitterly. He avoided looking at me, but when he did, his eyes still flashed with anger and hurt. I looked away with confusion and guilt for a crime I couldn't understand, and I felt the old loneliness again, the way it had been before Keith. I reached out and put my arm around him, but he pulled away. He'd never done that before. For the first time, I felt the pain that would make me a man of constant sorrow.

As that great storm rolled across the plains and engulfed us, the silence between us was broken only by the wailing chorus of the winds and the deep-throated thunder claps like a dialogue of male rage between us. I watched the rain first questioningly touch him and then possess him. I hated it. His wet tee shirt clung to his body like the desperate embrace of a lover. I felt angry that he would let a tee shirt touch him, but not me. Jagged bolts of lightning split the blackness, freezing Keith in statuary poses of deathly whiteness. This convulsive rage of nature expressed my own, and when Keith saw the anger in my eyes, he relaxed and put his hand on mine. His face seemed to say he knew I felt what he felt. Becoming gentle again, he said he would stay over with me on the last night. We left then; the storm was getting worse.

On Friday night, when Keith was to stay over, our last night together, the storm turned ugly. Everything became possessed by the massive blackness of it. Water flooded the streets, power lines broke, and sirens howled helplessly in the distance. My father paced from window to window. I watched the vacant lot behind our house, the way Keith would be coming. Our house shook with the blue-white strikes of nearby lightning. My dad said it was the worst storm he'd ever seen and told my mother and sister to get away from the windows. They moved to the living room and sat around a candle. It became so dark that I could no longer make out forms in the empty lot. Each imagined change in the blackness I believed was Keith—"There he is, Mom!"—but a lightning flash would illuminate only emptiness. I tried to call Keith, but the telephone was silent; the lines were down. I decided to run over to his house. "Absolutely not!" ordered my father.

I stared into the blackness for several hours. My mother came and put her hands on my shoulders. She said it was too late for Keith to come; I should go to bed. At that moment, a stroke of explosive lightning turned everything blinding bright as it hit the large cherry tree in our back yard, breaking it apart and splitting black high-voltage wires in two. My mother screamed. For too long a time, to the wailing of sirens, red lights flashing emergency, rain pounding, winds howling, I watched the darkness being slashed by the flaming blue arcs from those high-tension wires as they beat and flailed the earth, blocking the path Keith would have taken to come to me. That scene was the entrance to the dark realm that would lead to the very center of night itself. As this image entered me, I entered it. It was the beginning of my descent. My journey would be very long.

There is never enough time. In the morning, as we were about to leave for Glendale, the storm cleared briefly, and Keith appeared. We talked about the storm; its damage was everywhere. Too soon, it was time to go. Keith slowly waved and stood slumped in place as we drove off. I watched him watching me until I could no longer see him.

It seemed to me that we were simply taking a family vacation. My trip to Glendale would be something like Keith's trip out West; he'd be pleased with my adventures. I knew he would, because I couldn't think otherwise. My use of this defensive strategy of repression was a major obstacle to my becoming a person. Repression, one of the many forms of ignorance, protects us from the loss of value, or the imagined loss, by blinding.

Glendale was a well-manicured community with a country club and a self-deprecating awareness of nearby Ladeau, where those of real wealth resided. I took a job as a caddie at the country club, where I learned how men relate to one another when women are not around and what they really thought of women. I saw the many convoluted ways men courted one another and jockeyed for membership and status in the great fraternity of men. The male bond is of such immense power that successful membership requires its casual denial. Women often fear it with good reason. It is based on perceived power, and it concerns itself with shared power. Participation in team sports teaches men the power of collective action. It has been the joining together of men, not women, that formed corporations, governments, armies, and nations.

It was on the wooden benches of the dirt-floored caddie shack that I first heard the dehumanizing words for males who love one another sexually. We all know those lying terms of abuse. Those caddies obviously cared about one another and had an easy intimacy that many would never exceed or know again. Their affection for one another made it seem that they were playing a grotesque joke on me as they casually desecrated the most meaningful experience of my life. When I realized they truly didn't recognize their obscenity, I was shocked. I instantly became defensive and created a barrier within me to protect what I knew to be of value. I walled myself in—into a vault of silent solitary confinement where I almost died, where too many still do.

I didn't see these people as intending harm; rather, they seemed like children playing a game not of their own making, one I couldn't understand. I understand now they were rehearsing and claiming an identity in the fraternity of men by holding in check their natural tendencies to love and care about one another. They did this for the sake of power, because the more independent person has the greater power to control a relationship, while loving leads to dependence. The means they used to restrain their natural tendency toward caring for their own kind were calculated misdescriptions of what actually happens—the denial of reality contained in those blinding words of condemnation. I felt utterly alone in that dark room, surrounded by people who were suddenly aliens. It was like the experience we have when we meet a handsome stranger and suddenly discover that he is mentally retarded; it's useless to speak.

Later, as I walked toward home, one of the more outspoken of the caddies called me to wait up for him. He lived in the same direction I did. He unselfconsciously put his arm around my shoulder as we walked, but I drew deeper into myself. He was irritated with another leader of the caddie gang. He told me this guy, Paul, used to be his best friend until Paul expressed an interest in messing around sexually with him. I didn't understand why he was so angry, since Paul was his best friend. I asked why he wouldn't want to have sex with a friend like Paul, but he told me I was crazy. He said he'd never do anything like that, although he admitted he'd thought about it. I asked him again, and he said, "Because you might get caught, your parents might find out. You'd have to be crazy to want to do something like that—sick in the head." He told me he used to think Paul was "a real regular guy, being a good athlete and all," but he said if Paul so much as touched him, even by accident, he'd "turn that pretty-boy face of his into mush!" He was trying very hard not to be an irregular guy. God forbid.

For several days, he made sniggering remarks about Paul. Paul tried to humor him out of it, but eventually, at the height of the flashing sexual tension between them, he called Paul one of those names. Complete silence fell over the caddie house. The line of manhood had been crossed, and the caddies waited expectantly for the inevitable. The two handsome young men lunged at each other, coiled muscles exploding in violent motions. As fists thudded into solid flesh, the spectators, like mutants, cheered in savage excitement at the first sight of blood on one of the handsome faces. Then, clinching one another in a grotesque parody of the embrace of lovers, the two writhing bodies crashed together to the dirt floor. The old caddie master, hearing the noise, came into the room, stopped the fight, and fired them both. "I'll have no hanky-panky in my caddie house! Let this teach the rest of you!" After they left, the guy who was head caddie said, "Hey, good riddance! That's two more jobs for us. Besides, they probably are just a couple of fairy faggots! Who needs them?" The caddies assured one another that they certainly wouldn't miss them either. I never went back after that. Later that year, I saw the two caddies at a school dance together with their dates, their quarrel obviously over.

I telephoned Keith and told him I'd quit my job at the golf course. I told him about the fight but wouldn't say what had really happened—about those names for us. Although I was deeply troubled, I wouldn't inflict that harm on him. I had no one to talk to, so I remained silent and buried—planted—this disease of hate deep within me, beyond awareness.

Talking on the telephone was awkward for Keith and me. He knew I was troubled and said he'd try again to get permission from his mother to visit. Keith had become quite irritable and morose after I moved, so his mother, out of concern for him, called my mother, and they decided it would be better if we limited our contact, so he could have a chance to adjust. We were allowed to talk by telephone only twice a week, and he couldn't visit me until two months had passed. Keith and his mom had serious battles about that, and I felt completely helpless. At first, I thought about him all the time, and I talked with him constantly in my imagination and often out loud when I knew I was alone. When this became too painful, I began to practice not thinking about him. I bought a radio kit and spent weeks building it. It didn't work.

. . .

The telephone rang just after sunset the next day. It was a bad connection, but I heard Keith yelling my name and saying he could come a week early, the next Saturday. The arrangements were made, but my mother cautioned me that Keith and I wouldn't be able to get together very often; it was just too far. She said we ought to make new friends and that I shouldn't get carried away. During the week, I was excited but apprehensive about his visit. I'd practiced not thinking about him for some time, but the old painful feelings of longing were coming back again; I couldn't stand them. Several times I had the thought that I didn't want him to come, and this confused me. I thought this way when I imagined him leaving for home. I began to worry about what he would think of me, our new home, people in the neighborhood, even Glendale.

I worried about what my new friends would think of him. They were just beginning to invite me over. I worried that Keith might say something about how we'd been. What would happen to me if they found out about us? I reminded myself to warn Keith not to say anything about that, but then I worried he might forget. I wondered if there was something wrong with Keith and me, with what we did together. I couldn't understand why everybody thought it was wrong. Maybe it was wrong, I worried; we didn't know. How could we know? Why do people hate people who feel that way so much? Was it envy, I wondered.

I worried that maybe Keith thought it was wrong, too; we never talked about it anymore. I'd caught the disease of homophobia at the caddie shack, and my feverish young mind began to reel with the idea that maybe Keith and I really were sick, crazy, fairy-faggot-homo-pervert-queers and didn't know it. I worried that he might think I was that way—a projection of my own fears. I tried to minimize blame by reminding myself that he'd started our sexual relationship; I hadn't. I began to think that Keith might be a pervert, but I couldn't stand that idea, yet I kept worrying about it. It was the ugliest, most profane idea I had ever thought, yet the horror of it attracted me, like looking for the bodies at an automobile accident. But I decided that Keith was what he appeared to be—a good person, not like those people the caddies talked about. He had to be. We had to be.

When Keith arrived late Saturday morning—he'd gotten lost—I was filled with fear at the thought of meeting him. I worried about what he would think of the changes in me. I wasn't the same person he'd known. Maybe he'd changed, too. I was guarded, conflicted, and unsure of myself.

Then, magically, there he was, coming up our driveway, smiling as always, expectant, trusting, joyous, confident, and beautiful—so very beautiful. My mother ran to hug him. He closed his eyes and smiled with happiness as she held him. I hesitated. He ran up to me, calling my name. Then I saw his beautiful face dissolve in confusion when I didn't respond. I saw his expression turn to disbelief, hurt, anger, and sadness. His sadness tore at me and freed me from my immobility. I tried to disguise my hesitation as a bad attempt at humor. Although Keith played along with me, I knew he knew better, but he said nothing.

He was impressed with our house and commented sadly that we would never be happy living in Kirkwood again. When I showed him my bedroom and we were alone, he came over to me and put his arms around me. I was so conflicted; I worried about my mother or sister coming upstairs and seeing us, so I pushed him away and warned him about talking to my friends. He looked so pathetically confused.

I wanted to get away from the bedroom, so I took him to the garage to show him the radio I'd built. Everything seemed fine until several of my friends came over. I'd told them he was coming, and they'd been watching for him. One of the guys said that Keith's hair looked from a distance like it was made out of real gold. Keith laughed and asked, "What makes you think it's not?" For the first time, I saw Keith become uncomfortable around people. He said little and kept looking at me as if seeking approval. Eventually, the topic got around to baseball, and he relaxed. They joked with Keith about what a rotten ball player I was; he agreed and added that I was still the best friend he ever had. He immediately became self-conscious and looked over at me. I changed the topic, and eventually they left. He said he was sorry he'd said that; it just slipped out. I said it was nothing, that I'd already told them we were best friends. He smiled.

There were many awkward moments, silences and false starts between us that day. Neither of us dared mention our dreams about the West, not even once. We knew we would never go. We couldn't comprehend, much less talk about, all that was really happening between us. I wouldn't understand for decades. We were two people in love, with no present and no future, trying to relate. I was 14, he was 16; but he was no ordinary youth, not Keith.

In the evening, Keith asked me to show him the golf course where I'd worked. The sky was clouded over, and fog was beginning to descend. I didn't want to go there because of what I had learned there, but he pleaded, and I gave in. As we passed the caddie house, Keith asked if that was where the fight had been. He asked me to tell him more about why I'd quit. I avoided the truth, and I think he knew that, but he said nothing. I hated that savage place. We walked along in silence, lost in ourselves for a long time. I felt the old loneliness again and sensed his sorrow.

At the crest of a slight hill, with the damp fog rolling swiftly in, Keith grabbed my arm. He demanded I tell him what had changed in me. I didn't want to, God knows I didn't want to, but he was insistent. What happened next is etched in my soul forever. Keith looked at me for a long time, and then said, "Today in the bedroom, you pushed me away. Is it about that?" I told him I didn't want to tell him, that I had my reasons, but he asked again. He kept demanding. I pleaded with him to stop. I told him he wouldn't want to hear it, knowing I was about to tell him, warning him, so he wouldn't blame me afterwards. He wouldn't stop, so I said, "Because, Keith, what we've been doing together is wrong! It's wrong! ...I told you you wouldn't want to hear it!" I said that to him; I said those words. He seemed dazed and just stood there looking at me for a long time. I felt confusion, shame, sorrow, longing, fear, and, yes, pride and anger. I'd said it, and he wasn't going to change me.

He asked why it was wrong. And I said, "Because everybody says it is, that's why! *Everybody*! I'm not going to do it, Keith. It's wrong!" I said that to him. As I type this, I can barely see, because I'm crying tears of rage at those who, by fear, locked me in this cage.

Keith just stood there looking at me, then he walked slowly toward me. I will remember his exact words until my death. It seems to me that at that moment the god within Keith revealed himself and spoke, "It wasn't wrong, Denny. I'm going now. Don't stop me. I want you to remember always that I loved you."

We'd never spoken of love before. That idea seemed strange and confused me. He put his arms around me, and he kissed me. I just stood there. He smiled slightly, then turned and walked into the fog. I waited for him to come running back to me, laughing. He would do it, I knew! Further he went until I could no longer see him, yet I continued to wait. After too long a time, when I knew he was gone, I softly called out his name. There was only the fog. In a great seizure, I screamed, *"Keith!"* into the void. I slumped down on my knees on that damp grassy hilltop, and then I tried to caress and hold it as if it were him.

I have never seen Keith since, nor have I heard of him. In the Christian mythology, I have always understood that it was only Judas who truly understood the love of his Christ.

Chapter Five

When I raised myself up from that fateful hilltop, I was incapacitated and stumbled aimlessly through the fog. From time to time, I reached out helplessly to embrace nothingness and dropped, crying, to my knees in despair before the power of an indifferent universe. The conflict between my head and my heart, between what I thought I should be—what I believed others properly required of me and what I was—what I felt myself to be, short-circuited my ability to act rationally. Eventually, after I had waited long enough for Keith to have gone—I was not completely without purpose—I wandered home. With fear in her face, my mother pounded these words into my brain, "My God, Denny! What did you do to Keith? He came and got his things...and left! He couldn't even talk to us! What did you do to him? He'd been crying! What, *in God's name, did you do to him?*" That was exactly the problem.

"We had a fight. I'm not going to see him anymore. Now leave me alone!" I said. I went into my bedroom, shut the door, locked it and went to bed.

It was a very beautiful day—a day that was perfect. Surrounding us and extending to the snow-capped mountains before us were moving waves of flowers of every kind and color. Keith was dancing and laughing, his golden hair gleaming in the light of the sun's grace. "Denny, we're here! We're out West! We made it! We're really here!" With the perfect integrity of his body and being, Keith held out his hand to me, and with this gesture I understood without any possibility of doubt that I was known and loved by him completely. Every cell of my being flooded with love for his being, but just as my hand touched his warmth, the ground beneath my feet gave way, and I was falling backwards into a black, empty, deep, ever-widening shaft. I saw Keith's face at the opening, screaming my name in terror as he reached out for me. As I continued to fall, his face receded until the opening of the hole became a mere point of light; then I fell with increasing speed into total, silent blackness. I awoke from this horror to the sound of my mother pounding on my locked bedroom door. "Denny! Are you all right? Open this door!"

"I'm okay. I just had a nightmare, that's all. You can go back to bed," I said.

"You were yelling!"

"What was I saying?"

"You were calling out for Keith."

"I wouldn't have done that!"

"But you were, Denny. You kept screaming his name! You frightened me. Are you sure you're all right?"

"Yes. I'll be okay. Good night." I couldn't believe I was calling for

Keith. I didn't need him.

"Good-night, Denny." Around me was the black silent emptiness of my locked room.

I feared the abuse, degradation, and banishment that would be mine if my newly-discovered natural ability to love were to become known, and yet I couldn't comprehend how human beings could contain inside themselves such hatred and contempt for those who love and who harm no one by their love. My secure and beautiful world had become filled with powerful ignorant beings—aliens, enemies, Frankensteins! It wasn't until much later in my life that I understood that these defective people, the Frankenstein people, had learned their grotesque inhumanities in response to their own histories of dehumanization. They, far more than I, are the true victims of sustained abuse and oppression by our cultural institutions—church, government, media, family, school, and work. So violently oppressed are they that with perverse pride they blindly became the bodily instruments through which these inhuman histories survive the generations of mankind.

But do not think that I betrayed my gentle Keith simply out of fear alone—I wish that it were so, but I didn't. Now I know what happened, but because of fear and repression, I couldn't admit it to myself for decades. The truth is that as Keith and I walked toward that saddest place in my world, that tragic hilltop, I wanted him with such an intensity that I could barely contain it within me. But instead, using words as nails, I chose to crucify the one I loved, because I could not have him. Society and separation would see to that, so I killed the love to end the pain. By telling Keith that our relationship was wrong, I was claiming a membership in the community of my oppressors in order to end the love that could not be fulfilled.

Miserere mei, Deus,
secundum magnam misericordiam tuam.
Et secundum multitudinem miserationum tuarum:
dele iniquitatem meam.
Amplius lava me ab iniquitate mea,
et a peccato meo munda me:
Quoniam iniquitatem meam ego cognosco:
et peccatum meum contra me est semper.

(Have mercy upon me, O God.
according to thy loving kindness:
according unto the multitude of thy tender mercies,
blot out my transgressions.
Wash me thoroughly from mine iniquity,
and cleanse me from my sin:
For I acknowledge my transgressions,
and my sin is ever before me.)

My sin was the betrayal of love itself, and of one who loved me. This betrayal almost cost me my life.

Chapter Six

I was moody and withdrawn for several weeks after Keith left. I avoided my mother, because she suspected that Keith and I had been more than best friends. She almost asked once, but lost her nerve; I just stared blankly at her. She backed away, because she didn't want to know what she suspected, that she was the mother of a pervert. Both of my parents lived their lives in fear of what the neighbors would think, people they didn't even know. Part of me wanted to tell her everything, but this would have been suicide. She'd made her feelings about perversion quite clear when she lectured about sex when I was 12.

(During my head-shrinking sessions at 20, I impulsively told my mother that I'd been sexual with Keith. This greatly disturbed my psychologist, who feared for my welfare. Ironically, all my mother did was smile with a look of fond reminiscence and say, "Did you really? Well, yes, Keith was such a beautiful boy, wasn't he? I was glad you two were best friends." That's all she ever said about the topic, and I believed she was accepting—a mistake, as I would painfully learn later. My father, who also heard my confession, turned his head away, stared at the floor and, characteristically, never uttered a word, although the embarrassment of his flushed face said it all.)

My mother tried to help me by telling me her philosophy of life—of her life. I'd heard it so many times before: "I want to tell you something to help you through these times, Denny. My mother told me, and it's helped me in my life many times—many times! Your grandpa hasn't been good to her. She's suffered. You've seen those awful detective magazines he buys, the ones with the pictures on the covers of women being tied up and hurt by men, and when he drinks, well, he hasn't been kind to your grandma. She told me when things seem hopeless, I should say "This, too, shall pass.' I want you to say that. 'This, too, shall pass!' It will, Denny, sooner than you think, quick as a wink! Now, go and find some of your new friends! Remember, this, too, shall pass!" My mother passed her life reading murder mysteries and patiently waiting for the relief of an imagined heaven. She had been creative and alive as a young woman, a dancer and poet, but she married and became a trapped, kept housewife, a mother substitute for my father, with little to do but wait for this life to pass.

In my neighborhood in Glendale were many "young men and women," as our high school teachers called us, although the lavatories at school still read "Boys" and "Girls." About 20 guys my age formed a loosely confederated gang, whose main interests were companionship, sports, social climbing, ego boosting, and sex. We all wore the standard uniform of our tribe—white bucks, argyle socks, blue oxford button-down shirt with the sleeves rolled to the elbows, and 501 Levi's—cuffs rolled up twice—which, when new, were soaked and worn wet until they dried on us to an exact form fit. It was our rule that if someone were unfortunate enough to have the red tag pulled off his Levi's by a plier-toting enemy, a symbolic castration, the jeans could simply no longer be worn in public. Because I'd reached puberty early, I was larger and more muscular than most guys, so I was often asked to play lineman in our football games. It felt good to be wanted, and I made friends quickly. I had a new chance with these guys to learn how to be a regular guy, adjusted, well-rounded, popular, red-blooded and normal.

I quickly learned the pecking order in the gang. Status was determined by the degree to which one corresponded to the masculine ideal—the strength, athletic prowess and V-shaped muscularity of the warrior heroes; good looks, personality and intelligence; family wealth and association with the dominant "in-group." In our high school class, the "anointed of God" were our King, Terry Collins, his Queen, Corrine Eberhard, and the Crown Prince, Herb Travis, who was Terry's best friend and the star athlete of our class. Terry, who was from a wealthy family, was unbelievably handsome, tall and blond. He was an outstanding athlete, intelligent, warm and accepting, and loved. One day, when Terry was talking to me in the hall at school—a high honor in itself, he put his arm around my shoulder, then he turned facing me and rested both of his arms on my shoulders. I felt as though I had just been knighted. Many of my friends congratulated me that day: "Saw Terry talking with you, Denny! Don't get stuck on yourself!"

Terry's friend, Herb Travis, was the largest, most physically mature male in our class. His natural athletic talent impressed even the coaches. He'd been featured in several local newspaper articles, eagerly and enviously read by us all. He wasn't the brightest of students—Terry often helped him with homework, but he was one of the most open, sincere, warm, and friendly people I knew; he was liked by everybody.

Corrine, Terry's girl friend, was the pampered, socially ambitious, clever daughter of a wealthy doctor. She was vain and beautiful. The rumor was that she had so many clothes, she never wore the same dress twice; but this was just one of the many rumors spread about her by her rivals, who felt inadequate in her presence. She did, however, control Terry, and this power of hers awed us.

One evening, as I was walking home after visiting a friend who lived some distance from my neighborhood, I heard my name called. Terry and Herb waved for me to join them—a royal summons. They said they'd walk with me back to my neighborhood, and they were full of questions and good humor. My heart pounded with the excitement of their acceptance. The three of us walked along, me in the middle, their arms around my shoulders. I put my arms around their waists, and we began to sing and sway like drunken sailors on a spree. We did a mock Russian folk dance and for our finale, laughing in rhythm, we became the Rockettes' chorus line, complete with athletic leg kicks.

As we walked along, still holding on to one another, Terry asked if it were true that I said I'd never play football again. Surprised, I asked if they had a spy network. They both laughed, and Terry replied, "People tell us things. We have our sources!" I asked who they were. Herb grinned and with mock seriousness said if they told me, then they wouldn't be able to find out all about me. I felt fear.

I asked what they wanted to find out. "Your darkest secrets!" Terry said, laughing. I said they wanted to be like the Shadow on radio and mimicked the announcer's voice, "Who knows what evil lurks in the hearts of men? Only the Shadow knows!"

"Yes! I want to know what evil lurks in your heart!" Herb said.

"Why?" I asked.

"So I can tell every damned person in school—even the girls! Terry, do you think Denny has much evil lurking in his heart?"

Terry put his ear to my chest and listened intently, "Well, he's definitely got a heart—not like you, Herb! He might have a broken heart...or a sweetheart...no, not a sweetheart, because he's a virgin! I'd say, a broken heart!" I flooded with images of Keith and panicked with fear—a fear of rejection. "Wow, your heart is really pounding like crazy now, Denny! What happened? Maybe it's going to break! Herb, listen to this!" I pushed Terry away.

"I'm not a virgin!" I protested, camouflaging myself in my one hetero-sexual experience at 13. They both looked shocked at being one-upped.

"Oh, you are, too! We all are!" Terry asserted.

"But I'm not!"

"Your mother doesn't count, Denny!" teased Herb.

"Watch it, Herbie!" cautioned Terry, then teased, "But maybe it was your sister, Denny!"

"It was probably your sister, Terry!" retorted Herb.

I demanded to know how they knew I had a sister. "The Shadow knows!" they chorused.

"Don't you want to know what evil lurks in the hearts of men, Denny?" asked Herb.

With the shock of recognition, I answered, "Yes! Yes, I do!" The thought was exciting, but puzzling, since I didn't know what evil I unconsciously had in mind.

"You do?" asked Terry, surprised, "You really do?"

"Yes! ...What evil lurks in your heart, Herb?" I teased hopefully.

Bursting with laughter, Terry shouted, "He plays with his pecker!" Pinkness decorated Herb's cheeks like rouge as he cast his eyes downward until his embarrassment passed. Finally, this young hunky jock looked up and smiled shyly...until I shouted, "With his pecker?"

Again, I demanded to know how they knew I had a sister. Terry said a friend of his, Ronnie Ryan, told him. He said Ronnie lived near me and added, I ought to get to know him. Terry's emphasis on this last point let me know that Ronnie was a member of the royal court. He asked me once more if I'd said I wasn't going to play football again. I told him I had, at a game the weekend before.

"Why would you do that? Football's the greatest game there is! I love it!" Herb said.

"That's because you like to smash little guys, Herb! Now me, I like it, because a quarterback has to think. He's got to have brains!" taunted Terry.

"You brag about your brain, Terry, because you haven't got a build like this!" said Herb, slowly flexing his impressive muscularity. "If you had a body like this, you'd think you were perfect!" He grabbed Terry's hand and put it on his biceps. "Feel what a real man's arm is like! Here, Denny, you can feel it, too!" I was self-consciously defensive about the excitement of this intimacy with Herb's body.

"Herbie, I admit you've got a great body. The problem is your face!" taunted Terry.

"Hey, my face looks like a man's, not a pretty girl's like yours! If you put lipstick on, you'd get picked up, Terry!"

"What do you think, Denny?" asked Terry, who was expecting me to side with him. I said Terry would look better in lipstick than Herb.

"See! What did I tell you!" Herb shouted. "Hey, Terry, why don't you learn how to put makeup on? Get one of your sister's dresses, and I'll take you to a school dance! You'd look great! We could fool everybody! Let's do it!"

Terry snapped, "I'm no fairy faggot! You probably do want to go to a dance with a guy!" Calming down, he smiled a little at Herb and added, "That's what happens when you play with peckers!" Changing the subject, he asked, "So, why don't you want to play football, Denny?"

I told them about guys who were good friends before a game, but who left as enemies. The Saturday before, I had tackled my friend, Michael Arendes, so hard that his head smashed into the ground, splitting his upper lip. I described the way he looked at me as blood flowed over his chin—the way his eyes looked at me. My teammates were cheering me while his accusing eyes destroyed my insides. I didn't tell them how I felt about the beauty of Michael's face. I didn't tell them I'd seen the same look in Keith's eyes on that hilltop. When I took Michael home, his mother was devastated and angry with me. He told her it was an accident, that I was his friend, and he wanted me to stay with him. She relented, took off his bloody shirt and pants, gently wiped the blood from him, covered him with a blanket, kissed him and cried. I didn't tell them I envied her right to do these things. I just said it was senseless for me to hurt my friends and try to make them losers just so I could feel good about myself as a winner. It was stupid, I said, and I wasn't going to do it again.

Herb said, "I know what you mean. I hurt Terry pretty bad once, but still, football is, well, it's one hell of a good game! It's just a game, Denny. I hope you won't stop playing."

I said, "I'm not sure it is just a game. I'm not sure guys are just playing." (I know now that it's very serious business—a metaphor of our society, a way we learn American values and the power of team membership. It's training for the competitive life of males who strive for dominance in status hierarchies, with sex and property rights for rewards—as do our primate ancestors.) Terry looked at me thoughtfully but said nothing. We walked along in silence until we came to Terry's turnoff. Herb said he didn't have anything to do, so he'd walk with me to my house. I was glad he wanted to be with me.

"I like you, Denny," Terry said, "Get to know Ronnie. He's a good guy. Oh, yeah, and don't let Herbie here pull you into some dark bushes on your way home!"

"Oh shut up, Terry fairy," blasted Herb, "or I won't let you feel my muscles anymore!" The outcome of their status contest was a draw, as it usually is with friends. King Terry waved and disappeared into the warmth that night.

Herb kept his arm on my shoulder as we walked along together. Occasionally, he put his arm around my waist and pulled me close to him, and I did the same. These life-giving gestures of caring, friendship, and affirmation were commonplace and innocent for boys our age in that era. But for two years, I'd known sexual love. Our closeness evoked memories and my desire to love, my repulsive wisdom.

Herb talked while I ran from myself. I wanted distance from the rushes of excitement I was feeling, the forewarning of spontaneity—of being. But I noticed those dark hidden places where...concentrate, control, correct! But the oppressed parts of our human nature find ways to express the coded songs of our souls. "Hey, Herbie! ...Lots of dark bushes over there!" I said, carefully modulating the teasing tones so he wouldn't misunderstand...or understand.

"Oh, that darned Terry! I don't like it when he says things like that. And another thing, Denny, when he said...well...that I played with myself, it's not true!"

"I know. Besides, guys who do, get little hairs on the palm of the hand they do it with." Herb casually dropped his right arm from my shoulder; I waited. When he glanced at his right palm, I grabbed his hand and shouted, "I knew you'd do that! You fell for it!"

"But I don't see any hairs!" he said, examining his palm.

"Of course not! You do it anyhow!"

"Well, not that much. Do you ever do it?"

"Yes! Everybody does it as soon as they're old enough to do it. Didn't you ever hear about guys visiting Mrs. Thumb and her four daughters?" More of my camouflage. I wiggled my thumb and fingers, and he laughed.

"Do you do it very often?" he asked cautiously.

"Everyday. Sometimes a lot more than that. Everybody does it!"

"I don't think Terry does. He says it's against his religion or something, and he doesn't want to use it all up before he gets married. The coaches say you don't have as much strength if you do it often. That's why I try not to do it. I don't want it to spoil my game."

"Terry does it. He just doesn't want people to know he does. And those coaches are just worried that guys will get more interested in sex than sports. You can't use it up.

"How do you know?"

"Someone showed me a book—a book about reproduction."

"Who?"

I wouldn't admit it was my mother. "I forget, but the book said you can't use it up."

"Did Terry tell you he did it?"

"No, but he does."

When we came to my house, I could tell Herb wanted me to ask him in, but it was late, and I knew sports were his world. His love life was cheers in a stadium. "Thanks for walking home with me, Herb. Next time, let's try to find some bigger bushes!"

"You're getting to be just like Terry!" His comparison made me giddy; what a wish! I watched him saunter down the street. He was lonely, and so was I. He stopped and looked back. He was surprised I hadn't gone in. He waved. We waited for a signal. I knew he wanted me to call him back, and I wanted him to hold out his arms for me, but that would never be. I ended the tension by waving good-bye. From the dark dining-room window, I watched him slowly go. Just before he went out of sight, he turned once more and lingered, looking back at my darkened house, and I was heavy with loneliness and conflict.

The next Sunday afternoon, Allan Walpole came bounding up to my bedroom. He was one of the guys who came over to meet Keith—the one who said Keith's hair looked like gold from a distance. Allan knew everybody. He was my chief informant. If you wanted the latest information, joke, rumor or gossip, he was the man—well, boy—to see. Allan had a friendly energetic disposition that reminded me of a cocker spaniel, but he also had a heavy, a very heavy, burden to bear. Dear Allan Walpole, who was 14 going on 15, was not even within hope of the magic kingdom of testosterone called puberty. He had the physique of a short, skinny ten-year-old. Regularly, he listened in silent shame to this insensitive greeting: "Here comes little Allan Walpole, who still hasn't got his flagpole!" Once, when he was telling me his feelings about this abuse, he became enraged and shouted, "Those sons of bitches! I hope I get to be ten feet tall and it gets so big I'll have to carry it around in a god-damned wheel barrow!" He saw no humor in my comment that he would then be the biggest prick in town. He didn't understand that the teasings between males are often inverted kisses in their dominance game of king of the mountain.

Allan was Ronnie Ryan's spy, and Ronnie was the one who told Terry what Allan knew about me. Allan said that Ronnie was the leader of the in-group in our neighborhood, and he wanted to meet me, because he always checked out new guys to see if they would fit into his group. Ronnie was stuck on himself, Allan explained, but he was a big wheel. He was a prince of the royal court, because he was a friend of King Terry. Allan said Ronnie's dad was a big muckamuck in the local country club. He was a successful lawyer; Ronnie's attractive mother worked as his secretary. They lived in an expensive home beside the golf course. Ronnie was their only child. Allan told me to be sure to wear a blue oxford button-down shirt, just ironed, no wrinkles, because Ronnie made an issue of how people dressed. He said we had to be at Ronnie's at 7:00 sharp; Ronnie didn't like to be kept waiting. I was already irritated with the conceit of this Ronnie Ryan, but I knew if I wanted friends, I had to get along with him. I talked Mom into ironing my button-down. "You must be becoming a teenager!" she exclaimed. "I'll bet you're working up to asking some nice young girl for a date. How pleased she'll be!" I gave a reassuring nod. Allan came over early, but it was important for me to keep Ronnie waiting. I wanted to meet this friend of Terry's, but his imperious manner was too much like a target in a shooting gallery; besides, who was he to be playing king of the mountain with me? At about 7:20, Allan pointed to the Ryan's large white house surrounded by tall trees near the golf course. I felt some anxiety and excitement as Allan rapped the knocker ring held by the teeth of a brass lion's head. "Hey, Allan! I'm out in the kitchen. Bring him on back here," yelled Ronnie. The rooms were tastefully furnished, especially the wood-paneled library with its red leather, English wing-backed chairs. Ronnie was comfortably seated in the large, white-tiled kitchen with his feet propped up on a massive oak table. "You're late, Allan! I said 7:00, not 20 after!"

"I'm sorry, Ronnie. Don't get mad at me. Denny...well, he couldn't make it at 7:00." Ronnie was attractive, with the muscular body of a young athlete. His good looks were expected of an in-group member.

"No excuses, Walpole! You've been screwing up lately! You keep that up, and you'll be dropped from the group!"

"Ron, I'm real sorry. I am!" pleaded Allan.

I told Ronnie not to blame Allan, since I was the one who hadn't wanted to leave at seven. He slowly looked me over from head to toe, smiled, and said, "So...you wanted to keep me waiting, did you?"

I told him I didn't jump just because he snapped his fingers and sent his boy over to fetch me. I asked him just who he thought he was, bossing guys like Allan around, and I told him never to try that stuff with me.

Looking very nervously at Ronnie, Allan tried to harmonize, "Denny, Ronnie isn't really that bad to me, just sometimes. I don't mind doing things for him. When I do, he lets me be part of the group."

"You should tell him to go straight away to hell!" I said, looking steadily at Ronnie.

Allan really became nervous then, but Ronnie broke into a grin and started laughing. "Allan told me you had a mind of your own. He said you were an independent cuss! I like that! Allan, here, lets me push him around all over the place!"

Allan reminded Ronnie that he had said he would kick Allan out of the group if he didn't do what he wanted. Ronnie looked away with a touch of shame. I told Allan he should tell Ronnie to go to hell more often. Ronnie laughed and said, "You've got spunk! I sent Allan over to get you so I could look you over. I see your shirt was ironed. My mom custom-fits mine. Turn around so I can see if you have your red tag on your Levi's."

It was a shoving match—males testing the status hierarchy, like our monkey ancestors. I said, "Of course it's still on! Hey, Ronnie babe, you got this all backwards. The reason I came over here was to look you over, not the other way around!"

"Okay, okay...so what do you see?" he asked.

"A guy with a real ego problem!"

"We've all got ego problems," Allan said sadly. True for most people, but especially so for adolescents.

When our testing was over, our conversation and laughter began to flow until it became the heady, bubbly effervescence of adolescent trust. The three of us revealed ourselves—our dreams, fears, friends, families, tender triumphs and tragedies, heroes and hopes, and above it all, protecting us, shielding us, was our constant humor. Our peals of tearful laughter were the sounds of affirmation, communion, and growth—the music of souls playing. Only rarely would we as adults know again this spontaneous joy of discovery, born of such openness and innocent trust. For those who have known well this young soul play, its loss makes secret places of sorrow in our hearts forever.

Eventually, we initiates to the testosterone tribe talked about the sexuality we had become. Allan, being prepubescent, listened with fascination and respect. Ronnie asked if the guys in Kirkwood masturbated and how often I did it. Allan irritated Ronnie by saying that Ronnie kept getting Allan to jack him off. Ronnie claimed he was just doing Allan a favor by letting him see what it will be like when he gets to be a man—a good Samaritan. I said I was glad to know how much he would sacrifice for his friends. Ronnie changed the subject and wanted to know how much pubic hair I had, so Ronnie and I dropped our pants and stood there looking. Allan commented that Ronnie just wanted to know he still had the biggest one in his gang. I teased that Ronnie had to have something he could be proud of, even if it was being the biggest prick in town. After Allan left, Ronnie and I talked about the intensity of our sexuality. I said it was like being the wolfman, a teenaged wolfman. He gets hair on him—like us—and he can't stop himself; he has to have flesh before he can return to normal. "Yeah, exactly!" agreed Ronnie. The wolfman terrified me for years; it was my contradictory self, a normal human being with a deadly animal hiding inside, trying to take over.

As I was leaving, after showing me his chrome-plated barbell set and his newly bulging biceps and deltoids, Ronnie grabbed my arm and said, "I think we can be real good friends. If we do become best friends, I could make you number two in the group. What do you think?"

I told him I wouldn't be like Allan—no ones and twos stuff. I said I'd like us to be friends; I'd like that a whole lot...even if he was a prick with ears—big ears. Ronnie was pleased, so was I, and we both understood this.

Then Ronnie startled me by asking, "Denny, Allan said you had your best friend over—a blond baseball player?"

"Yeah." My mask slipped on.

"What was his name—Ken?"

"Keith. Keith Amadeus." I was completely on guard.

"Was he your best friend?"

"Yes."

"How long?"

"I don't know...couple of years."

"Then how come Allan said Keith left your house without staying for the weekend? How come?"

"We didn't get along."

"Why?"

"We had a fight over something, it was nothing."

"Are you two still best friends?" he asked. I noticed a nervous twitch in his left eyelid.

"...No."

"Good!" Ronnie said. The twitch stopped. "See ya tomorrow! Wanna play golf with me? I can take you free. We're members. I'll pick you up in the morning, buddy!"

The days that Ronnie and I spent on the fairways were happy times, except when we played the ninth hole. The slight hilltop where I watched Keith vanish into the fog was in the middle of the ninth fairway. I became superstitious about this hill and wouldn't walk on it. I made up excuses for us to not play the ninth; Ronnie often complied, but the ninth was one of his best-scoring holes. He knew my avoidances were irrational, but I couldn't even tell myself what had really happened there in the fog. The acknowledgment of my self-betrayal would take decades. At the time, I believed our friendship ended because Keith couldn't have his way. I didn't understand his wisdom—or his pain.

Once, Ronnie hit such a powerful drive that his ball rolled to the top of that hill. I watched him standing there, full of pride and laughing in the sunlight as he readied for his next shot. In my mind, as in a trance, I saw Ronnie's image blend into Keith's and back again in a flickering way. Ronnie looked at me in confusion and came down to me, "Are you okay, Den? Did I do anything?" I told him he hadn't. I said I felt dizzy; I'd better go home. He said he'd walk me home, so I'd be okay. He did, but I wasn't. It was afternoon, but I went to bed anyway. I was quite depressed, but I didn't know what to call those feelings then. I didn't want to be aware of them. I could only try to wait it out...in silence.

One Friday afternoon, Ronnie telephoned to ask if he could stay with my family for the weekend; his folks were going away. I was glad that Ronnie wanted to stay with me instead of his other friends, but I tested him: "Couldn't you get your other pals to put up with you, Ron?"

"No, you're the first person I called, I swear! I want to stay at your house."

"How come?" I needed reassurance.

"Because I'll have a chance to fuck your blond little sister, that's why! You pea brain! Now, do you want me to stay or don't you? You jerk!"

"Yeah, I'd like you to...but my sister will probably throw up!"

"Well, Den, that's what happens to them when it's as big as mine!"

"Ronnie babe, you know what you are?"

"I know! With ears! Don't say it!"

That Saturday night, as I watched Ronnie undress for bed, I remembered the times I'd watched Keith make those same motions. Sadness seeped into me unnamed. A lamp on a desk was still on. I watched Ronnie undress to his Jockey shorts, carefully put his shirt and pants on a hanger, and slide beneath the covers beside me. "You got that strange look on your face, Den. Are you sure you wanted me to stay over?" he asked. I reassured him, and we talked.

I wondered if I could ever tell him about Keith. Would he understand? Would he reject me? Who would he tell? I wanted it out of my mind forever! He was animated and happy, and my worried mood began to change. He chattered on about everything of importance to him. I asked if he was really joking about my nine-year-old sister—partly teasing him, but partly curious, too, because he'd remembered her blond hair. "You ninny!" he said. "I wouldn't touch her with a ten-foot pole—not after all the stuff she's caught from you!"

When the house had long been in sleepy silence, Ronnie asked about Kirkwood and Keith. He wanted to know if Keith and I had ever done what he and Allan had been doing—what he let Allan do. I noticed his throat sounded dry. I was silent and thoughtful before telling him yes. He wanted to know everything we'd done, every detail, and he was urgent and insistent. It was late, I said, and we needed to get to sleep. I added that there wasn't really much to tell.

He said, "I know you, Denny! I can tell when you're fibbing me! I can tell! Tell me all about it. I want to know the details about what you two guys did! I love the details!" He put his hand on my chest; it was hot.

I told him those things were between Keith and me, and it had to stay that way; Keith had a right to that, I said, but it was really me I was protecting. I felt those familiar feelings of longing beginning as I wondered if I could ever know the same intensity of feeling with Ronnie that I'd known with Keith. As I was experiencing my desire to love, I felt my fear, guilt, and shame.

Ronnie moved closer and pressed full length against me. His body was dry and hot. As I felt his heat next to me, I wanted to split off from my body, which I knew was then betraying me. I closed my eyes and imagined I was on the ceiling looking down on the two of us. We seemed from that perspective to be two lonely children, and just then, I became aware of the pleasant distinctive aroma of his body. It was different from Keith's, less sweet, and more like my own.

"Den, tell me what you two did. You can trust me. I want to know everything. Please tell," he whispered. My bodily yearnings, then powerful, became me, and I knew I would have him that night. I tried to plan ways to make it seem he'd been responsible for what I knew would happen, but my thinking melted into feelings of growing urgencies as I sensed him. I jumped from the bed and snapped off the small desk light. Moonlight flooded the room. I took off my shorts. "What are you doing, Denny? Why are you doing that?" he asked. I slipped under the covers and laid myself down on him. I was hard as stone. I whispered into his ear, "You know what I'm doing, because you wanted me to do it. Don't pretend. ...I'm going to show you some things you'll like." He put his arms around me and pressed me to him, closing his eyes and smiling, almost laughing, in the transforming glow of the moonlight. We quivered as we began the genetic, primeval dance that is the celebration of life, this most ancient of communions.

The many similarities of Ronnie's form to Keith's evoked the rebirth of my consuming passion for the realities of Keith; the many differences attached me to the unfolding realities of Ronnie. These two tactile beings separated and fused in my hands as I came to know completely this body, this redemptive other.

After we were sated, when the echoes of our passion became still, when Ronnie lay in peaceful sleep, I studied his gently breathing moonlit form...and remembered Keith. My constant sorrow entered my consciousness, and I realized that I would never again know my Keith. Several tears escaped my control, trickled down my face, bridged the distance between Ronnie and me, and connected with his sleeping body.

Chapter Seven

The next morning, Ronnie was in playful mood, while I was apprehensive and guilty. Ronnie insisted it had been his first time. He didn't want me to think he was the wrong kind of guy, not normal. We promised to keep our little secret just between us.

Ronnie's mother worked as his father's secretary, so Ronnie's house was his alone each afternoon. He often asked me to stay with him after school. We liked chasing each other naked around the house and having sex in each room, including—once—in his parents' bed, where Ronnie felt distinctly uncomfortable.

Ronnie was the first in our group to have the new RCA 45-rpm record changer. He was proud of it, and we'd often joke about what records we should play as background music when we sexed in his bedroom. We stacked the records so "La Vie en Rose" would be the last song to play; that way we would know when to stop to change the music. (That song still evokes clear memories of Ronnie's bedroom and of his particular fragrance.) It was sexuality we shared, not love, because Ronnie wasn't Keith. Keith was real, but Ronnie was primarily concerned with perfecting his social image, his act. I wanted to change, to be normal, and to free myself from my constant sorrow, my perverted longing. I didn't need Ronnie as I had Keith, and I didn't want to be vulnerable again. He sensed this, and it made him cautious.

Ronnie and I were separated for about three months that year. He and his parents had moved to the nearby community of Webster Groves. The reason they moved was that Ronnie and I burned their house down. He and I ignited pads of steel wool in the basement one afternoon. When we were done, Ronnie tried to hide some partially burnt pads, which he believed were no longer burning, by stuffing them behind a ceiling joist. When I rode my bicycle into their driveway the next afternoon and looked toward their house, I saw only charred lumber and a hole in the ground.

At first, his parents blamed me, but Ronnie told them truthfully that he'd been the one who initiated playing with fire in the basement. They relented and allowed me to visit Ronnie in their temporary home in Webster Groves. They weren't particularly upset by the fire, because the house had been heavily insured. I was very nervous the first time I visited them in Webster Groves, but they were friendly and talked excitedly about their plans for the new house. Ronnie was glad to see me and, as soon as we were in private, he blushed and said he was tired of making love to his pillow.

He bragged about new friends of his in more upscale Webster Groves. We were often invited to parties where we were jokingly introduced as "the peasants from Glendale." We retaliated by saying that the reason the Webster

Groves girls invited us was because they were bored with the little boys who lived there. Once, when one of the flustered Groves guys lost his composure during this territorial banter, which the delighted girls encouraged, he said, "At least none of the Groves guys are perverts like all you Glendale fairies!" With the same athletic skill I had often admired on the golf course, Ronnie smashed his fist into the eye socket of this stunned young man, who clutched his face and slumped groaning to the floor. We escaped easily and ran into the coolness of the night, but I was troubled. I told Ronnie that perverts did some of the same things we did; I asked if he didn't think that made us kind of like them.

He said, "What do you mean—perverts? Hell no! We're not perverts— you pervert! Do we look like perverts? Hell no!"

"Why not?" I asked.

"You pervert! We're not, that's why! We're different."

I started to tell him about a pervert behind some gas station I'd heard about. "Everybody knows about him," broke in Ronnie, filling in the details. "The guy's name is Bill; he's an old guy, about 35, who wears wire-rimmed glasses." Some of the guys Ronnie knew would meet Bill uptown and talk him into giving them blow-jobs at night behind the Shell station. He was a cop until he got fired; he'd been caught with five guys, doing it to all of them. Ronnie had heard Bill even offered to pay one guy to let him do it, because this guy was so handsome, but the guy told Bill he could do it for free. The guy said afterwards that he should've paid Bill, or so Ronnie said. I asked how Bill could earn a living if he got fired. Ronnie said he couldn't, he had to live with his mother.

I said, "Ugh! Can you imagine having to live with your mother?"

"Sure. We both live with our moms," observed Ronnie.

"I mean when you're a grown up, pea brain!"

"Oh! That would be awful—god-awful!"

I asked Ronnie if he didn't think the guys who got Bill to do things to them weren't kind of perverts themselves, but he said they were just normal guys like us—well, most of them. I asked him if he'd ever thought about getting Bill to do it to him.

"Are you crazy? I mean, I thought about it, yes, but I wouldn't be caught dead with a pervert! Look at what it would do to my reputation! Everybody who counted would drop me, I'd be finished for good." I said I still couldn't figure out why Bill was the pervert and not the other guys.

"Well, I don't know. He's older. He likes to do it..."

"They like it too," I pointed out.

"I know. Well...maybe it's 'cause they don't do it to him. That must be why." I said I bet they did it with each other sometimes, like the two of us.

"That's different! It's not the same! It's because...well...normal guys are supposed to like girls and grow up and get married and everything. That's it! We're not perverts, because we're going to grow up and get married and have kids! We like girls more than boys. That's it!" I asked him what girls we liked more than us.

"I don't know. I'd like to lay a girl sometime, but none of them will let a guy even touch her. You can't even get a finger under their bras. They have to stay in at night, and they always have parents or chaperones guarding them. I can't stand the way they giggle and squeal all the time. It drives me crazy!"

"I know. They giggle at you, and that's supposed to mean they like you, or something! They don't like to do any of the things we do. Do you notice how they always act so flirty and helpless when guys are around? They're always whispering to each other, and when you ask them what the whispering is about, they won't tell you. The only time you get to touch them is at dances. I like it when they put their heads on your shoulder. It means they really like you, and they want you to like them. Their tits feel real mushy!"

"Den, you know Christine? Well, her's were hard like rubber. I think she had falsies on. My mom wears a falsie, because the doctors had to cut off one of her tits. Remember, I told you it had cancer? Can you imagine walking around with big boobs flopping on your chest?"

"Or clopping around in those high heels! Have you ever tried to walk in those things?"

"Yeah. I tried my mom's once...a long time ago! I couldn't even walk in them. Why do they wear those stupid things? Women are weird!"

"They think it makes them look pretty, but I think it makes them look silly."

We were trying to reassure one another of our loyalty and male bond before the threat of impending heterosexuality. But then Ronnie said hesitantly, "Den, I've been thinking...maybe when I move back to Glendale, you and me...we ought to start double-dating. We should get some girl friends, you know what I mean? Terry's girl friend, Corrine, said we should start dating. She told me about some girl friends of her's who liked us."

"You mean so we won't become perverts?" I snapped with irritation.

"I didn't mean that! We're not perverts, you pervert, you! I just mean it's time for us to move on, that's all."

"Move on to what, Ron?" I asked. "Girls don't like to do the same things we do. They won't give you any nooky until after you marry them, and you've got to have a good job before they'll even look at you. We won't finish college until—let's see—eight whole years from now! And you better make lots of money if you want a pretty one; they don't come cheap. After you marry one, all they want are babies, lots of screaming babies. They really want to be mothers and run the house just like our mothers do. You just wind up with another mother! Why do you think our dads still go around calling their wives 'mom'?"

"God, they do, don't they!" he said. "Well, you and I would still be together if we double-dated. It might be fun. Corrine wants me to tell her if we want to double together. I told her we probably would...besides, Terry wants me to."

"Well, that settles it then, Ronnie baby! If you don't do what the King wants, he'll cut off your reputation!" I was angry.

"You jerk! He will not. I mean, I only do what I want to do! It's up to me, not him!"

"Sure, Ronnie! You'd screw your own grandmother until her eyeballs fell out on the floor if you thought it'd help your precious reputation! I swear-to-God you would!

"Fuck you! Your mother does it with Great Danes!"

"At least the dogs don't throw up afterwards like they do with your mom!" It was a lovers' quarrel.

Several days later, Ronnie called me with bad news. His parents had been confronted by the irate mother of the boy he'd decked. This—added to the fact that Ronnie had just burned their house down—caused righteous wrath. He was totally grounded until the house in Glendale was finished, several months away. He also told me that my mother and his had talked about finding semen spots on the sheets each time we stayed overnight together. My mother interrogated me, also. Her worry was that Ronnie and I were having sex with my sister. People tend to see what they want to see. Ronnie and I denied everything and suggested that the other had perhaps had a wet dream, or possibly beat off. Our mothers believed us, given the alternative, but we were not allowed to stay overnight anymore. My mother explained that Ronnie and I were getting to be young men, and men didn't sleep together in the same bed—obviously too much of a temptation for most men and the real reason why gay men aren't yet allowed to serve their country in the military services, though tens of thousands have, as did I.

As the weeks without Ronnie wore on, I thought of Keith more often. I knew that something important I'd known with Keith was missing in my friendship with Ronnie, but I couldn't name it. Whatever it was, I wanted it, and I knew I couldn't be happy until I had it again. Keith was gone, so I decided to get what I needed from others. I'd been aware for some time of the tense, lingering glances I got from some older males, especially when I hitch-hiked—a common practice for boys in those safe days. I liked their interest in me. Sometimes, when they were questioning me about my personal life, especially about girls, I noticed changes in their voices, and I understood their growing excitement. For their approval and attention, I posed, stretched myself, flexed my arm muscles, brushed against them, smiled longingly, spoke in allusions, and hoped for the drama of the moment when they would casually, but cautiously, put their hands on my thigh. I understood their deficiency. I knew that, in spite of their education, success, wealth, and families, I had something they wanted for themselves but could never have, something they hungered for but could never be again, and that was the healthy body of a youth in the peak of his sexuality, one who would live into the future far beyond their graves. Although these men, mostly married, would drive out of their way to be with me, and although our glances communicated it, and we knew the other understood our pleading eyes, for fear, the dramatic gesture was never made. I would have responded with gratitude. I'm like those men now. I'm often tense and reserved around beautiful young men. I fear that a clever one could easily control me—perhaps he wouldn't have to be clever. There is an unacknowledged and misunderstood love between men and between the generations of men—and it is love—which, in the vast variety of its expressions, has made possible the survival of our species. It's in the genes.

Sometime during this period of my search for human contact, I became enthralled with the fantasy that I could become invisible. Like a teenage Dracula thirsting for the intimate knowledge of others, I longed for a magic cloak of invisibility, so I could observe every aspect of the life of one who interested me. In this privileged state, I could even know their consciousness—their thoughts, sensations, perceptions, moods, dreams, impulses, and feelings. Several months before, when I was waiting at Ronnie's for him to return from a trip to the store, I felt this same stirring of the desire to know him even more fully. I began to search his bedroom—his closet, desk, dresser, bookcase—everything. In one drawer, I found his clean, neatly folded Jockey shorts, and I became excited. The room was saturated with everything that was him—the college pennants, the phonograph records, photos of himself and his friends, a muscle magazine, school books, a condom, and a perfumed note from a girl. Carefully hidden in the drawer of his bedside table was a single sock into which he ejaculated the secrets of his erotic passions. When I finished with Ronnie's room, I searched his parents' bedroom. I found old love letters under his mother's bras and falsies. When Ronnie returned, he joined me in the search. He found his father's condoms and wanted to put tiny pin holes in them, but I talked him out of it. I told him about the time I'd found some of my father's but didn't know what they were. I blew them up like balloons and played with them in the front yard until my mother screamed. Ronnie and I laughed and blew up some of his father's. As we began to make love in his parents' room, I told Ronnie I'd found his single sock. Ronnie, naked and aroused on his parents' bed, blushed.

My invisible cloak and my nostalgic reveries only increased my tension while Ronnie served his sentence of solitary confinement in Webster Groves. Allan and I often talked about Ronnie; he knew what was going on between us and understood our frustration. He confessed one day that he'd told two guys about Ronnie and me. I was threatened and angry, but he went on to say they were interested in what we did together. He pretended he didn't know the details and told them they should ask me. Several days later, I saw one of the guys, Kent, playing basketball. He waved and came over to talk. I was defensive, especially when he asked with a grin about Ronnie. He kept hinting that he knew about the relationship Ronnie and I had, but I acted innocent. Finally, he came right out and said he didn't care what we did together, he knew lots of guys did it; he just wanted to know how we did it—the details. Blankly, I said that there wasn't much to tell, we were just best friends, that was all. Kent gave me a dejected, skeptical look and returned to the basketball court.

Several days later, I was in my bedroom when my sister called from downstairs to say Kent was waiting to see me. He had never been in our house before, and he was curious about my prized collections of interesting gadgets and junk. I'd made several high-voltage sparking devices, one from an old Model-T Ford spark coil, the other from a discarded, very high-voltage transformer. Both of them sent sizzling blue arcs of electricity through the air, creating the smell of ozone. I told Kent about the time I had accidentally touched the electrodes of the high-voltage transformer with both hands. The resulting convulsion of my body knocked me off my desk chair backwards and onto the floor, unconscious.

"What happened then?" he asked with alarm.

I told him Denny died and I was really another guy who took the first Denny's place. It had seemed that way to me. I explained that as I gradually regained consciousness, I felt the greatest peacefulness I'd ever known. For quite some time, I couldn't remember what had happened to me, or where I was, or even who I was. It was as if I died and very gradually came back to life. This unintentional electroshock therapy was a beautiful and emotional revelation for me, but Kent seemed repelled by it and warned me about playing with electricity. I couldn't make him understand that what had been so positive for me about that experience was the relaxed wonder of very slowly regaining sensation, perception, feelings, thoughts, and memory—of being gradually reborn. I would have liked that then. Time, identity, and consciousness had been interrupted and altered. Although I couldn't verbalize it then, I suddenly understood that awareness, consciousness, is my life. Later, I would realize that this consciousness that I am has no experienced beginning or end.

We chattered on about the adventures and mysteries of our changing young lives. Eventually, Kent mentioned Ronnie again, and I became aware of my sorrow. I looked at Kent and pretended I felt about him as I had about Keith. As I did, Kent seemed to develop a depth, a spirituality, and a beauty that I hadn't noticed. The black pupils of his brown eyes were twin windows into his consciousness, and I wanted to know him.

"Why are you looking at me that way, Denny?"

"I want to see what you see."

"I see you. So?"

"I see you seeing me."

"Well, I see you seeing me see you! It's your turn!"

"I see you, but I don't know how much of what I see is just me—what I want to see—and how much is really you. You're like a different person for me now. It's weird!"

"I feel weird when you look at me like that! It's like it tickles! Do you get ticklish, Den? I sure do!"

As I continued to look at Kent, he seemed more complex and intense. I sensed his consciousness there behind his smiling brown eyes; and, as he became more vividly real for me, I told him to take off his shirt and lie down on my bed. I said I wanted to find out just how ticklish he really was. My obvious indirectness caused him to smile. Even though I knew Kent was athletic—he had his picture in the paper once for wrestling—I was amazed by his defined muscularity when he removed his shirt.

"You've got to take your shirt off, too, Denny!"

"Let's take everything off, Kent, and I'll show you what Ronnie and I do. Take all of it off—everything. Now! Do it!"

"Even my socks?" he asked, as if somehow naked feet went beyond propriety.

Afterward, when the sense of reality had returned, I felt alone, agitated, and empty. I couldn't connect with Kent or make the magic happen again. The experience had been the mere motions of skin, muscle, and body parts—

not a loving relationship. I knew even more painfully what I'd lost with Keith, and I felt more frantic about getting what I needed from others.

It had been a new experience for Kent and undoubtedly his last with a male. He struggled with the feelings he'd just experienced and was threatened by their intensity. I knew he'd learned something about himself he didn't want to know. I wanted him gone and told him so, saying my family might be wondering what we were doing.

As he left, I remember him saying, "You know, what we just did...well, don't tell anyone. Promise, Denny? It was...I don't know...well...it was just silly—sort of stupid, I guess. I don't know why a guy would ever want to do that again—unless it was with a girl, of course. I was just curious about it this one time. It was really just dumb, that's all—nothing else! ...Well, most of it was, anyhow." He looked at me with a fond questioning look, then smiled shyly and said, "You sure know what to do! See ya sometime."

"Probably not," I coldly concluded. The irritated look on Kent's face mirrored my rejection as he left. I was relieved. I knew he was deceiving himself, but I understood why. What saddened me, and what I couldn't understand, was why this self-deception was so easy for him and yet so difficult for me. That troubled me.

In those repressed times, the late '40s, sexuality was simply not discussed. Churches were still powerful then. Catholicism, which had been created by those few odd young men of each generation who were willing to deny their sexual natures to become church fathers, has always been impotent to conceive the passionate truth of our human sexualities. These celibate skirted wonders, who depended on the reproductive flesh of others for their empire, regarded sexual love with one's own kind as such a threat that they taught their flocks of brain-dead sheep that this love was an abomination, a mortal sin. It became the love that dared not speak its name, although today, we shout. And today, the rat-brained preachers of hate continue the lie; they tell us they love the sinner, but not the sin. Their lies are killing people, people I love, my people. That's why I write.

Because sex with your own kind was simply not mentioned by our elders, it didn't seem to be an important social concern for them. We certainly knew their views about the ungodliness of adultery, premarital sex, about Eve and the legions of fallen women who cause the downfall of Man, and—God forbid—about the punishment of pregnancy, but they were silent about the consequences of sex between boys. They simply seemed to ignore it, so we saw no great threat or harm. Boys in my neighborhood were fascinated with their new-found sexuality and were willing to experiment together, since girls couldn't and wouldn't. And, of course, we weren't perverts. We were just messing around a little before we had to grow up and settle down with a wife for life.

Like a lean, prowling leopard, I began a nocturnal hunt for prey during the many weeks that followed and became skilled in the subtleties of selection and swift seduction. It was easy—so easy. All I had to do was initiate and thereby assume the responsibility and blame. Since this allowed them to easily save face—"It was his idea; not mine"—they became enthusiastic quarry.

The word got out that I was on the hunt, and the prey began to seek me out. Allan fed the grapevine with lies that were irresistible to sperm-filled minds about my knowledge of exotic erotics. Like a vulture waiting for a few miserable scraps from the carcass of the previous night's kill, prepubescent Allan was rewarded by living vicariously on my deliberately incomplete descriptions. I wouldn't tell him that I was animated in my desperate search only by the memory of Keith and a dwindling hope. I was experiencing the loss of the only love I had ever known. I didn't want Allan to know that the meaning of my many contacts had been reduced to the novelty of body parts and various groans when they came. I wouldn't tell him, when I curled up like a fetus in my bed after a night's hunt that I thought of suicide and longed never to awaken. No one ever knew that I embraced with my naked warmth the cold blue steel of my loaded rifle.

Chapter Eight

With each dawning of the sun, the complexity of the world and its peacefulness returned to banish the solitary sorrow of my nights. The days brought relief, except for involuntary flashbacks of the sights and sounds of the latest prey. Almost anything could trigger these flashbacks—the register and timbre of a voice; a reminiscent, sinuous curve; odors; places and particular kinesthetic patterns. By the time the blue-green light of evening was fading, these flashbacks blended into a pulsating stream of sexuality, a collage of bodies in motion.

During one of these flashbacks while I was mowing our lawn one afternoon, I was suddenly grabbed from behind. The person jammed his arms under mine and locked his hands together around the back of my neck, bending my head down. He put his full weight on my back, forcing me forward to the ground on my knees. I could feel his cheek pressing against mine, but I couldn't see who it was.

"I got you now, you two-timing, baby-raping pervert, you!" It was Ronnie, a frisky, very happy Ronnie. Their house had been rebuilt, and he was back for good. Best of all, he was no longer grounded. Unfortunately, Allan had told Ronnie about my sex hunts, and Ronnie was peeved. He warned me that if I two-timed him again, he'd kick me out of the gang for good. He wanted to know how many guys I'd had and if I'd done anything with them that he and I hadn't tried. I lied and told him it had been just a couple of guys. I was truthful when I told him I'd missed him and had masturbated thinking about him. His mood changed, and he said he'd done that, too. Then he told me he'd bought a stack of new records for us, so we went over to his house and sexed with more feeling than usual. I didn't tell Ronnie about the flashbacks of other guys' bodies I kept having as we did.

Toward the end of the school year, I learned that most of the guys in our gang were planning to go to the first formal dance for our class. It was to be held outdoors in a park. Ronnie was excited and said he wanted to double date with me. He said Corrine knew a couple of good-looking girls who wanted to go with us. I wasn't enthusiastic and said I didn't want to go, but Ronnie kept stressing I had to go, since everybody else who counted was going. I gave in to this conformity out of the fear of loneliness, but I resented Ronnie's excitement about dating and felt threatened. I saw it as simply a status trip for him; but, since I felt rejected by his interest in dating, I became rejecting and decided to beat him at his own game. Ronnie was bubbling over about his plans for our double dating when I informed him that I didn't need Corrine to get a date for me; I preferred not to double date with him, because I wasn't afraid to be alone with a girl. I twisted the blade in his guts by reminding him that I, unlike himself, was not a virgin. We understand best the vulnerabilities of our own gender. My aim was accurate, but my communication, dishonest. He was hurt.

I knew the attractiveness of our dates would be the scores on the playing field where Ronnie and I would compete. Our dates were status symbols in our dominance games—as women often are for men. Like magic amulets, we believed these symbols would bring us admiration, respect, power, and even love from our male peer group. I was quite careful about my choice for this dance. I rehearsed many times before asking an extremely pretty girl, Elizabeth, the beloved daughter of a church deacon. When I finally felt confident enough to ask her, she was pleased but had to get permission from her parents. I worried and paced most of the day until she called in the evening with the good news. My mother was delighted, and my father, himself, took me out to buy a suit and new shoes. Ronnie kept trying to find out about the girl I was bringing to the dance, but I just said she was an ordinary-looking girl, nothing special. He was elated.

On the night of the dance, Ronnie called and said I could still double with him; if not, he was going with Allan. I told him I'd see him there, if I could recognize him in a suit. My father showed me how to put on a tie and carefully arranged the handkerchief in the pocket of my suit coat. When I was completely costumed, I was amazed at the image of the young man I saw in the mirror, and I waved at him and laughed as he waved back. My mother got all blubbery with emotion and told me how happy Elizabeth would be when she saw me. She went to the refrigerator and brought Elizabeth's corsage, a purple orchid, in its satin-ribboned box. She handed it to me with tears in her eyes as though she were giving me the key to the most precious thing she had ever known—the life-giving memories of the then distant time of the sweetness of romance in her lonely life. Her tears were also those of a mother who knew she was losing her son's exclusive devotion and love—such as it was—to strangers who did nothing to deserve it. My mother's tears evoked in me an uneasy sense of responsibility for a transgression I couldn't quite fathom.

The warm darkness of the starry night relieved me; but, as I came to the tree-lined street where Elizabeth lived, my heart began to pound with fear of the certain inquisition by her parents. They'd told her she could go to the chaperoned dance only if they met me and approved of the kind of young man I was. I arrived early, so I nervously paced up and down her street, rehearsing answers to every question I could imagine being asked. My greatest terror was that her deacon father might be someone I tried to seduce when I was hitchhiking. I was shaking as I walked toward their imposing front entrance. I saw a young, blond pigtailed girl of nine or ten peeking out at me from the narrow windows beside the massive door. "It's him! He's here! He's coming!" she shrieked and disappeared. I took several deep breaths and rapped the large brass door knocker. Silence. Again I knocked, but nothing stirred. I thought about fleeing from the horror of this time of judgment, but it was too late. As I knocked the third time, I realized they were trying to appear casual and unconcerned, but I knew this was Elizabeth's first date. I was amused by the thought that they were anxious, too, and that all of us would soon be in a play of pretense.

The intimidating door swung open to reveal Elizabeth's well-dressed mother staring at me in silence. As I recall, this memorable first date went something like this:

"Good evening, ma'am. I'm Dennis Hinkle, and I'm here to take your daughter Elizabeth to..."

"Yes, I know," she interrupted. "My husband and I have been expecting you, young man, but we forgot about the time. You prefer to be called Denny, don't you?"

"Yes, ma'am!"

"Forgive my staring at you, but you look so much more, well, so much older and taller than I expected. Do come in. How old are you, Denny?

"Thank-you. I'm 14, ma'am, going on 15. My birthday is at the end of this month. It's on the longest day of the year—June 21st!"

"How nice for you! My, you do look so grown-up and handsome in that suit of yours. I'll bet it's a new one!"

"Yes, ma'am. Most of the guys in our class got new ones for this dance. My shoes are new, too!"

"I can see they are. Betsy, come in here and meet this fine-looking young man." Betsy, the pigtailed girl who had shrieked my arrival, hid shyly behind her mother's skirt and stuck a thumb in her mouth as she studied me. "Betsy, what did mama tell you?" Betsy quickly jerked her thumb from her mouth with a loud plop that caused her mother to grimace. "Betsy, this is Denny; Denny, Betsy. Denny is going to take Elizabeth to a dance tonight."

"I know! You've told me that every day for a week!" wailed an exasperated Betsy. "Besides, Elizabeth can't go with him until Dad looks him over! Dad said so!" Her mother's composed face fell like a decorated cake in a rainstorm. Betsy turned to me and asked, "Mister, are you going to marry my sister?"

"No. I'm just going to take your sister to a dance."

"Then what are you going to do?" asked Betsy with a bratty smile.

"I'm going to bring her home safe and sound by 11:00."

"Is that all you're going to do?" Betsy teased.

"Betsy, right now, go tell your father that our guest has arrived," ordered her mortified mom.

"He knows he's here."

"Well, why isn't he coming in here then?"

"He said he was going to make this guy cool his heels for awhile."

"Betsy! Go get your father! I'm sure Betsy is just fibbing a little for fun. Pay no attention to her, Denny. She's just upset, because she can't go to the dance. My, I smell something so nice on you! It must be something you used on your hair. Here, come closer to me. What is that fragrance? It's familiar, so nice."

"It's Lifebuoy Deodorant Soap, ma'am."

"Oh. Yes, of course."

"My dad says I smell like I'm in rut if I don't use it. I don't know what rut is or even what it smells like. Do you know, ma'am?"

"I don't think...Oh, here comes my husband. George! We're in here. Over here, dear."

Elizabeth's stern hatchet-faced father stopped in the doorway, leaned against the door jam, scowled, and carefully scrutinized me. "How old are you, boy?" he demanded.

"Fourteen—almost 15, sir."

"You're mature for your age, son. Haven't I seen you somewhere before? You sure look familiar."

"No, sir! I haven't seen you before! I'm sure I haven't."

"I don't know...well, maybe it was somebody else. For a man of my age, all you young bucks look pretty much the same. Maybe I saw you in church. You do go to our church, don't you?"

"No sir. I don't."

"Where do you go to church, son?"

"Well, we've gone to several churches, sir."

"What denomination?" he demanded, knitting his brow.

"Ah...Presbyterian and Methodist, sir."

"Well, where are your papers?"

"Papers? Was I supposed to bring papers?"

"No, I mean, with which church do you have your papers of membership on file?"

"I don't know, sir. My parents would know."

"Are your parents good church people? Do they go to church as they should?"

"Yes, sir. They try their best, sir," I lied.

(The truth was my mother only went to church at Easter and Christmas— Easter, to show off her new hat, and Christmas, because she enjoyed the carols—these two times being sufficient to keep her space in heaven reserved. My father said he had no need for it and never went. I was forced to endure Sunday school "to learn good morals" until I could no longer stand it and refused to go. My most vivid memory of Sunday school was of a friend who forgot what God is. The exasperated teacher shook him so violently that his head flopped from shoulder to shoulder as she screamed, "God is love! God is love!" I never went back after that.)

"Well, I'm glad to hear that, son. We don't want our daughter going out with any Catholics or Jews or any of that sort of thing—if you know what I mean. 'Course, there aren't any Jews in this part of the country, are there?" he asked suspiciously.

"I don't know, sir. I never saw one. I don't know how I could tell if I did see one."

"Good. Tell me, son, what does your father do?"

"When, sir?"

"When? I mean, how does he earn his living?"

"Oh! He works for B.F. Goodrich Company."

"Tires? What does he do there?"

"He's a sales manager—or something like that."

"Oh, I see—a white collar worker, then."

"I guess so. He always wears clean white shirts, if that's what you mean, sir. My mom hates to iron them." Betsy came running down from upstairs, "Dad, Liz wants to know how much longer before you decide if she can go to the dance. She wants you to hurry up!" Elizabeth's father shouted up the staircase, "Elizabeth! We've been waiting for you! You're keeping your nice young man waiting. Hurry up now. Come on down!" We went into the hallway and waited at the bottom of the winding staircase. When I heard a rustle of cloth, I looked up, and there, at the top of the stairs, smiling and blushing self-consciously, was a transformed Elizabeth, a young woman of astonishing beauty. She lifted the skirts of her lace-covered, pure-white gown slightly and slowly descended. As she came closer, I noticed delicate white flowers in her intricately styled jet-black hair. I'd never seen such a vision of loveliness and light, and I suddenly felt a sob trapped in my throat. I was grateful that one so beautiful would want to be with me for an evening. I suddenly imagined I was her bridegroom. As she descended, she anxiously looked to her father for approval, and I felt jealous and resentful. I looked at him and thought, I can be sexual with your daughter and you can't! He looked at me, and I swear he was reading my mind. His face became drawn and serious, and I smiled defiantly at him. He had fathered her, blood of his blood, and had raised, loved, and cherished her; and I, a mere arrogant youth, who had done nothing for her, could ravish her and know her passion.

I presented Elizabeth with the corsage box. She feigned surprise; but, when she opened it, the size and beauty of the Cattleya orchid she found did surprise her. She thanked me and asked me to put it on her dress. I asked where. When she pointed to a place just above her left breast, my hands began to shake with the thought that I would have to touch her there while her father was watching. I was convinced that as badly as my hands were shaking, the pin would slip and puncture Elizabeth's left breast. I imagined a large red blood spot soaking down the front of her white gown. Her mother smiled and motioned for me to hand her the corsage. Her father shook my hand painfully, as men were taught to do, and we left. As we walked down the street, I looked back and saw Elizabeth's mother standing alone looking sad, watching us from a window. I waved at her, and she waved back and disappeared.

"I thought we'd never get out of there, Denny! Isn't my father the most awful man! I hope he wasn't too rude to you. He can be really loving sometimes, but he still thinks I'm too young to go to a dance. He says I'm still his little girl! Can you imagine that! I think he's jealous; I really do! You look really nice. I like that suit on you. It's good with the color of your eyes. Did your mom help you pick it out? You've got really long eyelashes. It's going to be funny seeing all you guys dressed up in suits and ties. I can hardly wait to see what the other girls are wearing. You know, my mom said this dress cost a fortune—a fortune! My dad said he didn't care how much it cost, I was worth it! They wouldn't tell me exactly what they paid, but I know it was a fortune. Do you like it? You looked at me strange when you first saw me.

You do like it, don't you?"

"It's the most beautiful dress I ever saw, Elizabeth. I was really surprised when I saw you. Those flowers in your hair—I wasn't expecting you to be...so beautiful! I mean, you're really pretty anyhow, but tonight, well, I still can't believe it. You'll be the most beautiful girl at the dance. Everybody will look at you. Aren't I supposed to walk next to the curb? Dad said guys walk on the outside."

"Oh, yes, I forgot. Let's change sides. I'm supposed to put my arm in yours...like this. There. Doesn't this seem silly? I don't know what I'm doing!" she said, laughing.

"I don't either. Let's pretend we're seniors—or going steady."

"Going steady! Oh, this is going to be hilarious! Neither one of us knows what we're doing. You're supposed to know, Denny!"

"Nobody else does, either. Let's just make it up as we go along and act like we're married or something."

"Married? You know, I thought about that when I was coming down the stairs. I thought about my father giving me away."

"You did? I thought I was your bridegroom! I swear-to-God I did! You know those little couples they put on the top of wedding cakes—those decorations? Well, I think we kind of look like that. I wonder if you can eat them?"

"Of course not, silly! You save them, along with your wedding dress."

"How come they don't make wedding dresses in colors?"

"Because white means the bride is a virgin. Didn't you know that?"

"No. What if she isn't a virgin? What does she wear?"

"You don't get married if you're not a virgin."

"But there must be some who aren't virgins. What do they do?"

"Well, I guess they could wear off-white or something. I don't know. I guess they'd just have to lie and wear white anyway."

"What do divorced women do? They can't help not being virgins."

"I don't know. I've never known a divorced person, but I don't think they could ever get married again."

"Why not?"

"Why, because, Denny, what man would ever want a woman who wasn't a virgin?"

"I wouldn't care if my wife wasn't a virgin. Most guys aren't virgins when they get married."

"I think you would. Guys don't have to be virgins, because somebody has to know what they're doing. I don't know if we should be talking like this."

"But what about the girls they do it with? What about all of them?" I remembered the older girl Keith and I had sex with.

"They don't get married, of course. They're called prostitutes!"

"I knew a girl once who wasn't a virgin, and she wasn't a prostitute, either. Her name was Sunny. She liked boys. She lives in Kirkwood."

"She'll never get a decent husband. I feel sorry for her. How did you know a girl like that? If my dad found out we were talking about this stuff, he'd go crazy!"

"A friend introduced me to her one time."

"You actually met her? You talked to her? That's disgusting! What was she wearing? Did she use a lot of makeup? How did she do her hair? Was she pretty? You actually talked to her? Did you like her?"

Images of Sunny's naked hip movements bounced in and out of my mind as Elizabeth's words continued to cascade into the night. I imagined sweet Elizabeth opening her decorative little hand purse and smiling as she pulled out a condom made to fit a horse. Then she asked me to go inside her, and I did—completely! I crawled in, and, holding a lantern, I explored her insides and even looked out at the world from behind her eyeballs. (I had that kind of a mind; still do.) "Denny, you're not listening to me! You didn't answer my questions! Where are you off to?"

The park came into view just ahead, and I was anxious with the thought of Ronnie's presence. The area for the dance was outlined by a perimeter of glowing red and yellow Chinese lanterns. A ring of picnic tables, loaded with potluck snacks, surrounded the empty dance platform where no one had dared to venture. Squeals and shrieks rose from the gaggles of girls as they greeted their friends and compared costumes. The boys, wearing their new suits and their fathers' old ties, stood around stiffly and self-consciously, because they had no script for their part in this initiation into these fertility rites. Occasionally, pairs of them would whisper obscene comments about particular girls, and, if the comments caused sufficient convulsions of carnal laughter, these remarks would make the rounds of the ring of boys. In the shadows of the perimeter stood the long-faced chaperones in still groups like silent sentinels who were ever vigilant for the slightest sign of dalliance—or were they only searching for what was theirs no longer amid the splendor, spontaneity and savage beauty of youth?

King Terry, Queen Corrine, and Prince Herb were holding court. As we joined the circle of sycophants, Terry studied Elizabeth, glanced nervously at Corrine, then smiled approvingly at me; he was always the good sportsman. Corrine's face contorted as she surveyed the details of Elizabeth's perfection, but then, with adolescent noblesse oblige, she embraced Elizabeth with diminished, but suitable, squeals of sisterhood. Herb said nothing, but later he came over to me while Elizabeth was away, put his arm around my shoulder, and whispered into my ear, "You got a winner, Den. I'd sure like to try to get my hands in her pants. She's beautiful!"

I asked if he'd seen Ronnie. He told me Ronnie and his date and some others went for a walk to a nearby stream. I felt a surge of threat and excitement when he said that Ronnie had asked him where I was. Just as Elizabeth was returning, I whispered to Herb, "She isn't wearing any panties!"

"What are you two boys whispering about?" Elizabeth asked suspiciously. Herb became pink-faced, excused himself, and left. Moments later, I saw him whispering to Terry, who looked at me incredulously.

Dancing was initiated by two girls because their boyfriends were too embarrassed to be the first on the dance platform. It was common for girls to dance together then, because most people had never heard of lesbians. Soon, we were all dancing. Holding Elizabeth and feeling her hold me was life giving and full of wonder, so different from the narcissism of today's solo dancing. Many boys cut in on us, including Terry and Herb. I resented their right to do this, and they knew it. But we were, after all, proving to each other that we were good sports on the same team, the men's team.

"What are you so jumpy about, Denny? Are you looking for someone?" Elizabeth questioned as we danced.

"I was just looking for a friend of mine."

"Who? Why are you so jumpy?"

"Ronnie. Ronnie Ryan. Have you seen him?"

"No, I haven't seen him. Is Ronnie really a friend of yours?"

"Yes."

"A good friend?"

"Yeah. My best friend."

"Wow!"

"Why do you say that?"

"Ronnie's real neat! All the girls think he's cute. He's got a dimple. You really are in the in-group, aren't you? What's Ronnie like?"

"I don't think you'd like him. He's sort of stuck on himself and kind of boring at times," I said defensively.

"This girlfriend of mine has a class with him. She talks about him all the time, but she says he doesn't even notice her. She says his folks are rich. Are they? Oh! I think that's him over there! Can you see?"

My heart started to pound with anxiety and my hands became cold and sweaty. "Elizabeth, do me a favor. Will you put your head on my shoulder while we're dancing now? Hurry!"

"Well, I don't know...people might think I..."

"Please, Elizabeth!"

I watched Ronnie and his date coming closer; he hadn't seen me. As he looked around, I turned so my back was to him. I held Elizabeth closer and studied the flowers in her hair to ease my tension. Time seemed to freeze. Eventually, the music stopped, and I knew the threatening moment had come. I turned and tried to look confident—even defiant. There, not ten feet from me stood Ronnie in his expensive, perfectly tailored new suit. He looked older and more mature, and very handsome and proud. His eyes were fixed on mine. We both understood one another. I was determined to make him look away first; after all, he was rejecting me by dating. As I held Elizabeth's hand, I wanted him to hurt inside the same way I hurt when I first saw him proudly wearing his date on his arm. While he looked at me, I vividly recalled his nakedness and his expressions of bliss at the moment of orgasm. I hoped he was remembering those moments, too. He eventually cast his eyes down; I'd won! He looked up slowly at Elizabeth. I knew he was hurting. As he realized how much more beautiful my date was than his, my victory was complete. He looked into my eyes again; my facial expression conveyed my thought, "How does it feel, Ronnie Baby? Now do you understand what you've done to me?" His face was sad in reply. He lowered his eyes again, and I knew he understood. He summoned some courage, looked at me and smiled, and nodded approvingly toward Elizabeth in manly acknowledgment of my victory. I relaxed and had this crazy impulse to go over to him and force him to dance with me with his head on my shoulder! Elizabeth's tugging on my arm brought me out of this trance state, and I was frightened about my impulses getting out of control or being known.

"Denny! What's going on with you and Ronnie? I thought you two were best friends. You didn't even speak to each other. You just stared. Why were you guys acting so weird?" questioned Elizabeth.

I felt fresh anxiety at the thought that she might figure out what was going on. The music began again. It was "La Vie en Rose." Images of naked, aroused Ronnie getting out of bed to turn over the stack of 45-rpm records jolted through my mind. "We aren't weird. Ronnie's just jealous of me, because of how much prettier you are than his girl."

"Oh, all you guys are silly! Compete, compete, compete! Is that all any of you know how to do? You guys even use dating to compete! I'm glad I'm not a guy. I don't think Ronnie should feel jealous. I know his date, Patty Mason. She's pretty and has a great personality. She can't help it if her front two teeth are too big. She told me that's why she doesn't like to smile or laugh too much, but she's a really nice person once you get to know her. My dad says I have perfect teeth. Did you see how white they are? And even? Did you notice?"

Ronnie and I avoided each other the rest of the evening. Just before the dance ended, Allan came over. He'd been teased about his date. She was taller than he was, so when the two of them danced, his face was at the level of her breasts. He filled me in on the gossip. As he was leaving, Allan said, "Oh yeah. I almost forgot. Ronnie wanted me to tell you to come over to his house after you drop Elizabeth off. He wants you to stay over. Okay?"

"Tell him it will be too late. I can't." I could have stayed with Ronnie, but I still felt rejected.

"Ronnie said you would probably say no, so he told me I should tell you he wants you to come over Saturday night. He wants you to call him."

"I don't know. Tell him to call me tomorrow if he still wants to."

"Oh, you guys are just a couple of peas in a pod! You both got fat heads! What's going on with you two? Ronnie's been in a mood all night. Are you two going to let a couple of silly girls break up your friendship? It's just not worth it."

"I know. Tell him I'll call him sometime tomorrow."

Elizabeth and I were nervous about what we should do when we got to her house. I told her I wanted to kiss her. She blushed, lowered her eyes, and said we shouldn't kiss on the first date, because then I'd think she was cheap. After much persuading, she finally agreed when I explained how horrible I felt about never having kissed a girl before.

"I've never let a boy kiss me before," she confessed.

"Has a boy tried to?"

"Well, not exactly. You're not supposed to ask about private things like that, Denny! Now, just to help you out, I'll let you kiss me, but only on the cheek."

I remembered some love scenes in movies I'd seen. I held her face between my hands and gently touched her cheek with my lips. With the feel of her delicate skin, the memory of this same gesture with Keith flooded my mind. His response had been powerfully erotic, hers, a wilting passivity. I kissed her other cheek, and we looked into each other's eyes for some time—just like the movies. She was smiling and very beautiful in the moonlight. I felt her warmth and my arousal and knew I was going to kiss her on those moist waiting lips. She resisted briefly before yielding. I closed my eyes and proudly pressed my hardness into her. She tensed, gasped, broke away, looked at me in confusion and anger, but also curiosity, and fled into her house. I never dated Elizabeth after that. I never wanted to; but, with the unfolding of the delicate white flowers of each spring, her loveliness lives again.

While I walked along deserted, tree-lined streets past dark homes where families slumbered, I wished my friends had seen me kiss Elizabeth. I wondered what Ronnie would have thought and if he'd tried to kiss Patty Mason. I worried about my crazy impulse to make Ronnie dance with me in public. I worried even more about remembering Keith when I kissed Elizabeth. I couldn't understand why I was so angry with Ronnie. He was just trying to grow up and be well-adjusted like any other normal, red-blooded, all-American boy, like me. We both went to the dance, because we were afraid we'd be rejected if we didn't. I couldn't understand why we had to pretend that girls were so special or important to us. I knew that guys liked guys, not girls, since no guy wanted to be like a girl. I liked being a guy, and I liked people who were like me. I couldn't understand why people wanted me to try to love somebody who was not like me—my opposite. It didn't make sense; and, the more I worried about it, the more upset I became. I knew there was something drastically wrong with me, and I became so agitated that I wanted to cry out; but I told myself—as my father would—to get tough and take it like a man, not a sniveling sissy. I had to make it home, but there was nothing there for me. Then I thought about Keith. He would be sound asleep, and I was calmed by the idea that the same moonlight that was touching my skin also connected me with Keith by shining through his bedroom window and touching him. I wondered if he often thought about me the way I did about him. As I walked on, I calmed myself by saying over and over again, "Yea, though I walk through the valley of the shadow of death, I will fear no evil, for thou art with me." It was Keith I was thinking about. But nobody was with me. Take it like a man, I thought. "If you step upon a crack, you will break your mother's back!" I repeated to focus on something else. But by the time I reached my dark, silent house, I knew that, unlike other boys, I was not able to feel for a girl what I felt for Keith. I was different in this way, and I decided I'd just have to live with that for the time. I resolved to find someone like Keith, so I could be happy again. I knew Ronnie and I would drift apart as he conformed; I understood his reasons, but I couldn't be like him—at least, not then.

(How different my life would have been if there had been organizations for gay teens then—other than the Boy Scouts. My father wanted me to join the Scouts and promised to go on one of their camping trips with me if I did. I was seduced the first night on that camping trip by an eagle scout who displayed his endowment with more pride than his merit badges. My father's tent was next to ours. I was terrified that he'd heard us, but when I saw him the next morning, I knew he hadn't. Scouts snickered knowingly at one another when our militaristic potbellied Scout master lectured us about staying morally clean—no masturbation, fornication, or perversion. He said it was our duty to report to him boys who were not morally clean. I dropped out soon after this. My sons are outraged by such gay discrimination and the hate campaigns of the religious right, but I remind them that they should be grateful. Good deeds can have evil consequences, and vice versa, I told them. Had it not been for the bigotry and sanctified hate of these fools, my sons would not have been born.)

During the summer, Ronnie and I continued to be friends, although he sought me out far more than I did him. I related to many guys in my search, even though this irritated Ronnie greatly whenever he found out. I remember one particular week when my parents went to visit my sister at a summer camp. They told me that under no circumstances was I to have anyone over to the house during that week for any reason whatsoever. Naturally, Ronnie and others stayed with me every night my parents were gone. One evening, a group of about five of us raided my father's liquor cabinet, played strip poker in our recreation room, and then jacked off together in a squirting contest. Ronnie wasn't there that night; and, when he found out, he was furious with me, but he wanted to know every detail of who did what to whom, how big each guy was, and who shot the farthest. The night before my family was to return, six of us had another orgy at Ronnie's insistence. After midnight, we were exhausted; so two of the boys slept in my parents bed, two in my sister's room, and Ronnie and I in my bed. I fell asleep with Ronnie's arms around me.

"What is this? Who the hell are you? God Almighty, what are you doing in my bed? Get the hell out of here before I break all of you bastards into a thousand pieces! Get out! Get out now!" my father yelled from his bedroom. They'd come home early.

My bedroom door burst open, and there stood my father, his nostrils flaring. Boys in underpants, and some naked, raced down the stairs past my astonished mother and sister. "Rube! For God's sake, calm down. You're going to hurt someone!" yelled my mother. I dressed and gathered the boys' clothes and fled the house to find them. I stayed at Ronnie's for three or four days until my mother said it was safe to come home. My father didn't speak to me for weeks, which made family life easier.

Later that summer, I was again awakened in the middle of the night, but this time to the pathetic sobbing of my mother. My father sat on the bed beside her looking confused, helpless, and frustrated.

"Denny, we just got a telephone call from your Aunt Julia in Florida. Donna's mother, your grandma, just passed away; she's dead," he mumbled. "Go back to bed. Mom will be all right. She *will be*."

Hearing this, my mother yowled between convulsions of sobbing. She looked plaintively at me with her red, puffy, tearful eyes and held out her limp hand toward me. It was almost exactly like my earliest memory of her lying on a stretcher.

My father, who greatly disliked emotions, much less their expression, became more agitated and yelled, "Donna! You've got to get a hold of yourself! You already woke one kid up! Do you want to wake up both of them? She wept louder. "Donna! You're hysterical! Control yourself! If you don't stop this, I'm going to have to slap you. Now stop it before you wake Judy," he demanded, but she continued. He looked helplessly at me and began to shake her. "Stop acting this way! Stop it now! I'm warning you." She couldn't. The palm of his hand smashed into the side of her face, knocking her head sharply to one side. She immediately became silent and began to shake with fear. The helpless anger in her eyes mirrored my own as I glared at him. "Get out of here before I do the same to you!" he snarled. My mother left for the funeral in Florida the next day. For the two weeks she was gone, I avoided my father completely.

I tried to stay away from my house as much as I could. One afternoon when I was killing time uptown, I saw a boy who looked like Keith. He was shorter, but he had blond hair like Keith, and his face was beautiful. Because his way of smiling and his gentleness were very much like Keith's, I was powerfully attracted. When he saw me looking at him—well, staring at him— he smiled and spoke; I was too emotional to make the first move.

His name was Bill Thomas. We went to the same school, but he lived some distance from my neighborhood. He knew Allan Walpole; they'd been in several classes and the Boy Scouts together. I was disappointed that he lived so far away, but we agreed to meet in town the next weekend.

I waited for Bill at the designated place, a Swenson's hamburger stand. Two hamburgers, one chocolate shake, and a hot-fudge sundae later, he still hadn't arrived. When I got home, I called Allan, thinking he might know Bill's telephone number, but he didn't have it anymore. He started his friendly prying into my reasons for wanting to call Bill, but I told him not to get nosey. I telephoned down the list of Thomases in the phone book, and the next to last listing was his. His mother told me Bill was sick with the flu, so I asked if he would call when he was better. I asked my mother every day if he'd called; and, every day, she would say no; and, every day, I simply couldn't get him out of my mind. Bill was very friendly when he did call. He wanted to know why I wanted to be friends, since we lived so far apart. I told him I liked to have lots of friends from different neighborhoods. I was nervous and wanted to impress him, so I launched into a rambling description of a party Ronnie and I had gone to in Webster Groves, where Auggie Busch, son of the wealthy St. Louis beer-brewing family, arrived in a chauffeur-driven car. I said Auggie was a regular guy, just like us, and he had been especially friendly to Ronnie and me. I said he had even invited us to their estate to see the Clydesdale horses his family owned. Actually, Auggie Bush barely spoke to Ronnie and me, because so many people were crowding around him—especially the girls— and he told everyone at the party there was a regular guided tour of the stables that was open to the public. Ronnie and I thought he was a stuck-up, spoiled rich kid, and we envied him. Bill seemed sufficiently impressed. I invited him to visit me the next Saturday, when my folks would be gone. He said he had to get his mother's permission first. I felt threatened by this and manipulatively asked if he was a mama's boy, but he confidently said he knew how to get past her.

The next Saturday, Bill Thomas, smiling, his blond hair glinting, came strolling up our driveway just as Keith had done. I was tense from trying to control my emotions and anxious about the unpredictability of myself. As he came toward me, I wondered if he could be the one—if it could be the way it had been with Keith. The way I was staring made Bill self-conscious. He looked down, and I understood his shyness. This pleased me, and I felt a rush of excitement, because I was able to affect him emotionally. With my hand shaking, I reached out and dared to touch him on his shoulder. I rarely touched people because that usually aroused my sexual impulses. He looked up and smiled. I was trembling all over. He noticed and asked, "What's wrong? You're shaking!"

Be careful, I thought, he doesn't know what I want; maybe he doesn't even know anything about it. He looks and acts like Keith; they could be brothers. Go slow, I told myself, because he might get angry when he finds out what I want and tell everyone. "It's nothing. Just a little windy out here I guess," I said.

"Windy? It's summer and it's hot! Gimme your hand. It's cold and sweaty. Are you okay? Maybe you're getting what I had. It was awful!"

Bill's hand felt hot. When I realized he was concerned about me, I trembled even more. We went in the house, and I tried to impress him in every way. Within a few hours, we were sharing the realities of our young lives. In my parents' bedroom, I showed him where my father kept his condoms. I was alarmed when this embarrassed Bill. I asked if sex interested him. "Not really. I don't like to think about it. Besides, I never saw a rubber before," he answered, turning his head away.

I asked why sex didn't interest him, and he said he was shy about it. It would upset his mom, he explained. He added that his folks never mentioned it, and his church said it was evil. He was Catholic because of his mother, but his father didn't believe in it. I said my dad was like his and told him how each Thanksgiving, my dad served everyone else at the table nice white slices of turkey, then he'd cut the tail flap off the carcass, put it on my plate, laugh his guts out and say, "Here's the Pope's nose for you, Denny!"

Bill laughed, and then, out of the blue, I said, "Do you masturbate, Bill? Does anyone call you Billy?"

Bill's face flushed pink. "No one ever calls me Billy! That's what my mom calls me, and I hate it! Don't you call me that, Denny!"

"Okay, okay! How about Billy-boy?"

"Don't you dare!"

"Okay! ...well, do you?"

"Do I what?"

"You know!"

"Know what?"

"Do you jack off, flog the dog, ride the rod, beat your meat, jerk the joint, skin the cat, climb the pole, shift gears, polish the rod, make cream? You heard what I asked you!"

"Well, I heard you, yes, but I can't believe you said all those names! I'm not going to answer you!"

"That means you do!

"It doesn't mean I do! It doesn't!"

"You do! Everybody does!"

He grinned and said, "Well, nowhere near as much as you do! I'm sure of that. I've never talked with anybody about that, Denny. Let's not talk about it anymore."

I brought up sex again several times, but each time he became uncomfortable and changed the topic. I knew Bill was completely inexperienced, but I was powerfully attracted to him. The gentle shy acceptance of his smile filled me with a grateful warmth, and I wanted him. I studied him and decided I'd have to back off completely for some time, maybe even weeks. He was too easily frightened by what he didn't understand, but I'd wait. Bill wasn't like most other guys; but then, Keith hadn't been either.

Bill trusted me and so, shared the intimacies of his 14-year-old life. His speech bubbled with the joys and pains of his years; and, since no one had ever listened to him with such concentration and avid interest, he cascaded these vital disclosures in an attempt to be completely known before the magic of these moments vanished. It was as though he had only this ephemeral time in which to make himself real, or else he'd return to the isolation of the imaginary world of self-reflection. The more he became real for me, the more I wanted to touch him and hold him, and my fantasies began to interfere with my concentration. "Denny! Are you okay? You're looking at me funny! Where are you off to? Aren't you interested anymore?" Bill asked several times with looks of confusion and exasperation on his angelic face.

I reassured him that I was completely interested. I calmed myself down by pretending Bill was the wanted brother I never had—my brother twin. He had a younger sister, as I did. As he was talking about her, I noticed the sunlight glinting from his golden hair, and I remembered Keith saying of his own hair, "What makes you think it isn't real gold?"

"Denny! You're looking at me that way again! Is there something caught in my hair?" I told him it was just the sunlight and that I was imagining what it would be like if we were twin brothers. I told him I had always wanted a brother and said I'd been good friends with the McBrides, identical twins in Kirkwood. They used to switch classes at school and could even fool their own mother sometimes. I didn't tell Bill just how intimate Tom McBride and I had been, or what sort of relationship the twins had been having together for years, or that I often wondered what it would be like to make love with your identical twin and often asked Tom for the details about it until he became bored.

Bill, having no brother, liked the idea, so we began pretending—that great masquerade ball of our human yearnings. As Bill Thomas and I were exploring brotherhood in the ways we could, I glanced out the side window and saw the grinning face of Allan Walpole. I told Allan I didn't want him to come in. "I just wanted to see what you guys were up to," said Allan. "I bet I know why you don't want me to come in, Den, but Bill wants to see me, don't you Bill?

Be fair, Denny!"

"Yeah, let's let him come in, Denny. I haven't seen him in a long time!" pleaded Bill.

Allan was in the room before I could reply. His smile revealed his delight at such a quick and easy victory. Confidently completing his triumph with a grin, he said, "Well, Den, have you guys done it, yet?"

"Shut your stinking, rotten mouth, Allan, or I'll kick your little ass out of here! I mean it, Walpole!" I warned.

"Done what?" questioned a puzzled Bill.

Allan saw the trouble that would surely be his if he spoke truthfully. "It was nothing, Bill. I was just trying to tease Denny, that's all. I didn't really mean anything by it."

While Bill and Allan chattered and laughed, I felt trapped and irritated by the slow, painful oozing of time. Within an hour, the hopefulness of my resentment eroded into helpless resignation, and I grieved my loss of Bill in sulking, self-centered silence.

"What's wrong, Den? You haven't talked in a long time. Are you okay?" This unexpected expression of Bill's concern reawakened the sharp pain of my longing for him. I said I was okay and pulled my legs up into a fetal position and locked my eyes in a frozen stare at the floor.

Then I heard Allan saying, "I know what's bothering Denny. He wants to take you up to his bedroom and do with you what he and Ronnie Ryan do together. I'm going to be going now, so you two can have some time alone. I'm just in the way. See ya!"

I was shocked and anxious, but also excited. I was grateful for what Allan was doing for me, but I sensed the sadness and pain he felt when he said, "I'm just in the way." I realized then that Allan knew he wasn't sexually desirable. I thought briefly about taking him to bed, but the idea seemed embarrassing, inappropriate, and even wrong. I was confused by this; after all, Allan was my good friend. It didn't make sense, but that was nothing new for me. For the past several years, not much in my life had been making sense. I was glad he'd told Bill what I wanted, though. If it offended him, I could deny it. I reminded myself not to push Bill, that patience was the key. I began to worry that Bill was upset by Allan's disclosure, because he acted as if Allan had said nothing. I knew he heard what Allan said, he must have. Eventually, I realized that Bill hadn't fully understood Allan, because he was so completely unaware of my sexual passion for him. I relaxed and felt safe again.

Bill continued in his same happy, playful mood. This reassured me that my craving was still safely hidden. I kept wondering how it was possible that Bill didn't know what I was feeling for him, because my confined passion was ready to explode. He looked right into my eyes, but he just kept talking about motorbikes. I started to get the shakes; I worried that my teeth would chatter, then what would I tell him? As I worried about my teeth, I suddenly had this erotic fantasy of biting deep into his flesh and drinking his warm blood! This was followed by the idea of a tasty, juicy Billyburger, which I believed I would enjoy. (My bizarre and frequent fantasies didn't disturb me;

I was used to them; I'd had them since puberty. I rather enjoyed them. My only fear was of what others would think of me if they knew.) I decided I'd just look at Bill's hands, but that didn't help. I began to wonder which one he used to jack off with. Impulsively, I asked if he was left handed.

"Yeah, I'm left handed. What's that got to do with what I'm telling you about, Denny? Don't you want to hear about Kent's new motorbike? Well, do you?"

I continued to watch his left hand as he talked. It seemed to swell up, and I imagined it had a life of its own. It flew around through the air, touched his hair and cheek, pointed a finger at me, and came to rest on his thigh, its thumb poking the bulge of his crotch. Defensively, I tried to study the pattern in the cloth of the chair Bill was sitting in, but I then imagined that the chair was actually holding him and feeling his body.

"Bill, let's go outside. I can't stay in this house any longer. Okay?"

"Sure, but just let me finish! So when I finally told Mom I wanted to get a motorbike like that someday, she said, `You've got a snowball's chance in hell of ever getting one as long as I'm alive! Just forget it! I'm not going to have you getting killed on one of those suicide machines.' I swear to God, Den, when I grow up, I'm not going to buy a motorbike. I'm going to buy the biggest goddamned Harley-Davidson motorcycle ever made and ride it until my ass falls off! I swear to God I am! Now, when are you going to take me upstairs and show me what you and Ronnie do?"

Panic and desire swirled through my insides. "What Ronnie and I...do? What do you mean?"

Bill grinned playfully at me; his eyes were warm and happy. "Messing around, sex, making love! I know why you wanted me to come over when your family was gone. I just wondered how long it would take you to say something! Are you afraid of me?"

"Jesus! Jesus Christ, Bill! No, I'm not afraid of you! I was afraid you might say no. I didn't want you to be angry with me. Do you really know what you're doing? Have you ever done this before?"

"No, I've never done it, but I want to. I'm a little bit scared, but that's okay. I want to!"

"I don't want you to feel bad about it later. Are you sure you really want to? Will you be bothered after?"

"I don't think I will. Why would I be? I haven't done it before, but I know what I'm doing, and it's my choice, so why should I be bothered? If I am, I won't blame you, Denny. I won't! I promise. So, what are you waiting for? Let's go upstairs!"

I was moved by the look of excitement and trust in his eyes. I locked my bedroom door and said, "I want us to go slow and take a long time. I want to remember everything. Don't hurry. We can do it until we can't do it anymore. I'm going to make your toes curl, I am! Unbutton my shirt...slow." Five decades have passed since that evening, and I remember everything as though I've just risen from that bed of tenderness. Faith and hope were reborn in my soul in the arms of that young lord of love.

Hours later, as Bill was leaving, he said, "Denny, I'm not bothered. I never knew it would be like that; if I did, I'd have done it sooner! Tell me one thing, though. One of the times when you were going crazy, you called me Keith. Who's Keith?"

Chapter Nine

The next morning, a sunny Sunday morning, I awoke from the depths of a dreamless sleep. I watched the dazzling patterns of sunlight on my crumpled sheets and remembered that Keith had stood in the sunlight from the same window a year before. The memory of Bill Thomas resting his head beside me on my pillow seemed like a gift. I pressed the pillow against my face and rolled over on top of the sheets where his loving body had been. I longed for him, but I glowed with the realization that, even though Keith was gone, I could love again. Crumpled sheets in Sunday sunlight, a sermon on love. I was 15. The year was 1950, a new decade, a new beginning, I hoped.

"Breakfast, Denny!" I heard my mother calling. "I've got Canadian bacon, scrambled eggs, and pancakes with real maple syrup! Come and get it, before your father eats it all! Bill Thomas wants you to call him."

I raced downstairs to the telephone, but my father growled at me, "You dumb dodo! Just who do you think you are, coming down here in your underpants in front of your mother and sister? You look like a stupid savage! Now, get upstairs and get dressed. Wash first and get rid of the stink from your armpits! You should have more respect for your mother and sister, you dumb cluck, you!"

"Rube, it doesn't bother Judy or me to see him in his underwear. After all, he sees us in our underwear!" Mom interceded.

He said, "Well, it should bother you! If your family had any sense of decency, Donna, it would! What kind of example is this for Judy? I won't have it in my house!"

My mother smiled sweetly and hissed, "Denny, your father comes from a hillbilly family of prudes, who think the human body is sinful, especially that witch mother of his, so you'd better go cover yourself up; we wouldn't want to upset your father, now would we?"

I got dressed and called Bill. Excitedly, he said, "Denny! I still don't feel bothered by you-know-what! You had me worried about it. I kept waiting to be bothered, but I'm not! I don't think I'm going to be, either! Isn't that good? Oh, I asked my mom about you staying over. She asked me lots of questions about you and your family. At first, she didn't like the idea—you know, your not being Catholic and all—but when I told her your dad was a real important man in B.F. Goodrich, and you live in a house bigger than ours and you knew Auggie Busch, she changed. I know how to work my mom! She said you can come over as soon as we get back from our vacation. Isn't that great, Den? I can hardly wait!"

"Yeah! I can hardly wait, too!"

"I know what you mean!" Bill giggled.

"Call me the minute you get back, Bill. Promise?"

"I will. I'll do it first thing! Denny, I'm real glad you wanted me to be your friend. See ya in just a few weeks, buddy!"

Allan and my mother commented about how much happier I seemed. Allan understood why; my mother didn't. Ronnie Ryan called and asked me to go swimming with him at the country club. He wanted me to meet him at the pool rather than his house as I usually did. I sensed he was up to something. When I got to the pool, Ronnie was sitting at the water's edge looking pained; he was having a charley horse. Leg cramps were common for us during our rapid growth. At first he didn't want me to massage his leg, something I usually did for him, but he relented when the pain became intense. When his calf muscle relaxed, we went swimming. We raced each other before we talked. Ronnie was evasive, but it was clear that he was upset with me. In a burst of anger, he told me he knew about Bill Thomas and me. Allan had told him he'd never seen me happier than after I'd been with Bill. What really irritated Ronnie was his firm belief that I'd done things with Bill I wouldn't do with him. I denied it, though it was true, and told Ronnie I wasn't going to talk about it. Ronnie was in no mood to hear about Bill's affection. Ronnie sensed that my feelings toward Bill were different from those I had for other guys he'd found out about. When he asked me about this, I admitted it. Part of me just didn't care what he thought. Ronnie looked at me with the same expression of fury he had when he decked the boy in Webster Groves, and I felt fear. He called me a two-timing son-of-a-bitch and said he'd warned me about what he would do.

Ronnie didn't call me again; and, when I called him, his annoyed mother said he didn't want to talk to me. I decided to give him plenty of time to cool off. A week or so later, I was talking with some guys I knew, and they were excited about a country club dance that Ronnie and his parents were giving. They asked if I would be taking Elizabeth. I hadn't heard about the dance and understood exactly what Ronnie was doing and why I wasn't invited. I was helpless, and I knew it. I thought about crashing the dance, but Allan called and warned me not to. He said Ronnie expected me to try something like that. After the dance, only a few of the old gang came by my house or called. When I called them, they were always busy. Even Allan stopped coming over. Ronnie had warned me. I began to panic with the return of the old sense of loneliness I had before Keith. I was glad Bill was away on vacation, because I was sure Ronnie would have invited him to the dance. I began to worry that Ronnie would win Bill's friendship just to get back at me. Thoughts of Ronnie in bed with Bill Thomas kept flashing through my mind; I knew Ronnie was capable of punishing me like that. As I became more depressed and lonely, I feared I would be a total outcast throughout high school. I knew Ronnie could be vicious. I suspected he was turning everyone against me by telling them I was a pervert—like that guy behind the Shell gas station. I worried that my parents or teachers might hear about my sexual behavior, then I'd be finished; maybe I'd even be sent to a prison or a mental hospital. My father would cut me off for sure. I'd be all alone, and I couldn't survive that; I'd rather be dead.

I had frantic conversations in my head with Ronnie, reasoning with him, begging him, but I knew I couldn't convince him; he wouldn't listen. What could I convince him of—that I didn't care about Bill? I wasn't going to lie about it. My friendship with Bill was my only hope, but I knew Ronnie too well; he'd get to Bill and turn him against me. I couldn't stop him—he had money and social status. Maybe there was something wrong with me, I began to worry, because my friends were turning against me. I began to think that Ronnie might be right about dating girls. Maybe I had gone too far. Maybe I was becoming...a pervert. I knew I didn't want to live if I were. I thought about how I'd kill myself. I had ammunition for my rifle, but I preferred the idea of using electricity, because there would be less pain. I could tape an electrical wire around my arms and another around my feet, then I'd hook the wires up to the 220-volt lines at the fuse box—that would do the job. The cords would have to be long, so if I thrashed around, they wouldn't break. I'd throw the switch and be free from all this. The last thing I'd know would be the sound of the switch, then nothing. I felt relieved; I had an escape hatch. In prison, it wouldn't be so easy to do, so I decided I'd better do it before I got sent there. My fears weren't totally unreasonable, given the intolerance, conformity, and religious bigotry of the McCarthy era.

There seemed to be no way to avoid my tragic future, but a few days after the dance, I walked into our house and heard my mother sobbing in the living room. Dad had his arms around her. She tried to speak to me but couldn't, because of her crying. Dad said, "Denny, I just got a call from Akron. It's final now. I'm being transferred immediately. We'll be moving by the end of next week."

"Where to?" I asked.

"Richmond, Indiana," he replied.

"Where's Richmond, Indiana?"

"It's a small farm town on the main highway across Indiana. It's not too far from Dayton, Ohio. You'll like small-town life."

"The hell he will!" interrupted my mother bitterly. "The hell any of us will! He'll have to leave all his friends again and start all over, just like us! If you had any guts, if you were a real man, you'd tell that company to go to hell!"

"Just shut up, Donna! I don't want to hear any more of your emotional whining," he roared. "We're going, and that's that! Now, no more of your lip!"

I went outside, lay down on the grass in the back yard, and looked up into the beauty of the swaying sycamore trees. What I felt was deliverance, because I'd just escaped from Ronnie's deadly trap. In a matter of days I'd be free. I could start a new life. Nobody would know about me in Richmond, Indiana. But I worried that Ronnie might telephone the school there and tell people about me, so I decided I wouldn't tell anyone where I was moving.

I thought about my future and my problem. There was only one solution. I promised myself that I would never have sex again, unless it was with a girl. I was never going to think about Keith, or Bill, or any other guy, again. I was never going to be an outcast in a looney bin or a prison. I was determined that

I was going to be normal, just like everyone else. Looking up at the tall, swaying sycamore trees as if they were witnesses, I promised that I would learn how to love girls more than boys; I would—so help me, God. Nothing could stop me. Nothing! I had to be born again...in Richmond, Indiana. I had to.

Several days before we moved to Indiana, my mother told me Bill Thomas called. He told her he'd just gotten home from his vacation and wanted me to call him right away. His mother had invited me to stay with him for a few days. Bill called several more times before we left, but I never returned his calls. I never saw him again. My mother was angry with me for not calling Bill; I was inconsiderate, she said. I thought I was staying alive.

My life permanently changed in Glendale, on the golf course. I learned about hate in the caddie shack and sealed myself in silent fear there. Then from the fear of love, I turned against myself and Keith on that hilltop in the middle of the ninth fairway. I still feel uncomfortable around golf courses—can't shake the memories.

On the journey to Richmond, miles of farm scenes streamed past my backseat car window, accompanied only by gentle rocking motions, the monotonous drone of the car engine, and the usual silence of my family. Somewhere in Illinois, I began to feel safe and believed I'd made good my escape. Because of this feeling of safety, I could then experience the horror of all that I feared. By that time, the people in Glendale would have fully understood the message of ostracism Ronnie had sent. The rumor would have spread that I was a pervert, a queer, a fairy. During the last leg of my freedom ride to Richmond, Indiana, this refrain kept racing through my mind like a dreadful warning:

> "Mine eyes have seen the glory
> of the coming of the Lord;
> He is trampling out the vintage
> where the grapes of wrath are stored;
> He hath loosed the fateful lightning
> of His terrible swift sword.
> His truth is marching on!"

During my high school years, it was Joe McCarthy who trampled the grapes of wrath and swung his terrible swift sword. Today, ministers and priests lead their sheep on a holy war against the civil rights of gay people. McCarthy reminded me of my father, but most men in authority did then—even God, I believed, was like my father, a vengeful tyrant.

In Sunday school, I was taught that God was all loving, all knowing and all powerful. He created everything and gave me freedom and knew what I would do, but if I disobeyed him, then in his infinite mercy and love, he would condemn me to an eternity in hell. It didn't make sense to me. I knew I wouldn't do that to people I loved; I wouldn't want to make evildoers in the first place. Everybody else seemed to have no problem worshipping this contradictory king of kings. What was wrong with me, I asked myself. Why was I different? They told me the ways of God were many and strange, but I

thought he was crazy and cruel. Did he really have to let his only son be tortured to death just so he could get his ideas across, I wondered. If he wanted to save mankind, why didn't he just clap, or burp, or something? They even say he was his own son. Since this seemed absurd, I began to worry that I might be the crazy one and not know it. I had to make a fresh start in Richmond; I had to!
"He hath loosed the fateful lightening
    of his terrible swift sword!"
The farmland sped by monotonously, disrupted only by my turmoil and the *Battle Hymn of the Republic*. The silent tension in the car was suddenly shattered by my father saying, "Okay. I'm going to make a pit stop at the next gas station. I want all those bladders emptied! Everybody out, whether you got to go or not! ...Oh, and you, too, Denny!" This afterthought didn't go unnoticed by me. The stabbing pain of my father's exclusion was nothing new; only this time, I was raw with the ache of alienation. My only experience of love had been with Keith. I had to belong somewhere. My mother saw me wince and lowered her eyes in sympathetic sorrow. I turned to my sister, but she was intent on picking her nose.

Richmond surrounded the eastern end of the highway crossing Indiana like a grimy nodule growing around an artery. It was an old town, a cluttered town, a plain town of modest means. "I don't like it here. Let's go back to Glendale where it's pretty," Judy whined.

My mother started to cry and said, "My God, Rube. What have you done to us?" I looked out at the clutter of dingy brick buildings and thought, here's where I'm going to have to learn to be well-adjusted; this is the place. It seemed to me that the bleakness of Richmond was a deserved punishment for my past desires, the vintage of some grapes of wrath, I had no doubt.

I knew no one, so I spent the time building the most powerful spark coils I could. The arcs from these coils reminded me of those from the high-tension wires that broke during the great storm that kept Keith from me. They were also like the electrical arcs used in old Frankenstein movies. Several of them would be snapping, sizzling, and cracking at once until my bedroom was filled with the smell of ozone. My father was upset about the number of fuses I blew out and thought I was crazy for spending so much time staring at hissing blue arcs. "You ought to be out there joining a football team just like any other red-blooded young buck your age. Your high school years will be the happiest time of your life, Denny, and you're just sitting here killing time!" But I couldn't help it; those deadly blue arcs were mysterious symbols of something alive in the core of my being. Maybe I wanted to create a monster.

In the house next to ours lived a hefty-breasted, 16-year-old girl who was actively interested in our family. My mother said the girl, Carolina, was really coming over to see me. One afternoon, Carolina asked if I would come over and help her move a chair in their basement, but there weren't any chairs. She explained that the story was an excuse for my mother. We talked for awhile, and then Carolina, hearing a creak in the old house, glanced nervously at the stairway leading to the first floor. In a few moments, she was reassured and said, "Do you like my breasts, Denny? They're bigger than most girl's my age, you know. Well, do you like them? You did notice them, didn't you?"

I said of course I did, and they were big, all right. I told her they stuck out like fins on a Cadillac. Pleased and blushing, she said, "Oh, you're so weird! Cadillac fins! I don't believe this!"

We sat in silence on the tattered green sofa-bed as a tide of adolescent self-consciousness washed over us. We both knew what the cultural script called for at this point, but with our awkwardness and stage fright, we waited for the other. Suddenly, Carolina blurted out, "If you really like my breasts, you can put your hand under my bra and touch one! Hurry before Mom and Dad come home! Feel them now! Hurry!"

I didn't really want to touch her breasts; I hardly knew who she was. I'd had my fill of groping the intimate body parts of those I barely knew and pretending it was otherwise, only to be jolted into the cold starkness of reality by our awkwardness, embarrassment, and loneliness afterwards. But I knew I should want to touch big breasts; my newly chosen straight identity demanded that, so I reached out hesitantly toward her left mammary gland. The screen door to the kitchen upstairs slammed shut. "Jesus, it's my folks, Denny! Tell them you came over here to borrow a tool from my father. Get a screwdriver from that bench over there. Remember, we just came down here to get it!"

I held the screwdriver conspicuously and explained to her parents that my mom had sent me over to borrow a screwdriver. At the same time, images of Carolina twirling long tassels from the tips of her tits flashed through my mind. I was relieved to be gone from her house. Carolina continued to be friendly, but I avoided her after that. I didn't know why, and this annoyed my mother. I understand now that I was afraid Carolina would discover my inability to be sexually attracted to females.

The people in Richmond were curious about me, the city slicker, the guy from St. Louis. One unusually handsome young man named Roger sought my friendship. He was tall and blond, and I was pleased that he was interested in me. His father had been killed in World War II, and Roger lived with his mother in a small walk-up apartment downtown. He was devoted to his mother, as were most boys of that era. The two things we simply did not do to a boy in those days were to insult his mother, because our code of chivalry required instant total combat, and to call him a mama's boy, which implied that a woman controlled him, proving he lacked masculinity. Most of us were, of course, mama's boys in rebellion against control by women, for we wished to be "real men"—those who had the power to dominate and control.

Although I appreciated Roger's interest in me, I was suspicious about his motives, since there was an uneasy lack of spontaneity about his behavior. I suspected he might be hiding an interest in sex with me—an obvious projection of my own unacceptable desires. He didn't send any of the usual subtle signals I'd learned in Glendale; but I thought, maybe Indiana guys did it differently. One afternoon as we were walking along, Roger, with his arm around my shoulder, suddenly stopped, turned to me, and with the pressure of strong emotions, said, "You know, Denny, now that I've gotten to know you...well,

I...I feel such a good fellowship with you! Do you feel it, too—the fellowship? Do you?"

"What do you mean, `fellowship,' Roge?" I asked suspiciously.

"You know, fellowship! Aaa...like we both belong to the same community. It's like brotherly love—kind of spiritual. You know? Do you have those feelings, too?"

"Well, I guess I do, Roge. I like you, and I always wanted to have a brother. We're the same that way."

"I hoped you would, Denny! I know I can trust you now. I've got a very important secret I want to tell you, but I don't want anybody to hear us. Let's go to my place, and I'll tell you there. It's going to involve you. I've been wanting to tell you, but I wasn't sure about you. Come on!"

As we walked to his apartment, my mind raced and rehearsed. I was convinced he was going to proposition me. He was handsome, and I wished I had a face like his. He wasn't even aware that he was so good-looking. Why am I thinking like this, I wondered; it's crazy. I watched the cracks in the sidewalk go by. "If you step upon a crack, you will break your mother's back!" Why did I want to step on every single one of them? I thought about my dad screwing my mother. He had to do it at least twice, I reasoned. I never heard them do it. I wondered if she even moved when he did it, like humping a pile of Jello. I imagined she probably pushed her fingernail cuticles back while he was huffing and puffing away. I thought about my dad probing her mushy mass and having to wear a rubber, everything soft and nothing pushing back, and I couldn't understand how he could stand it. She was such a bitch to him, but then, he just walked around the house ignoring her, bored, jingling the change in his pocket all the time and driving her nuts. I guess he liked to know he had money in his pocket after having survived the Great Depression. I thought it was sick for me to be imagining my own parents having sex. I even wondered what my father's penis looked like. I said to myself, you're sick in the head—thinking about your own father's dick! You're disgusting!

"Denny, you haven't said a word for blocks; are you thinking about something you can tell me?"

"No. It's nothing much, Roger. Things you don't know about."

"Okay. I don't want to pry. You were just so quiet."

I quickly submerged myself again after this brief breath of reality. I wondered what Roger would be like if he were sexual. He was much taller than I was, and I wondered what it would be like to do it with a guy that tall. He was so polite that I imagined when he came he'd just breathe faster and make little hissing sounds—ssss, sss. I'd scare him for sure. I remembered the night Keith and I thought we woke up the whole neighborhood. Old man Trapp screamed at us to get off his property. Thank God he thought Keith and I were just fighting. I wondered if he really knew. Then I remembered the worst time. It was the afternoon that Keith and I were bare-ass naked in the sunlight in the back seat of dad's car, and my father walked right by us. I could hear him breathing, and he didn't see a thing. I'd never been so scared; I thought my insides broke, the way they squeezed together. Keith started to laugh, and

I had to clamp his mouth shut with both hands, but he was still laughing so much that I thought the car was going to squeak, and then I imagined my father would turn and look through the window at us, roar like an enraged gorilla, drag us naked and screaming in terror from the car, rip our arms, legs, penises and heads off, and then crush what was left of us beneath his stomping feet. Why was I thinking like this again, I asked myself. I didn't want it to start again, I had begun my new life.

I calmed down, rehearsed the speech I was certain I'd have to give to Roger, and tried to forget about his arm on my shoulder. I practiced, and it went something like this: Roge, I'm glad you trusted me enough to tell me your secret. I used to have those feelings, too, before I moved here. No! He might tell other people I said that. Roge, I understand how you feel and what you want us to do, but I'm the wrong guy. I'm not like that, and I can never be that way. And you shouldn't be that way, either. If you give in to those feelings, you'll develop a craving you can't stop; you won't be able to fight it anymore; you'll wind up in a prison or a mental hospital; and you won't be able to get a job. Right now, they're getting rid of people in government, people with important jobs, successful people, but it doesn't matter, they fire them anyway and put them in jail. They're finished forever. How would you feel if your mother ever found out? Can you imagine that? Roger, you're a handsome guy. I wish I had a face like yours. Girls and old ladies will chase after you. Why make it hard on yourself? We can still be friends, as long as we promise not to talk about this again; we'll just forget it happened. My grandma used to have a saying: "As the twig is bent, so the tree inclineth."—so, Roger, be careful about how you're being bent!

But I suddenly remembered that my science books said plants always grow toward the light. They have to have sunlight to grow. Even if people bend them, they still grow toward the sunlight! It bothered me that my Grandma's old saying left out the influence of sunlight. I wondered if Roger knew that even bent trees continued to grow toward the light. Many people don't understand that. Plants die without light—so does the human spirit.

Roger's small, clean apartment was sparsely furnished. His mother, who lived on a war widow's pension, grew African violets in the window, the only colorful sign of life in the room. Roger took me into his small bedroom and locked the door. I reviewed my speech; I didn't want to hurt him; he was so serious and sincere.

"Denny, promise me you'll never tell anyone what I'm going to tell you now. Promise?"

"I promise."

"Have you heard of Jacques de Molay?"

He's having an affair with some French kid! "No. Where does he live?" I asked, trying to appear calm.

"He's dead."

The image of Keith playing dead flashed and vanished. "That's too bad. When did he die? Was he close to you?" I asked.

"No! He died in the 14th Century in France. He was the Grand Master of the Knights Templar. In 1314, he founded a secret society for boys, 14 to 21."

Oh, my god, I thought, a secret sex club for boys, and I thought Richmond was a hick town! I wondered what it would be like to do it with a 21-year-old guy or maybe a bunch of them.

"Denny, I've decided you'd be the right person to join our secret fellowship. It's a real honor to be invited, you know. I think you would be perfect for the organization, and it could really be of help to you."

"What do you do in this secret society?" I asked with mounting fear and excitement.

"Well, we learn the sacred rites and rituals. It prepares us to be leaders; and, when we become adults, we'll be leaders in the Masonic Order. DeMolay is sponsored by the Masons."

I surfaced back into reality empty handed, my fantasies sliding silently beneath my consciousness. I bobbed in a sea of sadness as Roger prattled through his recruitment speech. I wondered how many times he'd recited it before. I suddenly understood his lack of spontaneity and his mock enthusiasm. He's handsome, I thought, but a mama's boy. I asked if he was a member of the Boy Scouts, and he was. He had more merit badges than anyone else in his troop. I told him I was sure he would be an Eagle Scout and a 32nd degree Mason. Roger was missing something, and I knew it—something vital.

I often thought about Roger. In time, I realized that he was so lost in doing what other people wanted him to do that he didn't know who he was. His outside was what people wanted him to be; but inside, he was hollow, scared, and screaming to be loved. He couldn't love himself, because he was afraid to be a real person. I came to understand that there are many people like Roger—maybe most people. I thought about him often, because, without knowing it, I was trying to understand myself.

A couple of boys my age, Ted and Albert, took an interest in me and often invited me over to their homes after school. Ted, who had just entered puberty, was from a cultured family. Their home reflected complexity and refined good taste. And they owned a television set. It was one of the old, round-tube Zeniths in a wooden case, the first television I'd ever seen. Ted and I often stayed up watching boxing matches, since little else was on in those early days of the tube. I was revolted by boxing. I often thought about the fight I'd witnessed in Glendale between those two handsome caddies and the way I felt afterwards. I couldn't understand why two men would want to hurt each other, even if they were paid to do it. As for the expressions on the faces of the cheering crowds, it was like looking into a theater filled with human mutants, revolting to be sure but fascinating in their shared deformity. They were missing something, something essential for their humanity. Ted didn't enjoy the boxing matches either, but it was something for us to do together. What I saw were two little ghostly gray figures moving back and forth across the face of the small Zenith cathode-ray tube, jabbing at each other. Occasionally, the two miniature figures would clinch in a tired, sweaty muscular embrace, only to be broken apart by the ever vigilant tiny referee. I used to amuse myself by imagining that, when the two young boxers were in a clinch, they would suddenly kiss each other. I imagined them making love in the center of the ring, floodlights blazing like the sun and the crowd cheering! I imagined a title match for the heavyweight Lover of the World. But the more I imagined, the more alienated I felt, for mine was a society that rewards athletic youths for trying to damage the brains of their brothers for mere entertainment. I felt I didn't belong. I didn't even think I wanted to, but where else could I be?

One evening after Ted and I had been sitting together watching the ghost tube so long that it had become totally boring, Ted suddenly, with no apparent anxiety, reached over and felt my penis through my pants. "I didn't think you could be that big, Denny! It was just a fold in your pants. Want to measure and see who's got the biggest one?"

I felt no physical attraction to Ted, so I agreed, and he ran to get a ruler. With humor, we argued about the proper way to measure penis length. His was smaller, but he wasn't bothered. He explained, "I like to look at guys who matured earlier than I did, so I can see just how big mine is going to get. I saw this guy in gym class once; his was so big, I swear, if he sits down on a john, he could tell you how cold the water is. All the guys looked at him. I bet when he gets a boner, he'd scare a woman half to death! I hope mine never grows that big. Hey, I bet I can make yours bigger!" Ted grabbed me and began stroking with a practiced hand. I suddenly saw myself as from a distance, my pants down and this kid stimulating me; it had started again. I jerked my pants up, grabbed my jacket, and at the door, turned to a surprised Ted and announced, "I'm only interested in girls!" and left. As I walked home, I felt proud, self-righteous, and sad that I'd gone as far as I did.

I talked with girls more after that. They had illusions about big-city boys and our wild parties, illusions I nurtured. One day, I was surprised when Betsy, the cute, dark-haired cheerleader from the junior class and girlfriend of Bob, the star football player of her class, called me aside and told me she hardly saw Bob during football season. She said she was lonely on her baby-sitting jobs and asked if I would keep her company that evening. She wanted to hear about the wild life in St. Louis, but she asked me to keep our meeting a secret, especially from Bob.

That evening, I raced through dinner, set up the ironing board, asked my mom to iron one of my blue Oxford button-down shirts, and went upstairs and took a long shower. I washed my hair, polished my shoes; and, when I was dressed in the best I owned, went downstairs. My father looked at me in disbelief, "Was that the shower I heard running?"

"Yes, I took a shower," I replied.

He said, "What's the matter? You getting sick or something? What took you so long?" He looked at me with that conflicted suspicious look that fathers get when they think about what their teenage sons might be doing for so long a time in the shower.

"He must be getting sick! He hates water!" added my little sister.

"Now, Rube," chimed in my mother, "can't you see he's getting cleaned up to go out on a date or something? Do you have a date, Denny?"

"Kind of," I said.

"Who with?" she asked.

"A girl."

"Just make sure she's white. We're not going to be supporting any watermelon seeds around here!" chuckled my father contentiously.

"Oh, shut that West Virginia hillbilly mouth of yours, Rube! How can you talk like that in front of the children? You don't have to advertise your ignorance and unkindness to us!" scolded Mom.

I was excited as I approached the address Betsy had given me. My excitement was not so much about seeing Betsy as it was the exhilaration of the status conferred on me by her invitation. She was, after all, a cheerleader and the girlfriend of the star athlete of the junior class—a true royal princess of the court. Who knows, I thought, by the time they graduate, Bob and Betsy might well be the king and queen of the Senior prom. I didn't know what there was about me, other than my city-boy image, that caused her to grant this private audience to a mere sophomore, but I was pleased. I knew that evening would be a crucial one, because her opinion would establish my reputation with the other ladies-in-waiting, and the word would be passed to Bob and his friends— the heroic knights of the gridiron, members of the royal order of the jockstrap—the supreme male prototype, the athlete king.

Betsy seemed to be as concerned about pleasing me as I was her. She was alert, sensitive and warm. I'd always found girls easier to talk with than boys, although we didn't have much in common. They listened and responded to what I felt, and they didn't compete. In a short time, I was at ease, and we talked effortlessly. Later, I spun suggestive tales about the fast life in the big city. I talked about "my old buddy" Auggie Busch as though he had been a next-door neighbor and hinted about the wild parties "you people here in Richmond probably shouldn't even hear about." This proved to be irresistible bait. By the time I finished spinning my web of lies, she was trapped, caught by her own hopes and fantasies. Breathing heavily, Betsy confided, "Denny, the boys here in Richmond never do anything—none of them. Bob never lays a hand on me. He hasn't even tried. Don't you ever dare tell anyone I told you this! He'd kill you if he found out. He thinks it's wrong before marriage. He said if he thought about it, it would mess up his game. The coaches tell them that kind of stuff all the time. All the girls complain about Richmond guys. They're pretty immature. Bob won't even French kiss. He says it would be like using somebody else's toothbrush. I bet you've French kissed, haven't you, Denny?"

"French kissed? Oh sure—all the time. Some of us even Italian kiss— and a whole lot more than that! A whole lot more!" I said.

"Italian kiss? I've never heard of that, well, I mean, I've heard of it, of course, but I'm not sure I know exactly what it is. Tell me, Denny."

The Italian kiss was another filament in the web of my imagination. "Aa, well, you can't really describe it in words; too complicated."

"Well, Denny, I guess you'll just have to show me."

I had her! I could rehearse my heterosexual role. I'd prove to her what jock hicks from the sticks she and her girlfriends were chasing after. I told her it took awhile to do the Italian kiss the right way. I remembered my mom saying that women liked men to be gentle, affectionate, and very slow, and I recalled the movie love scenes again. I gently pushed her hair back, held her face between my hands, and looked into her dark eyes. Her features were delicate, flawless. I thought, my God, what do I do next? I didn't know what Italians did. Spaghetti, pizza, singing, artists, mafia—none of the associations helped. I'd just do a lot of things and call it Italian; she'd never know. I gently touched her forehead with my lips, then each cheek, and then I slowly let my lips come to rest on hers. I thought of Bob holding her like this and imagined him seeing us. He and his jock friends would break my legs, at least. I enjoyed the thought of Bob busting his butt practicing for the Saturday game, so he could earn sufficient merit to deserve a cheerleader like Betsy, while I could pluck his prize by simply responding to her.

Very gently, I ran the tip of my tongue over her lips and felt her move in anticipation. Slowly, so slowly, I eased my tongue between her lips and heard her moaning and yielding as it entered. I caressed her teeth with it and thrust it upwards to the roof of her mouth. She gasped and pulled back. "Oh, Denny! We should stop now. If Bob ever found out about this, he'd kill us both. Let's do it just one more time, though! Oh, I feel like I'm getting dizzy!"

I pressed against her and began to rub my hands over her body. She suddenly pushed me away. "Denny, be truthful with me. I won't tell anyone. Have you gone all the way with a girl before? Have you? I'll still respect you if you have. You're not a virgin, are you?"

"No, I'm not." I told her quietly.

She said, "Oh, I knew it the first time I talked with you! I could just tell! The way you look at people! Wasn't the girl worried about getting pregnant?"

"Which one?" I deadpanned.

"You mean...Oh! You did! You must think we're all a bunch of clods here, but not all of us are. I'm not, but I could never go all the way! Not until I get married, at least!"

I told her I knew things that were just as good as going all the way, maybe better, and she couldn't get pregnant doing them. "You mean, like petting?" she asked, smiling. I grabbed her and pressed her into me. She didn't resist as Elizabeth had. She groaned and rubbed me with her wriggling body. And so began our weekly trysts. Betsy would never let either of us undress for fear that one of the kids would get up, or the parents would return unexpectedly. These armored wrestling matches were frustrating, slow work for me and sheer romantic illusion for Betsy. She wanted to be ravished without being ravished—a budding whore-Madonna. As I went home sexually frustrated after doing my best acting job as romantic lover to Our Lady, I ached for the explosive power of naked male sexuality. The more I longed for it, the greater was the pain of my guilt.

As the weeks went by, I grew more confident in my relationship with Betsy. I could talk with her about my family and most topics, except for the truth about my sexual friendships in Kirkwood and Glendale; I was on guard about making a slip. "You never talk about your buddies. Didn't you ever have any boy friends, Denny?" Betsy once asked.

As our friendship continued, I resented having to sneak around so Bob wouldn't find out about us. Every day at school, I saw Betsy with him. She wouldn't speak to me for fear someone might figure out what was going on. I knew she liked me, and I began to imagine what it would be like to have people know she was my girlfriend. I would be part of the in-crowd then, and although Bob would be hurt for awhile, he and his buddies, good sports all, would eventually accept me. I thought perhaps I was using Betsy and becoming a social climber just like Ronnie, but I didn't care. It was no fun being an outsider. The only thing worse was being an outcast, but I had escaped from that fate.

Betsy put a swift end to my fantasies when I told her what I wanted. She said she really liked me but planned to marry Bob someday, because he would inherit the family business and be wealthy. This would provide security for her and her children. Her mother told her this was the most important thing for a woman. Betsy said we would always be good friends, because I understood her better than Bob did. He put her up on a pedestal, and I didn't. "So, diamonds really are a girl's best friend!" I said with a tinge of sarcasm.

"Oh, you're just awful, Denny!" she squealed, laughing.

Several days later, I became bedridden. I was exhausted and slept 20 hours a day. A physician was called and blood tests were taken and retaken. One morning, my parents came upstairs to my bedroom, they looked serious and sad. They made small talk until I could stand it no longer: "What's wrong with you two? You both look like somebody died! Did something happen to Judy?" My father looked away, mute with emotion. My mother began to cry and came to me. She lay beside me, shaking the whole bed with her sobbing. My father tried to quiet her. "What's happened?" I asked, flooding with panic. "For God's sake, tell me what's going on! Is it about me?"

My mother lifted her tear-drenched face, a mask of apprehension, and said to me, "Oh, my darling Denny, my little boy, the doctor says you have a blood disease!"

"Well, I sure know I've got something," I said, "What kind of blood disease?"

My father turned his head away, because he could no longer hide the intensity of his emotions. My mother choked out, "Leukemia! He thinks you might have leukemia!"

"He ought to know what I've got after all that blood he took from me. What's leukemia?" I asked.

"Oh, Denny, it's a serious illness, very serious. It can be fatal!" She began to cry uncontrollably.

My father cautioned, "Now Donna, don't go getting the boy all upset by jumping to conclusions! The doctor isn't sure. He just said he thought it might be that, so we would be prepared if it is. He's still waiting for tests to come back. Besides, he said leukemia isn't always fatal."

"Well," I said, "if the doctor isn't sure, I'm not going to worry about it. There's nothing I can do, anyway. I'm really tired again. I'd better go back to sleep. Wake me up if you hear anything."

"Oh my darling little boy! Yes, sleep well. I'll tell you as soon as we hear from him. I will!" My mom kissed me and left the room crying. My father glanced at me with embarrassment, said nothing, and left. I wasn't worried about the leukemia, and this surprised me; people are supposed to be stunned by this sort of news, but I wasn't. I thought about my dying, but it was out of my hands; besides, I wasn't looking forward to anything in a world in which I didn't fit. Since I'd conceived no future for myself, there wasn't much for me to regret. And because I was exhausted and longed only to sleep, death caused no fear and I welcomed darkness. Just before falling asleep, I paused and thought, this might be the last thing I'll ever know—these sheets, the pressure of this pillow on my face, the background pulsing of my blood, my breathing, the distant sound of a dog's bark, the expanding blackness I see. I don't care, I thought, if it's going to be, let it be. I don't care. I just want to go to sleep.

Several doctors eventually ruled out leukemia and decided I probably had a severe case of mononucleosis, or hepatitis, or both. Complete bed rest was ordered, and I lived in my bed for 21 days before being allowed to resume limited activities. Except for brief visits by the doctor, I saw my mother only when she brought my trays upstairs. Occasionally, I awoke to see my ten-year-old sister standing at the door looking at me with a sad, serious look. "Are you going to die, Denny?" she would ask.

"Yes! And when I do, I'm going to come back as a ghost and haunt you forever!" I'd tease. She would turn and run downstairs.

Once a week or so, my father accompanied my mother to my room with my supper tray. He and I would engage in ritualistic, but distant, exchanges concerning my health as good form required. His last lines were always, "Well, don't worry, boy; in a few days, you'll be on your feet again and just as ornery as ever!" I never thought of myself as an ornery person—just the opposite, in fact, but when my father decided something, his mind snapped shut like a steel trap, and I was caught in his view of me.

The weeks I spent in the solitude of my bedroom were a turning point, because I discovered my mind. I entertained myself endlessly with my imagination, and the theme I most liked to explore was that of invisibility—a way to get out of my closet without being caught. I imagined I could fly out my bedroom window as an invisible person and visit everyone in town. I imagined I could get inside anyone I chose and know everything they experienced, and they wouldn't mind, because they wouldn't know what was happening. That's still an exciting idea for me. "Who knows what evil lurks in the hearts of men? ...The Shadow knows!" Maybe this fantasy was a major reason I chose to be a psychologist, or was it because of that rainbow drop of water on Keith's skin that day at the magic pool?

During this period of illness and for the first time in three years, I had little interest in sexuality. I lost count of the days since I'd had even a brief erection. I was relieved and happy about this unexpected change, because I believed I was becoming normal. I began to understand what life must be like for most people, and it was amazing; no wonder I'd been so confused by their behavior. I had assumed all along that they were like me, but nothing added up that way. I realized other people weren't as obsessed and driven by the desire to love as I was, so I believed I was making strides toward becoming a wholesome, well adjusted, acceptable young man. I even felt closer to Roger and thought about telling him I'd join DeMolay. But, as my health began to return, so did the relentless urges of my body.

It frightened me that my body seemed to have a mind of its own. To reassure myself of my control over this body I owned, I held up my hand and commanded my fingers to move in patterns of my choosing. I couldn't understand how my thinking caused these muscles to move or how they seemed to know exactly what to do to carry out my orders, but it amazed me, and I spent hours testing my control over my body parts. I wondered what caused me to choose the commands I was issuing. Finding no answer, not even being able to imagine what an answer would sound like to such a question, I became frightened by the possibility that something completely unknown to me was controlling me, controlling what I chose. If it wasn't that, then my choices weren't caused, and I couldn't imagine that either.

My capricious erections began to frighten me. I remembered hearing a guy at school joking about his erections, "When little Henry here decides to stand up and take a stretch, he will! Even right in front of a class. He doesn't care; he's got no conscience at all! Henry's an independent cuss with a mind of his own, for sure. Sometimes the only way I can get him to lie down and go to sleep again is to rub him up and down fast and hard so he swells up real big, gets sick, and throws up all over! Then, he'll go to sleep."

Since I didn't will my erections to happen, I wanted to know what did. Was there something inside me that was using my body? Or did my body really have a mind of its own? It had a brain of its own. Where am I in this body? I wondered. The brain, I guessed, but the brain was a part of the body, not me. They taught me at church that the body was supposed to be a pure temple for the soul, but they also said it was the source of the most vile evil. They taught that the pleasures of the flesh tempt us to sin and corrupt our souls. The urges of the flesh are animalistic and unspeakable; they degraded our temples. This is why God placed the organs of sex together with that other repulsive place of foul function, they said. These unholy desires are the work of the devil, designed to lead us astray. We are to be pure of mind, and pure of heart, and pure of body; otherwise, we lose eternal life. Sex is sin. Holy is the man who foregoes it, but if he must burn, then let him marry. Because I'd been brainwashed with this religious nonsense, I believed that if I were to let my body be in control, then I'd be a monster—a hairy, wild eyed, fang-toothed monster. I didn't want to become my body, because I feared I'd become an insane pervert. I had to master my body. Bodies, bodies—always bodies! I thought, why do we always say everybody, nobody, anybody, somebody, busybody, homebody? Why? People say I should become somebody when I grow up, but I don't want to be some *body*! I couldn't live if I did! They'd drag me away and shoot me, and I'd die, frothing at the mouth like some diseased animal! By God, they would! That's what I believed, at 15.

I threw back the sheets and looked at my body. I felt like a prisoner locked inside his own house—a tiny, frantic little figure trapped inside this reclining giant's body—a body that was supposed to belong to this tiny master and do what he wanted it to, but not what it wanted to do. I thought about the little figure—me—and realized I imagined it as a body, too—a little spirit body, trapped in a big physical body. I tried to imagine me as something without a body of any kind—a ghost without form, a spirit or soul, but I couldn't. Then, with a shock, I suddenly became aware of the real me, the person who was imagining this little me inside this big skin bag of muscles and bones. This person seemed as big as my body. This me seemed to be what I, my body, was doing! It felt like I became my body and came home again! I felt whole.

I held up my left hand and looked at it. Earlier, it seemed like just a hand that happened to belong to me, an ordinary hand I used from time to time, a useful tool. But now, this hand was me, part of me. I was looking at me! I felt and caressed it with my other hand, and I experienced the intimacy of me caressing me. I ran my hands down my chest and sides, and I felt me touching me, holding me, loving me. At the same time, I felt touched, held, and loved. It was incredible! I watched me become aroused, and then I became my body, inflamed with the desire to love and to be loved. I was both the lover and the loved. I was whole and complete—the giver and the receiver. Then I was all love. And in the moment of fusion, everything was love.

Falling from the heights of rapture, the sure sorrow of separation began like a rehearsal for death, a little dying. In the distance, a dog barked, the exhaust pipe of a truck droned, children shrieked in play, a screen door slammed. I opened my eyes and counted the white splotches of semen on my chest. I stared at my body, and it seemed distant again. Let it go its own way, I thought; it probably wants to sleep. Let it.

Suddenly, it seemed like I was looking at some other boy's nakedness, as though I had just made love with him. The old memories crowded in as I studied the structure of this other guy's spent body. Ripples of revulsion rose as I realized what I had done. Oh God, can't I ever be free of this, I cried. Will it never end? What in hell am I? Who am I? Am I crazy? Why is this happening to me? I just want to live! Please...God...I just want to live! I covered my nakedness, rolled over, buried my head in my pillow and fought the sob erupting from the depths of my being until I couldn't contain it. I convulsed with tears, and there was no me anymore, just sobbing. I heard my mother running up the stairs in panic calling, "Denny! Denny! What's wrong with you?" I didn't speak. No one could understand my perversion. I was alone—always alone with it.

Chapter Ten

I realized during my illness that I had no important part in my parents' lives. I was simply the boy to be materially provided for while he raised himself. Their distance wasn't a personal issue, since they hardly related to each other. Only television lessened the tedium of their evenings together. They were solitary people who lived obediently by the rules of convention, so they never risked personal intimacy. To my constant adolescent questioning of every social custom, my resigned mother would only say, "Ours is not to question why; ours is but to do and die!" None of the significant issues of our family were ever discussed. Much to their credit, however, my parents left the care of my life in my own young hands. They made only minimal efforts to bend me, and when I resisted, they backed off.

Realizing that my parents couldn't help me with my conflicts, I vowed, more than ever, that I wouldn't be sucked down into the whirlpools of my abnormal desires. I'd heard that passion is easiest to stop before it starts; and, since I was unable to transform my desires, I resolved to starve them to death. I was determined to have nothing to do with physical intimacy. I remembered a minister yelling to his congregation: "If your eye offends you, then pluck it out!" In the earnestness and heat of my youth, I consecrated myself to mortifying my too eager young flesh. I had not yet learned that "whom the gods would humble, they first strike down with passion."

During my illness, one of the things I thought about when I imagined being invisible was the fact that there were the sounds and pictures of many other people in the form of radio and television signals passing right through my bedroom, even right through me—invisibly. How can this be, I wondered. What carries these sights and sounds? Why don't they get all mixed up? Is there a separate signal for each instrument in an orchestra? How does a picture stay together when it's sent through the air? Were there other invisible parts to reality I didn't know about? My mother brought library books to answer these questions. With relief, I entered the dispassionate world of science and technology. There was calmness in the cool Apollonian heights of logic, mathematics and reason. I learned the language of electronics. It was exotic, complex, precise, powerful and impersonal—exactly what I needed for my mission to mortify my flesh. Amateur radio especially fascinated me, because it seemed like a distant and safe way to relate to other males.

I built a simple two-tube, battery-operated radio that used earphones, and I asked my parents to come upstairs to see my prize. I wanted my father to be pleased with me and proud of what I'd done, but he wasn't. All he said was that if he'd known I wanted a radio, he would have bought me a real one, one that didn't need batteries and earphones. He said I'd been foolish. My mother explained to him that I wanted to build it to learn something about electronics, but that didn't alter his judgment. They left my room, and I, crestfallen, wanted to smash those radio tubes into a fine white powder with a hammer.

Later, my mom came back to my room: "Denny, don't pay any attention to what your father said. He'll never tell you this—and don't you dare ever tell him I told you—but he was a rotten student at college; he just barely got through. They kept him on, because he was a star football player. He wouldn't have made it except for that. I think he's just jealous of the brains you've got. He couldn't figure out anything as complex as this radio of yours, so he tries to whittle you down to his size. You've got twice his brains, and he knows it. Just don't let him get to you. Let it roll off you like water off a duck's back. That's what I do. I don't even listen to him anymore. I wish I'd learned to do that earlier in our marriage; it would have saved me years of tears."

"Why did you marry him then?" I asked.

"We were in love once. I was the beautiful Bohemian poetess, a dancer and a model. I showed you all my poems that were published and my photographs. I was invited to all the right places, even the Racquet Club. He was the star football player. I don't know, it just happened. We weren't right for each other even then, but it happened. We went together almost three years. I got sick and tired of waiting to get married, so I told him it was marriage or else. We were happy those first few years, but then that mother of his tried to break us up. Did I tell you she used to put lipstick and blonde hairs on his shirts so I would divorce him?"

"Yes, Mom, many times."

"He was her youngest, and she blamed me for taking her little boy away! He even had the nerve to have her live with us for awhile. I tried to get along with the old bitch, I really did! I tried, but she's just as pigheaded as he is. Finally, I couldn't take it anymore; I gave him the ultimatum: it's me, or her! I hope she rots in hell with the rest of his family! Did I tell you about that brother of his who got sent to jail? You met him."

"Yes, Mom."

"Well, they're all a bunch of thieves and liars, every one of them! His mother was the worst of the lot; she taught them. You've got to be careful, Denny. You can't believe how devious women can be when they want something. Imagine, lipstick smears on his shirts and perfume! She was a dumb dodo, though. She used her own brands. She didn't think I'd check."

"Why are women more devious than men?"

"Well, I don't know. We don't like to fight; besides, it takes real brains to be sneaky!" she teased. "Oh, all those years! I had a good mind once; I was creative, I danced, I wrote poetry, but now, well...my mind has just gone to seed."

"I know. If you don't stop soon, I'll start crying! You need sad violins playing in the background."

"Oh, you smart-aleck, you! I swear, if you ran across the poor little match girl freezing to death, you wouldn't even give her a penny! All you men are so hardhearted!" She was smiling though. She knew I understood her sympathy game.

I asked, "Why do you stay married to him? Why don't you get a divorce and find an artist or something?"

"People don't get divorced," she told me. "It's a disgrace to be a divorced woman. You get married for better or worse, 'til death do you part, and that's that. I didn't think there was going to be so much worse, though. Well, it hasn't all been bad. We've had our good times, too."

"Yeah? I bet you can't remember the last good time," I said. "The violins are supposed to get louder here, and a single tear should run down your cheek! ...You live on hope, Mom."

"What else can people live on? What?" she demanded. I remembered my own problem, and I understood. I felt compassion for her. She sensed this, caressed my cheek, and left. "Remember, not a word of this to your father!"

One day, while I was looking for new books in the radio section of our school library, an older boy came over and said he noticed I was interested in radio books. Tom Webster was his name; he was a senior. He said he was studying to take the exam for his amateur radio license and asked if I would be interested in getting a ham license, too. He was tall, somewhat overweight, unshaven, and had tangled, straw-colored hair. He was badly in need of some dental work on his lower front teeth. Since I felt no physical attraction toward him, I decided I could relate to him.

Tom came from a poor family; it was quite some time before he trusted me enough to invite me to his place. I'd never seen such poverty. They lived near a stream in a woods outside the city in a rickety house covered with tar paper and surrounded by trash. His mother was a frail, chain-smoking alcoholic. I never saw his father. Tom had an older sister who had run away from home when she was 16. Tom was very sensitive when he first brought me to his house; he watched my every move for the slightest sign of disapproval. His proud, defiant eyes seemed to be daring me to disapprove. Even though I was shocked to see how he had to live, I pretended nonchalance. He wasn't completely fooled by this; but, because he knew I was trying to keep my feelings to myself, his pride was satisfied.

We buried ourselves in the world of ham radio. The local hams helped us in every way they could. I'd never felt such acceptance by adults, nor had Tom. We were treated as friends and felt we were finally surrounded by the good fathers we both had longed for.

In the Spring of 1951, when I was still 15 and after many months of preparation, Tom and I headed for the Federal Communications Commission field office in Indianapolis to take the examinations for a commercial radio license and an amateur radio operator's license.

The examiners were excruciatingly slow in grading the exams. As we waited, each person withdrew into himself to cope with his own private fears of failure. At last, the examiner read the names of those who had passed. When he said, "Sorry, that's all who made it," long groans and a series of mumbles filled the smoky room like the chanting of monks in a Tibetan monastery. I passed the commercial exam by one point; Tom missed it by five.

We both passed the ham exams with nearly perfect scores. As the FCC examiner had predicted, half of the adults didn't make it. When we realized this, we felt giddy with our newly validated competence. We had competed with adults on their own turf, and we were their equals—maybe better.

On the long drive back to Richmond, Tom talked about life in his troubled family; it was worse than I'd thought. His sister left home because she'd been sexually molested by her father. Tom got a card from her each year at Christmas. She married a guy just like her dad. Tom's father had regularly beat his wife until the time when Tom, who had by then grown as large as his father, told him he'd kill him if he ever laid a finger on her again. Furious, his father had smashed his fist into Tom's stomach. Much furniture was destroyed in the battle that followed. Tom, having the greater endurance, was about to pound his father into a bloody pulp when he was stopped by the pleading of his drunken mother. After that, his father rarely came around. The last Tom had heard, he was shacked up with some floozy he'd picked up in a bar.

Tom planned to enter the Navy's electronics training school in San Diego in September. He checked off the days on a calendar he carried in his battered wallet. He said what saved him through all this was discovering the writings of the Stoics, the philosophers of impassiveness and indifference to pain and passion. He'd read everything on Stoicism in the Earlham College Library— Zeno of Citium, Seneca, Epictetus and Marcus Aurelius. A philosophy professor at Earlham had helped him with a reading list. Listening to him, I realized that my commitment to suppressing my own passions had an ancient dignity and justification. I was pleased. He told me everything he knew about the stoic philosophers, and then we debated the merits with our adolescent wisdom. Science and Stoicism would strengthen me against sexual sin, I believed, but the gods continued their relentless humbling ambushes, as they would until I worshipped them.

At one point, Tom said, "You know, they keep some of the books about the Greeks and Romans in a special room. You have to have a professor's permission to use those books."

"Why? Are they expensive or something?" I asked.

Tom was embarrassed: "Well, no. I probably shouldn't even tell you about them."

"Oh, come on, Tom! What do you think I am, a kid or something?"

He said, "Don't tell people I told you, but I looked through some of those books, and those old Greeks, well, guys back then fell in love with other guys, you know what I mean? I mean, the philosophers and aristocrats were all just dirty fairies who chased after the young naked guys in the gymnasium—that's a Greek word that means training naked. They didn't even feel bad about it back then. They put up all these statues of good-looking, young naked guys all over the place, right out in public. They didn't even cover their dongs. Can you imagine that in Richmond, Indiana? Did you know that 'penis' is a Latin word? It means a tail. You know the Olympic games? Well, they made all the athletes compete bare-ass naked. They did! I read it. The women couldn't watch, of course, but those old queers did. Professor Lane said it was a natural thing for them before Christianity. He said nobody cared if you loved a man or a woman or even both. Many of them had wives and children and still loved other men. He told me about some of those famous old fags—Socrates and Plato and even Alexander The Great and Julius Caesar. He said even their gods did it with guys. Their boss god was Zeus, and one day he saw this young guy called Ganymede. Well, he never saw anything as beautiful as Ganymede, so he just grabbed Ganymede around the waist and took him right back to heaven with him. I saw a picture of that in one of those books you're not supposed to look at. The title of the picture was "The Rape of Ganymede." They were both undressed. He didn't even ask the kid if he wanted to go. I didn't get it, though—the kid was smiling. Can you imagine a story about Christ grabbing some kid and carrying him away, because he was so beautiful! God, what a bunch of wild pagans they were! Well, they couldn't help it, they didn't know God was a Christian."

I asked Tom what this Ganymede kid looked like, if he was handsome. "How would I know?" he said. "I'm a guy. Guys don't notice if other guys are good-looking, unless they're a little queer. Do you notice other guys? No! And neither do I. I can't understand how a guy can love another guy—unless it's Christian love, of course, or Platonic. Maybe I shouldn't say Platonic anymore after what I found out about that old pervert Plato. Can you imagine! It makes me sick to just think about one guy making love to another guy. I even heard women used to do it. There was a whole island of them. I think it was called Lesbos or something like that. All that stuff is disgusting, don't you think? I can't understand people like that. I don't even want to understand people like that. They're just not human like us." I started talking about the advantages and disadvantages of various kinds of transmitting tubes, but I felt sick inside and alone with it again.

We got back to Richmond late in the evening. As I walked toward the front door of my house, I tried to calm the waves of excitement and pride I was feeling. I was always trying to control my emotions. I'd never accomplished anything so fine as passing the FCC exams. I imagined my sister throwing rose petals and my parents bowing to the ground. I remembered one old guy who flunked the test for the third time saying to us, "You youngsters are smart to get your license at your age before your brains start to rot like mine. When I was your age, radio hadn't even been dreamed of, much less invented. It's real tough learning this galldarned code when your brain has half turned to oatmeal. Well, most of me works some of the time, so I shouldn't complain too much. Sure would give anything to have a nice healthy young body like yours again. Everything goes but the old memories, and they get clearer than ever. Oh, I was a hot-blooded young buck, I was." I hoped he'd make it the next time. It didn't seem fair that I'd passed and he hadn't. But I was beginning to suspect that fairness had little to do with our lives. I decided to be very cool when I came in to heighten my folks' suspense.

My mother was the first to see me. She grinned at me and asked, "Well? Did you pass?"

"Pass what?" I replied, forcing my face into a mask. Suddenly, I could contain my excitement no longer, and a shy, proud smile cracked through.

"Oh, you did! Thank God! I knew you would! Rube, come here! In here! Your son is back!" Mom shouted.

My father came in, controlling a slight smile. He wanted to act surprised, even though he knew, "Well, how did it go, son?"

"I passed all three of the tests! The amateur tests were almost perfect! I'll get my license in about eight weeks! Over half the grown-ups didn't pass!"

He frowned at this last statement, as if I had challenged him personally. "Well, congratulations! That's something to be proud of for a boy your age. I don't know why you went to all that trouble though. You don't have any radio equipment, and I'm sure not going to buy you any. If you wanted to talk to your friends, you could just call them on the telephone. Why do you always want to do things the hard way? Why?"

"Because I like to do things the hard way!" I shouted.

His slight smile revealed that making me angry had pleased him, and the indirectness of my statement showed him I feared him, so he knew he was in control, as usual. "Well," he said calmly, "if doing oddball things pleases you, I don't really care. It's your life, not mine. You'll have to live with what people think of you, not me."

I raced upstairs to my room and dramatically slammed my door. Mother, Judy, and I were door-slammers. Mother came up later with my supper, and she gave me a few dollars she had taken from the grocery money. She said she would take some each week to help buy the radio parts I needed. She stroked my hair and said, "I'm proud of you, Denny. You showed him what you can do! He knows he hasn't got the brains to do what you did. Remember that duck's back! Sleep well."

My father continued to show no interest in my new hobby. When I showed him cards I received from around the world, he was indifferent.

In keeping with life's irony, some years after I was married, I helped him set up an elaborate ham station and taught him what he needed to know to get his amateur radio license. He was as thrilled as I had been and enjoyed the hobby for many years. I wasn't surprised when he flunked the FCC examination his first time round. He was greatly upset by this, and I commiserated with him, but I was secretly pleased. So was my mother.

Tom and I worked feverishly on our transmitters, and, of course, neither of them worked at first. The frustrating days we spent debugging them taught me the value of systematic experimentation, analysis and measurement as well as an appreciation for interactive causality, the view that an effect depends upon a complex set of interacting causes. I learned by agonizingly doing and undoing that the answer to any meaningful empirical question begins with, "It all depends..." and it really does. That old transmitter taught me to experiment systematically with possibilities and to think in terms of interdependent systems—not a bad way to live actually.

I often thought about the whole system of systems, the universe of which I am a part, as my fingers rested on the paddles of a Vibroplex code keyer. The slightest movement of my muscles, caused by the electrical signals on the nerves from my brain, closed the contacts of the keyer and sent current in a pattern of dots and dashes to the grid of the glowing transmitting tube. This caused millions of electrons to rush across the tube in waves at radio frequency and into the final plate coil, setting up the electromagnetic fields of radiation from my long wire antenna in the back yard. From there, the signals sped across the country, into the sky, out into the cold blackness of space, to the planets and stars, to galaxies and beyond, all at the speed of light. And I was doing it! When I listened to signals on my old army-surplus receiver, I thought of my long wire antenna as a giant feeler probing the invisible world of the radio spectrum.

In the months that followed, Tom and I racked up hundreds of contacts from around the country. In the years that followed, I talked with fascinating people from around the globe—an expedition to the Antarctic, a U.S. Senator, an Arabian sheik on his luxury yacht, a missionary in the jungles of Central Africa, a sheep farmer in New Zealand, a lonely sailor in the South Pacific, an Indian Maharaja, and Tom Christian, a descendant of Fletcher Christian of the H.M.S. Bounty mutiny fame on tiny Pitcairn Island, even His Royal Majesty, King Hussein of Jordan.

Because of my absorption in amateur radio, I rarely thought about that cross of passion my teenage shoulders had to bear. I was superstitious about even thinking about my burden, fearing that the mere awareness of this part of my life would somehow give it strength, and it would revive and overcome me. I heard a preacher say that God never lays a burden on a person's shoulders that is heavier than he can bear. I wanted to believe that, but deep down I didn't. It was as though I were running a race, my adversary just behind me, and I was afraid to turn my head to look at him.

. . .

Two things happened in the spring of my sophomore year at Richmond High to upset the pace of my race against self destruction. The first happened because Tom met two seniors who were interested in electronics and ham radio, and we became friends with them. Jack was an outstanding student who later went on to become a nuclear physicist. He lived with his elderly, German immigrant grandparents, his own parents having been killed in the war. His friend, Eddy, was a happy-go-lucky, frisky sort of guy with a boyish face. Everybody liked Eddy because of his friendly, outgoing nature, while Jack was scholarly, serious, and reserved. Eddy had dropped out of high school, in part to support his mother, but also because school bored him to death. He worked as a retail clerk in a department store and enjoyed the contact with customers. I couldn't understand why two people as different as Jack and Eddy were friends, and I was surprised to learn they'd been best friends throughout junior and senior high school. I often went over to Jack's to help him with complicated electronics projects. His basement was filled with his equipment, projects and experiments; he even had a fully equipped dark room. I could barely follow his complex thinking, but he was patient with me and appreciated my help. Although Eddy was often lost by our technical conversations, he enjoyed sitting in the basement with us as we worked and kept us entertained with his tales about odd customers.

Jack was building a transmitter. He thought he'd have it done by the weekend, so he asked me to stop by his house Sunday morning to help him test it. His grandmother answered the door when I arrived. She had trouble understanding English, but I kept saying Jack's name, and she pointed to the hallway leading to his bedroom. I was surprised he was still sleeping and thought he must have stayed up late working on his transmitter. I hoped he'd finished it. I opened the door, and there, completely naked in his double bed, were Jack and Eddy, arrested by my gaze, suspended in an incredible, tangled posture of lovemaking. What astonished me was not so much that they were lovers as it was the shocking and exotic configuration of their bodies. Their normally light-colored skins were flushed red and glistening wet. Jack jerked the sheet up to cover himself. While still staring at Eddy's body, I mumbled, "I'm sorry. I should have knocked. I didn't know..."

"We'll be dressed in a minute. Wait downstairs!" interrupted Jack.

Eddy grinned at me and said, "Well, it'll be a whole lot longer than a minute; more like 15 or 20, I'd say...unless you'd like to join us, Denny!" Jack looked at him threateningly. Eddy stopped grinning and said quietly, "I guess Jack is kinda shy today. See you downstairs."

I waited in the basement for what seemed like an hour or more, although it was probably only a few minutes. My blood was pounding through my head as I tried to rid myself of the image of their fused wet bodies. I kept remembering Eddy grinning at me and how red and glistening he was all over. I fought back the repulsive feelings of attraction for him that were growing in me. When they finally came in, nothing was said; we all just pretended nothing had happened, although Jack was noticeably irritated with Eddy, and Eddy said very little. I left as soon as I could. That night, I had a dream about Eddy being happy to see me. I stopped going over to Jack's after that.

Some weeks later, my mom took me to buy a shirt at the department store where Eddy worked. I hoped he wouldn't be there, but he was. When he saw me, he ran around the counter to get to us before another salesman did. He was very warm and cordial, and he impressed my mom with his attention to us. He even gave us a special marked-down price on an Oxford shirt for me. As we were leaving, he pulled me aside and whispered that he wanted to get together with me soon, after work that day, if I could. I knew what he meant. "What about you and Jack?" I asked.

"Jack's got nothing to do with it. I do what I want. Well, can we? How about tonight?"

"No," I told him.

"When, then? I'm sure glad to see you!"

I told him I wasn't interested. "Why?" he asked. "I know you like me. The way you looked at me that day at Jack's, I can tell!"

"I'm just not interested, Eddy. That's the way it is," I said.

"You are! Maybe sometime later?"

"Never, Eddy, never in a million years!"

Eddy sneered and spit out, "You piss ant!" loud enough for my mother to hear.

"Why was that nice young man angry at you, Denny?" she asked as we left the store.

"Oh, nothing, Mom," I said. "He just wants to have things his way all the time."

"Well, that's typical of you men. Always having to have things your way!"

"Look who's talking! Everybody wants to have things their way!" I snapped back.

"Not everybody, Denny. Some of us are kind and giving, but just look where it gets us!"

"See what I mean, you want things to work out your way, too!"

"I guess maybe everybody does," she sighed sadly.

The gods' second assault on my concept of myself that spring was a double whammy on the same day at school. Latin was still taught at Richmond High, rationalized by the notion that it would help one think more logically and better appreciate the English language. The real reason, of course, was that Miss Grey, the Latin teacher, had only three more years before retirement, and there had to be something for that sweet, loveless old maid to do until then. Miss Grey was almost childlike, innocent and timid. She worked hard to make the dusty declensions of Latin endurable. None of us doubted she was a virgin, a true daughter of her esteemed vestal virgins of so long ago and far away.

Had she ever known the sexual passion of her ancient gods, we wondered. We thought not and felt pity and protective, for she was like an unloved child who didn't know she was unloved. But the secret passions of our repressed natures cannot forever be denied expression. At the height of each passing spring, dear drab Miss Grey presented her Latin Club Diorama of Classical Statuary—the crowning jewel of her school year. Backstage, from the wings, I watched her prepare the statues.

The six young men she selected as sufficiently physically graced to portray Greek and Roman gods stood on large painted wooden pedestals and practiced their poses. They were clad only in clean, new, white jockey briefs. Dearest Miss Grey was no longer drab, but animated as she carefully used a powder puff to turn each supple athletic body into the milky white of Cararra marble. Each young man wore an overly large paper fig leaf pinned to the front of his shorts. When her tapping powder puff and brushing fingers came to this area, she handed the puff to the tense boy, who quickly finished the powder job himself and handed back the puff. She then diligently examined every square inch of his body, tapping and brushing uneven areas here and there with her puff and fingers. The faces of these chosen young gods were frozen masks of tension and torment as finger tips and powder puff caressed their already beautiful bodies into marble whiteness, purely for the sake of art and education.

Alex, by far the most handsome person in my class, was practicing his difficult, single-footed pose as Mercury, messenger of the gods. "Hey, Denny," he called from his pedestal, "hand me my caduceus. And would you mind tying those wings on my legs? They'll slip, so tie 'em tight."

There I was, putting wings on the pliable, muscular legs of Alex, who was marble white and wearing only a fig leaf over his bulging underwear. As I looked up at him, fear and excitement grew as I transformed him in my mind from Alex into the living, breathing Mercury, himself. I tried to imagine what message the gods were sending me. Just then, Mercury bent down, his startling face coming closer to mine. I pulled back in fear of his message. He grabbed my arm and put his lips to my ear—the sacred words of the gods must be whispered. "You know, if that biddy kept running her fingers over me for one more second, I'd have gotten a roaring hard-on. I guess that's why she made these silly fig leaves so big. They make us look like we've all got whoppers. I even had to think about eating a bowl of baby crap just to stay soft! I guess just about anything that feels good could turn me on. You'd better hurry up with that messing around with my legs, or I'll start humping you!"

I pulled away from him and said he'd have to catch me first. He laughed, "You can't run away from the gods!" Then he returned to his posing, this time with wings on his fleet feet. I often thought about him saying, "You can't run away from the gods!" It was so easy for me to imagine it was other than Alex who spoke that day; part of me—the dramatizing part—wanted to see it that way. I kept trying to figure out the significance of this strange message, but I couldn't.

I took a shower later that same afternoon at the end of gym class. The marble-lined shower room was large enough to hold several gym classes. It was filled with clouds of steam and the raucous laughter of pale, naked young men playing grab-ass and snapping towels at each other—the foreplay of unacknowledged and unconsummated love. Suddenly, in front of me, I noticed a strange dark form in a cloud of steam. I watched a person slowly appearing from this cloud, and when he became completely visible, he stopped, glanced down at his body, and then looked directly at me. His entire skin had the permanent tan of the Mediterranean sun, making him stand out against the background of the pale whiteness of the rest of us. His hair was glistening black, and it formed wet ringlets on his forehead. His face was the most beautiful I'd ever seen. When he saw me gape at him, he changed his posture to rest his weight on one foot so that the angles of his hips, shoulders, and head were in different planes in the classical contrapposto position of Renaissance sculpture. He slowly turned around as if looking back for a friend, then completed the circle and looked at me. His body was perfection and grace; never had I seen such flawlessness. A brief flash of puzzlement crossed his face as he studied mine, and then the calmness of comprehension and a gentle, pleased smile appeared in acknowledgment of this mortal's homage to a god. His pleasure became a warm laugh, and his smile, fondness. Then he turned again and disappeared into the cloud of steam. As his form became indistinguishable, I felt an overwhelming sadness and wanted to cry out for him. It wasn't a matter of sexuality, but rather, the realization of consummate perfect beauty. One is rarely in the presence of the gods, and it is agony when they are gone.

Later, as I was dressing, I felt apprehensive and looked up. There he was, standing beside me, smiling at me. Out of respect, I waited to be spoken to. When he did, I painfully realized that I was listening to a mere mortal who called himself Pete Ellis. The god had left him—probably in disgust—and returned to the heights. Pete, desiring friendship, wanted to get together after school, but I declined, fearing the enormous power of his beauty and my envy. He laughed, messed up my just-combed hair, snapped his towel at me, and left. I tried to stop thinking about him during the rest of the day, but I couldn't. That night, I had a dream. I was walking through a beautiful forest filled with peculiar flowers, like giant calla lilies, toward the lyrical music of a male singing. As I entered a clearing, I saw the source. On a rock beside a waterfall, standing naked in its mist, was Pete Ellis in the same pose I'd admired. He was surrounded by a rainbow and stood radiant in full sunlight, the god having returned to him. He called my name and held out his hand for me to join him. I started to walk toward him, only to suddenly awaken in the blackness of my bedroom. A dog was howling at the moon...a long, lonesome cry in the night.

I was greatly agitated during the weeks following this visitation. The revelation about Jack and Eddy was difficult enough for me, but my self-confidence was especially threatened by the double assault at school. I kept telling myself that Alex and Pete were just ordinary guys like everybody else, there was nothing special about them. It was all just in my head, the way I looked at things, and I could change that. So what if Alex and Pete were a little better looking than most other guys. It's what you do that counts, not how you happen to look, I told myself. My mother said that beauty was only skin deep; still, I kept searching for them every day at school.

I began to worry that Pete would notice the pimples I was getting. Acne. What an awful word! It sounds as bad as it looks. Ac...ne! I thought maybe I was being punished; my sin was coming to the surface for everybody in the world to see. I remembered how criminals used to be branded with hot irons so everybody would know to avoid them. I believed acne might be caused by sex and thought if I avoided sex completely, I'd clear up. But I knew some religious guys with acne who believed that even thinking about sex was sinful. Then I thought pimples might be caused by not masturbating enough and storing all that stuff inside for too long.

I became more confused, tense, and depressed with each day. There was no one I could turn to. Just before my 16th birthday, I reached a crisis point. I was unable to endure my confusion and depression any longer and became frantic with anguish. The more I struggled against this helplessness, the more ensnared I became; the more entrapped I was, the more I had to free myself; so I struggled until I was paralyzed, caught in the hideous web of my limited ideas. I saw myself impotently twitching, waiting forever in this helplessness. Then I began to ache for any change, even the fangs and venom of death. In desperation, I began to chant the 23rd Psalm of David:

"The Lord is my shepherd; I shall not want." I thought I don't even know who the Lord is. I don't think I believe in God anymore. He'll punish me for that, for sure! Maybe he already is, I worried.

"He maketh me to lie down in green pastures: he leadeth me beside still waters." Why does he want me to lie down, I wondered. The image of Pete Ellis, wet with mist, standing by the pool of water at the base of the waterfall erupted into my consciousness.

"He restoreth my soul: he leadeth me in the paths of righteousness for his name's sake." I was shocked; it was Pete I was imagining, holding his hand out to lead me. Terror gripped me as I fought against my perverted desire— this hideous spider of death steadily creeping leg by hideous leg up from my own black insides.

In even more of a panic, I chanted out loud until I was shouting:

"Yea, though I walk through the valley of the shadow of death, I will fear no evil: for thou art with me; thy rod and thy *staff* they *comfort me.*"

"Thou preparest a table before *me* in the presence of *mine enemies*: thou anointest *my head* with oil; my *cup runneth over.*"

"Surely *goodness* and *mercy* shall follow *me* all the days of *my life* and I will *dwell* in the house of the lord *forever.* Amen!"

Over and over, each time more rapidly, I chanted these words to keep my demons away, but my mind was at work. Each time I came to the "Amen," I became anxious. I was bothered by the idea that it really meant "Ah! Men!" Why never "Awomen?" I wondered. Why would the Lord's rod and staff comfort me, I worried. What is my cup that runs over? Does its running over refer to sex? Would dwelling in the house of the Lord be like living with my father forever?

I heard my mother coming up to my room. She thought she'd heard me practicing Bible verses. She said they would be a great comfort to me later in my life, and she brought me the family Bible. She said I would pass it on to my children and they would pass it on to theirs. I remembered the times I'd seen a preacher holding the Bible on high, or thumping his finger on a passage before a humbled and fearful congregation. It was a source of power over adults, the final authority they dared not question for fear of their lives. If it gave a preacher the power he had, then I, too, could learn the secrets of this Holy Bible. I committed myself to reading it in its entirety. For many weeks, I labored at this task. My mother was pleased. My father just smiled at me with a look that said I'd never finish it. "Good luck! I thought it was the most boring thing I ever tried to wade through!" he said.

He was right about much of it, but I began to view my labor as a kind of penance for my transgressions. I also wanted to prove to myself that I could do something he couldn't do.

I was shocked, but excited, by the cruelty, violence, and sexuality of the ancients. The book of Leviticus was frightening, for there was a demanding God of wrath, worse than my father could ever be, I believed. It was horrifying, even more so when I read late one night, "If a man also lie with mankind, as he lieth with a woman, both of them have committed an abomination: they shall surely be put to death; their blood shall be upon them." I was thankful I wasn't a man yet. I was just about to turn 16, giving me five more years as a boy. However, I was already guilty of the part that said, "For every one that curseth his father or his mother shall be surely put to death: he hath cursed his father or his mother; his blood shall be upon him."

The story of Saul, David, and Jonathan electrified me with excitement and bewilderment, though. I could hardly believe I was reading this in the Holy Bible:

"But the lad knew not any thing: only Jonathan and David knew the matter. And Jonathan gave his artillery unto his lad, and said unto him, Go, carry them to the city. And as soon as the lad was gone, David arose out of a place toward the south, and fell on his face to the ground, and bowed himself three times: and they kissed one another, and wept one with another, until David exceeded."

Exceeded? I rushed to my dictionary: "to go beyond a limit set." I couldn't believe it! But when I read David's lament for Jonathan, I believed:

"I am distressed for thee, my brother Jonathan: very pleasant hast thou been unto me: thy love to me was wonderful, passing the love of women."

I felt a strange kinship with David and Jonathan; and, for the first time in many months, I permitted myself to remember Keith. I knew then that I was not entirely alone in the world; there had been others of respect who understood what I knew. I caressed the leather of that gilded Bible. I was not entirely an alien; there had been others.

It was Ecclesiastes, more than any other book of the Bible, that impressed me. These words of the preacher, the son of David, king in Jerusalem, spoke directly to me:

"Rejoice, O young man, in thy youth; and let thy heart cheer thee in the days of thy youth, and walk in the ways of thine heart, and in the sight of thine eyes: but know thou, that for all these things God will bring thee into judgment. Therefore remove sorrow from thy heart, and put away evil from thy flesh; for childhood and youth are vanity."

Late one afternoon, having finished my labor, I thought about this Holy Bible and reread parts of it. The Old Testament seemed to me to be demanding blind obedience to authority, or else people and nations would suffer the horrible pain and death of one of God's many wrathful temper tantrums. I couldn't respect this God, who reminded me of my father, and in my adolescent rebellion, I believed I would prefer to die with integrity than to live cowering on my knees in submissive fear before such mere power. While the Christ of the New Testament preached compassionate love, I couldn't agree with his view of divorce: "And I say unto you, Whosoever shall put away his wife, except it be for fornication, and shall marry another, committeth adultery: and whoso marrieth her which is put away doth commit adultery." I'd only just turned 16, yet I knew I was more understanding of people's unhappiness in marriage than this. I reasoned that if God were all powerful, all knowing, all wise, all merciful, and all loving, then why did He make such a mess of man and creation? Why did He choose to allow sin and evil, and why does He let it continue? Didn't He know the consequences of what He was doing at creation? Didn't He care? If He's all knowing, He knows what people will choose to do before they're born. If he really cares, why doesn't He do something? If I had the power, I would—most everybody would, I believed. I looked at the red-lettered sayings of Jesus and thought these are supposed to be the words of God. They didn't seem all that grand, especially coming from the omniscient mind of God. Why do most Christians imagine God as a male and white skinned, I questioned. What if God is female or some form beyond our imagination? Yes! Or perhaps some form of our imagination! Yes! That's it!

I felt that tingling I get when I understand something important but don't yet know what I've grasped. Then the words came and insight. It was men who wrote this Holy Bible. It was the best they could do. Men created these images of God—in their own likeness! I held the Bible in my hand; it was a book, a better book than most, but just a book. To liberate myself from this book I'd always feared, I hefted it in my right hand, felt its weight, and then hurled it across my room with all of my strength. It smashed into the corner with such force that its gilded leather binding split in two. I waited for a moment or so, half expecting jagged lightning bolts to descend. With the silence, I relaxed and was free at last, so wonderfully free! I lay down on my bed still smiling, but I experienced a growing kind of terror. I'd cast myself adrift with no instruction manual, no divine Boy Scout manual for adults. I felt the terror of being completely free and utterly responsible for my life. I tried to return to my earlier sense of life, but my insight had transformed me, blocking the way back with the knowledge of alternatives. I'd taken my life completely into my own hands, and I realized I could make decisions that could destroy me. This was no game, no idle pretense, no second chances, and I felt utterly alone in the vastness of reality. How could I know what to do? "Ye shall know the truth, and the truth shall make you free." Yes! The truth!

With terror, I experienced the awesomeness of the cosmos and my complete insignificance in it. Know the truth! I understood that to take reality into me, to know it, would alter me forever, and I was terrified. There was no other way for me, except forward into the infinite cosmos. I sensed its overwhelming and incomprehensible vastness, its serene indifference, and I felt myself willingly climbing up onto it, naked, spreading my arms, and then opening my palms so I could receive the smashing agony of the nails of truth as I was to be crucified by reality's ultimate power. I bowed my head before the dominion of this universe and said to it in submission and surrender to reality's sovereignty, and even beyond that—wanting it to be as it was in preference to my confused illusions—"Unto your hands I commend my soul. ...Thy will be done." In that moment, I realized I had just become a man; I was 16. "When I was a child, I spake as a child, I understood as a child, I thought as a child; but when I became a man, I put away childish things." That was my hope...at 16.

Chapter Eleven

The conflicts never end for the caged gay person. We went to Florida for a vacation that summer to visit my aunt, uncle and their two sons, Stanley and Billy. Stanley was 25, dark-haired and tall, vigorous, ruggedly handsome, married, and the leader of a motorcycle gang. He taught me how to scuba dive. At the coral reefs off Key Largo on my first dive, Stan and I caught the interest of a large Mako shark just as our air supply was running out. (Perhaps because of the thrill of this and certainly because of the beauty of the ocean world, the sport of diving became a love throughout my life. I've dived many of the coral reefs of planet earth—Cozumel; the Red Sea, paradisiacal Micronesian islands, the deathly beauty of the sunken Japanese fleet in Truk Lagoon, Belau, and the awesome great walls of the Ngemelis Islands. With my sons, I came to know the North Wall of Grand Cayman Island, the Tubbataha Reefs in the center of the Sulu Sea in the Philippines, the glories of the Banda and Flores Seas, and the mystical islands of Komodo and Bali in Indonesia.)

Stan wanted us to celebrate my first dive; he was proud of me, he said, and told me he'd take me to the bar where his gang hung out. That night, Stan, dressed in a black leather motorcycle jacket with silver studs and a matching officer's cap, told me to get on the back of his big Harley-Davidson motorcycle. "Hold onto me for dear life, cousin. You'll be as safe as in the arms of sweet Jesus!" I knew Stan wasn't religious and that he would ride flat out to impress me. Like a wild stallion, the front of the great Harley leaped into the air in a perfect wheely, and we raced into the night, defying death. In a short time, we were racing along an empty long ribbon of highway beside the ocean in full moonlight. It was beautiful, and I was very happy that night. Stan and I were alike in so many ways, and that excited me.

The bar was old and comfortable, with pine-paneled walls, an open-beam ceiling, red and white checkered tablecloths, the smell of draft beer and hamburgers, and the clack of billiard balls on the pool table in the back room. The head of a large-racked trophy deer sadly surveyed the crowd from its final resting place above the brass-railed wooden bar. Nailed to another wall was a great blue marlin, forever frozen in its last leap for life. Hanging near these trophies was another, a cracked and faded painting of a reclining nude woman. The eyes of the deer appeared to be staring at her. Crescendos of raucous laughter punctuated the low-pitched, polyphonic melodies of male voices. I liked the place, it was a man's place.

Stan was the star. Everyone greeted him, and he introduced me to all as "My good buddy, Denny." He didn't mention we were cousins. I felt proud to be there with him, especially when a crowd gathered around as he told them of our skillful steel-nerved survival from deadly Mako shark attacks. I said nothing but nodded as witness to the reality of Stan's clever ballyhoo. After awhile, we went to a quiet table to talk; and, when we were alone, we both laughed so hard we nearly cried. I imitated his casual, sincere style, and he laughed until he held his sides in pain. The bartender was a close friend of Stan's, so he brought us both beers, even though I was under age. Stan said he'd just move my beer over to his side of the table if anyone suspicious walked in.

We talked intimately and long that night, and I was extremely happy, that is until Stan told me about a secluded beach he knew, a moonlit beach with palm trees. "We'll have it all to ourselves," he said. "Nobody ever comes there this time of night. I'll make sure you really have something to remember from this vacation. I've got a beach blanket in my saddlebag—and other things." He explained he was "a switch-hitter" who did it with guys "when my old lady puts me in the dog house." He pointed out several other guys who were "AC-DC." One of them smiled when I looked at him. I pretended innocence and fought my fantasies about Stan and me, hot with passion in moonlight on a deserted beach. The idea that Stan, an impressively masculine adult male, would want me to touch his body excited me so much that I got the shakes. I wanted to make love to the sounds of ocean waves and then swim naked and make love again in the warm ocean. But my innocent pretense didn't fool Stan; so, fearfully, I eventually confessed that I knew all too well what he was talking about. He said he'd known that by the way I'd looked at him in his bathing suit; I was embarrassed. I wanted him, but I couldn't stand the idea of love ending again and my perversion beginning. I explained that I was afraid I'd get into real trouble with it and said with pride that I'd stopped doing it for almost a year. He hinted about showing me some unusual things to try to tempt me, but I refused.

Stan looked at me steadily. He was irritated but said nothing. After resolving something for himself, he said, "Okay, kid. I understand. You can't help being a hick from the sticks of the Midwest. You'll be sorry you didn't, and you'll remember tonight. You will! Your loss...mine, too. Let's split. I'll take you straight back to your mommy's tits."

As we got on the motorcycle, I hesitated about putting my arms around Stan's waist, and he noticed this. I thought again about what it would be like to be naked on a beach in the moonlight with him, and I wondered which of the many ways men have of being sexual together he most enjoyed. When I did put my arms around him, he turned and smiled mockingly at me. I felt him there under the black leather of his motorcycle jacket; he was thin-waisted, broad-shouldered, and muscular. On the long ride home, I watched a lonely full moon in an empty sky watching me. Stanley said nothing and avoided me the rest of the vacation. Just as we were leaving though, I went over to him and hugged him. He was unresponsive; but, as I turned to go, he slapped me on the rump and winked. I rarely saw Stan after that; but, when I did, there was always a warm bond of affection between us. "Hey, Cousin, been to any deserted beaches lately?" he would ask me in front of my wife, children, and parents, leaving me completely flummoxed. He was right; I do remember that night...with a sad longing for what might have been. I should have gone with him, but now he's just a memory. He could have helped me accept myself and change my life, but I was in a cage of fear.

The remainder of the summer of my 16th year was tedious and lonely. I worked in a shoe store, my mind filled with stock numbers and the smell of new leather, so it was a relief when I began my junior year in the fall of 1951. As I walked the halls of the high school that first day, I feared and hoped I would see Pete Ellis, the Ganymede of Richmond High. I expected to see him almost everywhere but didn't. I asked a friend of his about him and learned that Pete had dropped out of school because of some family problems. The family had moved West to get a new start, and Pete had to work to help support them. I felt a great sadness for him and imagined him in some miserable job, struggling to keep his family together. But part of that sadness was for myself, because I knew I would never see him again. I fixed the details of his image in my memory and worried that time would erode it like a fading, tattered photograph. However, from this image and my desire, my memory's creative retouching has wrought an epiphany, the appearance of a god.

There was a boy in my class who, several years earlier, had been struck by an automobile. The car's front metal bumper had smashed his face; and, even after much surgery, his nose was a wide, flattened mass of twisted scar tissue. His skull fractured and his eyes were set much farther apart than seemed humanly possible. His left eye socket was higher than the right. He had no eyebrows, and part of his upper lip was missing. Children hid behind their mothers when they saw him. Mindless junior high school boys taunted him for being different; girls looked away. He was usually seen with his hand trying to hide his shame.

On the first day of school, he sat in the last row of one of my classes, hunched down behind the boy in front of him. I was sitting beside him. Our teacher, a rotund, friendly middle-aged woman began to call roll. When she called his name, he hesitated and whispered, "Here." Not seeing him, she called his name again. "Stand up, young man, so I can see where you are!" He hunched lower in his chair. With irritation, she marched back to his seat, "Young man, take your hand away from your face when I talk to you. How am I supposed to recognize you if you do that?" Trembling, he slowly lowered his hand and looked up at her. I saw her wince ever so slightly, then, with gentle firmness, she said, "You have nothing to fear in my class. You don't have to hide. No one will ever harm you here. I'll see to that. We all welcome you here, and all of us want you to be with us." He looked distrustful. Sensing this, she took his face gently in her hands, looked lovingly into his awed eyes, and slowly kissed him on the worst of his scar tissue.

His tears were my own, and I will never forget this woman and her wisdom. I don't remember the subject matter of her course, but then, we tend to remember only what is important to us.

As the class ended, I noticed a tall, slender student struggling to contain his emotions. He looked at me, and we understood what the other was feeling. I went over and talked to him, but he could barely speak. He was shy and embarrassed. I noticed his smooth, perfect complexion, his high cheek bones, and his angular face. It was David Rose, the young man whose love I eventually rejected at Purdue. Since I wasn't initially attracted to him sexually, I decided it would be safe for me to seek his friendship.

David had a budding interest in electronics, and soon he was inviting me over to his large, two-story brick house to teach him about ham radio. His home was fascinating. He was the youngest of three boys and a girl. His father was a reclusive engineer; his mother, Ruth, a warm and caring person. I felt accepted by her, and in time, was closer to her than I'd ever been with my own parents. Their home was filled with the many interests of each of the family members—art, photography, music, science, books. The large wooden table in the kitchen was the center of the life of the household. We spent many happy hours there; however, David's father never joined us. He was the dark specter in an otherwise happy home. I tried to be friendly to him but with no more luck than I had with my own father. Eventually, I stopped trying, as had the rest of the family, and simply accepted his rejection.

David quickly earned his amateur radio license, and we set up a station in a large room just off the living room. As our friendship became strong, we spent most of our free time together. When we were apart, we talked by radio in Morse code. Ruth said I was the best friend David had ever had, and this pleased her.

One weekend, shortly after David got his ham license, we decided to stay up all night to see how many distant stations we could work. We operated in relays; and, when it was quite late, I went into the living room to rest on a sofa. David eventually came in yawning and sat down beside me to tell me about his latest contacts. He was tired but excited. I motioned for him to lie down beside me. We talked for awhile and then drifted off into restful silence. My back was to him when he suddenly whispered into my ear, "Denny, I'm real glad you chose me to be your best friend. I've never had as good a friend as you. Thank you." He put his arms around me and hugged me and then held me in beautiful silence. I was at peace.

Slowly, almost imperceptibly at first, David began to press himself closer to me. Alarmed, I thought he was getting an erection, then wondered if I was just imagining it. I'd never thought of him in a sexual way. I began to think that maybe I wanted to believe it, that my craziness was coming back. I lay there in a state of suspension, afraid to move, afraid to know, afraid if he was, afraid if he wasn't. I remained in this state of willed paralysis until I felt madness swirling inside my brain. I had to know if I was just imagining all of this. I slowly pressed back against him to find out, and then David thrust his full hardness against me! Suddenly, his hand was slipping under the front of my Levi's and then under the waistband of my underpants. I jumped up and whirled around to look at him. His normally light complexion was flushed with the bright pink of sexual arousal. "Oh God! I'm sorry, Denny! I didn't think you'd mind. We were feeling so close. Please forgive me! I didn't know! Please! I'm so sorry. I meant you no harm. It was wrong of me, I know. We never talked about it. Please don't hate me. Can you ever be my friend again? I know I was wrong to do that. Can you ever forgive me?"

I felt the pain of his remorse and wanted to comfort him. I was moved by the realization that David's caring and respect for me was genuine and deep. I touched his face. He began to cry and grabbed my hand and kissed my palm. I raised him up and held him as he sobbed and held me, still begging for forgiveness. I felt his pain and fear, experienced my own conflict, thought carefully, and made the decision. When he was calmer, I told him he was my best friend. Then I slowly began to unbutton his shirt.

After his amazement passed, he asked, "Are you sure, Denny?"

"Yes," I answered. He was trembling.

We didn't need to speak. Our bodies told one another exactly what to do and when to do it. I knew immediately that he was experienced, and I was surprised by that. When we were finished, David fell into a contented sleep. It was then that the awful realization of what I'd just done began to devour me. I got up, quickly dressed, and went into the radio room to be alone with my guilt and shame; I'd gone for almost a year and a half without backsliding. My thoughts were like this: Why did I give in to it this time? Why? My God, I'll never be free of it. It'll destroy me! It will control me. I'll be powerless before it. I'll be a slave to this thing. Oh God, it was so wonderful to hold David and to feel alive again! It's been so long. All the loneliness went away. His skin was so smooth and hot...and he was huge. I'm sick to think like that! ...But what's wrong with it? We both wanted it and needed it. He felt so good! Oh God, there's no hope for me at all...because, now I love evil! I love the devil! I love the hard squirting cock of the devil! I'd like to come all over everybody in the whole world! Thousands of hot gallons of it! God, kill me to save me from myself! Destroy me! End me, now! I've become the very thing I fought against! Take me! End it!

I began to cry quietly in my total ruination as I waited for the imagined stern deity to end my humiliation and shame with merciful justifiable death. Suddenly, there was an arm around my shoulder. "Denny! What's wrong? What's wrong with you?" asked David, standing frightened and naked beside me. "I didn't know you'd feel so bad! I'm sorry, Denny. Forgive me."

I told him not to blame himself. I said I knew what I was doing and chose to do it. I explained that it was just that I'd tried to stop, that I'd controlled it for over a year and a half before backsliding.

"I don't know why you feel so bad about it, Denny," he said. "My brother Bill and I have been doing it for years. It's nothing to feel bad about. It doesn't hurt anybody. It makes people feel close and happy. I've wanted to touch you for months! I think about it every time I see you. I thought you'd never catch on. I used to think about you and masturbate all the time. I'm glad we're over that now. Are you feeling any better?"

Later, when I was home alone in my own bedroom, I decided that just one slip in a year and a half wasn't too bad; after all, I reasoned, I had five more years before I would be an adult—and kids were allowed to make mistakes without being as severely punished as an adult. I resolved to sin no more and to forgive myself my trespass. David didn't pressure me. He just waited. I lasted three days.

After that, we had sex whenever I weakened, because I, not David, was the reluctant one. I was conflicted, guilty, withholding, and struggling. I held back emotionally from David in the hope that I might eventually learn to control my sex drive, because I knew love irresistibly transforms. Real men needed to get their rocks off, I believed, but they certainly didn't love other men. Love hurts. Love can be lost. Love makes you vulnerable and weak. Real men are strong and independent. Whenever David said he loved me, I said nothing. I thought he was weak. Many men can't love, much less love sexually. Just ask legions of women. It's a matter of dominance and the fear of the loss of control.

David's mother, Ruth, and I became close. I would spend days at a time living with them. Ruth and I talked about everything in our lives, except for the fact that I was sodomizing her son—a mere detail, I tried to convince myself. Once, after staying two weeks with them—David and I slept in the same bed, I told her how angry my mother had been when I came home. My mom had screamed, "Have you forgotten you have a family? We haven't seen you for two weeks! You'd think David's mother was more of a mother to you than I am!"

I shouldn't have said it, but I did, and it was true: "Ruth is more of a mother to me than you've ever been! She listens to me! She likes me! And I like her!"

"Go live with her, then!" shrieked my devastated mother.

Ruth exclaimed, "Oh, Denny! How your poor mother must be suffering! You couldn't have hurt her more! You've mocked her very life! She's a mother! A mother! She loves you. Oh, you're young, so young. I forget that when you talk. I see you the way I want you to be. Someday, you may know the pain of parents who are not loved by their children. Thank God I've been spared that, at least for now. Now go to your mother and beg her forgiveness—for both your sakes! Go!"

What I said was the truth; she was like the mother I always wanted. I asked if I should lie about that.

"Oh, Denny," she said, "you know how proud I'd be to have you for a son, but listen to this middle-aged woman talking to you now. I didn't go to college, and I may not be as intelligent as you, but life has taught me this: love is far more important than the mere telling of truths. Loving is what counts in this life! Now go and ease your mother's pain. And when you have, and when she wants you to, you come back."

Ruth was right, of course. I picked some flowers for my mother and went home. When she eventually forgave me, she said, "The only reason you like it over there so much is because that woman fills your face with food all the time. Every woman knows the way to a man's heart is through his mouth and his pants. I'll bet she doesn't make a pineapple upside-down cake as good as mine!"

"No, Mom. No one makes one as good as yours! I don't think she even has a recipe for one."

"Just as I thought!" she said, smilingly sheepishly at our reassuring mutual pretense.

Soon the crisis passed, and I was back at David's. His grandmother was visiting for several weeks. Her husband was a photographer, and she was an artist of considerable skill. They had retired in Florida and continued their shared love of the visual arts together until two years earlier when this gentle and sensitive woman had gone totally blind. I would have done anything for her. She often asked me to sit with her and describe what I saw. In the beginning, she would say, "Oh dear! And to think I believed I was the one who was blind!" She taught me how to see. This blind artist helped me understand that my perceptions and descriptions of reality define who I am. What I perceive is myself in interaction with reality. "By the time I finish with you, young man," she said, "you'll find that view out there to be the most interesting thing you've seen in years. You'll never forget it as long as you live, because you'll be looking at yourself, Denny. And there's nothing more interesting or important than finding out who you are. I'm 78, and I'm still learning. My blindness is one of my best teachers. Strict, even severe, but one of the very best. Blindness introduced me to the beauty of music, the sounds of poetry and human voices, fragrances and the taste of fine teas. But I will admit to you that I would like to see the color red just once more before I die." She confessed to me that she had been suicidal when she first became blind, but resisted because of the grief that it would have caused her husband.

At the end of her visit, she asked if she could touch my face with her finger tips, because she had no idea what I looked like. Her fingers paused when they met my tears, then she hugged me and said, "I love you, too, young man!" She died the following year.

. . .

My need for intimacy and approval became more of a conflict. The more intimate I became with David, the more intimacy I wanted, but the more I wanted, the more I disapproved of myself, so I needed even more approval from others. But I couldn't reveal my strongest feelings for fear of their rejection, so I couldn't be close; I could only turn back to David and repeat the sad cycle.

I began to hitchhike more often. In those trusting times, hitchhiking was common and safe. I liked it, because most of the men who picked me up were lonely and wanted to talk. Some poured their hearts out, because I was a good listener and presented no risk. I remember one man in particular, about 45, average in appearance, balding, wearing gold-rimmed glasses he kept taking off. He was a salesman from Indianapolis who was unhappy in his marriage and quite lonely. Getting him to really talk was difficult; he wasn't used to it; but, when he finally did, he talked to me for hours. We stopped in a park, and he just talked to me. When he finished, he looked at me in amazement and conflict. I knew he wanted to hug me, maybe more, and I wanted him to, but he was afraid. I asked where he was staying the night, and he said he had planned to drive to Dayton but thought he would stay in the Richmond Hotel instead. The hotel was only a few blocks from David's house, where I was staying. The moment for us to part came, and we both knew it. I noticed his mouth seemed dry, and I knew what he wanted, but I also knew he would never say it, maybe not even to himself. We looked at each other in a long silence. He was filled with emotion and conflict, and I remember he turned away. Then I said quietly, "Would you want me to come up to your hotel room tonight?" Surprise, fear, terror, and revulsion crossed his face, and then confusion, desire, passion, and finally two tears as he simply nodded yes, yes, yes!

That evening, I told David I wanted to go for a walk. He wanted to come along, but I told him I had some thinking to do alone and didn't know when I'd be back. He was hurt but said nothing. I stood across the street from the Richmond Hotel for quite some time, fingering the business card of William Wilson, Sales Representative. I looked at the lighted windows and wondered which was his and what he was feeling. I wondered what it would be like for a married man his age to make love with a boy my age. I wondered why it meant so much to him that he, a grown man, cried when I suggested it. I was pleased by this and wanted to make him happy. I felt some anxiety and curiosity about going to bed with a middle-aged married man; I wondered what he would want to do. I kept remembering the tears in his eyes; it seemed to be such a simple thing for me to do and yet so significant for him. I wondered if I would feel that way when I was his age. I hoped I wouldn't. I remembered the hurt look on David's face when I said I wanted to be alone. I imagined how he would feel if he ever found out what I was planning to do. When I walked across the street toward the entrance of the hotel, I unexpectedly became quite sad. I wondered if Bill Wilson had really checked in or driven on to Dayton.

I felt fear in the pit of my stomach as I approached the reception desk. "Excuse me. Do you have a Mr. William Wilson registered here?" I asked.

"Ah, let's see—yes, Room 305. He checked in this afternoon. Shall I ring him?"

David's hurt expression flashed through my mind. "No, but I want to leave him a note." I wrote, "Dear Mr. Wilson (Bill), I'm sorry, but I can't see you tonight, because of a friend. I hope everything you told me about works out for you. I'm sorry. Your Friend, Denny" and gave it to the clerk.

I couldn't understand my sadness, so I decided to walk downtown before returning to David's. As I walked, I thought about the geometry teacher David and I had. He was a thin, gray-haired man in his late 50's and was one of the best teachers I ever had. He taught us how to think logically, and he knew how to convince us to do our homework perfectly. He was a master teacher; every one of his classes was a performance that dazzled us. He loved the Greeks and would often pretend he was Pythagoras teaching his devoted students on the warm sands of the Aegean Sea. He taught us the elegance, power, and mystery of mathematics. Each day, he carefully scrutinized our homework and returned it with comments neatly printed in the margins. It was said that his life was his students, and so it seemed; on his classroom walls, he kept photos of them, going back for decades. He'd never married. He lived alone in a seedy, third-floor hotel room in downtown Richmond, where he spent his evenings and weekends grading papers. Students often saw him through his window, working. For a week every Christmas, he visited his elderly mother at a rest home back East. Nobody knew where he went in the summer. Everyone in the school knew he was an old queen, but he was well liked and widely respected as the best teacher at Richmond High. He always helped Miss Grey with her annual Diorama of Classical Statuary—the old queen and the vestal virgin powdering beautiful boys' bodies.

I found myself in front of this teacher's hotel that night and, through his window, saw him hunched over his desk grading papers. I wondered if he'd ever made love; I doubted it. I sensed the dignified loneliness of his life and wondered what he lived for. His mother was the only person who had probably ever loved him. I imagined him in frustration and guilt as he lay on his back, holding a vivid picture of one of his students in his mind while quietly masturbating himself. I must have watched him for over an hour until he got up from his desk, yawned, looked out the window, pulled the shade down, and turned off his light...as he'd probably done for decades. I watched the dark window and imagined him dying in that small room, alone. I felt strangely close to this man, and I shuddered at the thought that I, too, might live alone and die alone.

. . .

My mother and sister couldn't stand the small-town life in Richmond, so my father built a house in Dayton, Ohio, and we moved there just before my senior year. As usual, we were the poorest people in a well-to-do neighborhood, but I saw this move to Dayton as yet another new beginning for me. I had to change myself; it would do me good to get away from David.

Many of the students at Fairwood High School came from privileged families, and I felt quite out of place. My classmates talked about their plans to go to various Ivy League schools in the fall. They found out rather quickly, that I wasn't of their social class. I was politely excluded from their long established cliques.

My loneliness was an incessant problem for me. My depressions became more frequent as did my parents' irritation with me. "I can't understand why a 17 year old just mopes around looking like you do. No wonder you don't have any friends," counseled my concerned father.

One weekend, when I could stand it no longer, I took the next Greyhound bus to Richmond. David was reading when I walked into his room. I told him I had just stopped over to see if he needed some help on his radio equipment or something. He was very happy to see me and just smiled knowingly. His expression conveyed, "That's okay, Denny! If that's what you need to believe, I don't mind." We just looked at each other, and then a shy smile escaped my control.

Each time I returned from visiting David, I promised myself that I would stop seeing him and start dating girls, but I wasn't interested. David occasionally came to see me in Dayton, but he felt uncomfortable around my parents. They didn't much care for anyone that Judy or I brought home. I was nervous when David was there because of the fear we might be found out. Once, in Kirkwood, my father had almost walked in on Tom McBride—one of the identical twins—and me in the middle of sex, but for some reason, he didn't open the bedroom door. I think he must have heard the noises of our frantically trying to get dressed.

I made a couple of friends, Tom and Greg, through amateur radio contacts. They were students at a different high school in the north part of Dayton. Tom was a Greek boy my age who lived with his mother. She didn't speak a word of English, but she loved to cook Greek food for me. For some strange reason, my father took a paternal interest in Tom, perhaps because he could identify with him. My dad had lost his father at an early age, too, and knew what it was to be poor. Dad encouraged Tom to go to college—he even insisted on it. Tom never thought he had a chance, but I helped him with his school work and reassured him that he was bright. He'd never thought of himself in that way, he said, but he was. Years later, he received his doctorate in electrical engineering from Ohio State University. He said our belief in him had made it possible.

My case was different. My high school experience had been deadly boring, except for my old geometry teacher's class. I made no effort to make good grades, and my parents didn't care. My grades were dismal; I graduated at the bottom of my class. Ironically, Greg, my other friend from north Dayton was the smartest student in his school—the introverted class brain who is now a full professor at a leading university.

One day, after getting to know him, I made a shrewd guess about his shyness and told him the reason for it was because he was fighting homosexual feelings. I went on to predict that he'd had homosexual relationships in his early teens. To make matters even worse for him, I told him who it had been, because I'd noticed how he talked about a certain rough-trade classmate of his—his muscle-bound, handsome, spontaneous, lower class, uncultured polar opposite. He looked at me in utter disbelief, then clenched his jaws in rage and hissed, "Yes, yes it was him! God damn you forever!" I'd never heard Greg swear before, but I'd just pillaged his sanctuary. He demanded to know how I'd found out, but he calmed down when I said, "You know the old saying, Greg, it takes one to know one."

"I'm not one! That part of my life is over for good!" he said. I didn't respond and locked my own closet door.

About five years later, after losing contact with him, Greg located me and called late one night. He was very excited; he wanted me to know that he had just had his first heterosexual experience—that evening. I felt somewhat rejected by this, as I had by Ronnie Ryan when he started dating.

I said it must have been a relief for him. "Now, don't go getting analytical on me, Denny!" he replied defensively. "I just wanted you to know, that's all."

"Why was it important for you that I know?" I asked.

"There you go again! Can't you just take things at face value?" he said with exasperation.

"No."

"Why not?"

"You know as well as I do. Don't play dumb with this one, Greg!"

"Okay, okay! Anyway, I'm really happy about the way things are turning out. Did I tell you I even graduated Phi Beta Kappa? I got lucky, I guess."

I congratulated him and told him we both knew it wasn't luck. He'd worked his ass off, as usual. Now that he has a girlfriend, I said, he wouldn't have to work so hard to prove himself. "You never stop, do you?" he countered. "Give a friend a break, will you? Did it ever occur to you that I don't like to be stripped naked by you?"

I told him I probably knew why, but then I told him my good news. I was engaged to be married to a blond girl named Truel. "Wow, that's wonderful, Denny. Congratulations! I'll bet you're very happy," he said with sincerity.

"Sounds like we both are, Greg," I replied. "It's nice to be normal, isn't it?"

"Sure is! Are you joshing me again?" he asked.

"No! I'm serious. We were both worried about the same thing," I told him truthfully.

A quarter of a century after Greg graduated from high school, and after two marriages and no children, he went to his class reunion. Ironically, he wrote this to me:

"If anyone says you can't go home again, they're wrong! The reunion was like that for me—going home again. The same old cliques, the same endless competition between the guys, the girls still trying for the guy they never got in high school. It didn't matter if he's married and has six kids. The same old jealousies and envies. It was disgusting. I was just as excluded as I'd been 25 years ago. For them, I'm still nothing but the skinny, bug-eyed class brain. It was a nightmare, Denny.

"...The only reason I went to the reunion was to see Ken and to find out what happened to him. You remember him—the one I used to have the silly crush on? I heard he still lives in Dayton, and I traveled all that way to see him, but the bastard didn't bother to show up! They said he's married and has five kids. He lives in a dump north of town and hauls trash for a living. Someone had a picture of him taken at a recent picnic. I got to see it. I honestly don't know what I saw in him. He's still got his set of muscles, even more now from slinging trash around, and that inviting smile of his hasn't changed one damned bit. I'll admit, it still gets to me! (I know what you're thinking, you dirty old man, and you're wrong—dead wrong! I'm happily remarried now.)

"He didn't even bother to come. I left when I found out he wouldn't be there. I thought about borrowing a car and driving out to see him, but what could I say to him—take off your clothes, I want to see what you look like? I thought about just driving by his place; maybe he'd be outside, but I didn't. Ah! That's the story of my life! C'est la vie!

"...Do you know that I've become so bored with life that the content of what I read doesn't interest me now? Blaa, blaa, blaa—that's what it is anymore. Only style amuses me sometimes. I even enjoy reading Anthony Trollope now. See what can happen to a good man, even a Phi Beta Kappa Eagle Scout? I've never even had any decent vices. If I'd known it would all turn out like this, I'd have said, to hell with the Boy Scouts and making valedictorian and Phi Beta Kappa, and I would have tried to fuck all those people I secretly longed for! Now, it doesn't matter anymore, not much does. Sex doesn't interest me. Mozart is still pleasant, and some of Bach. The one good thing I did for you, Denny, was to get you to listen to Bach. Remember? I'm a Full Professor, my friend. The 'Full' means I'm filled up to the gills with it, I am, and I can't take any more! Oh, for the days of yore, when life was not a bore. Remember?"

There are people who search for love and those fortunate ones who are in love. Then there are people like Greg, who were at one time in love, but who search no more for their bliss. I see many people like Greg in my clinical practice. Outwardly, they're normal and successful, but inside, they're without passion, zombies, the walking dead who merely mimic the rhythms of life. By the time I was a freshman at Purdue, I was becoming one of them. The life-threatening disease began with my betrayal of love, my bliss. Repression and denial were my chief strategies to avoid the pain of my soul dying. When I attempted suicide at 17, I felt I was an alien, without human resources, with no place to be, and with no future worth living. Because this view seemed so true, I repressed it, and one year later, I had no memory of that nearly fatal suicidal Spring evening. Keith was the only love I'd ever known, and he was gone, and I repressed the pain of that. Because our society severely punishes this love and preaches that it was wrong, at 18, I had hardly any memory of Keith. Even today, because society still viciously stigmatizes them—in God's name, the suicide and alcoholism rate of gays is four times higher than non-gays. I had to be normal, or I couldn't imagine living.

Being normal was why my new beginning at Purdue was so important and why I wanted to end my relationship with David Rose. Several weeks after I told him we had to stop having sex, David called me and shyly said he had a girlfriend...of sorts. I had to pry out of him the fact that Doris was married, more or less. He had told her about our three-year relationship, and she said she understood; her husband liked to have affairs with men. David wanted to get to know her better before being sexual with her. She offered to help him learn what it was all about, but he was nervous.

David often talked with Doris about me. She wanted to meet me. She was a writer and a painter, and her husband, Carl, was a graduate student. One Saturday afternoon, she gave David the keys to her apartment and asked the two of us to wait there until she came home. She left a note telling us to make ourselves comfortable. I was fascinated by their books, and I began to explore their apartment. This upset David. He didn't think I had a right to be opening their drawers, medicine cabinet, letters, and photo albums; but soon he was helping me. In the back of a drawer, I found a purse containing spermicidal jelly and a diaphragm container. We'd never seen a diaphragm before. When I opened the container, there was a note neatly lettered in Doris' hand, "I thought you would be looking in here, Denny. See you soon! Want to try this?" David laughed and said he'd built me up too much. He told me if I wanted to have sex with her, he didn't mind, because he wasn't ready for that, yet. The idea appealed to me, because it was what I was supposed to be doing. When she arrived and we talked for awhile, we both knew we would. We chattered away for several hours as the tension built, then she said she needed to get something from the store and asked me to ride along. The sun was just setting.

As we drove away from her house, she hinted that she wanted to have sex. I found a dark, secluded single-lane road leading to a farmer's house. We took off our clothes, she put in her diaphragm, and we played around with each other for awhile. Just as I rolled over on top of her, lights flooded our car. "Oh my God!" she shrieked, "The farmer's coming home! We've got to get out of here, Denny!"

In terror, I somehow managed to inch the car past the farmer's old Ford station wagon. He was yelling at us, and his wife and five kids were gawking in wild-eyed disbelief. I made it to the main highway, but the enraged farmer turned his car around and was in hot pursuit. I sped along unfamiliar country roads in the moonlight with him honking just behind, shining a spotlight in the rear window. Still stark naked, we were suddenly on the outskirts of Lafayette, heading toward the middle of town. I yelled at Doris to get our clothes from the back seat, but she was hunched down, hiding and laughing out of control. Several times, she even started to play with me, but I screamed at her and threatened to throw her out on the street, naked. She just laughed harder. I managed to shake the farmer; and, by the time we got back to her apartment, we were both convulsing with laughter.

Doris' husband was talking with David when we walked in. Carl was strikingly handsome, and he knew it. With a cheerful bounciness in her voice, Doris introduced me, excused herself, and went into the kitchen.

Carl sat there staring and smiling at me. I prattled on, nervously making small talk until he asked seriously, "Where have you been with my wife?" I said she needed something from the store. "Neither one of you brought anything in," he observed ominously. I told him the store didn't have what she wanted. "And what was that?" he asked.

"I forget. Don't you believe me?" I said.

"No," he replied. He was seated between me and the doorway.

"Well, where do you think we were?" I asked.

"You were out fucking my wife." He spoke in deadly seriousness, and I hoped he wouldn't try anything in front of witnesses. My pulse pounded like a steady military drum beat and my arm pits and hands were clammy. He was bigger than I and clearly well-muscled.

"I didn't fuck your wife! I didn't! I swear to God!" I said truthfully. David was laughing. I told David it was no laughing matter and asked him to tell Carl that we hadn't been gone more than a few minutes.

Carl yelled, "Doris! Get in here! Did this punk fuck you? You'd better tell me the truth!"

Doris glanced at me and said to Carl, "No, Carl. He definitely did not fuck me. ...He didn't! ...He was about ready to, but this damn farmer and his family came home just as we were about to start. You should have seen us riding through Lafayette without a stitch on! I was playing with Denny's thing, and he was screaming at me all the way. God, it was fun! I haven't laughed so hard in months!"

The three of them were laughing as Doris described the events. David explained that Carl had known about her plans all along and was just having fun watching my terror. After David left, the three of us talked and drank red wine. I kept looking at Carl, so Doris asked if I'd like to go to bed with him. He was smiling and looking at me with interest. Trying to appear casual, I admitted I was slightly curious about him.

"Well, you didn't do it with me, so you're not going to do it with him!" she chided.

"Oh, Doris, must you be so obsessed with fairness?" Carl complained. "Oh well, after seeing you undressed, the poor lad probably lost his interest in sex completely. Maybe some other time, Denny. You know, when the cat's away, the mice can play—that sort of thing. Did you know your friend David refuses to pop in the sack with me? He wants to be normal, he says. Can you imagine anybody actually wanting to be normal? My God, what's happening to your generation?"

"Well, I'm sure you have absolutely no idea what it's like to be normal, Carl," sniped Doris.

"Here's where I'd better be ducking out, folks. Thanks for the memories!" I said, inching toward the door.

Carl taunted, "Oh, don't go rushing off into the night. The fun is just beginning! You wouldn't want to miss our fighting over you, would you? Why, one of us will probably be dead by dawn. Besides, you were just beginning to grow on a certain part of me."

"Maybe all three of us should go to bed together, then the two of you wouldn't have to fight over me," I suggested, hoping for at least the novelty and partial normality of the experience.

"Oh, no!" replied Doris. "You'll never talk me into that! There's no way I⁴m going to just lay there and watch the two of you pawing at each other like two crazed animals in heat. I did that once with Carl, but never again. All you guys really want is the fast and furious basics—no romance at all. It makes me sick!"

"Denny, as I've said to Doris a thousand times, women want hours of affection and romantic illusion; men want to burst into flames of passion like an exploding fireball. Marriage is an institution that assures neither can ever be completely satisfied. Marriages are maintained by hope and belief in 'someday'and by guilt." He was quite serious and had a hurt, bitter look.

I asked why the two of them had gotten married, and Doris answered, "Carl and I are best friends. We always will be, and I know he loves me. Before we were married, he confessed he loved both men and women. I thought he just liked to be admired by anything! He's vain about his good looks, you know. I hoped I could convert him, I guess. I wanted to believe that. He's the best friend I ever had."

"Yes, and I wanted to believe in miracles!" said Carl, as he regained his sense of satirical humor. "You see, I was still suffering from a lingering case of chronic Catholicism, which—thank God—a literate mind, a decent education, or even a minimum of self-honesty can completely cure. So much for fairy tales! Do come again, Denny. It excites me when people come again!"

Some years later, when David graduated from Purdue as an electrical engineer, Doris was pregnant with his child. Earlier, she and Carl had gone their separate ways. David and Doris married and had two sons. Twenty-five years later, after losing contact with them, I learned they lived in the Bay Area, where I was also living. Late one afternoon, I stopped by their home on an impulse and was met by Doris. We talked and waited for David to return from work. "Are you the one I was with when we got chased by that old farmer and his family?" she asked, laughing and blushing. She and Carl were still in touch from time to time. She said she and David had gone through some difficult years together, but marriage counseling had been a great help. "David is a very private person," she observed.

When David came in, he didn't recognize me for several minutes. Then astonishment and joy came to him as he rushed to hug me. He said, "My God, Denny! You show up on my doorstep just when I was completely getting over you!" He showed me an oil painting I'd given him years before at Purdue. He'd kept it in his bedroom all those years. He and I went into his garden, where he spent most of his time, he said. He told me of the difficult times in his marriage and said he was sure they would be able "to go the whole distance." Counseling had helped them. He was open with me, and I remember him saying about himself, "I'm a strange bird, I guess. I don't talk much anymore. I just like to sit and watch my flower garden. My job is my whole life. I'm a technical person, you know. I'm at home with things, and I'm uncomfortable around people. I never could figure people out. They always seem so different from me. You're one of the only people I've ever felt at ease with, Denny. Maybe that's because I've always felt you understood me. Maybe it's because you're the only person I ever let know me. I'm really grateful to Doris, though. I don't think anybody else would have put up with me for this long. I don't make her very happy. I kind of lost interest in sex a long time ago; I don't know why. She never says much about it, but I know she's hurt. I just can't help it, it just became a mechanical thing. A fitting irony, isn't it? A mechanical thing for a technical person. How is it for you now, Denny?" he asked, shyly. How could I be so unfeeling as to tell him about my joy, my bliss? So I said little.

Doris was threatened by David's lifelong attachment to me and discouraged him from relating. I wonder what he thinks about as he sits alone in his garden watching his flowers bloom and fade, season after season. We were long-married husbands and fathers then, but from 16 to 20, in the full flaming of our youth, David and I had been lovers. This would not be spoken of by us, but it was remembered privately. When the autumn winds warn of winter, the roses of spring bloom more sweetly in our memories.

Chapter Twelve

In my clinical practice, I've seen many young men who were as frightened and lost as I was at Purdue. I'm generally effective in helping them, because I understand. All I have to do is remember. Take that day at Purdue, for example, when my mother told me Dr. Hadley feared I might have a paranoid schizophrenic break with reality. What a thing for a scared, 18-year-old in an identity crisis since puberty to confront! There I was, alone in my dormitory room, flunking out of college and seriously worrying that I was either going to commit suicide or become a criminally insane schizophrenic cocksucker! And I had pimples. Psychotherapists might describe such circumstances as "creative frustration," or perhaps, "an identity challenge." And, in retrospect, it was that.

People who have faced their own death—not an imagined afterlife, but nonbeing—often have a greatly enhanced understanding and appreciation of life. This was true for me, especially after my aborted suicide attempt the year before. Even when I faced the possibility of psychosis, I wanted to learn all I could about the life of a psychotic before deciding to end my life. I went to the university library and looked up paranoid schizophrenia. I read several textbooks on psychopathology and was profoundly relieved to learn that I wasn't schizophrenic—not even close. As for being paranoid, well, I had good reasons to be mistrustful, since nonconformity was punished. Students were expelled from universities for expressing the love that dare not speak its name, the McCarthy homosexual witch hunts were happening, and making love with a man was a felony punishable by imprisonment or indefinite confinement in a mental asylum until one was "cured" of this love. The textbooks said that electroshock therapy and castration were sometimes required to correct this affliction of the heart. (Over 20 years later in the mid-'70s, the American Psychiatric Association and the American Psychological Association both decided they had been wrong about classifying homosexuality as an abnormal behavior; they now recognize it as one of the natural forms of human sexuality. In a dramatic example of the sociology of knowledge, they officially announced that homosexuality was no longer a mental disorder or illness, thus instantly curing tens of millions of people of their psychopathology.)

Because I didn't fit the textbook descriptions of any other serious mental illness and there had been no history of mental illness on either side of my family, I decided that the extra responses I'd given to the inkblot cards had thrown Miss Evans and Dr. Hadley off the track. I've often observed that projective test interpretation tells as much about the psychologist as it does the client. It is still true that one of the best ways for a psychologist to understand what a person is doing is to ask him; he just might tell you. I would have told Miss Evans and Dr. Hadley what I was doing, but they never asked. I just wanted to talk to her, to let her know the truth but not have it used against me. I spent days reading abnormal psychology books; I never imagined there were so many ways for a human being to suffer. I didn't think for a moment that I was mentally ill. I knew what my problem was, or so I thought; I just didn't know how to change it, not at that time anyway. My reading convinced me that psychology was mysterious and powerful, and I believed it could cure me of my criminal deviant behavior. I looked forward to having my head professionally shrunk.

I clearly recall the first time I sat in the imposing reception room of offices shared by a psychiatrist and a clinical psychologist in Columbus, Ohio. One doesn't forget the drama of their first experience with psychotherapy. My parents moved to Columbus from Dayton, and I was home for the summer before transferring to Miami University in Oxford, Ohio, in the Fall. Dr. Hadley from the Purdue clinic had recommended that I see a friend of his, Dr. Henry Samuels, the clinical psychologist. Before I could see him, I had to be seen by the psychiatrist, or so insisted the attractive, young blond receptionist. I nervously noticed her looking at me from time to time and smiling, and I worried that she would read my clinical record as soon as I left. The psychiatrist, a rolly polly, thickly bearded, hairy armed, short man wearing the thickest glasses I'd ever seen came out and introduced himself to me, and escorted me back to his impressive office. He seated himself behind a massive, polished wood desk and glared at me with those tiny insect eyes of his.

"Well, young man," he said, "what brings a person of your tender age to a psychiatrist? How old are you, anyway?"

"I just turned 19."

"Well, why would a strapping young 19-year-old want to see a head shrinker? What's wrong with you?"

I said if I knew that, I wouldn't need to be there. I explained that I had been sent there, and he said, "Umm, defensive, I see. Sent by whom? The courts? Have you been convicted of a crime?"

I explained that Dr. Samuels had been referred to me by Dr. Hadley at Purdue University. He'd never heard of Dr. Hadley, he said, and that he would decide if Dr. Samuels would be appropriate for me. Then he asked me if I knew where I was.

"Yes," I said. I was beginning to think he was strange.

"Yes! Is that all you're going to say? What city are you in?" he asked.

I said Columbus, Ohio and asked why he was asking me that. "Young man," he said sternly, "I'm the doctor here. You're the patient. The doctor asks the questions, not the patient. Now, what month and year is it? Who is the president? What's happening in the world?"

I told him it was June, 1954, Eisenhower was the president, the Supreme Court ordered school integration and the Army-McCarthy hearings were on television. I asked if he thought I was crazy and told him I'd come there to see Dr. Samuels, not him.

"Yes, yes, I know, but I have to give you a mental status examination before you can see Dr. Samuels," he explained. "I can see that you're not seriously mentally ill—perhaps a bit neurotic and rebellious, but not psychotic—not now, anyway. I'll ring for the receptionist to take you to Henry. Good-day and good luck!"

Dr. Henry Samuels was a short, pudgy, middle-aged man with receptively intelligent eyes framed by gold wire-rimmed glasses. His disappearing hair was in the shape of a monk's tonsure, but his similarity to a monk was shattered when he spoke in his animated Jewish style. He was warm and gentle, and our sessions together were vitally important in the course of my life. They were like this:

"Ahh, come in, my young friend!" welcomed the good doctor. "I see you survived the ordeal with the hairy bear! So pompous, that man. And so rude! Well, what do you expect from a psychiatrist? They have such a poor education. You won't have to see him again. I've been expecting you. My old friend, Dr. Hadley, wrote me a nice letter about you. He said you were a most interesting, precocious young man, who would give me a real workout. I like that. I can't stand to be bored. If people start boring me, I just take a cat nap. So, if you see me with my eyes closed, start talking about something with meat on its bones instead of intellectualized yackity-yack. Now, tell your old Uncle Henry what's going on with you."

Initially, I saw Dr. Samuels three times a week. Most of the time, he just listened to me intently, occasionally asking for clarification, but when he did say something, it would ring in my head for days.

"Words, words, words! Such a smoke screen!" he said often.

"Next session, maybe I bring a shovel to get rid of the shit you're slinging!"

"You need parents like you need a case of terminal cancer!"

"Fair? You're 19 and you still want life to be fair? Maybe you do have a screw loose! Shake your head!"

"Who are you trying to convince? Me or you? Me thinks you do protest too much!"

"If you spend as much time avoiding the issues as you did today, I'll get rich; take your time, take forever!"

"Do you know that in all the weeks you've been seeing me, you've never once told me how you feel about me? Very interesting."

"You don't want to suffer, do you? Then I'm afraid life can teach you nothing!"

"You don't need anyone's permission to live, my friend. I'll tell you a secret. There are no judges—except in your head."

"So you think you're not like everybody else? Well, for that you should fall on your knees and thank God every day! You are blessed, not cursed, and you refuse to see it! Pull the scabs off your eyeballs and end your blindness!"

"Others are not rejecting you. They can't understand you. You're beyond them. They need your help and compassion, not your rejection."

"Ho, ho! How sad! I should whip out my violin and play sad tunes. You should tell your sad little tale to my relatives, the ones who were gassed to death in Hitler's death camps!"

"So, you think you are the only person who has suffered? Well, let me welcome you to the rest of the human race. None of us gets out of this alive, you know."

One day Dr. Samuels told me he'd gotten a report from Miss Evans at Purdue. "That young woman wrote one of the best psychological reports I've ever seen. It was 36 pages long. I had to chuckle over that five-hour Rorschach of yours. Shame on you! Such intellectual diarrhea! You really scared the hell out of them for awhile. When you decide to beat around the bush, you make an art form of it. But don't stop on my account! I still have to pay the mortgage on my house. Seriously, Denny, there is one area of your life that's conspicuous by its absence in your many talks with Miss Evans and me. Do you know what it is?"

"No," I answered defensively, suspecting the worst.

"Oh, come on! Con not thy therapist! You know!" he said firmly, but with a smile.

"I don't!" I insisted as I closed myself off and checked the locks on my closet door.

"You mean, you don't want to know," he said sharply. "Well, I'm not going to play cat and mouse with you. You never mention s, e, x...SEX!"

"You never asked me about it. I didn't know you were interested in that," I replied, trying to shift the blame.

"Doesn't it interest you, Denny?" he asked with a sly, accusing expression.

"Well, yes, but it's a personal thing," I answered with irritation, but I was thinking about walking out of his office. It felt like he was asking me to undress and expose myself.

He smiled knowingly and said, "Oh, I see. You tell me you've thought about fucking your mother, but we're not being personal or anything like that!"

"Well, what do you want to know?" I asked stoically. I was curious about what interested him.

"What do you want to tell me about it?" he parried.

"Nothing comes to mind." I made my face a blank mask.

"Oh, I see that mortgage getting paid off! Have you had sex? With a woman, I mean."

"Yes."

"How was it?"

"It was okay." He was going to have to pry the truth out of me.

"Okay? Hmmm, that bad, huh?"

"No." I was frightened by his perceptiveness.

"What do you think about when you masturbate?"

My mask shattered, and I exploded at him, "Geez, do you always ask your clients about their sex lives? You come across like a dirty old man! You are married, aren't you, or did your wife just cross her legs on you?"

His face broke into a large smile, and his eyes twinkled as he said, "Ho, ho! A spark of life in you! Good! I thought I was going to be bored again. I'm definitely not a dirty old man! Dirty, yes, old, no! Now, let's talk man to man about sex. It interests everybody, so Puritanism be damned! You Christians have never been at ease with your genitals! This Miss Evans writes that sex is probably an underlying problem area for you. She suggests that homosexuality may play a part."

"She said that? Or are you just making that up?" I asked. I was astonished and regretted that I hadn't trusted her.

"She says it right here. Look, Denny, large numbers of boys have homosexual experiences sometime in their lives, usually in their early teenage years. It doesn't mean anything. Almost all of them grow up and become husbands and fathers. It's a common experience for boys. Why, some psychologists have even had those experiences. Now, tell me, have you?"

"Yes." I caught his hint about himself and wondered if he was about to proposition me, then I worried that I was unconsciously wanting him to.

"Good," he said. "I know that took some courage for you to say. I'm glad you trust me. How many years ago was this experience of yours?"

"You mean the first time?" I asked.

"Aa...yes." I noticed his surprise. I told him it was just before I'd turned 12. "And did you have this experience more than once?" he asked.

"...Yes."

"Yes? That's all I get from you, a yes? Well, how many times did you have that experience—two times, three times?"

"I don't know. I didn't count. It was many times."

"Well, how long did it go on for? A week? A month?"

"A couple of years."

"Oh, I see. He was an older man, then? A relative?"

"No. He was just some kid in the neighborhood. He was a couple of years older. His name was Keith." What was completely repressed at that time was the profound emotional significance of my relationship with Keith. I had only vague, fleeting memories of him and rarely thought about that period of my life.

Dr. Samuels looked puzzled and replied, "Oh. So your only homosexual experiences were with this Keith? Well, that's not unusual. Many boys are curious and experiment that way shortly after puberty. Nothing to be worried about."

I told him that wasn't my only experience. "It wasn't?" he asked, looking troubled. "Well, how many years ago was your last experience?"

"It wasn't years ago," I said as I studied his face for his reactions, waiting for the disgust.

"Well, how long was it, Denny?"

"Two weeks ago."

"Two weeks! Oh! I see. Two weeks? I noticed a nice looking young man waiting for you in the reception room then. Is he the one you...have relations with?"

"No. He was just a friend, visiting from Purdue."

"He seemed to be agitated about something."

"He was. He wanted to get down inside the earth, and I told him I'd take him to a cave after my appointment with you. He had this thing about wanting to get down inside mother earth with me. It's all very Freudian. He's transferring to the University of Chicago—in psychology. He graduated from high school two years early."

"Why do you think he wanted to be down in the earth with you? Does he have feelings for you?"

"Oh, I know he has feelings for me—sexual feelings that scare him; he said that. Sex scares him. He likes symbolic things. He says all life is symbolic. It's just that he doesn't know what it's symbolic of, maybe it's God, he says. Going down into a cave was another one of his symbolic adventures— being in the earth womb together. He says I'm a symbol, but I tell him I'm also real. He laughs and says he prefers me to be a symbol. I think it's because sex scares him, don't you?"

"Let's not get off the topic, Denny. You're a slippery eel, you are! We were talking about you and your sexuality, not your friend's. People often shift topics when they're defensive."

"Well," I said, "you asked about him, I didn't!"

"...Hmmm. Yes, I did, didn't I? Well, the student is teaching the master a few tricks now! You're improving. I'm glad to see that. You've given me something to think about later today. Now, you were telling me you've had experiences with several people. Who was the most recent one?"

"David—a friend of mine from Richmond, Indiana. I used to live there."

"How many times did you and David...have relations?"

"I don't know. We've been that way for three years."

"Three years? Were there others?"

"Yes. I stopped once for a year and a half, but there were others—I don't remember how many."

He paused, thoughtfully evaluating and judging. I feared his verdict, but what he said was: "My! You really are a frisky little bunny rabbit, aren't you? Humping everything that hops! I suppose you masturbate in between times?"

"Yes."

"Wheeuu! Oye Vey! Such energy! I should have such a problem! Now I'm going to regret my own youth, thanks to you! The only memories I'll have when I'm an old man in my rocking chair are of my wife and one or two others. Oh well, we grow too soon old and too late smart. I'm glad we finally talked about these things. How are you feeling now?"

"Better. But I still think you're a dirty old man! Well, not old, but I think you enjoy hearing about this sex stuff."

"Yes, I do. You should put up with the boring stuff I have to listen to day after day. The dirtier, the better! Except, Denny, it isn't really dirty, you know. Sex is fascinating, and psychologists hardly understand a thing about this central human experience. Did you know the Chinese call sex 'the act of many significances'? It is, you know. Only fools and celibate priests think sex is just a biological urge to reproduce. Maybe it is for frogs and cockroaches, but for us, it's symbolic—the act of many significances. Oh, your young friend from the University of Chicago will have a field day with sex, he will. Well, our time is up until next week, and I'm feeling a strong urge to get home and take my wife to bed!"

At last, the barrier was down, and I was known and real. All those years, filled with the fear of discovery, and when I was finally exposed, dear old Dr. Samuels just laughed and called me a frisky little bunny rabbit humping everything that hops! The sense of acceptance and relief I experienced was incredible. That's why he was such a good psychologist. He got me out of my cage for awhile.

I didn't know much about him, because he always focused on me. I wondered if he'd ever had sex with a guy and believed he'd probably tried it when he was young. It was hard to imagine that he'd ever been young. I wondered if he thought about having sex with me. I knew he was uncomfortable talking about homosexuality; because, whenever he said "have relations with," he flipped his eyes down. As I listened to him, I wondered what it would be like to touch his bald spot—to ejaculate on it. I felt guilt, shame, and fear at the craziness of this idea, but I kept imagining it. I thought it would be like having sex with a father. I was deeply into psychoanalysis at this time and thought maybe I had a reverse Oedipus complex—I wanted to have sex with my father but was afraid my mother would be angry. Dr. Samuels noticed that I was off somewhere and asked what I was experiencing, but I didn't tell him. I was already worried about how he really felt about me now that he knew my darkest side. I didn't think he could handle incest or my coming off on his bald head. Besides, I thought he'd probably just say I was trying to avoid something by going off into intellectualized Freudian garbage. He would have been right.

The next session had far reaching consequences in my life and the lives of many others. My memory of what he said is clear. Dr. Samuels asked how I felt about our last session, and I told him I was ashamed and worried about what he really thought of me now that he knew. When I said this, he seemed to be deeply moved with compassion and pity, and I noticed that he struggled to control a surge of emotion. "Oh, my little bunny rabbit, you're much too young to be crippled by such a heavy burden of guilt and shame on your young back," he said. "I want you to listen carefully to what I tell you, Denny. I did much thinking about what you told me. Now, it's true you've had somewhat more sexual experience than the average boy, but it is clear to me that your experiences were just a part of the normal course of development. Your relations were perhaps a bit more intense and longer lasting, and you were somewhat overly aggressive, perhaps, in meeting your needs, but people show a wide range of variations in the duration of various stages of their psychosexual development. As a psychologist, I know you are a healthy, normal young man, who perhaps clings overly long to each of life's pleasures, but of this I can have absolutely no doubt: *you are not a homosexual.* You have not been, nor could you ever be, a pervert, an invert, or anything like that. Trust me. It's my job to know about these things, and I'm telling you that is simply not who you are or who you're going to be, because it's not in the cards for you. You're just slow in going through a developmental stage, that's all. Now look here, Denny, enjoying sex with women is learned; it's an acquired taste— like learning to love green olives or oysters. I guarantee you, after you have a couple dozen spine-bending orgasms with women, they'll be mighty attractive to you! Nothing builds confidence as much as success, and practice makes perfect. You know, I'm amazed at your skills in seducing males. It's damned hard for a man to get another man to go to bed with him! Why continue to do things the hard way? Denny, listen to me; for someone who has your skills, women will be pushovers! All you'll have to do is walk down the street and roll those blue eyes of yours. I'm serious! Women are damned easy compared with men, I tell you. Now, I want you to start trying it; you'll like it! Make it easy on yourself, okay? I want you to put your past to rest and be on with your life. You're a normal, healthy, red-blooded young man. Why deprive some young woman of the pleasure of loving you—of running her hands all over your sexy body? It's really not fair, you know! They're out there waiting for you right now. Take it from me—we all grow too soon old and too late smart."

I almost had tears in my eyes when he finished talking. I wanted to rush over to him and kiss him right in the middle of his bald spot, because he had just commuted my death sentence. He believed in me! He said what I most wanted to hear, but I was confused and surprised by my sudden awareness of a certain sense of sorrow. I didn't understand, and I didn't want to think about it, so I didn't. It was the sorrow of losing something of value.

After this session, Dr. Samuels showed no interest when I talked about my sexual past. He would say, "the past is past," and get me to talk about the present and future. But I wanted to talk about the past. Once when I objected to his putting me off, he looked irritated and snapped, "Look, do you want to wind up in a state prison? Then bury your past! It's over, forget it, Denny! ...I'm sorry...it's just that I'm concerned about you. Sex with a man is a felony crime. This society is going to start playing hardball with you soon. Wake up!" His mood softened, and his gentleness returned. "I remember a couple of sayings from a famous old Jew that I want you to remember: 'When I was a child, I spake as a child, I understood as a child, I thought as a child; but when I became a man, I put away childish things.' 'For whoever will save his life shall lose it.' And here's another way to say the same thing, Denny: 'The boy must die for the man to be born.' Let the boy die, Denny. Let him go! You don't need him anymore." My belief in the wisdom of Dr. Samuels was absolute; the alternative was unthinkable and unlivable. I had survived my trial by perversion and believed I was about to be transformed into a new life, the life of a normal adult.

. . .

In September of 1954, I transferred to Miami University as part of my new beginning. I was no longer interested in engineering, and I wanted to get away from David. Miami University is a sleepy, idyllic campus, with ivy-covered brick Georgian buildings, that lies hidden in the gentle, rolling hills of southwestern Ohio. It was founded in 1809, and the Miami tradition has retained a distinct fondness for that time period ever since. Miami is called the cradle of fraternities and coaches, and it insulates the conservative sons and daughters of the wealthy from the harsh realities of the society they will inherit. It was for me a place of transformation that sophomore year—as it would be again much later in my life, dramatically so.

My 19th year was filled with rapture and madness. The revoking of my death sentence by Dr. Samuels had freed me. The world suddenly seemed rich with the possibilities for a normal life, and I believed that I could at last safely confront my repressed past. Everyday, as I walked to campus from Fisher Hall, I passed under an archway above which was chiseled another saying by Dr. Samuels' famous old Jew: "Ye shall know the truth, and the truth shall make you free." I believe that, and I flooded with excitement whenever I passed that way, for I was well into my search for the repressed truths that were the keys to my freedom. I quickly learned that my classes had little of significance to offer me, so I spent my time in the Miami library, reading anything that evoked feelings. The library was a world of possibilities at my fingertips—a treasure house of the human spirit. The lamp of knowledge became the symbol for my hope and faith—the burning flame of truth, dispeller of illusion.

I discovered the writings and journals of Andre Gide, French Nobel prize winner in literature, who was homosexual. He wrote, "Nathaniel, I will teach you that all things are divinely natural!" When I read this radical intent, my mind burst into flames. I realized I was part of nature. My desires were the desires of nature! I was not an unnatural life form dropped into the world as the book of Genesis implies with its separation of God, man and nature locked in perpetual conflict. I didn't even want to have dominion over nature as the Genesis creation myth advises. Since I am part of this universe, I reasoned, I belong here. I was no longer an alien! Gide wrote of the spontaneous freedom to be, his gratuitous act, and I began to run and dance in celebration of the sheer joy of life. I was life celebrating itself. I was freeing myself from the crippling coils of institutionalized Christianity. I was pleased when a sociology professor cited research showing that orthodoxy of religious belief is inversely correlated with educational level.

Because of the many moves I'd made in my life—those many attachments and losses—I made new friends easily. My best friend, Bernie, was a Jewish pre-med student from New York City. Together, we dated Jewish girls he knew. I became attached to one, and she, to me, but one evening, she was astonished by something I said. "You are Jewish, aren't you?" she asked. When I answered, she was angered. "I don't date gentiles!" she declared and left me standing on the sidewalk. I didn't particularly think of myself as a gentile; I really had no idea who I was. I couldn't find a place for me in social institutions. I knew what I was feeling but not much else. I disliked it when people asked me what I was going to be, because I didn't even know who or what I was, much less what I would become.

Four of my friends and I decided to rent the top floor of a house to get away from dorm living. One of these friends was from Aleppo, Syria, and he taught me fencing and hypnosis. The old woman who owned the house was psychotic, and we would often wake up in the middle of the night to the sounds of her hallucinating downstairs where she lived. Sometimes, we would awaken to see her standing at the ends of our beds, just staring at us; but the rent was cheap, so we lived with it.

Another of my friends in the house, Charlie Barker, was the only son of a Cleveland family of significant old wealth. He introduced me to the exotic self-indulgent life of those of his rarefied financial status. Charlie was cynical, perhaps because his alcoholic father had divorced Charlie's mother to marry a young, blonde chorus girl, whose main qualifications seemed to be bulging breasts and a darting tongue. He lived with his father and "the whore," as he called her. Charlie was amused by my unsophisticated enthusiasm for the material trappings of wealth. I asked him why he was cynical about his rich and powerful friends, because I felt honored to be invited to their homes with him. He seemed surprised that I was so naive as to be impressed by wealth, then he explained, "I'm cynical, because I know them too well. I know what really goes on. All you see now is the surface, but you'll find out."

Charlie had a substitute mother, Mimi Burkhart, whom we visited one evening. "Don't be impressed by anything—look bored," he advised, "then you'll fit right in." Mimi Burkhart was reading a leather-bound volume of Chaucer near the large fireplace in her Tudor style library. I was introduced, and she read for us. She spoke the original Middle English with eloquence and drama and then translated for us. I was astonished by her and the grandeur of her home, her estate, but I remembered Charlie's advice not to look impressed. Mimi finished reading and looked at me expectantly, but my face was a contrived mask. She looked puzzled briefly, then smiled: "Oh, for goodness sake! Now don't you start imitating that deadpan face of Charlie's—as pretty as it is. He thinks it's very sophisticated, you know, but his eyes give him away every time, and so do yours. I could see you were enjoying Chaucer, and that speaks well for you. And who wouldn't be impressed by a grand room like this? I still am, and it gives me great pleasure to be able to share its beauty with you, Denny. Please, do sit down here beside me and tell me about yourself. Charlie says you're going to be a clinical psychologist. You would have a field day with my husband, but let's not ruin a lovely evening by talking about him; I'm interested in you."

Mimi's warm, receptive style, her inviting eyes, and her touches drew me to her as she followed the ebb and flow of my convoluted feelings. Our eyes began to communicate more than our words, and I knew she was sensing me physically. Charlie wandered off to find her son, Phillip. Mimi asked me to dance with her. "Dance?" I asked, suspecting a metaphor, since sex was usually on my mind. She smiled and went to the phonograph. She selected a slow dance piece and then returned and stood several feet from me, waiting. I took her hand in mine, put my arm around her waist, and watched her close her eyes as we began to dance. When the music ended, we looked at each other; her eyes were filled with kindness. Like a boy needing his mother, I put my head on her shoulder and pressed her close to me.

She stroked my hair and nurtured me: "Oh, my fine young man! You're lost, aren't you? You've lost your way. I should have seen that earlier. Hold on tight to me, then. Let me comfort you. So many young men your age haven't found their paths; it's all so sad. Life seems so confusing when you're young, but when you're my age, you know the pathways of your life and those of others."

Charlie and Phillip entered the library and saw us together. I stepped away from Mimi, and she looked amused: "Good heavens, Denny, you act as though we'd been doing something improper. I'm flattered you were conscious of such an idea with me. I keep forgetting all you young men have such hair triggers. I want you to meet my son, Phillip. Phillip is 16. He's been asking if he could show you his electronic equipment. It seems he's having trouble with a new gadget. Charlie mentioned that you know about electronics and amateur radio. Would you mind helping Phillip for a short while? That would give Charlie and me some time to catch up, but don't let Phillip keep you for more than an hour!"

Phillip was tall, with tousled honey-colored hair, and the healthy pink-cheeked look of a privileged English schoolboy. His green eyes glanced at me shyly, and his hand was warm and gentle as he shook mine. I immediately recognized his loneliness and felt I understood him. I readily agreed to help him, since I was strongly attracted. Because of his shyness, I took the lead in our conversation as we walked to his basement laboratory some distance away. Even though he was a high school student and I was in college, by the time we got to the lab, he knew he was accepted by me, because he most certainly was.

Phillip smiled proudly as he opened the door to his lab, which contained shelves of the latest electronic equipment. He was full of questions, and there was much I explained to him, but I kept losing my train of thought as my eyes photographed him in his countless fascinating images. At one point, when I was leaning over him from behind showing him how to operate a double-trace oscilloscope, I could no longer resist the temptation to touch him, so I rested my arm on his shoulder. I expected that he would show no response to this acceptable gesture—males were trained to discount such casual expressions of affection; but, instead, he looked back at me and smiled appreciatively. I then imagined myself putting my arms around him and pressing my cheek against his, then holding his head between the palms of my hands and kissing the back of his neck. I didn't regard this brief fantasy as a serious moral transgression. I didn't doubt that he would respond, and this frightened me. Just then, the telephone rang. It was Mimi telling him we were half an hour late. Just before we were about to enter the library, Phillip suddenly stopped me and asked if I had a girlfriend. I said no, and he blushed and looked away. We understood.

Several days after Charlie and I returned to the university, Mimi called me. Phillip had talked about me constantly. She wanted me to spend the summer in Europe with their family as a companion for Phillip. She said, "Denny, if you would prefer not to room with Phillip, we will provide separate accommodations. Phillip isn't keen on that idea, but he can't always have everything he wants, can he?" I told her I'd never been to Europe and was overwhelmed by the invitation. I thanked her and promised to call the following day with my answer.

I immediately phoned Dr. Samuels. "England, France, Switzerland, Italy? A free trip? Denny, why are you calling me? Ask them if they have room for a friendly psychologist for the family! I'll even carry the luggage if they'll take me, too! Why would you hesitate?"

When I explained my attraction to Phillip and what I knew about him, Dr. Samuels was silent for a few moments. "Denny, are you telling me you couldn't resist the temptation, even if the two of you had separate rooms?" I said I could for awhile but not for the whole summer, because Phillip and I had—using my newly acquired psychobabble—"instant rapport." "So, rapport, is it?" Dr. Samuels said. "Well, you understand the consequences of not growing up, Denny. You have an important decision to make about what you want for your future. You also have a responsibility for Phillip's welfare. As much as I like you, Denny, I don't make house calls in prisons; but perhaps I could give you a special telephone rate. A man must do what is right, my friend. Just take the temptations of life a day at a time. It's not my place to make this decision for you, but I'm glad you called to talk. I'm looking forward to our next appointment."

I called Mimi and told her I couldn't go because of my military draft status. The draft was still in effect after the Korean war, and I knew I'd be called to serve, especially with my low grades. The real reason, of course, was my attraction to Phillip. Charlie Barker said I was a provincial idiot, but I couldn't risk the truth with him. Many months later, he told me Mimi had been quite disappointed that I wouldn't go—she didn't believe my excuse, and Phillip was still bitter about my failure to answer a letter he had written. I accepted the guilt in silence; but years later, and even though I was married, during my first trip to Europe, I thought of Phillip constantly.

My life was filled with these trials by temptation. One sunny day on a class biology field trip along the Talawanda River, we were relaxed and playful. A classmate of mine, who had been displaying his tanned, muscular physique to girls in the class, was given a large, red wild flower by one of them. He admired it and casually placed it just above his ear in his wavy, jet-black hair. The effect was beautiful, and he noticed my eyes etching his image into my memory.

As we returned to campus, I was surprised when he walked along beside me. "I noticed you looking at me earlier today. Were you interested in flowers...or me?" he asked.

"Well," I said, "it was just that, when you put that flower in your hair, you looked like pictures I've seen of South Sea islanders, that's all."

"So, are you interested in flowers or me?"

"Aa...neither, I guess."

He moved closer and whispered, "It's okay if you're interested in me—do you know what I mean? I mean, being around all those great looking girls all afternoon and getting all hot and sweaty, well, I'd sure like to mess around right now, you know what I mean? You could come over and take a shower at my place. How 'bout it? ...You know what I mean?"

I looked at his expectant face and the red flower in his black wavy hair and said coldly, "No, I don't understand, and I don't think I want to. Sorry. I've got homework to do when I get back."

His smile indicated he knew I wasn't truthful. I immobilized my face, but my brain was generating stroboscopic images of the two of us in a shower. Still smiling, he took the flower from his hair and placed it in mine; then he walked away, and I was depressed.

One Friday evening, a student who had become friendly with me called to invite me to "a real bohemian party" at some professor's house. I should be prepared to meet some unusual people, he said, and I should be polite, no matter what.

At the party, I was introduced to the dozen or so guests by the two bachelor professors who shared the elegant home together. I was surprised that my friend had told them so much about me and even more surprised that they'd bothered to remember. The guests were unusually friendly, and their conversations, punctuated with hilarity, were scintillating and sophisticated. I began to feel self-conscious and out of place.

A very handsome, boyish-looking young man with impeccable manners and dress was the center of attention as he charmed the group with stories of his recent trip to Italy. I'd never seen such refined graciousness, intelligence, culture and wit, and I envied him. I was even more astonished when he came over to me later and introduced himself. He'd noticed me looking at him, he said, and wondered if we'd met somewhere before. He was socially perceptive, and I felt I was being charmed into a trance as he politely examined each layer of my being. I asked about him, and when I told him how impressed I was by his self-confidence, he grinned and said it was a well-rehearsed act. He admitted he'd practiced his stories before he came. I don't recall our dialogue exactly, but it was like this: "If I had real self-confidence," he said, "I wouldn't need to do things like that. It's all just show. I know I make people admire me, but I'm really just lonely. I'm afraid to let people get to know me."

"You're letting me know you. Why is that?" I asked.

"Maybe I'm not!" he said. "Maybe this is just more of my act. You can't be sure, can you?"

"Well, there must be somebody you let know you," I countered. "How about your girlfriend? Does she know you?"

He laughed, and his face flushed pink. "My girlfriend! Do you see any girls around here? You don't know where you are, do you? I'm sorry, I shouldn't have laughed. It wasn't at you but at this crazy world. Let me explain. All of us here are looking for boyfriends. That's right, we're homosexuals, or fairies, if you prefer. Does that shock you?"

One of his friends came over, whispered something to him, said goodbye, and kissed him on the cheek. I was uncomfortable. The friend left, and he continued, "That surprised you, didn't it? You seem to be tense. What a pity. Oh, you Midwest types! I don't understand why I ever left the East Coast; perhaps it was fantasies of cowboys...or was it Indians in loin cloths? Could you be just straddling the fence? That can be very uncomfortable on the male anatomy. Perhaps you just have a purely academic interest in the psychology of the sexually disparate, not to mention the desperate. Would you like to interview me for your research? I'm a willing subject."

"Aren't you afraid of getting caught?" I asked.

"Well, of course we are—all of us. I think about it every day, but what's the point of staying alive if you can't love? I used to be terrified, but I've reached the point where I just don't care anymore; if I'm caught, I'm caught. I'm sure there would be someone in prison who would interest me."

"But how would you earn a living when you got out?" I asked.

"Fortunately, I don't ever have to worry about that. I have a substantial inheritance."

"Well, why do you think you are like you are?"

"Like I am?"

"I mean...that way." I didn't know any polite word for it. "Gay" was not in use then.

"Oh, you mean queer," he replied with a teasing look. "Well, I have no idea. I've always been like this...for as long as I can remember. I think I was born this way."

I asked him if he ever wanted to be a girl. "Of course not," he said with irritation. "Who would want to put up with what a woman has to? No, I've never had the slightest interest in being a woman—neither have my friends. We sometimes tease one another by using female names, but that's just a parody of the way you provincials think we are. You think if a man loves another man, then he has to be a woman. How stupid."

"Why do you think there are laws against it?" I asked.

"Oh, because of churches that want to increase their power by out-populating the competition, parents who want lots of children and grandchildren to take care of them in their old age, more hands to work the farms and factories, a bigger power base for politicians. Who really knows? Maybe misery loves company, or maybe wives are afraid of losing their husbands if they discovered really good sex. Maybe it's because men define their masculinity in terms of dominance, so they believe a love between equals means a loss of masculinity. Men often need a weaker partner they control to feel like a man. Perhaps they're just afraid of their own pleasurable impulses. Pleasure might tempt the majority, those gutless cowards, to dare to question their blind obedience to authority, and God knows, disobedience is an evil for which all rule breakers are to be severely punished. This I know, for the Bible tells me so! ...I don't really understand it. I wish I did."

I asked if he didn't think his sexuality was a case of arrested development as the Freudians thought. "From what I've seen," he answered, "one could just as easily argue that heterosexuality is a case of arrested development. Just look around at the battlefield called marriage, my friend. Besides, who cares what causes it? No one chooses what they love. I certainly didn't, did you? Look, why would anyone object to a sexual relationship that harms no one? Either we believe in personal freedom in this country or we don't—and the laws of this land of liberty make it quite clear that we don't."

"I think you're somewhat biased," I said defensively. His logic was threatening.

"Do you?" he said with an indulgent, sarcastic tone. "You know, we understand you better than you understand us. We know all too well about bias. For centuries, and in the name of your loving Jesus Christ, you have condemned us, burned us at the stake, imprisoned us, cast us out, denied our existence, put us in mental hospitals, and castrated us. Yes, we live with your bias everyday of our miserable lives."

"I think you're getting a little too hot under the collar," I said. "I didn't do any of those things to you."

"No, but you think like those blind hypocrites. You're uncomfortable just being in this room with us, aren't you? What will people say about you, Denny, if they knew you were here? But don't worry, we'll never tell. We're quite good at keeping secrets; after all, our very survival depends on it. The truth you people just don't want to see, and that we understand all too well about you, is that, if you weren't so tempted by the alternatives we represent, then you wouldn't hate us as much as you do. What you're threatened by is your own freedom. Did you know that 'heretic' comes from the Greek word meaning 'one who has an alternative,' one who is able to choose? Rather interesting that Christians have made freedom a heresy. Now, aren't you going to ask me about what we like to do in bed together—strictly for your research, of course? Don't you want to ask me questions about that? Aren't you even a little bit curious?" he teased.

"Not really. I have a pretty good understanding," I answered, feeling fear, threat, and a warning twinge of excitement while looking at the pupils of his iris-blue eyes.

"Oh really?" he asked. "And just how did you come by this precious bit of forbidden knowledge? Perhaps I've been misreading you."

I told him I'd had some experience, but I was in psychotherapy, and my therapist believed I was fixated at a developmental stage and I could learn to move on to a higher level. "A higher level?" he questioned with a disapproving expression. "There's your bias, again. Can't you see that? Different doesn't have to mean inferior."

All I knew, I said, was that I didn't want to be miserable and hated by people. "I know what you mean," he said sympathetically, but with sadness. "I'm the black sheep of my family. They pay me to stay away from home, so I won't be an embarrassment. I can't go home for holidays, because the relatives and family friends will be there. I visit with them briefly when they travel away from home. My mother calls me on the telephone now and then. I don't know...maybe it is a developmental stage or whatever you called it. ...I get so confused. ...I don't know how else to be. ...Maybe it can be changed...but I don't think so. It doesn't seem like that. ...Are you attracted to me?" he asked, looking up from his sorrow.

"Attracted? I wish I were as good-looking and socially skilled and intelligent as you—oh, yes, and as rich, too! You're a very impressive person, and I think you know it. You like to get compliments, don't you?"

"They feed my soul with the vain hope that someday I can be loved. I'm not sure I have anything else I'm living for. ...I know it would be pointless to ask you if you would be interested in experiencing the rapture of the gods with me this evening...or, from your perspective, slipping further into the abominable pit of perversion, because I know you're hoping your psychologist can cure you. Maybe he can, and you can be normal and live happily ever after. ...Do you really think I'm all that good-looking?"

"Yes. Quite! Extremely!" I replied. "I hope you find the love you're looking for someday. I really do. I appreciate you talking with me."

He looked at me very thoughtfully. His intelligence was frightening. Then he said, "I wish you well, too, but I think your journey will be the harder one." When I left that house and looked up to the stars, I felt relief. I worried that someone might see me leaving there, but nobody was around. I was glad I hadn't told anyone my last name. I kept seeing the face of that young man saying, "I think your journey will be the harder one." What did he know about me, I wondered. What did he really mean? I decided that he was just trying to get me to go to bed with him. I knew I wasn't like those people. I still had a fighting chance to be normal; they had obviously given up all hope, and I pitied them. I thought about Dr. Samuels and carried on an imaginary conversation with him. He would have been proud of me. But I kept recalling the face of that young man—his knowing, longing eyes—and wondered if I should go back. But because of fear, I didn't.

After that evening, I became more frightened of myself, and I began dating girls more often. My friend and housemate, Gene Best, and I double dated. He was older than I was and had been in the military in Korea. He was the best man at my wedding years later. Gene was quite popular with women and very sexually active, usually in the back seat of his car. One Saturday, Gene and I spent the day with our dates on his parents' farm in central Ohio. It was late when we returned to campus. My date was shy and sweet, a virgin for sure. At her dorm, I kissed her good-night, but she suggested we sit in the bleachers for a few minutes to look at the stars. We sat there in silence, waiting to see some shooting stars, but the way she kept looking over at me told me she wanted me to kiss her again. I didn't feel like it, but it seemed like such a simple thing to do to make her happy. I leaned over and embraced her. Suddenly, she began to kiss me all over my face. Then she started groaning, and she unbuttoned her blouse and flopped her large breasts into the moonlight. "Oh, Denny! Feel me! Rub them! Hold them! Kiss them! They're for you. Put your hands around them. Oh, Denny, I've waited all day for this. Denny, take me! I'm yours!"

Fortunately, the girl's dorms were closing in ten minutes, so I reminded her of this, and we went no further. As I walked home, I thought about how most college guys dreamed about that opportunity, but I felt absolutely nothing for her but sorrow, because I couldn't be the stuff of her dreams, and I didn't understand why. I imagined Dr. Samuels frowning when he heard about this, but I couldn't help it. I knew I'd have to work harder to find out what I was repressing that had arrested my sexual development. I decided to keep a daily journal.

My new strategy for my archaeological digs into my unconscious was to outline as much of my past as I could remember. It quickly became evident that I was unconsciously blocking out large chunks of time—as most people do. When I told Dr. Samuels about my new plans, surprisingly, he encouraged these expeditions into my past. He probably knew he couldn't stop me. I went through photo albums and talked to my parents about where we'd lived and what I'd been doing. Slowly, I recovered vast portions of my past. There was a painful price to pay in retrieving each repressed time period, but I'd begun my journey into the darkness that was me. I was convinced about the reality of repression, and my hope was for full awareness. "Ye shall know the truth!" I said to myself, and I didn't care if it made me free; I wanted light.

It was a detective game—clues, fragments, hints, hunches, false leads, but I became skilled. The most elusive and disconnected parts of my past were the years from age 11 to 15. I dug there for weeks but collected only unemotional, insignificant fragments. I was astonished by the way that time period resisted the light, how it seemed to shrink back into blackness. The harder I pressed, the more it retreated. I tried to sneak up on it, but it was no fool. Even though I was armed with the powerful technique of free association, it wouldn't yield. I became totally preoccupied with recovering those memories; I was convinced that they were the key to my difficulties. I worried that the resistance I was encountering indicated the power of the buried psychological material. Could I bear it, I wondered. Dr. Samuels gave me several telephone numbers where he could be reached. I carried them in my wallet.

Pages of my diary were filled with frustrating fragments of memory, yet something was always missing, something essential. Because of my growing anxiety and excitement, I knew I was on the right track. Like a mountain climber making a last dash to gain the summit before a gathering storm, I skipped classes for several days to engage the darkness within me with total concentration. I vowed I would make it yield or be shattered in the process.

As this internal battle raged on day after day, I became highly agitated, yet excited. Could I survive the insights, I wondered, or would the truth send me into uncharted realms of madness? Would the very structure of reality be shattered in my brain forever? Would I live only unending horror, would my humanity disappear, leaving only this animal body smearing its feces on the tile floor of a solitary cell in an asylum for the insane? That was one of my many fears. Or would I be free?

My roommates worried about me, but I told them to leave me alone, that I'd be fine. Inside, I was afraid. I gave the one who was most concerned Dr. Samuels' telephone numbers in case I got into trouble.

One hot afternoon, when I felt nearer than I'd ever been to ending the repression, I became highly agitated and began to pace around like a caged tiger. When I could no longer stand the confinement of being indoors, I walked for miles around the campus, lost in swirling smatterings of memory. I became fatigued from my efforts and the heat. As I stumbled around in circles on a neatly trimmed field that looked like the fairway of a golf course, I thought if I pray to God, even though I'm no longer a believer, maybe something will happen. I was exhausted, and anything seemed worth trying. I fell to my knees. "God, if you do exist, hear me! Forgive me and help me now. I must know. I can't retreat. All I ask from you is a sign. A clue. Anything."

When I got up, I noticed a slight hill nearby. I walked to the top of it to be closer to heaven and waited expectantly. I looked at the clouded sky and spoke directly to God these words of Martin Luther: "Here I stand, for I can do no other!" And I waited. God, I believed—when I believed—was a Protestant. The earnestness of my teenage dramatizing seems humorous now.

There was only silence, and I thought I was just desperate and superstitious, but still I continued to hope for the slightest sign. I noticed some movement of the clouds overhead, and I imagined the heavens parting, great beams of light, and God in a nightgown, looking the way Michelangelo painted him in the Sistine Chapel, appearing to me dazzlingly bright and speaking in a thunderous voice. There was only silence. Feeling depressed, I turned to walk down from this slight hilltop toward home. I glanced one last time at the sky, toward heaven, and thought I noticed just a tinge of color on one of the clouds. I strained to see it. There was a slight reddish tint. A sign! Or was it from the sun? I flooded with anticipation and terror. The clouds were changing! Something was happening behind those clouds, and I wondered if other people could see it. I looked across the field where two guys were walking along, oblivious to the sky. I looked up again and saw rapidly changing pastel colors, then suddenly, all movement stopped—the world was suspended—and I knew the moment of truth had come! Just then, the colors in the sky became kaleidoscopic and brilliant, and the patterns began to form an image—or so it seemed in my excited, exhausted state. Time stopped, and then I saw it! It was vast, covering an entire quadrant of the sky in clear detail, and it was brilliant, radiant, and sublimely beautiful. In the heavens, crowned with graceful blond curls that were backlit by the light of the sun, framing his head in a golden glow, was the gentle, loving, eternal face of Keith Amadeus. His sky-blue eyes were looking into mine with infinite compassion, and his face actually drew nearer as if to kiss me!

My world shattered, and there was a fleeting impression of blackness. When I regained consciousness, I found myself being carried toward a dormitory by two young men. "Hey, are you all right now?" one asked. "The heat must have gotten to you, buddy. We'll get some medical help for you; just hold on."

It wasn't the heat, I thought, it was the light! I had seen the face of God. I passed out, because my need and my guilt were so overwhelming that I couldn't bear it.

Our gods and demons, our heroes and villains, are the creative projections of our human potentialities. Through them, we learn what we are and what we aspire to be. I understood that the epiphany I had just experienced was created by my own fertile brain, and I began to develop a profound new respect for the being I was beginning to know, the person I am. Dr. Samuels' confidence that I was not homosexual allowed me to end the repression of my feelings about Keith; and, as the countless memories of him cascaded into my consciousness, I ached for him in a way I'd never known was humanly possible. Because it was no longer threatening, I realized that knowing him had been the most significant experience of my life and that to be out of his presence was unending pain. I drew countless pictures of Keith and made a trip home to search for a photograph of him. I found only one small one, part of a class picture, but I carried it with me everywhere.

One day, I went deep into the forest along the Talawanda River to be completely alone with Keith. With a ceremony befitting his status, I placed his picture on the altar of a large fallen tree and spoke to him. I begged him to forgive my betrayal and denial of him. I undressed completely; and, in the light of the sun, lay face down, weeping in the dirt before him in total humili-ation and remorse. Then I sobbed and clawed at the earth longing for him until no more tears came. His last words echoed through my mind with such realism that I thought he was there, "I want you to remember always that I loved you" ...and I realized that he had forgiven me even then with his kiss. He was just a youth of 16 ...or was he? I experienced once more the eternal face of his unlimited compassion, and I knew that he was no longer Keith Amadeus, the person, but he was now a sacred conception. I felt immense sadness for the loss of this beautiful young man, Keith, in my life, but I knew he must die for the god to be born. I knelt, still naked, before his photograph. I took it in my hand and looked deeply into his face. I felt those incredible, startling words forming deep within my soul and consciousness. I had never felt them before about anyone. I said to Keith Amadeus, the person, "I...love...you! I love you, Keith. I love you! And I always will!"

Then, with solemnity, I lit a match and slowly touched it to the corner of my only photograph of Keith and watched the purifying yellow flames lift him beyond time. I ran my hands over my naked body. I was a transformed being, because I knew I had just created a god. Worshipping a god is safer than loving a male.

Chapter Thirteen

My sophomore year at Miami University was a time of significant personal growth. I read voraciously, and my greatest achievement was the recovery of the memories of my two years with Keith Amadeus. But no academic credit is given for becoming a human being; I was flunking out of Miami. I hardly went to my classes, because what was taught was of no use to me. My French class was typical. About 50 of us were taught in a starkly plain room in the oldest building on campus. One could probably still find the brown tobacco juice stains from Miami's founding fathers on the old wooden floor around the missed spittoons from a century and a half before. In this class, I learned to hate French, Frenchmen, French culture, and France. I even avoided traveling in France until much later in my life; a sad mistake. What made this class such a horror was the professor, Mr. Harris, a small, weak, balding, middle-aged man with the charm of a pit bulldog. His principle pedagogic technique was sadism—a sign of his weakness. He required us to rise when he entered the classroom and when he called on us to recite, a sign of our submission and respect for his power to flunk us. Ridicule and scathing sarcasm were his weapons as he attacked the unprepared or the inept. He seemed to delight in the tears of humiliated females, especially the good-looking ones, the ones who skillfully used their fortunate genetics to attract and reward. Males just stared straight ahead or bit their lower lips—as in a military boot camp. Mr. Harris became animated and aroused when he flaunted his little power and dared our defiance. Rumor had it that he had divorced his first wife, because she was sleeping with other faculty members; he was, of course, the last to find out. His second wife, it was said, enjoyed being reamed out by the well-hung members of the football team.

There I sat in his classroom fearing that this stalking sadist would suddenly call on me and break the trance I was usually in. These trances were caused by the blond young man seated in front of me. He was the cultural ideal, the quintessential preppy boy-next-door. He was beautiful, and he basked in the easy grace of the homage others readily paid, including myself. It was his instant value in the eyes of others, their acceptance of him, that I envied. He was eye candy for sure; and, in all of my classes, there were always some of his genetically gifted kind, the paradigms. "Mr. Hinkle, s'il vous plaît! La page suivante de *Candide*—translate, now! Or would you care to share what was going on in that little mind of yours?"

I felt no sexual interest in this student or his kind—that would have required a caring relationship, but I did want to touch him—the way people touch admired statues in museums, or other objects of beauty. It is the ideal that attracts, like a magnet for our souls. Particular people are sometimes incarnations of this invisible world of our gods—as Keith was for me. Without conceptions of the ideal, we are completely lost in darkness. The easiest part of this ideal realm to grasp is physical beauty, but it takes maturity to recognize wisdom. Perhaps that's why our youth culture is oriented toward style and image, rather than learning and substance.

At 19, I was an iron filing being pulled this way and that in the presence of the cultural magnets among my peers. It was also easy to recognize exceptional beauty in women, but I felt no envy as I did toward ideal males. Men wanted to be "real" men, and women were expected to be feminine and facilitate. Women didn't cross-dress then. They were primarily housekeepers, cooks and mothers. Men saw being feminine, effeminate or womanly as utterly unacceptable and highly repugnant for themselves; it was a profound stigma, supported by religious traditions, that is still with us. Because of this rejection of the feminine in themselves, I couldn't understand why college guys bragged about how much they loved women. How could they love in another what they hated in themselves? I decided they were really proclaiming their heterosexuality to other males, an essential requirement for membership in the fraternity of "real" men and to share in their collective power. These men described women primarily in terms of their physical attributes and sexual receptivity, but the personhood and subjective reality of women held little interest for them, because they wished to be completely masculine and untainted by femininity. A common revealing expression of that time was used to describe a man who'd fallen in love with a woman: "he's gone soft on her." Soft is feminine. So is loving.

Every day I was painfully aware that I was different from most guys I knew. Unlike them, I understood the overwhelming experience of loving someone like yourself, someone you desire to be like, an ideal person who loves you in return. I'd had that experience for two years with Keith. On good days I believed I was just more perceptive, intelligent, and fortunate than they; the rest of the time, I suspected I was an anomaly, a mutant, a yet undetected alien life form. I'd never met anyone I could deeply identify with, other than Keith. I feared that someday the authorities would come for me, having found out that I wasn't an acceptable human life form, and isolate me so that I would no longer offend society with my hoax of being human.

For my own survival, I decided I had to understand the psychology of the normal college student. Since I wasn't motivated to go to classes, I had plenty of time to read, travel, and get to know people. When I saw someone who interested me, I introduced myself, said I was studying psychology, and offered to buy them coffee, beer, or whatever, if they would talk with me about themselves. No one refused. I remember one young man of 19 that I particularly admired. His personality reminded me of Keith, and he looked the way I imagined Keith would look at 19. He was the happiest person I interviewed, and I wanted to know why. He was gifted, enthusiastic, loving, and heterosexual, and he was loved by many people. I was astonished by how open and trusting he was, but then, he had little or nothing to hide. His life simply hadn't gone wrong in any of the countless ways it could have, and I envied him completely.

I remember asking him if he was aware of how good-looking he was. He blushed, looked away, and said, "Well, let's just say, between me and you, when I look in a mirror, I'm pleased." He also knew that people were attracted by his happiness. He attributed his good fortune to his family of seven. They were close and loving. He was especially close to his father; and, with a little embarrassment, he admitted that he still kissed his father good-night when he was home. He didn't believe he could ever do anything to make his parents stop loving him, for which he was grateful. I was depressed when I thought about my family. I told him how much I envied him, but this distressed him. He quoted what a pastor friend of his family had said about each person's journey in life being unique, that each person must find his own way and discover what he cares about and what he can do. Envy, he told me, diminishes the unique importance of your own life and gets you off the mark, off your own path.

Later, we talked about women and sex. Pretending it was an afterthought, I asked if he'd ever made it with a guy. "Whoa!" he said, "That'll cost you another coke, buddy!" When it came, he grinned, took a slow swig, and said, "If I did—I'm just saying if I did—I wouldn't tell, because my friend, sex is a private affair." He sensed my interest went beyond the academic and suggested we go to nearby Western College for Women where we could talk with girls he knew. He wanted us to go there "before you start getting carried away—in the wrong direction, Denny!" I protested that I wasn't heading in any direction, especially not that one, as I thought about using my skills to get him into bed. I believed I could do it. He'd almost admitted that he knew the experience, but I also knew, for him, it could only be once. I couldn't stand the pain of loss again, so I did nothing—except resent the casual privilege of the Western College girls as they touched him fondly.

It was late when the two of us ambled back from the Western campus. I felt the warmth of his arm resting on my shoulder as we walked in silence beneath the archway inscribed with large capital letters illuminated by pale moonlight:

YE SHALL KNOW THE TRUTH,
AND THE TRUTH SHALL MAKE YOU FREE.

Those words meant nothing to me at that moment, for I, the alien, was briefly happy in the warm, accepting touch of my ego ideal. The feeling that I was touchable by one of his human status filled me with the hope that I couldn't be as different from him as I believed myself to be, and that perhaps I, too, could one day be as he.

I eventually admitted to myself that it was pointless to continue college. I'd flunked out of Purdue and now, Miami. I simply couldn't concentrate on academics while I bobbed helplessly in a surging sea of emotions beyond my comprehension. It was inevitable that I would be drafted into military service; so, with relief, I volunteered for the draft at the end of the summer. This would give me a two-year moratorium and time enough to find myself, I hoped—although I was afraid of what I might find. The recruiting posters promised that the Army would make a real man out of me. That didn't seem like a bad idea.

I stopped in Richmond to see David before returning to Columbus for the summer. We hadn't gotten together much during the school year, although he occasionally made the trip to Oxford when he was home from Purdue on holidays. I was always in conflict about seeing him because of the sexual tension between us.

I wanted to see Dr. Samuels before going into the Army. So much had happened, and I wanted to know what he thought about the changes in me. When I told him about seeing Keith's face in the sky and speaking to him along the river, Dr. Samuels kept shifting positions in his squeaky chair and seemed uncomfortable and troubled. "Denny, I know all of this means a great deal to you. You seem to know where you're going with all of it. I'm having trouble following you, but just go on. I don't want to slow you down."

I thought he was uncomfortable because I was so emotional about a male. What he couldn't understand was my guilt. He understood why I felt guilty for wanting to love Keith fully, but he couldn't grasp that my greater guilt was for not having loved Keith fully. That was beyond him. I had to suffer guilt no matter what I did. I had been trapped until I realized that Keith had already forgiven me. More importantly, by burning Keith's picture and making him into a god, I was acknowledging the loss of the only love I'd ever known. I wanted to put Keith into the past and end my desire to love the living flesh and blood of a male.

Poor, sweet, old Dr. Samuels. He tried, in his way. He said, "But Denny, you were just a couple of kids messing around with each other, discovering sex together. What's all this love stuff? And gods? And betrayal? So dramatic! I should get out my violin—and handkerchief. Stuff and nonsense! You didn't betray anyone. You just wanted to grow up, that's all. It was a stage, just puppy love. Why, this whatever-his-name-was probably doesn't even remember you. Now, tell me again about that girl in the bleachers, the one with the big breasts. Does your mother have big breasts?" When he degraded my relation with Keith by calling it "puppy love" and pretended he didn't remember Keith's name, I felt hurt and distant. It was as if Dr. Samuels had become like all the others, and I was alone again. For awhile, I thought he said what he did because he was jealous, but that was just a wish.

Dr. Samuels had a serious car accident late that summer and was hospitalized for six weeks. Initially, it wasn't known if he'd survive, and that was a difficult time for me. He was hope, the hope for the normal life.

I worked in a warehouse with other college students that summer. The regular warehouse employees hated us, primarily because we were temporary nonunion help and could read. I sometimes feared I'd wind up like them because of my difficulty with school. I felt sorry for the way the regulars were treated and sorrier still for the way they treated each other. I saw two of them get into a knife fight one hot afternoon. Both were hospitalized, one with his stomach slashed open. They'd been trying to date a girl who worked in the front office. She had encouraged their attention but wasn't seriously interested in dating blue-collar workers.

One of the students I worked with was a fashion model for some local department stores. His picture was in a national magazine. I often ate lunch with him, and he talked about going to Hollywood to be discovered. He knew he would be the next James Dean or Marlon Brando. I asked him why he was so sure he could make it, and he said, "Because I'll do anything to be discovered! If I have to, I'll jump on the casting couch and sleep my way to the top."

I said casting directors were men. "Oh, don't be so naive," he admonished. "And don't pretend you don't know about these things. I know the way you look at me. And you know damned well what can go on between men. I know you'd like that with me, too, so anytime you're ready to show me a good time, we can just slip down one of the aisles behind those big cartons and go to it. But I think you're too chicken." I was, but I thought about him often. When temptations like this would pass, I felt virtuous and believed I was developing as Dr. Samuels had predicted I would. But it did seem to be taking a long time.

Some years later, I saw this same person walking along the streets of Columbus. He was out of work and had lost some of his youthful beauty. He appeared hardened and cynical. When I asked about the West Coast, he looked away bitterly and said only that it hadn't worked out. I still felt tempted, and we both knew what was on our minds, but we each waited for the other to give a sign, so nothing happened, and I grew slightly more in virtue. I felt sorry for him. He had turned himself into an object for the pleasure of others...and, as it always is, lost.

There was another student at the warehouse, 22 and recently married. He had the ideal look of the all-American boy-next-door: wholesome, handsome, and outwardly happy. One day, he was arm wrestling with a couple of guys at break time. One of the guys admired his well-developed chest muscles. He saw me looking at him and insisted I feel his pectorals, too. He was proud of himself. It must have been the way I touched him, because he became serious for a fraction of a second, then he laughed and went on his way. At the afternoon break, he stopped to see me and said he wanted me to go for pizza with him that evening. His wife was in the hospital, and he didn't want to spend the evening alone.

We met in a quiet pizza parlor, drank beer and talked. He'd dropped out of college, too. He told me about the affairs he'd had, even after marriage.

"Those chicks really like this body of mine," he boasted, "especially when they see how much I've got. I'm not the kind that can pass up free, good juicy pussy. Not me!" I wanted to find out why that was so easy for him, especially since his detailed descriptions of sex left me feeling slightly nauseous. What he kept describing were body parts, not people.

I asked why he married, and he said, "She's got a great pair of legs, good thighs, and she's real juicy and tight. I don't like those frigid, dry bitches; they're not worth the time or effort. Well, she really digs my thing, you know. I make her beg for it and all, and she does!" He said she started getting serious about him, but he wasn't interested in that. Then she got pregnant. She was in the hospital that night, ready to deliver. He said he was fairly sure the kid was his, and he guessed he would stay with her for the kid's sake, as long as she did what he wanted and didn't interfere with his life.

I asked why he was sitting around having pizza and beer with me instead of being with his wife who was delivering his child. He told me he didn't want to sit around bored for hours and that her mother, who was "a real bitch's bitch," was there. He thought his mother-in-law had the hots for him, but then, he thought everybody did.

I asked why he had wanted to get together with me, and he said, "Well, you looked like someone I could be buddies with. I can't really get through to women. It takes a man to understand a man, you know? You looked like you liked me today, and I thought we could really talk. I was right!"

I wanted to know why this particular night. "Okay, I won't play games," he answered. "Today, the way you looked at me when you touched me, I knew you liked me, I mean...really liked me. I know you dig the way I look and the way I'm built. I'm proud of it, too. But wait 'til you see the rest of me. I want to show you. Besides, I don't want to be alone tonight. Come stay with me. Sometimes, I've just got to be with my own kind and connect all the way—man to man—know what I mean? A man knows what another man needs. Will you? Please?"

I was shocked by his unselfconscious directness, but curious and in conflict again. Pop went my illusions about him. Coldly, like a self-righteous bitch in heat, I told him I'd seen enough of him, more than I'd wanted to. I admitted that he had a great body, but I told him I wasn't up for committing adultery with a body that had its head missing. I added that he needed people to worship him, because he had a fatal defect—he didn't love people. I was angry at him for tempting me and wanted to create distance. He protested, "But I am a good lover! I'm a damned good gymnast, so I can make those dippy broads scream for more pretty good." He didn't even know what I was talking about, so I told him he was a living dildo with gonads for brains. He just laughed and said he bet I'd never touched a body as fine as his, a truth that only irritated me more. He offered me a deal: he promised to do anything to me that I'd do to him. Scenes of sweaty, gymnastic sex flashed through my mind, but I said nothing. Noticing my hesitation, he offered, "Hey, if you really don't want to do anything, just come over to my place and look at me. I'll do it to myself, and you can watch."

I couldn't believe it. Sitting right there in front of me was a missing evolutionary link, stuffing pizza in his face. Tens of thousands of years of human evolution and culture, and he somehow managed to avoid all of it! I thought this way because I needed more distance. His offer to watch him jack off didn't really seem so morally objectionable, and I was tempted, but I didn't know if I could just watch. It was very important for me to be morally scrupulous, especially given the persistence and intensity of my gross, unnatural, criminal desires. (This is often the case with the morally self-righteous, those irritating little people who are uncomfortable with the vague suspicion that someone somewhere might be happy.)

I became coolly rational and aloof. He became angry and snapped, "Don't try to lay intellectual bullshit on me! All you eggheads are at war with your puny bodies, and I'm not. What you don't want to admit to yourself is a fuck is just a fuck, and you'd like to fuck until you drop, if it weren't for that brain of yours fighting you every damn day. So why try to make it more than it is?

Fuck your brain! You know, one time this cute little prick-teasing cunt came on to me real good, but she just wanted to play games with me. Well, I wanted her, and she said no, so I raped her little ass hard, and you know, it felt good— real good. ...Well, if you're going to pass up this chance I'm giving you, I'll just call up my neighbor's wife. He's gone on a business trip, and she has the hots for me. She's a dog, but I'll do her a big favor tonight. See ya, sport. Maybe that brain of yours will let you play with yourself when you're in bed all alone tonight. Bet you think about me when you do." And I did, damn him. Later, I tried to bolster my wounded self-esteem by wallowing in the passionless sense of my imagined intellectual and moral superiority, but I envied his masculine spontaneous sexuality. I feel sorry for him now and all those who are like him. He was a victim, too, a victim of the hard-core macho ethic—independent, unfeeling, unyielding, and unloving. Those poor souls are some of the loneliest and most oppressed. But I do wonder what he looked like when....

I became more lonely as that summer wore on, especially since I couldn't see Dr. Samuels during his recovery. My mother told me about a woman she'd met whose son, Paul, was my age and was interested in classical music. He'd asked some of his friends over to listen to music and invited me to join the group. I knew no one in Columbus except the guys at work, so I accepted.

Paul's home, with its circular driveway, was impressive, as was the large music room, the Steinway grand piano, and the best high fidelity system I'd ever heard. I was introduced to nine other college guys. They loved classical music. Several were music majors, and one—a pianist—performed. I was completely impressed by his emotionality...and his expressive face. After awhile, I noticed that the guys still seemed somewhat tentative and uncomfortable with me, and I couldn't figure out why until I happened to glance at an ornate wall mirror. Reflected there was the startling view, through a partially opened door into the library, of one of the young men passionately kissing the handsomest one of the group. Paul, suddenly realizing what I was staring at, announced, "Well, guys, I guess the cat is now officially out of the bag! I hope this doesn't offend you, Denny, but that's the way we are. If you want me to show you the way out, I will. Please don't say anything about this to your family." All eyes were on me, and I imagined Dr. Samuels looking distressed. I muttered something about live and let live, but I was shaken. I was attracted to these people, because they were gentle, emotional, aesthetic, intelligent, cultured and they cared about one another. They were the kind of people my father would detest.

They became more friendly. The young pianist and a dark-haired student from Yale infatuated me; I couldn't keep my eyes off them. What unnerved me were their blushes when they noticed the intensity of my gaze. I imagined each guy in the room in bed with the person he happened to be talking with; I knew they probably had been.

Paul sensed that something was going on inside me. "So, this is a new experience for you!" he said. "Your mom didn't know what she was getting you into, did she? My mom isn't aware, either, but I think she sometimes suspects. She doesn't really want to know. People see what they want to see, don't they?"

He asked what it was like for me to be there with them now that I knew. I said it reminded me of a party I had gone to at Miami and that I was feeling nervous. He wanted to know why. I hesitated, then told him how I kept imagining each guy in bed with every other guy. He laughed and said, "Oh, don't I wish it were true! Let me tell you, my dreamer, there are several of these fallen angels I've been working on for years, but they have no mercy in their vain hearts! Ah, but where there's life, there's hope. C'est la vie; c'est la guerre. Some...day...my prince...will come! So tell me, what else makes you nervous about us?" I said I couldn't understand why they were all so relaxed and calm, especially with McCarthy right-wing groups and all that was going on in the country at the time. They seemed to be sticking their heads in the sand, and I wanted to know why the serious risks they were taking didn't seem to matter.

"It does matter," he said. "Do you think we want to be locked up like criminals? Do you think a day passes without our worrying about it? We know all too well that most people believe that anyone who is not heterosexual must be sick, evil and inhuman. No, our heads aren't in the sand. We always watch the horizon for danger, and we're skilled at blending in. Our detractors don't even realize we're sometimes their best friends; almost all of us are invisible, you know. They believe we're all just wrist-flapping nellie queens, but we're not like that, as you can see. Even for us, it's very difficult to spot a kindred spirit. What affectations we do use are just ways of signaling our membership in our secret little society. People see only what they want to see, and they don't want to see us, so they don't. We would never do anything to upset their heterosexual assumption or to offend them in any way."

I asked what would happen if his luck ran out someday—as I was sure it would. "Prison, I guess," he said. "But I've tried it the other way. I deceived myself for years. I still have a girlfriend. Here's her picture. She's beautiful, isn't she? She doesn't suspect a thing. ...I don't know what else to do. Life has to be more than pretending, doesn't it? I didn't choose to be this way; no one ever does, but I don't know how I can be happy if I can't be real. Do you?"

I told him about my hopes for psychotherapy. He asked me to let him know if it worked, and I promised I would, knowing I wouldn't. I thanked him for inviting me and was relieved when I left. I felt sorry for them, because I saw only tragedy in their futures. I knew that our society would crucify them some day. I could hardly wait to tell Dr. Samuels, knowing he'd be proud of my progress.

The next night, I dreamed about the young pianist I'd met. He and I were playing a piano sonata for four hands. We were naked in moonlight. I decided not to say anything about that to Dr. Samuels. Those things made him uncomfortable, and he squeaked his swivel chair.

When I told Dr. Samuels about Paul and his friends, I expected that he would be pleased with my progress, but his chair squeaked more than usual. I watched him and thought maybe he is attracted to me, and that's why the topic bothers him so much. But I decided I was just projecting again. I worried about his disapproval. As he was talking, this crazy fantasy happened inside my head: I saw myself getting up and walking over to Dr. Samuels, who was sitting in his swivel chair. He looked up with an anxious, fearful expression. We looked at one another for a few moments, then I knelt down and slowly unzipped his fly. His looked almost terrified but did nothing to stop me. The fantasy was upsetting, even frightening, but I had trouble suppressing it.

Dr. Samuels sensed the change in my mood, but I denied it. His expression indicated he didn't believe me, but he was a patient man. After I left the session, I worried about myself. I had to be a moral person. It had been easy for me to feel morally superior to the gymnastic sex machine from the warehouse; but, when I thought about Paul and the warmth of his friends, I felt inferior and vaguely guilty, and I was again disturbed by dark thoughts about my betrayal of Keith. It was always the same: attraction and repulsion, thesis and antithesis, my endless conflict with no conceivable resolution.

The rest of the summer was even more depressing for me. I worked, slept, and, in loneliness, read books during my time off, nothing else. I was struck by a line from a Joseph Conrad novel. I didn't understand why, but I memorized it; and, for many years, it would drift in and out of my mind: "Ah, Davidson, woe to the man whose heart has not learned while young to hope, to love—and to put its trust in life!" It would be decades before my intellect could grasp the essential wisdom known then by my heart.

. . .

The tapestry of our lives is woven with unexpected interactions—the patterns of colorful people entering and leaving. A kind old medical doctor and his wife lived next door to us, and they were among the many who touched my life in important ways. This doctor took care of me when I had the flu— well, what I mean to say is that he gave me a series of embarrassing penicillin shots. He liked to tease me about pulling down my pants. With exaggerated care, he would feel my rear cheeks for a good spot, pinch the skin between his thumb and forefingers many times, and give me the injection. As I began to recover from the flu, I got aroused a couple of time when he did this and was scared to death he might notice. I was afraid he might tell my father. This old doctor often came over to talk with me when I was reading in the back yard, but he developed cancer. He took experimental drugs, but nothing worked. He told me he'd seen too many people suffer through the last, painful phases of cancer, and he wasn't going to allow that to happen to him or subject his wife to watching this useless agony. Everyday, I watched the two of them in their back yard lovingly talking, hand in hand, admiring the last roses he would ever know. One day, his wife came over to tell me he'd chosen the time, and he was gone. She said he enjoyed his many talks with me, and he wanted her to give me a gift he'd chosen. She took me back to his study, where he had neatly packed his literature books in boxes for me. With the calmness that came from her acceptance of reality, she comforted me like a mother as I wept in her arms. While weeping, I became aware of the pain of my own father's indifference to me.

I told her what her husband had said to me the last time we talked: "My young friend, you and I have enjoyed many fine talks about literature, philosophy, and life. We haven't quite solved the world's problems, but I want to thank you for being so kind to an old man in his last summer. My life has been very good, and I'm more than grateful for that. Yours will be, too, my young friend. Never doubt that. Never! It's not easy at your age, but life is better the older you grow. I mean that. Now, I want to tell you a story that has meant a great deal to me in my life. I often remember it. I think it can be especially helpful to you in yours. Charles Lamb, the English essayist and critic, was walking with a friend in London one afternoon. He suddenly turned to his friend and said, 'See that man across the street there? I hate him!' His astonished friend exclaimed, 'But Charles, you're such a kind person! You could never hate anyone. Why do you hate him?' Charles Lamb replied, smiling, 'Because I don't know him!' You think about that, Denny."

As I told her this story, she had a fond look of remembrance. I asked her what he was getting at by telling me this story. She laughed and said he'd known that I would ask her, and he'd made her promise to say nothing. He said I would understand when the time was right. This caused me to think about his story for many years. He was a gifted healer; I know now that he was giving me the key to compassion.

My life wasn't going well that summer. The monotony of the warehouse was soul numbing, but I had to have the money. I had no close friends, no transportation, I'd flunked out of two universities, and I was afraid I might end up like the workers at the warehouse. Even reading began to bore me, because it was a lonely monologue; and, without dialogue, our humanity is lost. The only thing in my future was a two-year hitch in the Army. David was too far away, and I didn't really want to start that again, not with the progress I'd been making in therapy. Dr. Samuels was taking longer to recover than expected. I believed I was becoming the failure my father had predicted I would be.

From that summer when I turned 20, I'll always remember one awful, magnificent weekend. What I experienced then gave me insight into the heart of my existence and that of humanity.

I was sitting alone in my bedroom struggling with the anguish of my worthlessness, loneliness and boredom. I couldn't stand doing nothing, yet there was nothing I could imagine doing, and I couldn't stand that, either. I knew I was already mired in a great depression, but I believed that if I waited long enough, it would pass, but the depression became more massive than any I'd ever known. I waited for the battle. After my close call in high school, suicide was out of the question. I knew I would suffer anything, and I would win, no matter how long it took. Like the biblical Job, I would survive. This cyclone of depression was dramatic; I even welcomed it.

Hour after long hour, I slipped steadily down into blackness, but always retaining a modicum of faith and free thought. I never imagined depression could have such vastness and power. I kept waiting for the bottom, the sure sign for the upward journey to begin. Sometime long after midnight, I found myself on a psychological plateau, inching toward the edge. I believed if I didn't do something to stop myself from slipping over this unknown edge, I would never survive. I forced myself to get up from the easy chair in which I was dying. I whispered, "Please, God, let there be someone; I'm dying!" I managed to open my bedroom door and stumbled hesitantly toward my parents' bedroom. When I entered, I was groaning. My startled father snapped on the lamp on the table separating their twin beds. All I could do was stand there, holding my arms out to him. It was a pathetic scene.

"What's wrong with you?" he demanded. "It's 2:00 in the morning, for God's sake! Don't just stand there moaning and holding your arms out like an idiot! You didn't knock before you came into our bedroom. Why aren't you dressed for bed? What do you want at this time of night?" He was annoyed, but I couldn't make the words come. I just kept reaching out to him, silently begging. "Donna! Take care of the boy!" he growled and rolled over to go back to sleep.

My frightened mother asked, "Denny, did you have a bad dream? Your eyes look so wild!" I turned slowly toward her and could only stand there, mute, holding my arms out to her. I thought, oh, my God, can't you see, can't either of you see, can't you understand? Hold me! ...Hold me! ...Just touch me! I'm going to die! But I could see fear in her eyes as she pulled her blankets further up around her. "Denny, it will all be better in the morning. It was just a bad dream. Now go back to bed and sleep well."

Dazed and rejected, I stumbled to my bedroom and slumped down in resignation into my overstuffed chair, which seemed like an electric chair. No longer resisting annihilation, I closed my eyes and quickly slipped over the edge of the abyss. This realm of depression is beyond all action, all hope, and all caring; in it, one is selfless. There is only nothing.

I waited for any change, but there was none; hour after hour, nothing. Then, just before dawn, I thought I detected the slightest change in the uniform blackness, but it was an illusion. Then again, an imagined change, so very faint, but again, nothing. Slowly, almost imperceptibly, I saw the faintest, smallest dot, not quite so black. I waited and waited. Then it became slightly brighter. It was the tiniest dot of white. Oh God! A change! Something! A sign! Is this death? Is this the end? Will my last experience be...a dot? It just stayed there, remote from me, suspended in nothingness, just waiting. If I dared to hope, I believed it would disappear. I wanted to go closer, but I couldn't, and I couldn't make it come closer to me. I was helpless. I resolved to wait for it...forever, if I had to. At least something was happening! I waited, and so did it. Then I pleaded with it, "I accept you, whatever you mean! I want to know! Please!"

It moved closer and became a white disk about the size of a pencil eraser, and lines seemed to be moving within it. "I accept you! Please let me know! Please, let it be now!" I pleaded out loud. Everything about it stopped; nothing moved. Then it rushed full speed toward me, growing brighter and larger, as if coming from a great distance. And then it was all encompassing and blinding, overwhelming the blackness everywhere! There, looking into my eyes, was the gentle face of Keith, flooding me with the certain knowledge that I had been loved beyond all time. I was overwhelmed with love and uttered his name as his lover. Then very slowly, I returned to the world of time, reborn.

This was a pivotal revelation. It changed forever my fundamental status in society. Never again would it be possible for me to doubt my reality as a sacred human being. I remember looking at my hands, these same hands that had so often touched him, and they seemed miraculously transformed, for they were now of the same flesh as his own. Keith and I were at last of the same body and being, inseparable. He is of me, and I am of him, for we are brothers, born of the same conception—born by love. And so it shall be forever, I vowed.

I drove my father's car out to a hill to wait for the rising of the sun that magnificent dawn, and when the sun's disk revealed itself to me, like a young, enthralled priest of ancient Egypt, I raised my arms to it and worshipped its new gift of warmth and light, for I was alive in a new universe!

I do not know if, in the darkness of that black night of my soul, my fertile brain created this startling sacred icon of Keith to save me from despair, or if it merely remembered and reminded me of his reality and therefore of mine. And I do not know if Keith was simply a person who loved greatly, or if he was in fact an incarnation of a reality beyond appearances. And I wonder if such a realm exists merely in my conceptions or if I intuit it. And so, I remain suspended, where I want to be, between my head and my heart, between truth and faith, between fact and metaphor, between what I can believe and what I wish to believe. Is this not the very creative tension of life itself, this conflict of reality with desire? What this experience teaches me about myself is that it is my nature to seek meaning and to construct my views of reality in ways that increase the meaning and significance of my life's drama. We are the symbolizing, dramatizing animal. A life without symbolic significance is not a human life, although it may be the life of a member of our biological species. If this world of appearances cannot be construed in sufficiently meaningful ways, we invent invisible worlds to add richness and fulfillment to our comic cosmic tragedy. Our symbols draw together the vital structures of significance in our lives; and, through them, we can learn what we are. The opposite of the symbolic is the diabolic—that which disintegrates and thus makes meaningless. Keith, the icon of Vishnu, Buddha, and Christ, became at the dawn of that summer's day, the central integrative symbol of my existence. I was a man sinking knee deep into certain death while worshipping his god. Is this not the description of our human condition? What I recognized and made real that day was that Keith and I were incarnations of a far more significant reality. I created greater meaning for my life by recognizing that his essence was also in me. We were part of the same greater whole—the conception of love.

Our descriptions of reality are always given for our own human purposes; descriptions describe the describer as well. So, what then is the knower, and what is the known? Are they not one, part of a whole? Is not the known part of the knower? Is not the knower part of the known? And what, then, is Keith? And what am I?

Chapter Fourteen

The day after that extraordinary night while I was asleep, my parents called Dr. Samuels out of fear for my sanity. He arranged to see all of us that day, even though he hadn't planned to return to work until the following week. I was glad to see him again, but when I tried to explain my experiences of the previous night, I couldn't adequately communicate what had happened.

What I experienced in that state of depression was not pain but indifference. In this state, nothing is wanted nor not wanted—there is no motivation, no animating spirit or soul, no god within, no enthusiasm, no inspiration. Lacking motivation, there is no action; and since I am what I do, there is no sense of self. Our lives as persons begin with desire—preferring, wanting, valuing, caring and loving. Without a conception of what is of worth, I cannot behave as a person, as a human being. Catholics are taught that hell is the state in which one is out of the presence of God, the conception of ultimate worth. In suffering, agony and hatred, there is still valuing. Beyond this is the indifference of apathy, the inner circle of hell in which we are no longer able to desire. What I experienced that night was this living death, the indifference born of my helplessness. I was saved from this death by the conception of what I had experienced to be of ultimate value in my life, of one whom I loved who loved me.

Sadly, it is often only absence that enables us to know the value of what is present, as in the grief of one who suddenly goes blind or the death of a loved one. After I experienced this depth of nothingness, reality became endlessly rich for me, and I was flooded with gratitude for its contrast with the void. I realized that the shimmering luminescence of Keith's face was generated by his skull. Great wisdom can be gained from the vantage point of a corpse.

Dr. Samuels frowned when I talked about Keith's face again. "There's that boy again!" he said. "Denny, not only are you fixated at the homoerotic level, but now you present me with a full-blown case of object loss identification. You pretend Keith's flesh is your flesh, because you miss him. I'm very disappointed with you. Why must you always try to swim upstream? Why make life so difficult for yourself?"

"That's what my father always says to me. He says I like to do things the hard way," I rebuked.

"Denny, you know I'm not your father. I've told you that. I'm not like him at all. All authority figures are not like your father! Denny, I *do* care about you. You know the seriousness of the issues we're working on. I don't want you to wind up in a goddamned federal penitentiary! I guess it's just a case of two steps forward and one step back. You've been making steady progress, but remember, the Army is not going to treat you with kid gloves.

It's the big leagues there; if you slip back even once, you'll be kicked out of the game for good. But I'm sure you'll continue to make progress. This reminds me of something I want to talk to you about. I saw both of your parents today for several hours. We talked candidly, and I reassured them that people in your phase of psychotherapy sometimes do things that seem strange to others, but this is to be expected. I told them you've made excellent progress and will continue to; they shouldn't worry about you. But there is one thing. Based on the report from Purdue, what you've told me about them, and my own observations of them, I want to tell you quite frankly that you would be well advised not to return home after you leave the Army. Build a life of your own, Denny! Neither of your parents can give you what you need. They want to love you, but they aren't able to be loving people—even to one another. I warn you, Denny, if you continue to involve them in your life, they will harm you. I'm serious about this, completely serious. It's not because of you, but they have problems they'll never face. It's tragic, and I fear for your kid sister. Look out for her, she'll need you someday. We don't get to pick our parents, but we can choose not to be harmed by them."

"You mean I shouldn't even write to them or see them when I'm on leave?" I asked, knowing that he was right but clinging to what little hope I had for at least their acceptance. I knew that their love was out of the question.

"There's no harm in a birthday card or an occasional letter, but make the visits short. Spend time with your new friends instead. Part of growing up is learning to be emotionally independent from your parents. They can't give you what you need, Denny. They can't even give each other that."

I was surprised that he understood them so quickly. What he said was sadly true. "When you talked with them today, did they say something to make you feel so negative about them?"

"Yes, they did," he said, "but because of confidentiality, I can't discuss that with you. And don't try to ask them, because they won't be honest with you. Let me just say, you would be very wise to follow my advice. If you don't, you will be harmed. I'm sure you'll do what you want to do, and that's as it should be, but remember what I'm telling you now! ...I see our hour is almost up. I know you'll make the best of your military experience. I have great faith in you, Denny. You know, women really get turned on by guys in uniforms. It's true! You'll find out. Write me from time to time. Someday, I hope you'll remember to send me a picture of your wife and kids. Okay? ...You know, Denny, in all the time you've been seeing me, you've never once expressed how you felt about me. Today was the first time you saw me after my automobile accident; I saw tears in your eyes when you saw the sad shape I'm in, but not a word from you. Very interesting! Well, that's an issue for another time, isn't it?" I was leaving for the Army in a few days; we both knew this would be our last meeting.

"I know. Those things are hard for me. ...You didn't tell me how you felt about me, either," I said, feeling even sadder. I knew he was wanting some expression of caring from me, but I withdrew to protect myself from the loss of him. If I learn not to need the warmth, then the cold wouldn't hurt, I believed. I hadn't planned on frostbite.

"So! The student is teaching the master again, is he? Well, that's something for both of us at another time, I hope," he said with a sad and somewhat hurt look. "Good luck, my young friend. Remember, women are easy, and keep those uniforms pressed!"

I never did express my feelings to Dr. Samuels; men then weren't supposed to feel such sentimental slop about other men, even if they did. Anyway, I never saw him again, but he helped me create a bold new pattern in the fabric of my life. His warning about my parents eventually proved to be true, as were his fears for my sister. His psychotherapy with me was entirely appropriate given the oppression and intolerance of our society in the '50s; it would have been unethical and illegal for him to encourage me to become a criminal. He and I were pawns in society's control game. Liberty and justice is not yet for all.

My parents drove me down to the dingy Greyhound bus station in Columbus on the morning I was to be inducted into military service. We arrived early and made painful small talk as we waited for the moment of departure. None of us looked forward to the conflicted emotions of that moment. My mom and I talked, and my father paced the platform, jingling his pocket change. The great bus pulled in, disgorged the passengers from its innards and waited with motor running to ingest a fresh set of bodies. The wanted and feared moment came. My mother hugged me and cried while my father paced behind us, avoiding eye contact with me and biting his lower lip. Just as I started to board, he turned to me, his face contorted as tears formed in the corners of his eyes. He hit me forcefully on the arm with his fist and said, "Don't get in trouble!" He quickly turned and raced away to hide his emotions. As I entered the belly of the bus, I thought, my father can only care about me when I'm gone, but at least he cared! My arm was still sore from his male love tap. I couldn't remember the last time he'd touched me. I felt sorry for him, because I realized that his loneliness was far greater than my own. Men like him live only by fear and rules and never listen to the songs of their souls.

It was dark when our group of frightened inductees entered the gates of Ft. Leonard Wood in the back country of Missouri. Such arrivals are at night to heighten the dramatic impact of our initiation into the eight-week ritual called basic training. These rites of passage were carefully designed to transform peaceful civilians into obedient, willing killers. We were stripped of all remnants of our former life. We stood naked and shivering for hours before our superiors, who viewed us with disgust. The hair was ritually shaved from our heads as we were made uniform. To function as an individual in the military was regarded as a form of treason. It was an offense against God, country, and military honor.

The concepts of honor and manhood were skillfully linked by our trainers. It was this linkage that gave them the power to transform us. We were being trained to be efficient murderers, but this was described as defending the honor of our country and protecting our sisters and mothers from certain gang rape by inhuman foreigners. The tragic truth of our rifles, bayonets, hand grenades, land mines, mortars, bazookas, machine guns and the other tools of death was washed clean by the holy water of honor and masculinity. If honor were taken away, the soldiers of this planet could not live with the guilt of their collective murder.

A gray-haired bird colonel lectured about the long history of our regiment. He told us of men who had sacrificed their lives for buddies and country. He told of the terrors of the stockade and of the iron-fisted Uniform Code of Military Justice "that now owns your very asses, troopers! Do...you ...hear...that?!"

"Sir! Yes, sir!" we shouted in unison.

He recited the penalties for various acts of treason and disobedience and read a long litany of thou-shalt-nots. And then he said, "And one last thing, men. I hate to insult you by mentioning such a thing, but it is my duty as an officer. You're young, and the sap of springtime is rising in your veins, and you're confined together with few women around. You'll form many close friendship in these next two years, and some of your buddies will be your friends for life. You'll be closer to them than your wives, because we men have a bond that no woman can enter. Mark my words, you will all miss the comradeship you'll have in the service; it will never be so good for you again. You'll always remember it and long for it. But, sometimes, because you're confined, some of you might be tempted to do things with your buddy, things that would cause both of you to lose your masculinity forever! If you do, you'll never be able to get married and have children. It just takes one time! Just once—and you will have no manhood left. When you're caught, you'll be sent to the stockade, stripped of your rank, and dishonorably discharged. A dishonorable discharge means you'll never be hired for a decent job by anyone. You'll be avoided by all honorable people for the rest of your miserable life. Now, if you find out about such criminal activities, even if it's your buddy, it is your duty as a soldier of honor to immediately report it to your superiors. In combat, our very lives depend on our buddies, and we don't want our buddy to be a pervert fairy queer...do...we?!"

"Sir! No, sir!" they shouted and looked around at their buddies, laughing and teasing.

Because of our extreme loneliness and the conflict caused by our growing need for one another, most of this great cross section of young American males began to imitate a crude macho style to distance themselves from their need for tenderness and intimacy. We were the lowest class in the military caste system, and we mimicked the postures of macho power to mask the fact of our complete impotence: "Hey, man! You see that mother-fuckin' little squad leader order me around today? Man, he so much as looks at me, and, man, I'll knock his goddamn teeth right down to his fuckin' asshole, I will! Shit, man, I'll hit him so hard he'll never wake up! Ain't nobody goin' to mess with me, man! Nobody!"—this from the mouth of a skinny young man, a recent graduate in English literature from an Ivy League college.

The kid in the bunk next to mine was from the hills of rural Tennessee. Everyday, he carefully spit-polished his new boots, even though they had a mirror finish. When I told him he wasn't required to polish his boots every single day, he said, "I know, but I ain't never had such a fine pair of shoes or such good clothes." When he looked at himself in a full-length mirror in his dress uniform, his face filled with the wonder of new pride and honor; he was no longer a poor hick from the sticks—he was a soldier in the Army of the United States of America. And his country needed him. He showed me a color photograph of himself in his uniform that he was wrapping to send to his mother. I reassured him that it was a very nice picture, and he took out a wallet-sized copy and gave it to me. I didn't want it, but I thanked him, and he seemed pleased to have done something for me. "I hear tell you been to a college," he said. "I never met a person who'd been to a college before. You don't look much different to me."

There was a guy in our barracks, Billy, who seemed to me to be mentally retarded. One day near the barracks, I saw a ring of about 30 men laughing and tossing an envelope among them and chanting, "Billy fucks his mother! Billy fucks his mother!" Billy was crawling on the ground in the center of the circle, looking wild-eyed and crying in rage as he tried in vain to recover the precious letter from his mother that they had taken from him. Occasionally, one of his tormentors would read a line or two from the letter in a mocking, suggestive style, and Billy would convulse in helpless anger and beg them to stop. This only whetted their appetite for more of his humiliation and suffering. I looked at the faces of these men; some were handsome, and one reminded me of a photograph I'd seen of a smirking, good-looking young Nazi soldier holding a rifle to the bowed head of an old rabbi in the Warsaw ghetto. I grabbed the letter from one of the men and yelled at them in a rage to leave the area, or I'd report every one of them. For some reason, they thought I had authority, so they left immediately.

I stayed with Billy until he stopped crying; then I walked him back to his barracks, where he just sat on his bunk clutching his mother's letter to his chest. With embarrassment, he finally handed me the letter and asked me to read it to him, because he couldn't read handwriting. It was a short letter, crudely written, and he asked me to read it many times as he memorized it word for word. Each time I did, his face had a look of wonder at the amazing grace of the love of his mother. The letter ended, "Billy, I pray to God every night for I go to sleep for him to keep you and let no bad come to you. I miss you so. I think about you most all the time. Your dog is fine. The chickens and the ducks is fine. We all miss you and want you to be all well. Come home to us soon as you can. Love, Mother."

I went to the sergeant major and reported what had happened and told him that Billy was mentally retarded and shouldn't be in the service. The sergeant major just frowned and waved me away; but, several weeks later, Billy came to me all excited and showed me papers for his immediate discharge. He asked if I would help him telephone his mom; he didn't know how. I'll never forget Billy's face as he told his beloved mother, the only person on earth who loved him, that he would soon be coming home. "And Mom, tell my dog, Patch, too—will ya?"

. . .

Bayonet practice was held on a large graveled area. At one end of the field were rows of stuffed dummies waiting helplessly to be slashed apart by us. We lined up two-by-two in long rows facing each other to practice the mutilating movements. As we executed each movement, we had to shout, "Kill!" as if we meant it. If we weren't convincing enough, we'd be pulled out of line and made to scream, "Kill!" into the face of each soldier in our long row, who would have to scream it in return.

As I stood there looking at the healthy faces of several hundred of my countrymen, at least half of them seemed excited, even enthusiastic, about this training; and it made me sick. Their excitement wasn't about competence in defense, but rather, the exhilaration of power, primal aggression, and the illusion of invulnerability. About a quarter of the men were probably feeling as I was, and the rest couldn't be read because of the way they masked their emotions.

I thought about young soldiers in other countries practicing on their bayonet fields for the honor of their invisible abstractions, and I realized why we have wars. I looked at the youth standing opposite me and wondered, if he were an enemy, could I plunge my long bayonet with its blood grooves deep into the side of his abdomen, slash across it, and pull his intestines out in one movement as we were being trained to do? I realized that I could kill only in a clear situation of self-defense, and nothing else. That was the way I was, and that was the way I wanted to be. I looked at the hundreds of vital young men yelling, "Kill!" in unison; and I thought of all the soldiers in every country lost in the grand illusion of us and them, and I realized the tragedy of our human natures. We are the most vicious of the animals on the planet, kings of the food chain. We even kill for the mere excitement of the hunt. We are the only species that is its own worst enemy, yet we love one another, sometimes enough to die for that love.

One day, I was watching a company of soldiers resting after calisthenics. One young man caught my attention, Kevin Rogers. I watched him for some time. There was something quite different about him, something ideal, but something I couldn't name. Later, I went to Kevin's company area and asked about him. I eventually found him sitting far from the others under a tree. He was obviously deep in thought, yet when he became aware of my presence, he just looked up peacefully and smiled. I introduced myself, and he continued to smile as he said, "I remember you. You were watching me." We talked for awhile. I explained that I had noticed something about him that made him stand out from others; I wanted to find out what it was.

"You're perceptive!" he said. "I'm glad it shows. I know exactly what you see in me. What you see is a kind of radiance in my face, a happiness, don't you?"

"Yes! Exactly! What is it?"

"I'll explain only if you'll agree to hear me out and not make snap judgments. Okay?"

"Sure, Kevin. I've got all evening. Fire away!"

He told me about his upbringing in an emotionally cold family and his attempts to find happiness through sports, fast cars and women; and of his growing emptiness. Something was always missing in his life. He went to Europe and hitchhiked around by himself, searching, always searching; but thoughts of suicide were frequent. What he said was something like this: "You know, Denny, I always thought religion was just prescientific, superstitious nonsense. I was proud to be an atheist, because at least I could still think. So there I was, the 20-year-old suicidal atheist going to see that masterpiece of Gothic architecture, the Chartres Cathedral. Well, it overwhelmed even my cynicism, Denny! And on that day I grasped the importance and complexity of the living concept of God. You see, what makes me different, what you see in my face, is the unfolding spirit of the conception of God within me. I'm a convert to Catholicism, and I now appreciate the spiritual realm. I never knew I could be so happy and filled with love. Don't get me wrong, I'm not one of the Pope's trained sheep. Maybe I should just say I'm a student of Catholicism. I don't know if God exists, or if Christ was really born of a virgin and was resurrected, or if partaking of the flesh and blood of God at Mass is symbolic, literal or cannibalistic. None of that has any real importance for me. It wouldn't matter if it's all a myth. Sometimes I believe it is, but it doesn't matter, because doubt makes faith meaningful. But what matters is the conception—the spirit. That does exist. I don't care about the god games and Bible babble of churches competing for power and money. They're scams. What my life is about is the growing understanding and experiencing of the conception of God. Everything is symbolic, like a clue; everything speaks if you listen with an open heart. God is an idea. In the beginning was the word, then there was God! Did you know that the words 'enthusiasm' and 'inspiration' come from the roots meaning 'the god within' and 'the spirit within'? Interesting, isn't it? I hope you see I'm not just another religious nut. So what do you think, Denny? Tell me about yourself."

I was moved by Kevin's spirituality. I wished I could make his leap into faith, but I was more comfortable with the evidence of my senses; besides, my idea of God was linked with punishment and fear—and my father. Kevin and I got together often after that. We were like brothers. I trusted him completely. I thought of him as an incarnation of St. Francis; it made drinking beer with him more interesting. I told him about my family, Keith, my sexual problem, and psychotherapy. He asked many questions about Keith and said he and a close friend had a relationship like that once. "I'm glad Dan and I had the chance to express our feelings. He and I are more comfortable with women—he's married, and you know I'm engaged to be, but neither of us will ever forget. I'll always be grateful for his love of me. It was a holy thing, Denny, and I think it was that way with you and Keith, too. God, you see, hides right out in the open."

Toward the end of basic training, Kevin and I and several others were concerned about our advanced training placements. We learned that the assignments would be made at post headquarters by some enlisted person, a clerk. We found out who he was and offered to take him to dinner. He was quite likable, and we got along well. It was his job, he said, to pick out "the killers" and the "cannon fodder" for the infantry assignments and to give the better jobs to the ones with brains or political influence. The ones with political pull had their folders specially marked, he said. He told us what kind of placements were coming up for our companies and indicated that for 30 dollars apiece he'd see to it that we got what we wanted. (Bribery was commonly practiced in the military.) One of the guys in our group tried to rationalize the ethics of this by saying it was just another example of the natural law of survival of the fittest. We offered the clerk 20, and he took it, as a special favor to us, he said. Kevin and I wanted the medical corps, because we could save lives rather than take them.

The assignment clerk was true to his word. I got my orders to report to Ft. Sam Houston in San Antonio, Texas, for medical corpsman training. Kevin was to go there, too; but, because of his record performance in calisthenics, an officer intervened and had the orders changed for assignment to the infantry, where his physical prowess would be of more use. Kevin was despondent. He was eventually sent to a bleak outpost in Korea, and I never heard from him again.

One day, our company was ordered to line up at the supply office window. A blank statement of charges was presented to each trooper with orders to sign it. This meant he would be authorizing unspecified amounts of money to be taken out of his monthly pay allotment. This was theft, and some of us refused to sign and warned the others. We were immediately herded into a room and harassed, threatened and humiliated for hours. Many gave in to escape the promised punishments, including cleaning the infamous grease pit of the mess hall. We had all been forced to witness some poor naked soul who was ordered to climb down into that pit of unspeakable slime and spend hours in its stench cleaning it with his bare hands.

Something clicked inside me, the sense of who I was, and I knew I'd never give in to them no matter what they did to me. I prepared myself to accept whatever these mutants had in store for me. In exasperation, two of them pinned me to the concrete floor as a third began to burn my hand against a potbellied stove. A second lieutenant, who was sitting quietly in the background, ordered them to stop, came over, and tried to sweet-talk me into signing. When I refused, he said I'd just signed my own death warrant, because he was going to send me to the captain to be court-martialed for repeated, witnessed instances of insubordination.

The lieutenant and two sergeants escorted me to the captain's office, where I was made to wait at attention for 30 minutes. When I was finally motioned into the captain's office, he asserted his authority by continuing to read some papers for ten more minutes.

When he did acknowledge my presence, he barked, "We'll make this short and sweet, private. Sign this goddamn paper right now, or I'll make you wish you'd never been born! Sign it, or I'll court-martial you." I had been in this same drama too many times before, with my father.

"Sir. I won't, and you know why. You wouldn't dare bring charges against me, not with my witnesses."

"Look, you slime ball," he said, "just remember this: I have to certify that you successfully completed basic training. If I don't sign, you'll stay here and keep repeating this crap until your discharge date. I'll make it so hard on you, you won't survive one more cycle of this. Now sign the goddamn thing! Just do yourself a favor and sign it."

All the time I was being harassed, I'd been making plans. "Sir," I said, "you have a good point. May I have your permission to think about this for a few minutes? I'll probably want to change my mind. I need just a little time."

"Now you're acting like a college boy, son. Sure. Think it over, and report back here in 30 minutes. Dismissed." That's where he made his mistake.

I rushed back to the barracks and told my buddies my plans and what they should do if I got into trouble. I slipped away from the company area without permission—a court-martial offense—hitched a ride to Post Headquarters and demanded to see the bird colonel in charge of the Inspector General's Office, the watch dogs of the military.

When I was allowed to see the white-haired colonel, I explained all that was happening, but he just sat there looking tired and glared at me. When I finished, he asked, "Private, who gave you permission to leave your company area?"

I told him, "No one, sir. They wouldn't have given me permission to go to the IG's office."

He leaned forward and frowned. "Private, do you realize you just committed a court-martial offense? If this were war time, I could have you shot! I think you're headed for a visit to the stockade, young man. Now, what's your company commander's name?"

"Captain Rodebaugh, sir."

"Captain James Rodebaugh of the 235th? You mean him?"

"Yes, sir. That's him."

"Well, I'll be goddamned! I've been trying to get something on that son-of-a-bitch for five years now! I never did trust him. Will your buddies swear to what you've told me?"

"Yes sir! In writing, sir."

"Good! I'll finally have that bastard's balls, I will! Now, return to your company area immediately. I'll call over there giving you my full protection. If anyone so much as looks cross-eyed at you, I want you to contact me immediately. Got that? ...Oh, yes, you were damned lucky, private. If your captain was one of my friends, you'd be on your way to a gang rape in the stockade right now."

Much later in my tour of duty, I met someone who knew the fate of Captain Rodebaugh. He'd been convicted of a variety of charges and was serving time in prison. I felt sorry for him and was somewhat uneasy about the part I'd played in his downfall.

In our last days at Ft. Leonard Wood, we participated in a full regimental march, complete with jeeps, trucks, tanks and helicopters. It was awe-inspiring to be part of a great moving column of companies that stretched from hilltop to hilltop—a vast living organism of macho power and death. The exhilaration of this collective power was as palpable among us as the steady cadence of military drums. Our personal power and sense of community were vastly magnified by identifying with this moving organism, and I understood the emotional sense in which war has a deep, primitive, territorial appeal. It was the ultimate football game of life, or so it often seems to invincible youth and old generals.

On the reviewing stand, in a special place of honor, was the only soldier on the base to wear the Congressional Medal of Honor, the nation's highest military award. All officers and enlisted men were required to salute him. When I first saw him, I was shocked; the memory still overwhelms me with sorrow. He was an old sergeant, standing at attention on the reviewing stand, but looking bent and weary. His eyes were expressionless, as if he were not even there, as columns of healthy young men marched past with their heads turned sharply right to see him. Chunks of his expressionless face were missing—blown away by shrapnel, so I was told.

A couple of enterprising sergeants took orders for bottles of booze that they would smuggle onto the base for our celebration of the end of our basic training. We were no longer individuals, but real soldiers, GIs ready for a blow out. A group of us college guys went to the post canteen for the evening, knowing that most of the troopers had little experience with alcohol, and we knew what would happen. We returned to the company area about 11. It was strangely lit, with patches of light here and there between odd, shadowy shapes. Bodies of drunken troopers were strewn randomly about the graveled grounds. I checked them to see if they were breathing. A couple of guys were hauling these bodies into the barracks to prevent them from freezing. As we got to the door of our barracks, I saw a quite drunk, pink-cheeked, boyish-looking 18 year old chug-a-lugging a bottle of beer. He complained of the taste and how warm it was, but he was reassured that it was just a different brand by some laughing GIs who were busy filling up another beer bottle for him with their urine.

I went inside and saw partially clad bodies strewn across steel bunks. The barracks reeked with the acrid odor of vomit. One poor soul raised himself up, leaned over the side of his top bunk and puked into the sleeping face of his buddy below. Two guys in their shorts were passed out in the middle of the center aisle with their arms wrapped affectionately around one another. Moans and groans of suffering echoed from the large toilet area, where a row of naked young men were on their knees, paying homage to Dionysus, god of drink and revelry, at porcelain commodes. The large hissing shower room was a scene worthy of Dante's Inferno. There at its huge gaping mouth, two tired sergeants labored to fill its belly by undressing half awake GIs and sliding their vomit-covered bodies across the slippery layers of puking, naked manhood wriggling beneath its shower sprays. It was for me a moral allegory—a celebration of the greatest perversity of mankind: the destruction of the individual.

I had several weeks of leave before reporting to Ft. Sam Houston for medical training. I was going to vacation in Florida with my family, but I stopped at Richmond to see David on my way home. His family was impressed by my military metamorphosis and touched my uniform with respectful curiosity. The way David's mother, Ruth, carried on, you would have thought I was going into combat the next day to die for my country. I described the drama of basic training with spine-chilling details, especially the moral melodrama of Captain Rodebaugh and his henchmen. What most moved them was my description of crawling under barbed wire with live machine guns firing just above our heads. Ahead of me, a youth from my platoon had panicked, stood up, and was cut in half. Ruth cried for him and his family.

David was fascinated, in a horrified way, with my adventures. He said my uniform made me seem almost like a different person. The way I looked excited him. It was clear what he wanted, but I hesitated. David wasn't pleased with my enthusiastic description of Kevin, but I understood that, too. On my last night in Richmond, David and I were sad with the certain knowledge that we would be apart for several years, if not forever, but we didn't want to talk about that. Our conversation was interrupted with silences as we simply looked at each other. I knew this might be the last time I'd ever see David, but I kept thinking about Dr. Samuels. Eventually, I came to my senses and went over to David. We searched each other's eyes, then I told him to come with me. He smiled, excitement blazed in his eyes as he followed me. Neither of us spoke as I drove to a motel outside town and took a room. We didn't speak as we showered together, aroused, in preparation. He knew I'd make love with him as I never had before. Nothing would be held back, not this time. We had no need for words, because our eyes and bodies communicated it more accurately. In a last gesture before contact, I removed my stainless steel dog tags. Then, for the first time, David spoke: "Leave them on." I never knew I could want and be wanted by another as much as I did that night. We didn't sleep until the birds of morning sang.

Chapter Fifteen

My plane from Miami, Florida to San Antonio made stops in New Orleans and Houston. In New Orleans, waiting to board the flight to Houston, was a woman about my age wearing a skintight black dress. She fascinated me. I talked with her, and discovered she'd moved to Glendale shortly after I'd moved away to Richmond. She knew most of the people I knew there. She said Allan Walpole reached puberty at 16, grew quite tall, and became a star basketball player. Ronnie Ryan became the big wheel he'd always wanted to be, class president, and was at the University of Missouri preparing to go into law, politics or insurance—she wasn't certain which. He was in a fraternity and was engaged to a sorority girl. I asked about Bill Thomas. "Bill Thomas? Oh, I had a real crush on him, Denny. He's so cute! He wasn't much interested in dating, though; he was always studying. He was our valedictorian, and I heard he wanted to be a priest. Such a waste."

Since I had a layover of several hours until the flight to San Antonio, we got something to eat and necked for an hour in the back seat of her car. She said she really liked my uniform and made me promise to visit her on my first weekend pass. I promised I would, but I didn't.

At Ft. Sam Houston, I was assigned to Company C of the medical battalion, otherwise known as Sgt. Tracy's company. Sgt. Tracy had the reputation of being the meanest, most fearsome sergeant major on the base. Those of us who were assigned to his command were viewed with compassion and pity by our luckier comrades. Our tension increased each day as we stood at attention during reveille waiting for our first glimpse of him, but he never appeared. Sgt. Tracy was a master of manipulation and suspense.

One misty morning, we were told Sgt. Tracy would speak to us. All eyes were on the door of the day room where he would appear; there was complete silence. The door eventually opened, several Mexican shoe-shine boys came scampering out, then two officers marched smartly out and took positions on the raised platform in front of us. More time passed in silence; then, there he was, resplendent and awesome, framed by the doorway. Soldiers gasped. He was a very powerfully muscled, handsome black man with inhumanly intelligent dark eyes. His tailored uniform was creased to perfection and his boots gleamed in a flawless challenge to us. He had a thick black mustache and carried a leather riding crop with a carved ivory handle as a symbol of his undisputed authority. He just stood there and glared at us with all-knowing eyes. I was instantly fascinated by him. As Sgt. Tracy began the long, slow, steady walk to the platform, we heard the sharp clicks of unauthorized steel taps on his boots. This open defiance of military dress code heightened his commanding power; we were awestruck. He mounted the platform and silently looked down at each one of us with disdain, yet familiarity, until, one by one, we lowered our eyes in submission to his unspoken will. When he spoke, we knew we were at his mercy. He was commanding, stunning, articulate and cunning. No one doubted that everything we'd heard and feared about Sgt. Tracy was true. I thought he was one of the most extraordinary people I'd ever met. I was strongly attracted to him and felt a strange kinship whenever I saw him. I went out of my way to see him.

Shortly after this initial meeting, Sgt. Tracy stormed into our barracks at two in the morning for a surprise inspection. He was somewhat drunk and wore no shirt, revealing his powerfully muscled upper body. I believed this was a deliberate part of his superb showmanship. He found an unauthorized radio in a frightened trooper's foot locker and smashed it into fragments before the boy's disbelieving eyes. He verbally harassed one delicate, blond young man so badly that tears of humiliation streamed down his face as he stood at rigid attention. Seeing this, Sgt. Tracy taunted, "Just as I thought. The little boy with the pretty face is a mama's boy! Here, son, you want to suck on Sgt. Tracy's big sweaty tit here just like it was your mama's? Since you got such a pretty face, I'm going to give you some real milk, baby, some sweet man's milk from my big billyclub! You want to suck on a big black snake? Do you, angel face?"

Hatred blazed in the young man's eyes. Tracy studied his face and said quietly, "You hate this stinking nigger, don't you? You'd like to smash my face in, wouldn't you? You'd like to cut my belly wide open, wouldn't you? But you won't, and I know why! Pick up that bayonet there! Now! ...Feels good in your hand, doesn't it? Now put the point right here on my throat, just under my chin. Do it! Think about how good it would feel to shove it in! You want me to fuck your pretty face? Do you? Feel your arm muscles twitching! You won't do a thing, because Sgt. Tracy owns you, little trooper! I own your white ass, and we both know it." Tracy just stared at the helpless GI until the youth lowered his eyes and the bayonet. Tracy's face softened, he smiled, leaned over the humiliated youth and whispered for a time into his ear. The trooper looked astonished and confused, then he smiled and looked at Sgt. Tracy with admiration. I never could get him to tell me what Tracy had whispered to him, but I noticed he never had guard duty or KP after that. I saw him one night several weeks later riding in a red sports car headed into the country with Sgt. Tracy at the wheel. They were laughing.

Standing at the bunk next to mine was a large Sioux Indian shaking in his shorts as Tracy approached him. Tracy asked him a question, but his speech was slurred, and the Indian didn't understand him. Tracy became irritated and demanded to know what tribe he belonged to. The Indian told him, and Tracy said that since this was probably the first time the Indian had been off his reservation, Tracy would help him, and he began to speak to the Sioux in a strange tongue. The big Indian let out a yelp of fear and fled to the back of the room, where he slumped down, covering his ears, shaking in terror. Sgt. Tracy roared with an evil, sustained laughter.

When Tracy left, I asked the Indian what had happened. Still frightened, he told me that Sgt. Tracy had spoken to him in the sacred Sioux language.

He was afraid that Tracy was a Sioux god in disguise coming for him. He said Tracy spoke with no accent. After that, I tried to find out everything I could about Sgt. Tracy, but he was a very private person. No one seemed to know anything about his personal life. One old-timer warned me not to try. I considered paying Sgt. Tracy to tell me about himself, but he was too unpredictable. I kept remembering the old-timer's warning. He knew something about Tracy.

I liked my medical training; but, once again, I found myself in a new environment in which I knew no one. There was a red-haired guy who bunked near me, Fred Hessel, who really liked me and sought my friendship time and again; but, for some unknown reason, I detested him. I often wondered why; perhaps it was his red hair. I felt badly about the many times I rejected him, but I just couldn't help myself. I now understand that I felt threatened then by males who were overly friendly; they tugged on my closet door.

There was no privacy in a barracks. Loneliness and sexual frustration were everywhere around me. I'd been emotionally jolted by a figure on a carved stone plaque outside the Alamo. It was a nude male soaring skyward, and this image kept invading my mind as I wrestled with my desires. I thought of it as representing Sgt. Tracy, and also, me. I held imaginary conversations with Dr. Samuels and tried to visualize life in a military stockade, but desire grew. I knew I shouldn't think about it; but once I dared to admit to myself that I wanted somebody, my thoughts became almost uncontrollable and constant. Then I stopped fighting and became a different creature. I sat in the warmth of the sun on the steps of the barracks watching troops of young men my age pass in review. I was the hunting leopard again and soon spotted my prey. He was by far the most handsome soldier I'd ever seen, tall and muscular, dark brown hair, and urgent, soul-telling brown eyes. The beauty of his extraordinary face astonished me. I ached for him as if I'd been wounded. He was intelligent and had that desirable look of loneliness. I studied him for several hours and asked some guys in his platoon about him; then I began to stalk him. I figured I'd have him by the weekend, about three days away. His name was Ted Giampaolo.

Our friendship developed rapidly, because I could easily read him. His face was expressive, and his style open. He was an avid and skilled horseman, and we made plans to go riding that weekend. I suggested we take a weekend pass and spend Saturday night in San Antonio. This puzzled him, but he gave in to my insistence. It was easier than I'd thought, and I dreamed about him every night. Then disaster struck.

The guard duty roster was changed at the last minute; I was scheduled for duty that Saturday night. I found someone to switch places with me, but only Sgt. Tracy could authorize the change. I rehearsed a phony story about my aunt and uncle flying in from Miami to see me that weekend; and, when I felt confident enough, I went to Sgt. Tracy's barracks, hesitated, and knocked on his door. Two Mexican shoe-shine boys opened the door, smiled, and left laughing. Tracy, in his shorts, was seated in an overstuffed chair reading a book. What overwhelmed me was the sight of ceiling to floor book shelves on every wall of his room. I saw sections on philosophy, the arts, and languages.

"You didn't think Army sergeants owned books, did you, college boy?" he said with a touch of pride. I was surprised he knew I'd been to college. "Keep your eyes on me," he said, "and quit trying to find out what I read. It's not your business to snoop into your sergeant major's life. Eyes straight ahead!" He was awesome, even in his shorts.

I told him my story and requested permission to switch guard duty. He studied me for a moment, smiled slyly, then granted permission. It was all so easy. Relieved, I hurried down the hall, excited with thoughts of Ted and the weekend and proud of having pulled something over on Tracy. Just as I reached the barracks door, Tracy's voice entered my brain, ordering me back. I stood at attention before him, filled with fear, yet attraction, at the sight of his anger. "College boy," he said, "you were feeling good you pulled one over on ol' Sgt. Tracy, weren't you? Don't ever think you could be smart enough to do that! I know you lied to me; don't even bother to insult me by trying to deny it. We both know it."

He glared at me and paused to let terror bloom. When he saw it had, he grinned and said, "But you did a fairly convincing job, better than most who have the guts to try. You were impressed by my books, weren't you, and you're curious about me, aren't you? You know I'm damned smart, and that scares and excites you, doesn't it? Well, you've found out more than you need to know about me. You'll wonder about me for years; I know your type. Don't ask any more questions about me around here; I don't like it. Oh, yes, you can switch guard duty as you planned, because I wish it, and because you had the guts to try to take me on. But don't ever try anything like that again, or I'll show you why I have the reputation I do. ...Enjoy your weekend with your pretty new friend, college boy!"

I thought he might be bluffing, the old fortune teller trick. "My new friend? What do you mean?" I asked, feigning innocence.

Tracy smiled; he knew. He locked his eyes on mine and became serious and silent, then he said, "...Ted Giampaolo. Yes, college boy, Sgt. Tracy does read minds, and he has eyes in the back of his head just as people say he does. Your heart's pounding now, isn't it? I can read you like a page in a book, but I'm not going to tell you what else I see. Now get out of here, and be grateful for ol' Sgt. Tracy. You won't forget me, not you! And I know why," he said with a self-satisfied laugh. Then he smiled in a friendly way, almost like he was expecting me to say something. My terror left, and I felt again that strange sense of identification with him.

I figured that one of the sergeants had seen Ted and me sign out for a weekend pass. Tracy had everybody feeding him information. I wondered what he really knew about me, about my wanting Ted. I believed it couldn't have been much, or he wouldn't have let me have the weekend pass. Maybe he was sympathetic with my desires, or was he trying to trap me, I wondered. I decided he had more important things to do, because that's what I wanted to believe.

Ted and I spent the day riding on prairie trails through sagebrush country around San Antonio. In the evening, we talked for hours over dinner and

Margaritas on the patio of a Mexican restaurant beside the river that ran through the center of town. Four Mariachi players were singing romantic ballads as I watched the light of our table candle play with Ted's elegant face. He said he was glad I'd picked him for a buddy and wondered why. "Because I was feeling so lonely, I couldn't take it any more, Ted," I answered truthfully. "I have to be close, and you're someone I know I can be close to."

"I'm lonely too, but what do you mean, close?" he asked warily.

"I mean close, not distant, Ted," I hinted.

"Well, how close is close?" he asked with a worried look, but I noticed a "tell," just the slightest beginning of a smile.

"As close as we want to be, Ted," I said confidently, knowing I had him. I'd known for a long time about the power of responding to the loneliness of another, and I understood that loneliness is a daily part of everyone's life. Some people are simply more honest about it than others. "Haven't you ever had a really close friend before?" I asked. "I bet you've never talked with anyone as openly as we did this evening. Why do you keep pushing people away? It just makes everyone feel more lonely. It makes me feel lonely...and you, too.

He broke eye contact and just stared at the bright Mexican tiles of the patio. I knew he was in touch with his loneliness. When the timing was right, I began the closing. "Ted, let's go up to our hotel room and talk some more in bed. I want to do that. Okay?"

Ted was a little edgy at first, because there was only a double bed in our room; he didn't know I'd requested it. But he relaxed, and we talked in bed like a couple of kids on a camping trip, pouring out our souls. Suddenly we heard pounding on the damned door. It was Fred Hessel, the redhead, and a couple of his friends. I couldn't imagine why Fred had gone to all the trouble of locating us. I told Ted not to make a sound. Fred kept banging on the door and saying he knew we were in there. After too long a time, he gave up; and, as he was going away, we heard him say to his friends that he thought we were in there making love. Ted said, "That son-of-a-bitch! How can he say such a thing? It's not true! God damn him!" His response didn't worry me. Hostility often hides insecurity, longing, and fear.

"I know, Ted," I said. "We haven't been making love—not yet, anyway."

"What the hell do you mean by that?" he demanded.

"I have to be close to you tonight, Ted. I have to express how I feel about you. Don't push me away. Don't do that to me—not now, not as close as we've been. Just once in your life, relax and let yourself feel something. Quit fighting yourself! Let me be close to you."

"I'm not that kind of person, Denny," he said. "You've got me all wrong!"

I told him what I honestly believed. "I know you're not, Ted. Neither am I. We're just a couple of regular guys, but we care about each other right now. We're lonely, and there's no one else involved. I need you tonight, and I know you need me. There's no reason for us to hold back, none."

I put my hand on his chest. He pushed me away and cried, "Oh, Jesus!" as if calling for help, and we began to wrestle. It was very erotic. When he fought back with little of the power of his impressive physique, I knew he wanted it, too. I knew his fighting was symbolic, a way for him to save face. He began to hesitate and then to yield, and when he knew I was aware of how hard he'd become, he grabbed my hand and began to rub it over his writhing body while he groaned and thrashed around, starved for affection and human contact. But what I didn't expect was the extent of his untapped need and new-found passion; it was as great as my own. He was embarrassed about being uncircumcised, but my curiosity about that relaxed him, and he laughed when I teased him about wearing a turtleneck sweater to bed. He said he thought of it as a monk's hood; he was a Catholic. Then it was all man-sex, sweaty, athletic, urgent and demanding, ending only by the exhaustion of many orgasms. I wish we'd taken our dog tags off, though, all that stainless steel jangling, clattering, and clanking. Our chains got tangled up together, and his broke after nearly choking us. Our awareness of the intensity of our desires created much guilt, and we avoided one another after the revealing heat of that night. I knew I shouldn't have done it, but I didn't care. I was entirely satisfied...in my shame. I believed it had just been a single slip-up, that's all; I could get back on track.

When I finished medical training, I was assigned to a hospital at the Army Chemical Center, outside Baltimore, for the rest of my tour of duty. There, chemical weapons were developed and tested, including nerve gas. I was pleased with the assignment, since I would be near Washington and New York. Unfortunately, Fred Hessel, the guy I disliked, the Red Baron, was also assigned there.

Because of its scientific and technical mission, the personnel at the Chemical Center were educated, making strict military discipline a joke. Once, when the aging post general made his entrance at a ceremony, he was astonished to hear the military band playing When *the Saints Come Marching In*. Another time, a group of psychologists trained a dog to attack officers' uniforms, then released their four-legged weapon during a ceremony. This delighted everyone, except the commanding officer, whose pants legs were ripped to shreds in front of his troops. Leaders of this resistance movement met weekly at a pizza parlor in a mock staff meeting to plan each week's adventures. The members were assigned either to the corps of active resistance or to the corps of passive resistance. Typical of their scheming minds was their permanent solution to the problem of having to wax the linoleum floors of some of the supply rooms each week for inspection. A draftee—a chemist—and a witness went to the captain in charge of the building in question and got his permission to use trisodium phosphate to clean the linoleum. The troopers then mixed a solution strong enough to destroy the linoleum, and the problem was solved.

I arranged to be assigned to the dental clinic, because it was air-conditioned, and to the hospital emergency room, because it was dramatic. Relations between the officers and enlisted men were casual and relaxed. Several officers often invited me over to their bachelor officers' quarters for evenings of conversation and drinking, even though such fraternization was prohibited by Army regulations.

The people of the Chemical Center were fascinating. There was a 200 lb.

female MP who had a black belt in karate and who enjoyed knowing that most men feared her. She was the leader of a gang of WAC lesbians who rode their belching Harleys out from the post into the darkness of Saturday nights, dressed in full black leathers and headed for unknown meeting places. The men who saw them stood silently, feeling confusion, fear, disapproval, curiosity and envy at such a forceful and proud display of masculinity.

Sgt. Tom, a shy little man who'd been married for five weeks once, ran the medical lab. I watched him perform autopsies. At the end of one, Tom was surrounded by body parts and covered with blood. I teased him and asked if what he was doing didn't make him feel just a little bit guilty. He looked at his bloody hands and the body parts, then he screamed like an hysteric and ordered me to get out of the room. The degree of Tom's loneliness was beyond my comprehension. I felt compassion for him whenever he was around.

There was also a sadistic surgeon I had to awaken at two in the morning, because a black guy and a white guy had gotten into a drunken fight with broken beer bottles. Both had deep, multiple lacerations. This colonel was so angry at having his sleep disturbed that he told the unfortunate soldiers he'd teach them a lesson they'd never forget; he stitched them up with no anesthesia.

A tall, broad-shouldered, good-looking staff sergeant with 15 years in the service was transferred into our unit. Everyone knew he was gay. (That polite term was not used then.) He would never directly admit it because of the military policy of discrimination, but he did little to hide the fact. When another sergeant asked if he was "that way," he just laughed and told him to go jerk off in the shower instead of trying to get decent people to go to bed with him. Everyone laughed, especially when he pinched his startled questioner on the cheek and said, "But now that I think about it, you are kind of cute!" Another old sergeant, who wasn't laughing, said, "Well, I think you're one. I can tell." The gay sergeant, still laughing, replied, "Why, Charlie, my God, after all the things you begged me to do to you last night, I hope you could tell!" Even the old sergeant laughed. The other sergeants—whose lives consisted mainly of drinking, poker, and old war stories—enjoyed his quick humor enough to invite him to their Friday night, high-stakes poker game. No one knew he was a master card shark who had memorized tables of poker statistics.

The captain of our company took a dislike to this popular sergeant and made his attitude known. "I know his type all too well," said the gay sergeant. "His frigid wife lets him have it once a year if he's good and doesn't muss her hair. He's the misery-loves-company type. His imagination about my life eats his insides out. Well, I'll fix his little red wagon."

Later that day, I overheard him making a call to the Pentagon: "Yes, I'd like to speak to General Smith. Just tell him Sgt. Allan Peck is calling, he'll talk to me. ...Hello, George? Surprise, it's Allan! ...Yes, I know I promised to write, but you know how those things go. ...Of course I do! You know that. Come on now, nothing has changed. ...I promise, George! ...Hey, this assignment is definitely not working out. The captain is after me. I want you to get me assigned down there as soon as you can. ...George, you're just trying to make me feel guilty again. Okay, I'm sorry! How much longer are you going to make me pay for one little mistake? ...No, I haven't had any contact with him. How could I after you had him assigned to Alaska! ...I know you were, but that's all in the past now. ...This weekend? Of course, yes, I'll arrange it. ...I do too, George! ...Hot fudge? Whatever happened to your West Point tradition? ...Yes, you know I do. ...Just get lots of sleep and eat egg whites." A week later, Sgt. Peck received his orders for transfer to the Pentagon. "I warned that silly captain not to mess with me," he explained.

Military units had been racially integrated only several years before. One of the guys assigned to our barracks was a young black man who fascinated me. I wanted a friendship with him. He was quite physically attractive, but he almost never spoke and resisted all my efforts and those of others to befriend him. He always showered and shaved alone late at night. I'd never had any close contact with blacks before, and I was hurt by his rejection of my offers of friendship. I complained about this to one of the old-timers, and he explained, "Hell, I know exactly what's going on inside that boy. He's from Mississippi, same as me. This is the first time he's been with white folks, much less using the white man's john, and he's scared shitless. He thinks we're all KKK members just waiting to cut his black balls off in the middle of the night. All he'll say to you is 'yes, sir!' or 'no, sir!' He's all alone with us, and he misses his own kind real bad. He'll never trust you, Denny, not after the way we raise them up in the deep South. I kind of feel sorry for him."

I did become good friends with a black dental lab technician I worked with, though. He was a married civilian who lived in Baltimore. He told me hundreds of stories about black ghetto life. He kept offering to fix me up with a black woman, and he delighted in shocking my white, middle-class, Midwestern view of the world. Later on, we trusted each other enough for him to tell me how blacks thought and felt about whites. He told me what it was like for him to watch his young children receive the heavy yoke of racism they would bear for the rest of their lives. Racism was a warning to me about what would happen if my sexual deviation was exposed.

One afternoon, we got an emergency call from post headquarters. A handsome young lieutenant had been running around on his pregnant wife, the mother of his two children. She was so despondent when she accidentally found out that she pumped nine bullets into his convulsing body in front of post headquarters. She was tried for murder, but the jury was sympathetic and let her off on a temporary insanity defense—a warning to unfaithful husbands, they said. While she was under sedation at the post hospital, a corpsman from Oklahoma, who had the nasty habit of spitting chewing tobacco into a paper cup he always carried, came from her room and wryly told us that the post chaplain was trying to calm her down.

"How?" I asked.

"Oh, he's a' reading her scriptures from the good book."

"Like what?"

He spit deftly into his cup and grinned. "Oh, that one about the wages of sin is death." And what of my sin, I wondered.

The next night, I was at a cheap, honky-tonk, hillbilly bar in Baltimore with a friend of mine. We were only 20, but nobody checked ages in joints like that. Near us, two handsome guys in their early twenties, wearing cowboy hats and boots, were arguing loudly about who was going to take home a drunk blond girl sitting at their table. They began to scuffle, and I heard the click of a switch blade knife. I saw its long blade flickering in the red neon lights of the bar. Fear crossed the face of the threatened one. Then, as if in slow motion, I saw the deep thrust of the blade as it entered his body and consciousness. I heard the gasp of his disbelief and pain, then I saw the upward movement of his pleading eyes as if he were beseeching heaven, then the final closing of those beautiful eyes into unconsciousness as he fell backwards. His equally handsome murderer stood frozen in place, the bloody knife still joined to his hand, as the bartender held a shotgun to his tragic face until the police came. His young friend had died almost instantly, his aorta having been severed. The drunken blond girl continued to complain loudly that she was out of beer until someone gave her one.

My friend and I hurried to get away from there. We went to a bump and grind burlesque bar and watched young soldiers and sailors with serious faces watching old men feeling the sagging breasts of aging strippers. At another bar, I met a beautiful young woman about my age wearing a tight, sexy, white dress and talked with her for about half an hour. Because of her warmth and intelligence, I asked if I could take her to dinner and dancing. She blushed and said I was a nice young man but that I didn't understand. She said it would cost me 50 dollars to spend the evening with her, one hundred for the night. I was heartsick. She said, "I know, you want to know what a nice girl like me is doing in a place like this. All you young ones always ask the same thing. Well, the answer is money. I make more now than you ever will. If I'm smart, I can retire at 30. Can you do that? So don't look down your nose at a successful working girl. But thanks for asking me for a date; it gives me a nice feeling to know you didn't think I was a whore. If I could ever really enjoy going to bed with a man, it would probably be with someone like you."

After this, I began to spend as much time as I could in Washington and New York. I visited Bernie Grey, my friend from Miami, and his family in Brooklyn. He showed me New York City as he knew it. We saw concerts and plays, an opera at the old Met, but what I most valued was the art. The paintings by Sandro Botticelli at the Metropolitan Museum of Art touched something vital within me. Scenes and faces in the style of Botticelli became frequent elements in my dreams. In the first of these dreams, I was viewing an actual painting of his of a street scene, when suddenly it became real. The people began to move about and talk, and I began to live with them in all the color and drama of Renaissance Florence. I was in ecstasy; but, when I awoke, I became depressed and remained that way all day, so great was the beauty of the experience. It was probably the sensuous beauty of Botticelli's men, but I was a budding culture vulture then, thriving on sublimated sexuality. I hadn't yet learned that Botticelli had been a lover of "beardless youths" until he came under the influence of Savonarola and produced little thereafter. The loves of Leonardo da Vinci, Michelangelo, Shakespeare and hundreds of other world-renowned gays and lesbians were completely unknown to me, as they are to most people today. The love that dare not speak its name must be silent, and truth suppressed. Some progress has been made, however. Censorship is no longer advocated for adults, only children, who must, of course, be protected from truth and choices.

One evening, Bernie and I talked for hours in a booth at a crowded bar in the Village. He asked if I noticed anything unusual about the bar. I saw nothing out of the ordinary. "Do you notice any women, Denny?" he asked.

"No. So?"

"This is a fairy bar! How could you miss it? I thought you wanted to be a psychologist! You've been sitting here for hours, but you didn't notice. How could you be so blind? Guys are holding hands, and two guys just finished dancing together over there! I thought you'd notice the minute we walked in. You've got a blind spot—to talk to you in your native Midwest language—the size of a barn door. What's with you? Haven't you ever been to a bar like this?"

"No" I said, then I suddenly remembered Charlie Barker taking me to several bars like this in Ohio, but that hadn't registered at the time. As the memories were vividly coming back, I was troubled because I hadn't seen the obvious.

"Does this place interest you?" Bernie asked.

"No. Why should it, Bernie?" The bar threatened me.

"You better tell this to your shrink," he said. "This is juicy clinical material, real mother lode! When I told my analyst I wanted to bring you here, he said we'd better start addressing the issue of my latent tendencies."

"Do you have latent tendencies?" I asked, half hoping.

"Well, Zia, my girlfriend, sure doesn't think so, as often as I plug her. She says she wishes I did, so she could get some rest. I think everybody has some homosexual tendencies, don't you?"

"I suppose so."

"I've always been curious about what it would be like...I mean, with someone you really liked...a good friend. Haven't you wondered, Denny?"

I told him I believe most people are curious; if not, they're either experienced or repressed. He asked if I'd ever tried it. I felt very defensive and asked why he wanted to know.

"Just curious, that's all."

"Have you done it before, Bernie?"

"No," he said, "but I think you have. Have you?"

"I think your analyst is wise," I said. "You better start working on your latent before it becomes blatant." I never did tell him; I knew he loved his girlfriend, Zia. I thought I was doing him a favor, but I was really protecting myself.

Months later, I received a letter from Bernie. His analyst had encouraged him to write. He said that because of me, he doubted himself and his love for Zia and that he was forced to deal with homosexuality in his psychoanalysis. He and Zia were fighting. What most angered him, he said, was that I hadn't been open with him about my life or my feelings toward him, that I'd rejected him when he needed me—whatever he meant by that. He thought hell was too good a place for me. This hurt, so I wrote him a bitchy note saying I could appreciate how difficult it was for him to deal with reality, but using me as a scapegoat would only make his analyst richer. I ended by pointing out that hate is often the outcome of frustrated love. I knew this would drive him crazy. We never wrote again; rejected people often become rejecting people.

There was no escape from my conflict, it was everywhere. I flew to Boston for a weekend to visit my Syrian friend from Miami University, Hortune, the one who taught me hypnosis and fencing. He had transferred to Harvard. He showed me the sights of the Boston area and invited me to dinner with his girlfriend, her parents, and her 17-year-old younger brother. My friend had been dating this girl for seven months, and I simply couldn't imagine why. She was pleasant enough but was neither attractive nor intelligent. Hortune was both. Michael, her younger brother, however, was a cultural ideal. Life for Michael was joy, and it was this way to be around him. He lived in the present and gave no hint of mortality or sorrow. His beauty was his virtue, and he was confident and spontaneous in his celebration of life. His body expressed his soul. As my friend was driving me to the airport for the trip back, I realized why he dated this plain girl. "My God, Hortune," I said, "you keep dating her, because you want to be around her younger brother. You're in love with Michael!" I remember how Hortune just kept driving and was completely expressionless, but a tear formed in the corner of his eye, then several tears, and he said with shame, "How could Michael not be loved? You're the only one who knows, and you'll be the only one who ever knows."

On the flight back to Baltimore, I thought about Hortune's disturbing question: How could Michael not be loved? Not to love Michael would require a history of cultural conformity, repression and fear. To love Michael required only the recognition of what is of value. This disturbed me, because if I didn't love a lovable male, then like Oedipus, I willfully blinded myself to truth. And, if I loved a lovable male, I would be tormented by desire or condemned for its consummation. I wished there were a way for me not to love the Michaels of this world; but, I thought, perhaps I can learn not to desire the complete knowledge of them. Why was I so different, so abnormal, I wondered. It always seemed to come back to that question.

Fred Hessel, the Red Baron, was ordered to Germany, an assignment he didn't want. We tried to change places, but it was impossible. He'd never been to New York, so he asked if I'd take him along before he went overseas. Since he'd soon be gone, I decided I didn't need to be quite so rejecting of him. Besides, a weekend with Fred might help me figure out why I disliked him. He was excited about going to New York and talked most of the way there. Occasionally, I was even interested in what he had to say. We checked into a room at the top of the YMCA and went sight-seeing. At a French restaurant that evening, our snobbish waiter complained about our tip. Fred took the tip back and told the waiter he was a French-fried asshole. The waiter began hissing insults at us. Fred and I walked menacingly toward him as he continued to insult us. Fred jerked a table cloth, sending dishes all over. Shocked patrons stared as we yelled Army profanities and left, laughing.

Back in our room that evening, Fred talked as if he'd just gotten out of solitary. I felt closer to him. I noticed the pressure behind his speech and remembered the time in San Antonio when he'd come up to the room where Ted Giampaolo and I were staying. I wondered.

"Denny, why are you staring at me like that?" he asked.

"Just trying to understand you. Go on, I'm listening."

"Well, what are you trying to understand about me?"

"If you've ever had sex."

"No, I never have."

"Why not, Fred?"

"I guess I never had the chance."

"Do you want to have the chance?"

"Sure! Who wouldn't?"

"Then let's do it right now, Freddy!" I said to test my suspicion about his interest in me, but while saying this, I realized that I wanted sex—even with him. He'd be leaving for Germany soon, so there was no danger of getting hooked.

"What?!" he said, not believing me.

"Oh come on, Fred. I know you've thought about doing it with me before. I can read minds, you know."

"Geez," he said, "I don't know. Yeah, I've thought about it, I admit, but..." Fred stopped and looked at me questioningly. "Wow! You really are serious about this, aren't you?"

I got up and shut off the light, leaving the room dimly lit from the chromatic glow of the city below through the uncurtained window. Fred looked at me with astonishment, but then he smiled in a shy way as I walked over to his bed. "Slide over, Fred," I said. "You're about to be born again!" I took off my tee shirt, shorts and dog tags and lay down beside him. As I began to hold him, I remembered that in just a few months I'd be 21, the legal age of adulthood at the time. For some reason—perhaps it was the sex talk with my mother when I was 12, or the fear of the law, or maybe my ego ideal—I always understood that I would never do this as an adult, so that night was to be my last time forever; and, with this thought, the magic, the very special soulful music, began within me. Just enough light from the city far below entered our window, so I could watch the transformations of his face as he acquired this special consciousness of being. My passion was incredible, because it was to be the last time, and I let myself go—a farewell, forever. When all had been known by us, I felt the warmth of Fred's tears on my face and tasted their saltiness as he held me, kissed me and cried the relief of ending a long, great loneliness.

In the morning, as I sat watching a new Fred Hessel eagerly downing a breakfast of sausages, eggs and blueberry buttermilk pancakes, I couldn't believe how beautiful he was—every single part of him. Even to this day, I'm still slightly speechless around males with red hair. I understood then that it must have been me who had changed, but it didn't seem that way. Fred Hessel was suddenly a beautiful, valued person. How much is reality, I wondered, as I watched him, and how much is me? What is melody and what is harmony in the sweet songs of the interplay between loving and knowing? Our sex had been lovemaking; good sex makes love.

Looking back on these experiences of my youth, I believe that every person, to learn more about what they truly are and to feel free and alive, should make love at least once with someone of their own sex, the other half of the human race. And I mean, make love, not just awkward body contact. I know this belief is one of the most threatening ideas for most people, a heresy for some—even repulsive for those who are especially threatened. It is threatening because it fundamentally attacks sexism and mindless conformity, so it will be quickly and emotionally rejected by the obedient majority. Sadly, I also know that most people who choose to avoid this significant source of knowledge have no rational basis for their choice other than fear and an absence of desire based on religious and social prohibitions. Who can desire to do what is punished? Just listen carefully to the rationalizations given: God's will, mother nature's way, the attraction of so-called "opposites," reproductive biology and the survival of the DNA molecule, the complementarity of body parts, passing on the family name, absence of desire and so on. Except for the promise of fidelity, these objections to a same-sex experience are not at all rational, factual, logical or ethical. Sexual desire is influenced by social learning. Surely a human being wanting freedom will aspire to be more than the victim of the history of his social emotional conditioning. A person is the history of his choices. Feelings and unquestioning obedience to authority need not be the only basis for our human choices. Changes in our thinking and actions often cause a change in our conditioned feelings and emotions. New ideas and new behavior can alter how we feel about ourselves, one another, and the world we share; and this is a source of hope for our species. Life is a process of change, and if a person can't be changed, he is the living dead. His soul rots, yet he can't smell it; because, for him, the sweet stench is so familiar, so ordinary, and so normal that it seems natural.

. . .

There was a Professor of Medicine from Johns Hopkins University who often worked on weekends as the physician on duty for the hospital emergency service. I admired him and arranged my duty schedule to be with him. For some reason, he liked me, and we spent many pleasant hours talking. He was enthusiastic about poetry. We would often wile away the hours reading and discussing his favorite poems. He said he regretted that he and his son weren't close. He wished he could talk with him the way we were able to, but his son wasn't interested. We often discussed religion, because he was an intelligent Catholic, whose views reminded me of Kevin Rogers.

One weekend, he and I were on duty when a 20-year-old soldier was brought to our emergency room. He'd been injured in a serious automobile accident just outside the Post. I recognized him and saw that his condition was critical. His extraordinarily beautiful face hadn't been injured, but the rest of him was mutilated. We rushed him, mercifully unconscious, into the operating room. Under brilliant blue-white surgical lights, I cut off his boots and his bloody clothing. His red-smeared, but still handsome, body was covered with rips and gouges. His smooth white skin seemed like a canvas torn by an insane artist who desecrated it with bizarre decorations of blood red. As I handed hemostats to the doc, who was frantically clamping off arteries and veins, I wondered if this youth had loved. His face was so peaceful. Whom had he kissed with those perfect lips? Who had touched his beautiful face?

A corpsman anxiously said that the youth's blood pressure was dropping. Doc ordered an increase in the IV fluids and probed the boy's flaccid abdomen, then he ran his fingers through the boy's jet black hair, feeling his skull. "Oh Jesus!" he shouted. "The back of his skull is fractured! Somebody call the neurosurgeon at Aberdeen Proving Grounds! Hurry!" Doc looked at me with a frightened, pleading look. I nodded my understanding.

The corpsman shouted, "Sir, I've lost his pulse!" Doc put his fingers over the boy's carotid artery and the stethoscope to his heart. His face clouded over as he began the physicians' last rites of hope. "Clear!" he yelled again and again as he tried to put the spark of life back into the limp body. I prepared a syringe to inject a stimulant into the boy's heart and waited. We medics looked at one another; we all knew, but doc just worked frantically. He held out his hand for the syringe, positioned it, and plunged the long needle into the boy's heart. All eyes were on doc, everything was silent, except for his hurried movements and the hum of the surgical lights. I watched his face. How could his son not be honored just to be with him, I wondered. I'd gladly be your son, I thought.

He stopped and looked at me. He looked so helpless. We both knew. Then, in one of the most memorable scenes of my life, this loving man bent over the beautiful boy's still warm body, ashen and red-splattered under the blue-white surgical lights—this body kissed by death on the cold, stainless steel table. He placed his hands on the boy's body as if he were touching a sacred altar, a shrine of God, and he closed his eyes and raised his face to heaven, and I saw his lips move in prayer. When he'd finished, he looked at me, then down at his hands on the body of the youth, this incarnation of sacred life. He made the sign of the cross on his own body, then went to his office and closed the door.

Later, I heard him weeping. When he'd had enough time alone, I knocked on his door, but he didn't answer. I told him who it was, and he opened the door. I had brought him a mug of hot coffee and his favorite candy bar; I didn't know what else to do for him. He understood, because, after we'd talked and shared our feelings about the death, he grinned and pointed to the coffee and candy. "Well, Denny, I know you're a tough-minded agnostic, but I prefer to believe. I think you're like a young priest restoring my faith, offering me this coffee and candy bar as if it were the blood and flesh of Christ, himself. I'll eat and drink them in remembrance of you! I think God is already with you, Denny, but you don't know that yet. May his light shine down upon you, someday. ...Youth is such a blind ordeal. Please don't think I'm trying to patronize you; I'm not. I sincerely believe these things...but I confess I do like to watch the way you squirm when I talk to you like this! You're a God seeker, my young friend, a doubting Thomas who spent too long in Missouri. Like most youth, you'll have to wander the earth; and, if you're blessed enough to find what you seek, you'll discover it has been with you all along. Life is like that. Now, let's do something practical; go get me a death certificate."

The young man who had died was only 20, and so was I. Some days later, I asked a technician to take a profile x-ray picture of my skull. He didn't see the point, but I did. I was trying to understand what I was. I still have this x-ray; the skull appears to be grinning.

Chapter Sixteen

Bob Roberts described himself as "a right sociable hillbilly from the feudin' and fightin' green hills of Harlan County, Kentucky. Bob's my name, and women are my game!" He said he'd never met anyone he couldn't get to like him, and I knew this was true because of his native social intelligence. He was a wily master con, who knew how to read the "tells" of his marks with unerring accuracy. Even when I knew Bob was taking advantage of me, he saw to it that I didn't really mind.

No one who knew Bob Roberts ever doubted his skill with women. He often said that the luckiest guys in the world were gynecologists. He'd worked his way through most of the non-lesbians in the WAC detachment, and he claimed he'd even talked a couple of the lesbians into giving him a try. Several times I'd seen WACs sneaking into his barracks room in the middle of the night. It wasn't that he was such a good-looking man, he was rather ordinary, but he knew how to listen to people and learn what they really wanted. He made everyone believe that he had a special fondness for them. He knew I was impressed with his skills with women, which he liked to show off for me. I learned more useful psychology about women from this Harlan County hillbilly than I did from my professors in graduate school, who weren't interested in the psychology of women, gays or minority groups. All my professors, both undergraduate and graduate, had been white males.

Bob Roberts was my make-out coach, my hope for survival in this society. We spent our free time in dance halls and bars. I quickly became sexually involved with a number of women; because, he pointed out, as a college man, I was great marriage bait. I learned that the best looking women were often not exciting in bed. They wanted to be loved, but they weren't into loving. Most women of that era used sex as a means to get affection, love, and marriage, unlike most men for whom sex is a positive end in itself. For those women, sex was bait; it was the romance they valued. That really bothered me. But who was I to talk, I baited my hook with my earning potential, so I could use them to practice being normal.

I was an inept, sexist lover. I had no empathic understanding of a woman's body or cultural experience. Bob preached to me about the importance of foreplay and a woman's "magic button," but what a woman experienced sexually was mostly a mystery that made me feel lonely. Women's breasts particularly puzzled me. I tried to imagine what it would be like to wear a pair of them. I asked women to explain what their bodies felt like, but they had the same difficulty I did when they wanted to know what it felt like to get an erection. So there I was, groping with the dimly understood bodies of the other sex, who were always called the opposite sex then. This was so unlike my intuitive grasp of the bodily sensations of males that I often felt lonely with women. For me, it was like having sex with a friendly mannequin; I knew what was on the outside, but the inside was hollow, empty. Sex seemed solitary, like masturbation. With a male, this never happened, because we both understood.

There were other differences, too. Bob warned me that I'd have to be patient about getting a woman "into high gear." I shouldn't get discouraged, he said, because women have slow starters—that's just the way they are. A number of them liked to talk during sex. This drove Bob and me crazy. Women wanted sex to be slower and much gentler than most men did. They didn't like sudden starts, quick dominance reversals, or the deep muscle, uninhibited athleticism of male sexuality. Not many women, for example, would enjoy having their butts forcefully smacked, their biceps bitten, or their nipples pain-fully pinched, or group sex, or silent sex with lust-crazed strangers. And these women never doubted that it was up to the man to satisfy them—to perform; such were the sex scripts of the '50s and well beyond. Even afterwards, when I longed for sleep, women often wanted to cuddle and pillow talk. I often felt I was using. Using was a popular word with women then. Occasionally, some would make snide remarks about males' strong interest in sexuality. I felt a silent hurt when they did. This mocking filled me with the lonely sense that I was with a person from a foreign culture. In a sense, I was. Women belonged to the pink tribe, the she's; I was a blue, a he, and the division was lonely. The foreigner can be beautiful, exotic, even fascinating; but, after a time, we long to be with our own kind. When a group of couples got together to visit in those days, the women generally went into one room to talk about people, relationships and their feelings; and the men went into another to talk about business and sports, to brag, and to compete. These sexist tribal mem-berships are maintained in many ways—dress code, jobs, distribution of power, law, history, mythology, religion, but primarily by the constant reminders of the language of he, him, his and she, her, hers. Our personal pronouns reveal and support the sexist foundation of our culture. Significantly, the first bit of information given about a newborn is its gender tribal membership.

Fortunately, I met Barbara White. Bob Roberts had told me that the shy, less flashy women were generally the best in and out of bed, because they didn't take a man for granted. I wanted to find out for myself. Barbara, a brunette, was taller than average and older, 26; and she wore glasses that she kept taking off at every opportunity. The signs of shyness, a need to please, and some depth of personality were there, so I approached her and watched for the "tells." The way she looked at me when I asked her to dance sent an adrenaline rush through my insides and made my testicles tighten. I knew this particular look of sexual urgency all too well, but I'd never seen it in the eyes of a woman.

Barbara invited me to a picnic with her uncle's family the following af-ternoon. In the evening, we went for a swim in the bay of Baltimore. Barbara was in the water when I finished changing into my swim suit. As I walked toward her, she studied my body, then I noticed her beginning to tremble. She looked into my eyes and we both knew. As I put my arms around her, she shook so much that her teeth chattered. All she could say was, "Later. Stop!" The next evening, I took her to dinner. We just looked at each other as we ate and said little. Then we went to a motel. I've been with many women, but Barbara was the only one whose sexuality approached that of a man's. I was stunned and ecstatic. We sexed everywhere and in every way. Something was missing, but I wasn't going to let that bother me. I was one of the boys, and Bob Roberts was proud of me. I remained with her for over a year, until my tour of duty was finished. What a relief to be affectionate right out in the open without guilt or shame—to have people smile as we kissed and caressed in the sunlight before the knowing eyes of children. I was convinced my shrink had been right about my sexuality. Men will do extraordinary things to earn the respect of other men.

One weekend, Barbara and I visited some of her relatives along the Maryland coast. We went for a crab roast and stayed overnight at their home. The folkways of the time dictated that she and I couldn't sleep together, so I was assigned to share a bed with her 15-year-old cousin. He was fascinated to talk with an honest-to-God soldier. He was impressed with my uniform, and when we got undressed for bed, I let him try it on—even the dog tags. He studied himself in the mirror and looked proud—this was before Vietnam. I told him many Army stories, but he wanted more. It was late though, and we were tired, so we quickly fell asleep. I remember having wild dreams about crabs coming alive in my stomach and crawling around in my insides. I woke up and saw moonlight streaming through our window. In the distance, a dog was howling. The beautiful youth beside me was illuminated by the milky light. I watched him breathing, then I became agitated when I realized that I desired him.

I thought about Barbara and this youth I hardly knew. I realized that the essential difference between them was that this soul sleeping beside me was of my own kind; we were brothers in the male tribe. I identified completely with him and instinctively understood his moods, gestures, impulses, fears and desires. I reached out my hand and gently touched his warm skin. You are like me, I thought, that's why I desire you. I believed that if I sexually aroused him, he would willingly make love with me, but I was aware of the extreme danger I would be in. I was an adult; he was a minor. I couldn't fully understand the purpose of these restrictions; because, in my teens, I would have welcomed sex with an adult, or practically anyone who cared about me. You certainly don't have to be very old to know if you want to be sexual with someone, and I couldn't understand how sharing such simple affection and pleasure could harm anyone. But there was much I didn't understand then about this strange society of mine. I rolled away from the boy and cautiously masturbated to the vivid memories of what Barbara knew how to do so well that I liked best.

In the morning, I woke up feeling the teenager curled up beside me with his arm around me—a beautiful warm feeling. During the day, he kept smiling at me in an odd way. Just before Barbara and I left, I asked him what his smile was all about. He whispered into my ear, "Denny, I saw what you did last night! I woke up when you touched me, but I pretended to be sleeping. I got so stiff watching you, I did it after you were asleep. Some of it got on you! I won't tell Barbara what you did if you promise to tell me more Army stories when you come back."

My two-year tour of military duty was about to end. I was admitted to the Ohio State University in Columbus for the fall quarter of 1957 with the help of a couple of letters from Dr. Samuels. Barbara begged me to take her along. She said she could get a job and work while I went through school; she didn't plan to go to college. But at 22, I had no interest in marriage; besides, I'd always planned to marry a college girl—it was a kind of class identification, an issue of status. Status is important when people are having problems with self-esteem. I also knew that there were many years of academic study ahead before I could become a psychologist and properly support a wife and family.

Our last night together was frantic with lovemaking as we tried to deny what was true. Barbara cried...so many times. I stayed at her apartment as late as I could. When the parting came, I drove my old green Dodge a couple of blocks, but I just couldn't keep going. I pulled over and sat there, crying my heart out. God, I hurt. I worried that someone would see me. Real men didn't cry, especially in front of women. In a fit of lonely anguish, I pounded on the steering wheel so hard that I bent it.

Like ocean waves incessantly seeking and caressing the land and then inevitably retreating, our life is the ebbing and flowing of our attachments and losses, of our loving and grieving. And what of still waters?

I said my farewells to friends at the Army hospital. The nurses threw a surprise party for me and gave me a gift of initialed gold cuff links. I never imagined I'd been valued by the staff that much. I wondered why I was so blind to being liked by others. It was a problem of self-esteem; they didn't know about beautiful bodies in my closet. The doc from Johns Hopkins was there. He shook my hand, winked at me, and said, "May God be with you, always...my son!" I hugged him and felt tears stinging my eyes.

On my many trips to Washington, I'd often visited the National Gallery of Art and attended concerts there. In the Gallery's fine collection of Italian Renaissance art, there was a portrait that deeply disturbed me. I would often go back and stand before it. The face invaded me. In its presence, I felt anguish, turmoil, and pain, yet it drew me to itself. It was a superb master-piece of Florentine art painted about 1485 by the son of Fra Filippo Lippi, Filippino Lippi, who studied with Botticelli. Some authorities even attribute the portrait to Botticelli, himself. This humanistic Portrait of a Youth is the embodiment of the physical and intellectual qualities that were the quintes-sence of the Renaissance Florentine ideal of perfect manhood. The youth is in his late teens or early 20's. His long, wavy brown hair surrounds his well defined, elegant face—softening it and giving him an androgynous appeal. He has the full potential of youth and age, male and female. His wide, pen-etrating brown eyes look directly at the viewer from any angle. These unfor-gettable eyes show a confident, clear and supreme intelligence. Through them, he sees your soul, or so it seemed to me. I saw the youth as calm, centered, receptive and totally comprehending. His expression had a slight suggestion of aloofness, of a certain disappointment in the character of the viewer, yet there was a compelling compassion.

Because this portrait was so disturbing, I knew it had a deep elusive psychological significance for me. It shouted the truth, but I was stone deaf. Because of this, I made a special trip to Washington to buy a reproduction of this enigmatic painting and had it mounted in an appropriate gold frame. I lived with this irritating picture for almost 17 years before I understood its profound significance. There is more of the story that I must tell first, however.

Like a monk in a cloistered order, I dedicated myself to the goddess of knowledge and upward mobility and began my years of study at the Ohio State University where I earned my B.A., M.A., and Ph.D. degrees.

The most important undergraduate class I took was quite by accident—Ancient Greek Philosophy. This class changed my life, because it was the first time I'd heard significant human values discussed and debated in a classroom—a sorry commentary on our educational system. At 22, the question of how a man should live his life was central for me. Among other books, we read the *Dialogues of Plato*—the infamous Benjamin Jowett translation that he had secretly censored and distorted to satisfy Victorian prudery about explicit homosexuality. The first time I read the *Symposium*, that immortal discourse on the nature of love, my understanding of the possibilities for my life changed.

I was surprised enough by the open homosexuality of the speakers in the *Symposium*, but the famous description of the stages of love by Socrates gave me an honorable way to understand my own experience. I understood that my love of Keith was the first rung of this ascending ladder of love. Ronnie and all the others were the next step in my realization of the aesthetic ground of human life. When, as the lonely leopard feeding, I hunted for the beauty and joy of bodies, my nocturnal kills were followed by despair as I realized that I hungered not for the body of Keith alone but also for his mind and soul. And when I pursued Bill Thomas, I wanted both the beauty of his body and intimacy with his mind and soul. I thought of the beauty of other minds and souls who had touched my life in so many ways; then I thought of the whole human race, past and present. I imagined the countless beauties of this earth and the heavens, and I grasped for the first time the wisdom of the idea of having a love affair with the universe. I'm a sucker for grandiosity.

I was grateful for Socrates and his band of gay friends, especially because they were treated with respect in a public classroom in the Midwest in the 1950's where the topic was unspeakable. I still wonder why it was that the spark of creative genius touched so many men in that small town of Athens for such an extraordinary moment in history. This creative outburst didn't happen again until the flaming of the Renaissance in Florence, with the rediscovery of Greek culture. In all of the centuries since, why have there been no men of such stature from the cities of Athens and Florence? Human nature is the same, people are at least as intelligent as they were then, but something special happened in the social life of those cities, something quite uncommon.

In that class was a girl who wore a heavy, tarnished silver crucifix. Once, she angrily questioned the respect given same-sex love by the ancient Greeks.

Professor Weiss, who was Jewish, smiled and said the Greeks were that way because there weren't any Christians around then to harass them. The class laughed, except for the uncomprehending girl, who nervously fingered her crucifix.

My best friend at this time was Frank Robertson, a social worker I'd met in the Army Reserves. He and I went out for beers—human contact, really—after our weekly reserve meetings. He was married and had two kids. His wife, Marilyn, resented our weekly night out, because we would usually stay until the bar closed at two in the morning. Frank and I could connect in a way that astonished us—in a way he and Marilyn couldn't. She saw this, and it hurt her. It wasn't that Frank didn't love Marilyn; he did. It was simply that Frank and I understood one another deeply in a way only males can. The relationships between most adult males in this society are somewhat distant, defensive, competitive, unemotional and boring. Such males usually talk about business, sports or how to do things, or they competitively brag. Rarely do they say something personal or express feelings, especially about one another. Frank and I were well beyond this, partly because he was trained in counseling and psychotherapy.

It was Frank who got me involved in weekly training sessions in gestalt therapy for professionals with Fritz Perls, father of gestalt therapy. Fritz was unforgettable. The first time I saw him, I sat nervously with a group of about 12 professionals, who were quietly looking at me, the self-conscious new member. Frank was smiling from ear to ear; he knew what would happen. Fritz stared at me with curiosity for too long. Then his thickly German-accented voice boomed out, "Vhat do you vant?" I gave him some intellectualized pap about learning the principles and techniques of gestalt therapy and understanding myself better. I thought it sounded pretty good, but he just sneered at me and said sarcastically, "Vell, you have shown us your brain. Vhy don't you show us your cock!" I panicked about what I thought he suspected.

Once, he asked me to describe everything that I was aware of in the present moment. I rattled off a catalogue of internal events, but he became angry: "You are a basket case! There is no hope for you! You are an idiot!" He got up from his chair, came over to me, pressed his large nose against mine and shouted, *"Now, vhat are you avare of?"* I suddenly understood: "I'm aware of *you*, Fritz." He relaxed and said, "Vell, perhaps there is some hope for you after all. I varned you about the subject-object split!" Perls was anti-intellectual, rude, and a great therapist. He deepened my appreciation for the range of human experience and helped me live in the present—where reality always is.

Frank and I attended these weekly happenings for almost a year, but the main reason we could be open with one another was because Frank wasn't defensive about his sexual feelings. Because of our easy openness and unusual degree of honesty, we developed a sexual attraction that was playful and harmless. We were secure in the knowledge that neither of us would ever let it go anywhere. Frank had no objections to same-sex relations; he'd even experienced some but preferred women. And he had no intention of being unfaithful to his wife, whom he loved. I, on the other hand, had no regrets that

I, then an adult, would never again participate in same-sex relationships. The last time had been with Fred Hessel over two years before then, and I was completely relieved to be free of it. Unfortunately, Frank knew I was attracted to him, so he enjoyed teasing me with outrageous suggestions. He particularly enjoyed watching me fidget and squirm as he described graphic details of his sex life with Marilyn.

Frank and I had to attend a two-week Army Reserve training camp each summer. Nobody took the training seriously, so nothing much happened except for gambling, letter writing, and serious drinking every evening as lonely males made ambivalent attempts to reach out to one another. At the NCO club, just before the end of our summer camp, Frank got stinking drunk while pouring his guts out to me about missing Marilyn. He could just barely walk; I helped him back to our barracks room. I put him to bed and managed to pull his boots and uniform off. Just as I was putting a blanket over him, he came out of his stupor, grabbed me, pulled me down to him, said he loved me, and tried to kiss me on the face. In slurred speech, he said I was the best friend he'd ever had. He started to cry, then lapsed into unconsciousness. I sat there, stunned, looking at this sleeping hulk, this big galoot, and I was flooded with feelings of love for my drunken friend. It was so easy for him to love and care, so effortless and honest. That's what I could never do. That's why I loved him.

The next morning, Frank was his usual, chipper self. "Wow, Denny, I really hung on a lulu last night, didn't I? Let's get over to the chow hall early, I'm starved! Hope I didn't throw up on you."

"No, you didn't, but you were really out of it, Frank. You probably don't remember much, do you?"

"I don't remember leaving the club or how I got back to the barracks. ...I do remember one thing. I remember telling you I loved you, and I mean that, Denny. I know it was a thrill for you to undress me, but I hope you didn't take advantage of me when I passed out. I'd want to be wide awake for that, old buddy, if you ever got up the nerve to try to take me on!"

"I'll never tell!" I said. "You'll just have to wait a couple of months and see if you get morning sickness, Franky! You'd still never know if it was me, because maybe I rented your body out to these horny guys around here for 20 bucks a shot!"

"You know, Denny, in the condition you and I are in, after we get back, Marilyn and Truel won't be able to walk for a week—maybe two. We're a couple of cowboys without our mounts. Back in the saddle again! Ride'em cowboy! Say, when are you going to get engaged to that little filly of yours? Marilyn and I think Truel is a fine woman. You two would make a great couple."

I'd met Truel in a class on the History of the Ideas of Western Civilization, on the day I decided I needed a girlfriend. What I noticed was her flowing mane of golden hair. My sister had beautiful blond hair, so had Keith and Bill Thomas—Pavlovian conditioning, perhaps. Anyway, after class, I asked the owner of this bright stream of hair out for a coke. Truel was a fun-loving person, a registered nurse. We liked each other immediately. We became good friends, even though I wasn't sexually attracted. What mild feelings of sexual attraction I occasionally had for a woman required a close friendship and good sex for a period of time, usually several months.

Truel lived with her divorced mother. Her father, a broken and frightened man, lived alone and related to no one, except for Truel on her occasional visits. Two years earlier, he had been released from prison after serving a sentence for embezzling from a bank. He was a tragic figure; a man who had only contempt for himself, waiting for the end of his disgraced life.

Truel and I became friends with an English professor and his wife, Bernard and Marcia O'Kelly. Bernard and Marcia were an amazing couple, and evenings in their home with their friends were treasured by me. I was particularly impressed with Marcia, because she was intellectual, beautiful and gracious. Truel was jealous of my friendship with Marcia, and with good reason. Bernard disparaged the pretentious scientism of psychology and said if I really wanted to understand people, I should study literature. Shakespeare, Kafka and Dostoyevsky understood people better than any psychologist ever had, he said. I've never had a reason to doubt that.

Truel became more sexually suggestive because of her insecurity about my admiration of Marcia; so, to reassure her and with Frank Robertson's encouragement, we got engaged. She'd said she was a virgin. Good girls in those days were supposed to be, but I strongly doubted her and couldn't have cared less. After our engagement, she said she was willing to give me her precious gift of virginity, if I wanted it. I wasn't overly enthusiastic, but I was willing to do my part and reminded myself of Dr. Samuels' comments about acquiring a taste for green olives and oysters. We had sex, because the script called for it; we were both acting, faking it, pretending to be in love.

Truel's performance the first time we had sex was a parody of the innocent virgin. I assured her that, for me, virginity was a state of incompetence at best, and that I knew she wasn't a virgin. I begged her to be honest, but she persisted in her deceit. I lost trust and respect for her. Months later, she admitted the truth, but it was too late for us.

I dated extensively then, because I wanted to be married. I had to put an end to my loneliness. I remember one woman in particular, Cathy. She did modeling, and I was pleased that she would date me. On an impulse, I drove to a motel with her, and she just smiled. We undressed and she lay back on the bed like a corpse. I asked her what she most wanted from me; she answered that she wanted me to put her on a pedestal and treat her "like a real queen." I wanted her to be real with me, but all she wanted was a romantic illusion, and I couldn't play her game. I abruptly got dressed and told her nothing could work out between us, because our values were in conflict—truth versus illusion. I didn't tell her that her undressed body looked silly. She asked if I wanted to make love, but I said no. She was surprised and told me I was the first man she'd been with who hadn't wanted to. She said I was odd. I made a bitchy reply, then I said, "Cathy, it's a lonely life living on top of a pedestal. Someday you might want to risk being real with someone and then, if you're lucky, you'll discover that loving is more fulfilling than being loved." Such projection; I was the one who couldn't be real. She told me I was a conceited, pompous ass who could go to hell and stay there.

"Besides, Denny," she hissed sweetly, "from what little I saw, I don't think you have the right equipment to satisfy me."

After that, I decided to be systematic about sorting women out. Dating became careful auditioning, nothing more. The romantic approach to life, as emotionally beautiful as it is, is based on idealized illusions about reality, appealing fictions. Romanticism is popular with the reality-challenged. The tendency of women working on their MRS. degree to say what they think potential husbands want to hear troubled me, and so, the auditioning. I withheld information about myself until they told me about themselves. I took my dates to foreign films I'd already seen and watched their reactions. I didn't waste much time with warm-ups and dating games. If a woman wasn't comfortable disclosing, I dropped her; defensive people usually have good reasons to be defensive. The variety of personalities and approaches was fascinating as I learned more about myself and what I wanted. After months of dating, I met Joyce.

Joyce worked at the psychology library. I was impressed by her openness, warmth and kind receptivity. Our eyes spoke, but I was hesitant. She surprised me one day by asking me out for a lemonade—the best investment she ever made, she used to say. This was far more honest than the usual waiting game played by most women of that era. She lived in the Scholarship House, a fact that impressed me, because this required a high grade-point average. She was a member of the University Symphonic Choir, voices of exceptional quality. Joyce had studied voice for many years. She was also singing in the university production of *Showboat* and invited me to see her. She was majoring in chemistry at the time. I was impressed by her academic ambition and her interest in science. I was growing tired of dating women whose primary scholastic interests were interior decoration, child development, home economics, kiddie literature, and elementary education—women who wanted to get married in order to be mothers. Joyce effortlessly passed the tests of my audition, including the foreign film. When I realized I'd found what I was looking for, I worried if she would have me. On our way driving back from a trip to Cincinnati to visit Gene Best, my friend from Miami University, and his wife, I asked Joyce if she would marry me. I knew the custom was for the man to be on his knees with a sufficiently large ring in hand, but that seemed too much like a john bargaining with a whore. She looked surprised, but not too surprised, smiled, hesitated a second or two, and said yes. In September of 1959, Joyce and I were married, 90 days after we met. She was 21, and I was 24.

Before we were married, Joyce asked if I'd ever been in love before. I was afraid she might reject me, but I said yes and told her about Keith and what Dr. Samuels had said about the delay in my sexual development. I told her what I believed, that I was beyond that psychosexual stage; it was finished. She seemed reassured. However, many years later, she told me that the way I'd talked about Keith made her believe then that I probably would prefer to be with men. She said she had always suspected I was gay, but she believed she could make me happy and never doubted that I would be faithful. The risk for her was minimal, because how could a homosexual man ever find happiness in the society of the '50s? We never discussed the topic again.

Joyce was not pleased, however, to learn I'd been with so many women, including an engagement with Truel and a year with Barbara White. She asked many questions about them. We weren't sexual before our marriage, because Joyce was a virgin and wanted to believe she was giving me something of value. That was the way it was in those heydays of unconscious sexual politics.

Before our wedding, I went off by myself to study our marriage vows, because a man's word was his honor then and marriage was a sacred covenant for me. The only promise that concerned me was faithfulness, forsaking all others. I had no doubt I could remain faithful to Joyce when it came to women; that would be easy, but it was my ability to love men that concerned me. With Joyce, I would be able to know the love of a woman, but could I also forsake the love of a man? As I thought about it, I realized that, if this were a society in which we were all truly free to live and love as we desired as long as we harmed no others in any way, if we were really free, then in truth, I knew then I would have preferred to share my life with a man—out West, somewhere. Sadly, I couldn't deny it. However, in 1959, such relationships were crimes in every state. Even today, over four decades later, nearly half the states still have such laws, and they were upheld by a 5-4 vote of the Supreme Court of the United States in the infamous Bowers v. Hardwick, 1986 case in which a state's right to deny specific sex acts between consenting adults in the privacy of their own home was upheld. The conservative justices cited the centuries-long tradition of religious discrimination against homosexuality as a justification for their opinion, an argument that could also be used to justify bigotry, racism, slavery and the oppression of women.

The only choice I saw society permitting me then was either marriage or a lifetime of fear and loneliness. Dr. Samuels had assured me that I would outgrow my homoerotic desires, and who was I to doubt his professional conclusions? I had to believe him, given the alternative, and these desires were less frequent and not as intense. I also believed there must be something of great value in traditional marriage, because it had remained so popular throughout history, something Dr. Samuels reassured me that I, too, would come to know and appreciate. I had enjoyed my year with Barbara, and Joyce was the kindest person I'd ever known. She was all that I looked for in a woman and more. I felt proud to be with her. Marriage to Truel would have been a mistake, but even she had been sweet to me in her own way.

I didn't worry about being sexual with a woman; because, at that age, I probably could have come off if I'd simply stood naked in front of a fan. I didn't experience emotional passion with women, but the physical stimulation was sufficient, and I believed that the passion would come with time, or so Dr. Samuels had assured me. I was worried about getting through the wedding night with a virgin; it seemed like the molesting of an uncomprehending child. I wondered if my father would be jealous of me because of how young and attractive Joyce was; I hoped so. I thought I might even like having children; I could then be the kind of father I never had. Then I worried if I would be able to love a daughter as much as a son. I had doubts about that because of the limited roles of women in those days. Women were outside the status hierarchies of society. What status they had came from their husbands—even their names. It was a son I wanted, but if we had a girl, then, as we used to say, I'd give it the old college try. I thought more about the advantages of marriage. I hoped Joyce could bake bread, because I imagined—in a burst of staggering originality—kids, a house with a white picket fence, a dog, a fireplace and fresh baked bread. And so I decided to forsake all others—meaning men—for her. When I realized I could make this promise in good faith—I saw no livable alternative—I glowed with the realization that I was about to be a married man, a normal, married man. And Joyce would be my lawfully wedded wife—forsaking all others, for better or for worse, for richer or for poorer, in sickness and in health...'til death us do part. Yes, yes, yes, Joyce! I do!

I was filled with compassion for Joyce as I watched her prepare for our wedding. This was the fulfillment of all she'd ever dared to dream of, this most significant of days in the life of a woman, and she loved me. Just before the ceremony began, Charlie, her father, an Archie Bunker bigot of the left, pulled me aside: "Denny, a friendly word of advice. As a union man for many years now, I've seen too many men who couldn't handle their women. Just remember this: if that little girl starts to give you a hard time, just take her shoes away! I mean it!" And he did. His Edith Bunker wife, Laura, seemed to know only two words: "Yes, Charlie!" Joyce, her younger brother, Phil, and Laura lived in cowering compliance to this tyrant, a college graduate in English who worked as a carpenter, cried over poetry, and had no status or authority outside his captive family.

The wedding ceremony was intensely emotional for everyone, even my father. The minister we had chosen held such tolerant views about religion that he said he would lose his job if the fire-and-brimstone old-timers in his congregation ever found out. We liked him, and he liked us. He said he would be proud to bless our union even though our beliefs were "unconventional." We were humanists, agnostics, closet atheists. I could barely control my emotions enough to get through my vows, because they were so sacred and meaningful for me. I remember looking into Joyce's eyes as I promised to forsake all others. I thought briefly of Keith then and felt ashamed that I'd thought of him during my wedding. The flaw was still with me, but I would continue to rise above it. As Joyce flooded with feelings while saying her vows, I watched tears dripping off the end of my sister's nose and wondered why she was crying. (Years later, she told me she'd cried because she believed she was losing me.) At the end of the service, the minister was crying, too, such was the sincerity and youthful idealism of our love and everlasting commitment.

At our reception dinner, my wife and I looked at our flawless new gold rings and at one another and were hardly aware of anything else, except for the glory of the music in the background of the immortal love duet from Puccini's *Madama Butterfly,* our own song. My God, how I loved that woman as she sat there beside me in the virginal white of her wedding dress, sewn by the fingers of her loving hands, this trusting woman, my wife...and my life. I do! I do, Joyce! I do!

We had little money, so we honeymooned in our tiny one-bedroom apartment near the university. On our wedding night, Joyce readied herself for the long-imagined moment and came to me with curiosity and a tinge of anxiety. She looked up at me and said her wish in life was to please me. I held her face in my hands and said it would please me more if she did not try to please me but pleased herself with me in our life together. I hoped sex with Joyce, my wife, the woman I loved, would be passionately emotional, unlike my pleasant experiences with other women.

I couldn't comprehend what it would be like to be a virgin giving herself away to the man she loved on her wedding night, and I hardly understood female sexuality. As I look back on that era and my own ignorance, I'm not surprised that so many women mainly valued the attention and affection of the sexual situation, because that was generally all a young woman would experience in the beginning. I was distressed that Joyce would know some pain when I first entered her, but her doctor had assured her that it would be minimal. Even so, as gentle as I was, I felt I was violating her. The deflowering—a sad metaphor, the reaming out was required, but it felt like rape to me, and I hated it. If Joyce was disappointed, she didn't say, so astonished was she by my insatiable sexuality and my vain and naive hope that she would know ecstasy in the consummation of our marriage. Physical exhaustion put us to sleep at dawn. I told her the experience had been wonderful; but, even with all the orgasms I had that night, I couldn't make the passionate magic happen in me. I knew it would take time, but I was worried, and I continued to worry long after my bride was asleep.

The next afternoon, I watched Joyce dress and realized that what was so familiar to her was strange for me. The differences between us, while initially interesting, made me feel lonely. It was like watching a friendly foreigner, a Hindu, getting dressed. Yet when we went out that day, I felt as though I were walking three feet off the sidewalk as I watched the sun glittering on our wedding rings. I wanted everyone to see my wedding band. I wanted to shout to everyone that I was a married man. I was at last what I was supposed to be!

My selection of Joyce had been correct in every way. Each year together was better than the one before. I was admitted to the best clinical psychology doctoral program in the country on full scholarship, and during my years of graduate study, Joyce finished her degree in science education and became a high school science teacher. Later, she earned her Master's degree in Counseling Psychology. We lived a fantastic year in the San Francisco Bay Area during my pre-doctoral internship at the Palo Alto V.A. Hospital and came to love the freedom and cultural diversity that is California. I completed my doctoral dissertation and received my Ph.D. degree in 1965; I was 30. My father became friendlier with me after I was married; but, true to his competitive character, when I received my doctoral degree, his only comment to me was, "Well, now you're a certified egghead. I guess they never managed to catch you in all those years of graduate school!" My mother told me he'd bragged to his coworkers about my degree, but she asked me not to tell him that she'd told me; he'd be angry with her, she said.

During my entire graduate education in clinical psychology, the subject of homosexuality was rarely mentioned by the faculty—white heterosexual males, not because it wasn't important, but because, for them, it was one of those unspeakable topics—like rape, incest, child molest, and necrophilia. Most people are far more comfortable discussing homicide than homosexuality, perhaps because violence is more socially acceptable than sex.

During my graduate training, however, I did see large cell blocks of homosexuals at both the Ohio State Penitentiary and the Chillicothe Federal Reformatory, where I did psychological evaluations. Some of these men had been sent to prison because of the crime of this love; others had been convicted of it while in prison. At Chillicothe, I interviewed a startlingly beautiful, blond, 19-year-old who was so strongly desired by inmates that the warden had ordered all prisoners to stay at least ten feet away from him. In the center of the large mess hall, this youth ate alone, his beauty framed by a ten-foot ring of empty tables. Beyond this ring were hundreds of eyes looking at him, but he never acknowledged their praise. That scene etched itself into my mind. Wherever he went, his beauty was like a protective force field that caused others to veer away. He told me that inmates had offered him money and protection if he would let them touch him. He'd done more than that he hinted as he searched for my response. He wouldn't be direct because of his fear of conviction for the crime of lovemaking. I hid behind my professional mask, but I was awed and threatened by him. He must have sensed this; because, when I left, I held out my hand to shake his, but he looked amused and hugged me instead. That brief moment of touch was beyond the boundaries of time. I was profoundly shaken; he saw this and was very pleased with himself.

Against my better judgment, on my next visit to the prison several weeks later, I asked to see him. The guards told me he wasn't there. He wouldn't be coming back, they said. He was in the hospital recovering from major surgery and would be there for some time. Rumor had it that the strongest guy in prison, the "king man," and five of his lieutenants had gang-raped him in a seldom-used supply room. It was the most brutal rape the guards had ever seen. A blanket had been thrown over his beautiful head from behind; he never saw his attackers, he said. They didn't speak but just grunted and groaned as they raped him. When they were done, they savagely raped him with the threaded end of a metal water pipe, perhaps proving to one another that they were not gay. He was found hours later unconscious in a pool of blood.

. . .

After I graduated, Joyce and I took the summer off and went canoe-camping deep into the mystical and transcendent beauty of the Canadian wilderness. Weeks went by before we could fully live in harmony with the natural rhythms of ourselves and nature, there being no need then for artificial time. We ate when we were hungry, slept when we were tired, woke when we were rested and made love in the elegant extravagance of nature. We became at one with ourselves and the universe. Because we wished it to be so, everything spoke to us of the universal presence and of Indian gods, who visited in endless manifestations preceded by fanfares of meteors and the stately dances of northern lights in the star-clustered sky. It was a magnificent summer, there in the wilderness with Joyce, just the two of us and the universe.

In a forest clearing—encircled by graceful ferns, overlooking the clear, dark, sky-hued waters, on a soft bed of lush emerald-green moss, in the warmth of the sun—Joyce and I, by choice, conceived our first child in the joy of our love. I expected sex for reproductive purposes would somehow feel different, but it didn't—so much for the propaganda of celibate priests. The next day, Joyce knew she was pregnant. Soon her cheeks were blushed with a healthy pink, and she was more beautiful than ever, as most women are during the marvel of pregnancy. We were what our society most wanted us to be, married and with child—Joseph, Mary, and Jesus—hope of the world.

We moved to Massachusetts for my post-doctoral fellowship at the end of this wilderness summer, and the following April, when I was 30 and Joyce was 27, I watched a healthy nine-pound son be born to us. A son! My son! My joy was so great that I didn't get a good night's sleep for an entire week. In the middle of the night, I'd wake up thinking about him, and I would cry at the very thought of his existence. My son! I was so moved by his birth that I named him Nathaniel, because the name means "the gift of God;" and he seemed like that. I was a psychologist, but I couldn't understand why my joy was so overwhelming. I now understand that this joy was born from my loneliness, as it is for many parents. I also knew the birth of a daughter wouldn't have brought as much joy, and I worried deeply about that.

As every parent knows, all is not bliss when a newborn child is plopped down in the middle of a marriage. We had been happily married for almost seven years; then suddenly, there was Nathan. Some months later, Joyce and I were exhausted, because she was nursing him every four hours. The impact of our irreversible decision to have a child was with us, and one night, when I had trouble sleeping, Joyce asked what I was thinking about. Hesitantly, I told her the truth, "Well, don't be upset with me. I love Nathan, but honestly, I was thinking if we cut him up into little pieces and put them down the garbage disposal, well, nobody would ever find his body!" There was a painful silence, then Joyce started to laugh almost uncontrollably as she confessed that she'd thought about burying him in a garbage bag underneath the house. Don't misunderstand, we loved Nathan deeply, but the stress of our ineptness as new parents had gotten to us.

What was married life like for us? Well, our close friends often commented about the exceptionally good marriage we had, and we knew that was true. We communicated well, had many interests in common, rarely argued or fought, and even did marital therapy together after Joyce got her Master's degree in Counseling Psychology. We played out many of the traditional male and female roles, but we became aware of this and worked on it long before it became a popular issue. She taught me how to sew, and I taught her how to ride a motorcycle. We helped one another learn the many subtleties of our pink and blue subcultures. This helped me feel closer to Joyce and to women in general. Men do have more trouble understanding the behavior of women than vice versa. The privileged don't need to pay much attention to the feelings of subordinates. Regretfully, I still took advantage of my male status, as most men do even today. Joyce accepted this unfairness without complaint, as women continue to do.

Joyce wanted me to be more physically affectionate, but I felt comfortable touching her only during sex. I thought this was because I'd grown up in a family that hadn't been affectionate, but I wasn't sure I felt affection. Sex had been the only affection I'd ever known. I couldn't understand how a person could be touched without thinking about sex, and I couldn't stand sexual frustration, so I rarely touched people, and then only briefly. I was often uncomfortable being touched, especially by men. It was easier for me to touch women than men, because I didn't feel anything, but Joyce wanted more affection than I was able to give. I was aware of this and constantly felt guilty, but I couldn't fake what I couldn't feel, although I often tried. Our sex life was uninhibited; we enjoyed sex almost every day throughout the marriage. Joyce was easily orgasmic and often had multiples, much to my envy. The passionate magic never happened for me during our sex, but this became unimportant for me as the years rolled by. Our physical sex was always good, an orgasm is an orgasm. I didn't fantasize during sex, but only concentrated on physical sensations. On rare occasions, I had sexual dreams about males, but never females. These dreams distressed me. I would withdraw into myself in shame for a day or two.

In spite of theses "glitches"—that's how I thought of them—Joyce was my best friend and the primary source of my happiness. I loved being married. It was warm and secure, and I was a respected member of the straight community. I had family and friends, my career was going well, and the future looked very good for us. We did all of the things couples and parents do. We shared learning, travel, nature, friends, gardening, backpacking, fishing, amateur radio, canoeing, photography, astronomy, gourmet cooking, psychology, the arts (particularly music—she sang and I accompanied with the classical guitar), and we loved our children. We raised three fine sons and made a cultured home for them. Joyce was very good to me and loved me, and I loved her as my dearest friend. Life with her was comfortable, secure and enjoyable. Our marriage was better than most. There's really not much more of significance for me to say about my married life; and that fact is the most telling description of all. We were married for 20 years. I didn't notice that I was slowly dying inside, but then, I wouldn't have noticed. Many married people don't. We see only what we believe is livable and deny the rest.

. . .

The relationship of a son to his father is of central importance in the life of a man. Young men long to be initiated into the powerful fraternity of men, to be accepted into manhood. These vital rites of initiation can only be performed by men—older men, the tribal elders. We have precious few of these essential rituals, much to our social detriment. If a son is not accepted and loved by his father, he will be haunted by demons throughout his life. But these essential rites of passage can also be performed by other older men—mentors. I was not accepted by my father, and I did live with demons until I underwent my five-year test of manhood called doctoral education. My spiritual father, my mentor on this difficult journey, was Professor George A. Kelly, one of the founders of clinical psychology.

George Kelly was a formal person and somewhat shy, but he was one of the most perceptive observers of people I've ever known. His skills were so great that he adopted a kindly grandfather facade so as not to threaten people. He was deeply compassionate. He taught me so much, but what I most cherish were the lessons he taught by the example of his life. He was his own best lesson. He once said to me, "In the final analysis, the most important truth we will ever know in our lives is the truth of our human relationships. Never forget that." There is so much to say about this mentor I loved, but I'll describe only two rites of initiation he performed, releasing me from many of my demons.

After receiving my doctoral degree, I went to Massachusetts to continue my research with him; he was at Brandeis University then. George Kelly was in his early 60's when he moved to Brandeis at the invitation of Abraham Maslow. Early in my graduate career, George Kelly had suffered a serious heart attack. His response to this had been to write a detailed phenomenological account of his experience. He described what he thought and felt as he lay helpless on his living room floor, looking into his wife's terrified face. He was in agony and believed he was going to die. After he had recovered, he took a leave from teaching and traveled, against medical advice, around the world for a year and a half, something he'd always wanted to do. Years later at Brandeis, he was again having heart trouble.

His wife, Gladys, called and invited my wife Joyce and me to dinner at their home, just us. This was extraordinary. On the infrequent times that the Kellys entertained, it was usually a gathering of people, but certainly not for dinner. Joyce and I were apprehensive; we knew this invitation signaled something quite special, but we couldn't imagine what. In keeping with their style, the dinner was formal, with heavy silver, crystal, linen, fine china and candelabra. They were painstakingly gracious. George, quite tired, was having angina pains. Occasionally, he would discretely slip nitroglycerin tablets under his tongue. On the floor beside him, not quite fully hidden from view, was a green oxygen cylinder and a mask. This fact chilled me and established the dramatic context for his every comment and gesture. When I asked about the oxygen, he made light of it for our sakes, but I saw the look in his wife's eyes and the way she bit her lower lip.

At the end of dinner, I reached for my water glass, but it was empty. I turned toward a water pitcher on the buffet behind me. Ever vigilant, George intervened: "I see you're in need of some water. I'll get you some."

Being painfully aware of his condition, I insisted, "No! It's no trouble. It's right here. I'll fill your glass, too."

As I started to rise, he said firmly, "Denny, allow me. You are my guest, and I am your host."

"Please, George, it's no trouble," I protested.

But he said, "No, I insist!" and I knew it would be rude to press the issue. All eyes were on him as, with the effort of illness and age, he slowly rose from his chair, took the water pitcher from the buffet and carefully filled my glass.

I choked back the sob struggling in my throat, because I suddenly understood. I looked up in awe at my beloved mentor, my good father. He saw this change in me, and it pleased him. He smiled slightly, and unforgettably spoke: "I see you understand I've just given you far more than a glass of water." This was the purpose of the dinner. I looked at Joyce. She understood, and her tears were flowing for me...and for him. Even to this day, when I see a person pouring a glass of water for another, I remember. Yes, George Kelly, the truth of our human relationships is the most important truth we shall ever know.

The second and most important rite happened several weeks later. George called me one morning and asked if we could get together for most of that afternoon. He knew I had clients to see, but he told me I would soon understand why he was making this unusual request. He insisted on driving to Worcester where I was. Of course I agreed, but I was apprehensive. When we met, I talked with him about a client who had just told me she was terminally ill with cancer. He made many helpful suggestions for counseling the dying and then said our discussion was pertinent. He said he'd just come from Massachusetts General Hospital in Boston where he'd been told he needed immediate heart surgery or he would soon be dead. Unfortunately, the odds of surviving this difficult surgery were estimated to be no better than 50 percent. "Of course, it makes sense for me to have the surgery, Denny, but it also makes sense to anticipate the alternatives. One should never be caught with his alternatives down! Now, I've led an extraordinarily rich and full life. I've been quite fortunate and privileged, but I've also been aggressive in doing the things I most wanted to do, so I have no real regrets about dying. I don't want my life to end, but I've realized most of my important goals. I wanted us to get together today to help you anticipate the possibility of my death. It would be more difficult for you if you were to be suddenly shocked by such unexpected news. Most importantly, you and I have the opportunity to say all the things we need to say to one another. Do you understand what I mean? I can spare you the awful pain and burden of never having said what you needed to say to me. Let's talk, Denny. Let's talk from our hearts...while we can."

And all that long afternoon, we did—in the rapture of a wedding of love and death. Calling on all my courage, controlling all my fear, willingly risking my career and crying as I spoke, I finally found my voice; I told George Kelly, my good father, that I loved him. He smiled and put his hand on mine. "I've known that, Denny. And I think I understand why it was so very difficult for you to say. Some people are so terribly frightened that they think white is black, and black is white. I'm glad you had the courage to speak the human truth to me, and you will be glad, too—all of the days of your life. My actions demonstrate my regard for you. Now, my friend, I'm going to teach you my final lesson in my long and productive years with you. I'm going to give you a gift of great value. You see, I intend to leave you a psychological legacy that will be with you forever, Denny. Until recently, I'd always seen my death as the final defeat of my human values, but now I realize that even the fact of my death and dying can be put to my own human purposes. This insight gives me great happiness. We both know death is inevitable. You, too, shall one day follow me in this certain event. Inevitable events are our circumstances. What is important is not our circumstances—they are the givens of life—but, rather, how we choose to confront our circumstances. That is our humanity—our choices. The legacy I leave you is this: I intend to show you by the manner in which I approach my own death and dying that you have absolutely nothing to fear when you inevitably follow me. This shall be my final gift to you."

George Kelly said what he needed to say to the many people in his life. He put his affairs in order and arranged the details of his funeral. He told me, "Funerals are so lugubrious, Denny! My casket will be closed. Corpses are morbid. I'm not very good-looking, anyway. Funerals are for the living, not the dead. It is to be a time of coming together, of joining. My casket will be in a separate room away from the group. Caskets are so depressing to look at. I want you all to celebrate your coming together and one another. Remember, life is for the living, not the dead. Enjoy it! Be on with it!"

George hired his physician on the condition that he be informed of the truth of his medical condition at all times. He told me that he'd said to his doctor, "I've always been a man of truth, Dr. Nelson, and I don't intend to stop now. Never dishonor me with deception or partial truths." The operation was performed, and it was a success. He would be coming home soon.

George's wife told me what happened next. At eight o'clock that morning, Dr. Nelson told George about the results of the latest blood tests. The worst had happened. He told him that his internal infections were now uncontrollable because of his diabetic condition. Death would be soon he said.

"Dr. Nelson," Kelly replied, "what you did took courage. You have been a man of your word. I honor and thank you for that. God bless you. Now, call my family, and we shall spend these last hours together in truth." The rest of his family came, and those hours were spent in truth, and on that ashen-gray rainy afternoon, George Kelly died.

During the memorial service at the Brandeis Chapel, hundreds of students stood silently outside in the rain, there being no more room in the chapel. I feared that the minister would use George's death as an opportunity to slip in a commercial for Jesus, but he didn't. He said, "I know there may be many here who may not believe in an afterlife, and sometimes I'm not sure of that myself, but I had the good fortune to be a personal friend of George's, and because of that, I hope he is up there somewhere, still asking his wonderful questions." Never have I wanted to believe so much as at that moment. I have often held imaginary conversations with George Kelly ever since.

. . .

For my first academic appointment, George Kelly wanted me to accept a position at Harvard, but I had always wanted to live out West. I had my heart set on the beautiful University of Colorado at Boulder at the foot of the magnificent Rockies. Even though he opposed my going to this school, his secretary told me he'd written the strongest letter of recommendation she ever typed. After two grueling days of oral exams, I won the faculty appointment in the doctoral clinical psychology program, and Joyce, Nathan and I moved to Boulder in the summer of 1967.

Joyce and I were looking over the campus one day when I felt a strong emotion, and this startling thought flashed through my consciousness: I don't want to be a university professor! What a completely alien conception, a craziness, I thought. I quickly disregarded it, although I was puzzled and troubled by its emotional force. I should have listened to myself instead of trying to validate idealized theories about who I should be. Theories are speculations. What we need are descriptions of what actually happens. This was a very hard lesson for me to learn, because for most of my life, I couldn't trust my feelings, my grossly abnormal feelings.

During the excitement and turmoil of the '60s, I thought that universities were islands of freedom and sanity amid the seas of mindless social conformity. I cheered and celebrated the free speech movement, begun at Berkeley, because I lived in silence in my closet, fearing the loss of my job. But a famous professor who befriended me said: "Oh, you bright-eyed, bushy-tailed, optimistic young Turks who think you can save humanity and change human nature. So you think universities are islands of hope? All of us were like you, once...so long ago. Well, my little idealist, you will come to know that universities, far from being the cure for social ills, are a major cause of them. Welcome, Denny. I'm not sure you'll like it here. Your heart isn't sufficiently hard, nor your skin thick enough." His cynicism revealed a jaded, but passionate, vision of our human potentialities.

My scientific research on the psychological significance of change in the self-concept—quite personally relevant for the closet case I was—attracted interest in Britain. During my first year as an academic, when I was 32, I was invited to address the British Psychological Society. It was an impressive experience, with toasts of sherry to the Queen, groups reading poetry in the evenings, and a town house in Chelsea. I went without Joyce, because the Society paid only my expenses, and our second son, Brendan, had been born just four months earlier. This trip changed the direction of my life.

One day while I was there, I was invited to breakfast by an Oxford don who abruptly informed me, "You racist Americans are up to it again! You have just assassinated Dr. Martin Luther King. Is there to be no limit to the violence of your people?" Seeing that I was heartsick, another more empathic English colleague offered to take me to Canterbury Cathedral. He was a student of history and something of an expert on the American Civil War. He made the silent stones of Canterbury speak of what they had witnessed. The tale of the friendship and crisis between King Henry II and the extraordinary Thomas à Becket, Archbishop of Canterbury deeply moved me. When, in silence, my friend took me to the spot of the martyrdom of Becket, the place where this man had been hacked to death by four of the King's swordsmen in 1170, I wept for him. "I don't understand why I should be so moved by the death of a man eight centuries ago. Who is he to me? I don't understand the significance," I lamented to my English friend, who was somewhat embarrassed by my open display of emotion.

"Why, indeed," he replied, and said no more.

What impressed me about Becket was that he believed in the worth of something, rightly or wrongly, enough to die for it—that was what was important. I thought about how Becket had been transformed by his sudden elevation to the position of archbishop, and I recalled these words of King David: "Let us fall now into the hand of the Lord...and let me not fall into the hand of Man" (II Samuel 24:14). That was my own deep longing—to have something I cared for deeply enough that I would die for it. I suddenly realized that, for some unknown reason, I identified with the martyred Becket...as I had with the victims of the Holocaust. My tears for him were also for me, thus setting in place another piece of the puzzle of my life. Today, I realize that those tears were also for all the oppressed people of planet earth.

Some days later, I visited Westminster Abbey for the first time. Several of my English colleagues offered to go with me, but I wanted to go alone to this special place whose history I'd studied so well, this spot where 900 years of English Kings and Queens had been crowned. I walked around the dark exterior of the Abbey and felt my excitement mounting; then, knowing this experience would be unforgettable, I approached the north entrance. I walked in, glanced up at the soaring Gothic splendor of the vaulted, carved stone ceilings of the transept, and rushed outside again, so convulsed with emotion that I feared I would collapse into a quaking mass and be carted off to a British mental hospital. I sat quietly and self-consciously on a park bench trying to calm myself from the emotional impact of the shattering grandeur of Gothic spirituality. Eventually, when I could think again, I made a plan. I'd enter the Abbey and just look at the stone floor. I'd sit down immediately and practice relaxation exercises, still looking only at the floor. Then, very slowly, I'd look up at a small part of a wall. When I was relaxed again, I'd look at more. I followed this plan, and when at last I dared to raise my eyes to look at the glory of the whole...just at that exact moment...the choir began to sing. For the first time, I heard the purity of the soprano voices of English choir boys, and this sound was like an ethereal blue flame pervading holy space. My intelligence, this faithful old servant of mine, respectfully suggested a coincidence but didn't argue with my yearning heart that longed for it to be otherwise.

In time, I was able to walk about this sanctuary, this shrine of cultural significance, and I stayed there the rest of the day. It was like a homecoming for me. The reason I was so emotional was because this holy place was in such contrast to the spiritual wasteland of my country and self. I had been slowly dying for a very long time, and I was nearly empty inside. The self-absorption and vain status-seeking of individualism and the emptiness of materialism and hedonism were gods in America, now that the memories of meaningful community were fading in the indifferent crowds of cities. I had paid them homage as well. I wondered what it might be that modern man would fall down on his knees to worship...only himself, it seemed. The churches are run by fools, I thought, science can't save us, the government is corrupt, corporations exploit, schools are prisons, families are dysfunctional, people are self-seeking...so one can no longer rely on God, or Man, leaving only Nature...which is utterly indifferent to our fate and which we pollute and destroy. Cynically, I believed there was only the individual left—our frightened, floundering, pathetic, lonely self, and I couldn't trust that. Why am I kidding myself, I asked; I'm a man of constant sorrow, and I don't know why.

I was damn good at depressive thinking.

My sorrow was overwhelming that day in Westminster Abbey. Joyce and my sons depended on me to lead them, but I was lost; I couldn't find the path. I couldn't even remember where I was trying to go. Yet in this holy place, I was taken beyond myself, and I sensed the cosmic, eternal context of what I am. There, in the cathedral, I knew I was a part of this incomprehensible whole. I exist, because it exists. I am of it, and it is of me. In that sacred, clear moment, I knew what was real and what I ultimately am. I was at peace in this awareness which is beyond time and space. Yet, when I left there, I knew the separations and divisions would begin again. Which is truth? and which is illusion? or are they one? I asked myself. I knew I ached when I was separated from this timelessness. Was the sense of separateness the source of my constant sorrow, I wondered as this piece of the puzzle entered my consciousness.

I often intellectualized like this in my depressed states. What I couldn't dare admit to myself was that I was dying of separation and loneliness, 12 years of solitary confinement in my cage. I needed to be fused into one with a loving man, but I couldn't even think that thought.

That evening, I attended vespers service, not because my capacity for rational thought had suddenly weakened, but I went to hear again the voices of the angels, the English choir boys. When individual people join in concert in such harmony to create beauty, it is what is best about us. After the service, the choir led the procession of robed churchmen down the main aisle beside me. In the middle of the procession was the elderly Senior Vicar of the Abbey, resplendent and gentle. I was flooded with the glory of the music and the sanctity of the Abbey, yet troubled by thoughts of the emptiness of the life to which I would soon return. I noticed the old Vicar studying my conflicted face as he came toward me; he looked puzzled, even distressed, by what he saw. I looked at him, and our eyes communicated as one human being reaching out to another. Then, just as he walked beside me, he stopped, turned, and looked deeply into me, his face troubled. Then he became calm and made the sign of the cross, blessing me. He paused as he noticed tears forming in my eyes, gently smiled in satisfaction, and quietly moved on. I sat there until the Abbey was empty and silent. I knew then I could no longer return to my former life, yet I didn't know what the future would bring, much less what I wanted it to be. I was only 32 at the time, but this was the beginning of a predictable mid-life crisis—a destination crisis, a crisis of purpose and meaning. It was like waking up from a long coma and realizing I was on my death bed. Everyone is; most are dreaming.

It was dark and cold when I left the Abbey. I went to St. James Park, where I walked, remembering the elderly Vicar. What had this perceptive old man understood about me? I wondered. He was distressed by what he saw. Why was it important for him to bless me? It seemed to me that he realized I would have to face some terrible ordeal and perhaps lose my life. He blessed me to protect me, or perhaps out of compassion. It seemed like that to me. I remember that throughout St. James Park that night, thousands of large daffodils, their golden trumpets heralded the spring in the cold of that night.

Chapter Seventeen

"Love, you might say, is the burning point of life, and since all life is sorrowful, so is love. And the stronger the love, the more the pain, but love bears all things. Love itself is a pain, you might say, that is the pain of being truly alive."

Joseph Campbell

We often avoid knowing our own greatest happiness, because not having what we most inwardly desire is the source of our greatest suffering. This is why the normal habitual existence of apathy and indifference is preferred by most to the suffering of the truly passionate life. Love is the pain of being truly alive, of being awake to our own greatest happiness, and grief is often the pathway to this wisdom. Those who will not grieve...cannot live. I learned this in a convincing way, the hard way.

In England, I became aware of my constant sorrow, my separateness and spiritual emptiness—as I thought of it then. For a time, I believed my sorrow was related to the turmoil of the '60s, the decade that was the best of times and the worst of times—of civil rights and the peace movement and of assassinations and body counts. I watched too many graduate students become drug addicts as they tuned in, turned on and dropped out into a world of subjectivism, self-absorption and despair. I cheered the freedom movements, but I couldn't recognize my own oppression, because of the heterosexism of this culture.

I also thought my sorrow came from the cynical goal expected of me as a professor to publish quantity. I knew most psychological experiments were worth little, since the findings were rarely cumulative and had little generality. Academic psychologists tend to study journal articles and journal editors more than the psychology they actually use everyday to make sense of people. I shocked the psychology department when I resigned and accepted a promotion at a university where the pressure to play the publication game was not so intense. Ironically, that school was Miami University, the school I'd flunked out of as an undergraduate.

Before we left for Miami University, Joyce earned her Master's degree in counseling psychology and gave birth to our third son, Brett. The three children were a compromise between my desire for two and Joyce's hope for four. I think she wanted to try for a daughter. On the morning I was scheduled to have a vasectomy, Joyce urgently called from her gynecologist's office to tell me that he had just found a large tumor needing immediately removal. He said she could have her tubes tied at the same time. The tumor was benign. We were finally free from the worry of contraception. Our sex life became even better without the fear of pregnancy, a fear that had always lurked in the background.

In the summer of 1970, we moved to Oxford, Ohio. I was a professor in a congenial graduate department. Joyce was a warm and charming wife, who was devoted to me; and we had sex almost every night. We lived with our three healthy sons in a beautiful white home. Joyce had an excellent position at the University Counseling Service. We baked bread, planted a vegetable garden, played the piano and sang around our traditional fireplace. Norman Rockwell, the painter of mythical America, would have liked us. We even had a white dog, a West Highland White Terrier from California named Toulumne—after the white waters of the Toulumne River where we'd back-packed—and a white cat named Percy. We planned to live happily ever after, playing with our many grandchildren and dying contentedly while asleep in each other's arms at an overly ripe old age in our white bedroom. But the gods of Olympus were slapping their naked thighs and laughing, for whom the gods would humble they first strike down with passion.

One day, after walking through the archway inscribed with the words "Ye shall know the truth, and the truth shall make you free," I became somewhat nostalgic and decided to make a pilgrimage to the slight hilltop where 16 years earlier I'd seen Keith's face in the sky and lost consciousness. I rarely thought of Keith, but his image was powerful and precious. Only in moments of great distress would I allow myself to step up to the altar of my sacred memories and open the golden doors of the tabernacle to see his radiant face for a brief moment or two. His presence always restored my soul. I'd even hoped that this life-giving image would be the last thing I would see before my death, so I was very careful not to misuse his icon. I felt guilty for wanting that. It was also true that I didn't want to think about him. After telling Joyce about Keith before we were married, I never spoke of him again to anyone. I was a married man. I wanted him to be simply a pleasant memory from my childhood.

I found the exact spot where I'd stood when Keith's face appeared in the sky almost 17 years before. The dormitory where I'd been carried was the same, except more ivy was on the old brick walls. Several of my undergraduate students, who were the age I had been then—19, greeted me, and we talked for awhile. Was I that young then? I wondered.

I hiked down to the Talawanda River and found the place where I'd burned Keith's picture. The fallen tree was gone, but I recognized the curve in the river. It had been so long ago; I'd changed. Everything was so passionate then, so intense; but, at 36, I didn't feel much of anything. I was well-adjusted and successful doing what I was supposed to do. I was normal, almost. So why my constant sorrow? Life was easy, but I was dead inside and couldn't smell the rot. I was born a man, but I'd become a career—not unusual for men. About the only thing I valued was my contact with a few graduate students and my psychotherapy clients. I thought perhaps I was just getting burned out in academia. I didn't know anyone on the psychology faculty I'd call happy. There wasn't a good friendship between any two of them, not unusual for straight men. They were frightened and off center, so obsessive-compulsive, but so was I. Most of them secretly knew their publications meant nothing to anyone, including themselves. What a fate. Professors who have nothing to profess...or to confess.

I was invited to give a workshop on the self-actualizing personality—a case of the dead leading the blind. We were doing small group exercises, and I asked the groups one evening to do some expectancy-free fantasy work. In this exercise, a person is asked to imagine that he is waking up on the morning of a perfect day in his life, a day in which anything can happen, a day with no reality constraints. Most of us tend to want only what we expect we can get; but when we free ourselves from expected outcomes and circumstances through fantasy, we can tap unconstrained desires and motivations that are the well-springs of our psychological lives. What people tend to fantasize is what has high reward value for them, but what they believe is unlikely to occur at present. Most people initially imagine a beautiful home and scenery, great food and friends, being loved, good sex and traveling to exotic places. Such people are often lonely, live in a cramped apartment in a dirty city, haven't enough money to travel, are either unhappily married or divorced, and are on a perpetual diet.

The group I was leading that evening was coming up with the usual things, until we came to Jack Wiseman. Jack was 30 and married. He had two young children: a boy and a girl. He worked as an engineer designing rockets. He was taking biology courses, so he could be admitted to medical school. As an undergraduate student, he had earned almost a perfect grade average. Physically, Jack was striking. He was an inch or so shorter than average height, but he was a body builder, perhaps to compensate. He was broad-shouldered, well tapered and powerfully muscled. His head was classically handsome, with casual curls of thick, jet-black hair, and his sensitive, intelligent eyes were of the darkest brown, almost black, with long eyelashes. His manner was shy, perceptive and gentle. I was stunned when he quietly began to tell his fantasy. I'd listened to many fantasies over the years, but Jack's was the most unusual and moving one I'd ever heard. In his gentle way, he spoke of a truly human community, a spiritual utopia of the highest human values where people could be fully human with one another. The more details he gave, the more deeply moved I became, because his dream was my own. When he finished, we were all so emotional that no one spoke. He looked around shyly; and, when he realized the effect he'd had, he smiled and blushed and looked down at the floor. The last time I'd felt emotions like that had been in Westminster Abbey years before.

When the class was over, a number of people stopped to talk with me. I noticed that Jack was patiently waiting until everyone finished. He asked if he could talk with me privately sometime to get my advice. I explained that I was busy with clients, extra teaching, research, committees, other responsibilities and my family and told him I couldn't. He looked pained and pleaded with me to reconsider. He said he would come any time, day or night. The look in his dark eyes was frantic. I remembered how moved I'd been by his fantasy, so I reluctantly agreed to see him once.

The following week, Jack and I met for an hour. His concern was about his marriage. His wife had been somewhat psychologically disturbed when he'd first met her in New York, and, in part, he had married her out of compassion. Things went downhill in their relationship, and he blamed himself. They were in marital therapy at the time, but he said he had a sexual problem. He confessed that he suffered from premature ejaculation with her. He wanted to know what I knew about the treatment of this disorder and whom I'd recommend he see. He was surprised when I suggested that premature ejaculation might mean that his wife was taking too long to have an orgasm. He'd never thought of it as possibly being her problem and neither had she; he laughed at the fitting novelty of the idea. I told him other factors that might be involved, whom he could see, and suggested a number of techniques for them to try. He was delighted; and, for the remainder of the hour, we talked about his extraordinary fantasy. He was a fan of Theilhard de Chardin and the utopian architect Soleri. He and his wife had even visited Arkasanti, Soleri's experimental community. The hour was too quickly over. We both wanted to meet again, so our friendly Friday afternoon get-togethers began.

Our one-hour meetings quickly became three and four hour sessions. Even this was not nearly enough for us, because our lives became the topics. Jack's visits were the high point of my week; and, one warm spring day months later, I remember walking across campus from the faculty club to meet him after having lunch with Joyce. I suddenly felt an incredible lightness, as if I were walking three feet above the sidewalk on a soft, springy cushion of air. It actually felt like that. I thought perhaps I was dizzy, but I wasn't. Everybody else was walking normally, but there I was, springing along in air. I thought of Jack waiting for me, and my insides contracted in a rush of joy. Then I knew: My God! I'm in love! Oh, my God, I am! I'm in love with Jack! I'm in love with a man! ...But I'm married and a father—three times a father! I've been faithfully married for 12 years! Oh God, what's happening to me, I asked.

I slumped down on a stone bench, depressed and guilty. One of my students noticed me and asked if I was okay. When I nodded yes, he went on his way. What could I say to him—no, I'm in love with Jack! I couldn't believe it; yet, each time I thought of Jack, I felt an unbelievable surge of joy. Why was I worried, I wondered. These feelings would harm no one, and I'd never do anything improper. They're just feelings. He's a married man and a father, too! Just enjoy your good fortune, I said to myself; you haven't felt like this in years. I tried to remember the last time. Maybe it was when Nathan, my first son, was born. I told myself, just enjoy the present and turn that analytical brain of yours off for awhile. Accept life as you find it. Jack's waiting for you!

Jack was an enthusiast of the human potential movement and had gone to many workshops. He went through therapy as a result of having been raised by a Jewish mother, or so he said. He was psychologically perceptive. When I met him that day, he immediately noticed my mood. "Denny, what's happened to you?" he said. "I get these vibrations that you're buzzing with happiness inside, or something. Maybe you're going manic! What's up?"

I said I wasn't sure, but that I was happy, because I was thinking about our friendship. I couldn't tell him the shameful truth. I told him I really valued his friendship and was very glad to see him. He said, "Hey, these Friday afternoons are the best part of my week. We never have enough time, though. You're strange! I keep asking you to do all sorts of things with me on the weekends, so we can have more time together, but you never want to do any of them! Why not? Don't you really want to be friends?"

I lied, "Yes, I do, Jack, but I've been so busy, and I like to be with my family on the weekends. We have faculty cocktail parties to go to and other things. I'm not trying to avoid you." Lying to him made me feel lonely and ashamed. The truth was that I had avoided close male friendships throughout my marriage—as do many married men.

"Well, then, lets do something!" he said. "I've invited you to my home, we could go camping, fishing, hiking, out to dinner, I don't care. Let's just do something!"

"Okay. What do you suggest?" I asked, not wanting to initiate anything; I was too threatened by my feelings for him.

"Well, you're the big outdoorsman, Denny. Let's take a camping trip! You've got all the equipment. We could take one of your canoes. I've never been canoeing. Let's do that!"

"Where would we go?"

"Kentucky. A friend of mine says the Green River near Mammoth Caves is beautiful in spring. How about it?"

"Well, I don't know. Maybe we could do something else. Something for an afternoon," I said with no enthusiasm.

And he said, "Denny! Look, I don't like it when you won't talk straight with me. I've mentioned going camping with you a couple of times before, and each time you back away from the idea. I know you love camping. You've spent months and months in Canada, the Rockies and the Sierras, but you won't spend a weekend with me. Why not? Won't Joyce let you? Are you just pretending to be friendly? Is that it?"

Jack was right; I did owe him an explanation. I couldn't stand the deception and the lonely feelings anymore, but I was afraid to tell him. I thought for a few moments and decided to risk being honest. If he couldn't accept my reality, then to hell with him. In a controlled voice, I said, "Jack, I'm sorry. I do want us to be friends, I really do. The reason I won't go camping with you has nothing to do with you or anything you've done. The reason is, I'm afraid of my homosexuality."

"Your homosexuality? ...You aren't homosexual, are you?"

"No, I'm not, but I'm aware I have a potential for it," I admitted.

He said, "Well, everybody has feelings like that sometime. Kinsey says most people have a bisexual potential; you ought to know that."

"I know, but I've experienced those relationships."

"How long ago? Recently?" Jack's face was tense and serious.

"No," I said, "I've been completely faithful to Joyce. Let's see, the last time was...16 years ago, when I was in the Army."

In a flat voice, Jack said, "Oh. Well, at least now I understand you better. Thanks for telling me. That must have been very difficult for you to admit. I'm glad you trust me. I won't mention this to anyone. I'd better be getting back. See you next week." Jack looked troubled. I expected him to reject me and thought that might be for the best, the end of a temptation.

After Jack left my office, I sat at my desk and remembered a similar time years earlier, when I was finishing my doctoral degree. There was this student, Bill Pearloff, a senior in the introductory psychology class I was teaching. What I remember noticing first about Bill was the graceful motion of his body—odd, what we remember. He was an athlete, a varsity baseball pitcher, and his movements flowed. He always proudly wore his cardinal-red Ohio State letter jacket, but he didn't need it for people to notice him. He was exceptionally beautiful, and he noticed me watching him. He signed up as a subject for a psychology experiment I was running. I took the opportunity to give him a battery of personality inventories in the hope he'd have feet of clay, but he didn't. He was one of the healthiest people I'd ever tested, and I felt unnerving envy. He was the only child of wealthy parents, who adored him and made leather-bound scrapbooks about his life. He said he loved his father so much that he French-kissed him; he wasn't joking. Bill had also just been admitted to a prestigious medical school, and his future was assured. One day, he asked me to have a beer with him, and I did. He told me he knew I was attracted to him. I denied it, of course, but he just smiled.

When he went away on field trips with the baseball team, he sent me clippings from the local papers praising his pitching skills. I would become depressed, because he wasn't in class. He liked to show up in places where I least expected him, like the stacks reserved for graduate students in the main library or a hangout favored by psychology graduate students; he would ask me to have coffee with him, and I always did. I knew I'd fallen in love with Bill when I began to dream about him—wonderful dreams of him calling my name and running gracefully toward me, hugging me, his face filled with joy and relief at finding me.

Bill pressured me into having dinner with him once. I resisted for one or two seconds. We met in a Chinese restaurant near campus, and there, over hot egg rolls, he told me he knew I loved him and that he loved me, and it didn't matter what I said, he knew what I felt. He said, "Denny...or should I start calling you Professor again? I want you to come to my apartment tonight. I want to show you my sports trophies. Will you come?"

I was irritated and said, "Trophies? Are you sure it's your trophies you want me to admire, not your perfect body?"

"Knock the sarcasm off!" he said. "I know how we both feel. Don't pretend with me anymore, Denny! I'm not exactly blind or stupid, you know. Why go on frustrating each other? Let's go after dinner tonight. Now...if you want to."

I told him, "Bill, for God's sake, I'm a married man! You're my student!"

"Denny, love is where you find it," he said. "No one will ever know. I know you love your wife, and that won't change. It'll just be for this one night—you and me—a night you'll always remember. That's all I want. I'm only going to ask you once. You want to, don't you? I can see it in your eyes."

I couldn't hide it anymore, so I told him the truth, "Christ, Bill, I've dreamed about you! You're the cultural ideal. You're beautiful, and you know it. I wake up thinking about you with my wife sleeping beside me and the moonlight coming through the window, and I think about that same moonlight touching you—night after night! But I can't, Bill. You want to be loved, but you're not a lover—you don't need to be. I won't be just another trophy in your display case. I've got too much self-respect for that. And I love Joyce. I would never hurt her like that. You think you're god-like and believe you have the world by the tail, don't you? Well, the fatal flaw in your plan is death, Bill; medical school can't save you from that." He winced and looked irritated. I didn't tell this laureled idol that the real reason I wouldn't go with him was that I loved him so much that I couldn't stand the pain of the loss of the relationship, the inevitable loss.

Bill was no fool. He looked steadily into my eyes and said, "You may love her, yes, but you can love me more. You admire me. You merely care for her out of compassion. You don't want to be like a woman, but you envy me, and I envy you. We want the same things. We're like brothers! We understand each other. We both value our competence and our masculinity. We love it! We worship it!"

His aim was devastating, and I was furious. "How dare you say such a thing about my marriage! You conceited ass! Joyce has devoted her life to me. She's loyal and loving. She knows what it really means to love, to give, to care—unlike most guys like you who only know how to take. You're a fly-by-night. You aren't even fit to be in the same universe with her! You disgust me!"

He wouldn't stop. Taking careful aim again, he said, "But she's still a woman. Seems like I hit a raw nerve, Denny! I'm sorry, but I thought you were a good psychologist. What I said is true, whether you admit it to yourself or not. You'll regret your decision. Let me know when you come to your senses. Do you want that last egg roll? I'm starved!"

"Obviously, Billy-boy, but for more than food!" I said.

He had the last word: "So are you, so piss off and pass the damned egg roll!"

I avoided Bill after that, because I was afraid of him—I mean, I was afraid of myself. He took his revenge, though, by coming up to me from time to time at the end of my class and whispering into my ear with 60 students milling around, "I love you! I want you! Come with me!" Then he would glide out of the classroom, stop, turn, look at me, smile and wink—that son-of-a-bitch! At the end of the semester, his last, I gave him a book—*Siddartha*, by Herman Hesse. I wrote an emotional inscription. I wanted to make peace and give him something to remember me by. I never saw him again. He was a magnificent illusion, a conceited ass, and I loved him very much.

I hadn't been bothered by anything like that until Jack. I was actually proud that I'd resisted Bill Pearloff's allure, but I dreamed about him from time to time. In one, we made love in a tropical sea. He was so incredibly beautiful! So, what's in a wet dream, I thought; no harm done. I even told Joyce about him, that I was having dreams about him, but I didn't say what kind. All she said was that Bill sounded like a special and beautiful person. Years later, she told me she had worried about my "enthusiasm" for him.

Enthusiasm? The root of the word means "god possessing," so perhaps it did fit. She suspected I had an affair with him.

Jack canceled our meeting the next Friday; he said something had come up at work. I suspected he couldn't handle what I'd told him about my homosexual fears; but, the following week, he was there, just as happy as ever. Weeks went by, and we never talked about what I'd said. Then one day Jack said, "Denny, you know what you said about why you felt uncomfortable going camping with me? Remember? Well, I've been thinking about it ever since. I've really thought about it, and—well—I don't care about that. I mean, whatever happens, happens. I never thought I'd feel like this, but I don't care if it happens or not. I just want us to have time together, that's all. Let's plan a camping trip and not worry about it. Okay?"

I panicked. "My God, Jack! Do you know what you're saying? We're both married men! We're fathers! How can you be so matter-of-fact about it?"

He told me, "I've done a lot of thinking over the last month. I don't see any danger for either of us or for anyone else. We're not going to become homosexual! Besides, it might not be an issue for you anymore. The last time you acted on those feelings, you weren't even an adult. What's the danger? What's your fear? So what if we're sexual? What's the big deal? We're not going to leave our wives and children. So, will you go?"

I told him I needed time to think, because I wasn't going to do anything impulsively; I wanted to be fully responsible for my actions. I thought about the issue every day for the next three weeks. I had to trust my knowledge and intelligence rather than my confused emotions. I was relieved that I wasn't sexually aroused by Jack. Yes, I felt love for him as a person, but the idea of making love with a body builder seemed comical at best. Besides, it had been 16 years since I'd been with a man. By then, Joyce and I had enjoyed sex almost every night for nearly 12 years. I reminded myself that I'd resisted the temptation of Bill Pearloff with no ill effects and that behavioristic psychology and learning theory would predict that after all these years of extinction, of no reinforcement of homosexual behavior and thousands of reinforced heterosexual trials, I ought not to have anything to worry about.

So why was I worried, I asked myself. I wasn't a homosexual, I didn't want to be one, and I wasn't going to become one. Neither was Jack. He said he'd never had a sexual relationship with a man, but he was curious. I loved Joyce and my family, so my fears seemed, most likely, groundless. I believed that Jack and I would probably enjoy the weekend and nothing would happen, and that would be fine with me—a relief. Even on the outside chance it did, so what, I thought. It's not like I'd be having an affair with a woman; it's not the same. It didn't seem like adultery, although I supposed that technically it would be. I just couldn't see how my love for a man would adulterate my love for a woman; enjoying apples didn't lessen my enjoyment of oranges. I reminded myself that we all have a bisexual potential, whether we admit it to ourselves or not. What else could possibly explain the irrational, emotional overkill to the idea of same-sex relationships except for the threat of this bisexual potential in all of us? So what's to fear, I asked myself. Would I tell

Joyce, I wondered. Yes, of course, I would. We agreed to have no secrets. She might initially be upset, I thought, but there would be no threat to us. If she wanted me to stop seeing Jack, I would. I knew where my priorities were; besides, there couldn't be any future with Jack. How long could two men get away with living together without people finding out? I thought it might be possible in a large city, but I'd never heard of a male couple staying together for very long.

I obviously knew next to nothing about gay people, even though I was a professor of clinical psychology. I wondered why, in my many years of graduate training, we had been assigned only a dozen poorly done research articles on homosexuality and why the topic had rarely been mentioned in all those years. Why the silence, why the denial? I should have looked to myself for the answer, but I decided I'd better go to the library and start reading about it. I was afraid to check out books on that stigmatized topic, but there were only a few poor books anyway. I eventually decided that my conflict boiled down to the single ethical issue of whether harm would come to our marriages.

Day after day, my threatened brain droned on and on as my heart waited patiently for the final verdict. My heart didn't want to scare my cerebral cortex—my frantic reconnoitering intellect—with the brute fact that it had no doubt what the decision would be.

It was a fine spring day, warm and sunny, as Jack and I drove the winding roads through the verdant hills of Kentucky with one of my canoes tied securely to the top of Jack's car. We were like teenagers, best buddies off on an adventure. I remembered the many times Joyce and I had gone canoeing. They'd been good times, but marriage tends to remove men from the joys of male camaraderie which are so valued in our youth—a bonding that is essential for our survival on this planet. Jack and I felt the bonds of this brotherhood, and I'd never seen him so happy. He was still having difficulties in his marriage, even after all their counseling, so he was glad to be free of those conflicts for a weekend. We agreed to stay in the present and to be open about everything we experienced. This intimacy initially threatened Jack, yet he was intrigued, because he'd never risked this with anyone. Most people don't, out of the fear of rejection and the threat of too much self-knowledge. As we drove, I suggested that we practice this openness by sharing free associations and censoring nothing.

Jack started: "Road, curve, breast, milk, wife, knife! Damn, I'm still angry with her. I can never please her. Okay, let's see...tree, roots, family, mother, dance; I'm blocking! I used to have to dance with my mother when I was a kid. I hated it, but I knew how to please her to get what I wanted."

Denny: "Hill, climb, challenge, sky, fly...die, dirt, worms, flowers, spring, growth, death, birth, life...Nathan. Nathan? All I can think of is his trusting smile. God, I love that kid; I'd do anything for him. Okay...stop sign...Joyce. Wow! I should stop relating to you! Dangerous intersection! I'm feeling sad now...silence, loneliness, longing, sunlight, tears—I'm completely blocking."

Jack said, "Hey, Denny, if you're having any hesitation about this trip with me, let's just turn around and call it off right now."

I told him I wasn't rejecting him; my free associations weren't the whole story. I said I wanted us to share everything without censoring it. And talk we did, all that day as we canoed along the sun-dappled banks of the Green River, and then beside the crackling, orange campfire in the quiet of the evening, with red wine, the smell of smoke and pine, and the occasional lonely sounds of a distant whippoorwill. With the coming of the night chill, we went into our green wall tent; it was large enough to sleep six. Our two red sleeping bags, discretely separated by several feet, seemed lonely to me on the empty expanse of the green canvas floor. We continued to share the realities of ourselves in the warmth of a softly hissing Coleman gas lantern. Jack and I were lying on our sleeping bags, clad only in our boxer shorts and tee shirts, and I noticed his powerful muscularity beneath his clinging shirt. Our hours of talking had been just a warm-up for Jack, a testing time, for his soul songs were then soaring, harmonized by my laughter and tears. At one point, he was so ecstatic that he grabbed me and hugged me and, sobbing in my arms with joy, said, "Denny! My God, I can talk again! I can talk! I thought I'd lost that forever! Oh, God, it's been so long—so many years now, but I can talk again! How can I ever thank you enough? I can speak! I don't feel lonely anymore! I don't think I've ever felt this much trust in anyone! I'm free! I can be *me* with you! I've always dreamed of having a friend like you."

"Me, too, Jack! I've ached for a friend like you most of my life!" I said, somewhat surprised by this truth. I asked if he remembered how kids used to cut a finger with a knife and press their bleeding fingers together in a ceremony of becoming blood brothers, best friends. I told him I had a fantasy of doing that with him and said I didn't want anything to ever weaken our friendship. He smiled and nodded agreement. We were both tired. I told him it had been a wonderful day for me, and I turned off the lantern.

It takes awhile for a gas lantern to go out—to die. We watched the brilliant white of the twin, hissing mantles becomes dim, then turn yellow and faint, and finally transform into small, pure-blue twin flames dancing in unison to a pulsating rhythm for a few moments, then all was blackness and silence.

"What are you thinking about, Denny?" whispered Jack.

"About us. About how happy I feel," I whispered back.

"Me, too! Anything else?"

"A few thoughts about my problem," I said.

"Oh. ...Do you want to talk about it?"

"No." There was a long silence, and I listened to Jack's relaxed breathing.

"Denny? Are you still thinking about it? Are you having conflict about it?"

"Yes."

"Well, just let yourself be human," he said. "Be free to be yourself. I'm here if you want me. If I fall asleep, just wake me up. Okay, buddy?"

"Okay."

My brain was running in triple time. I don't remember all the details, but my thinking went like this: I still don't feel sexual attraction toward him; I'm glad for that. Maybe I can just drift off to sleep, after all. He's really built;

he's stronger than I am. God, I've wanted a friendship like this! Jack's so easy to understand. The way he cried in my arms! He's known the loneliness, too. It feels like I've come home again, to a brother, after years of being away. I wish he was my brother! God, I do! I don't know when I've ever felt as happy as I do right now. What does that mean? Joyce is home asleep now, all by herself, and that's so sad, so very sad. She's done nothing wrong. Why can't I ever feel this bond with a woman? Why? God knows I've tried, all these years! I do love Joyce, but being here with Jack—oh, God, why can't I have this with Joyce? She's everything a man could want and more! She's love! But as much as I want to, I can't deny what I'm feeling! ...If that son-of-a-bitch has fallen asleep, I'll beat the living shit out of him! "Jack!" I said. "Are you awake? Are you?"

"Yeah. What do you want?"

"Oh, nothing. I just wondered if you were asleep, that's all."

"Just wondered? Bullshit! You're fooling yourself now! Just relax and be yourself, Denny. I'll be here."

My frantic brain droned on: Damn him! I'm the one who taught him that "just" is often a clinical red-flag word. He learns fast. He's smart, he's forcing me to face my conflict head on. Well, I can't avoid it anymore. To be...or not to be! That is the question, isn't it? So dramatic and unoriginal, but it fits, doesn't it? Very existential. And what about those goddamned slings and arrows of outrageous fortune? What will happen to me? What if I get hooked? If the faculty even suspected, I'd never be granted tenure. Well, thank God I'm a clinician, I don't have to be stuck in academia like the rest of them. What in the hell am I doing here now? Am I fucking crazy? God, I could lose my marriage and my kids. And my job. Who'd hire me? What if I got really hooked? I could wind up in a cell in a goddamned mental hospital playing with myself and eating my feces. Think clearly! My life depends on it, and so do my wife and kids. Why is Jack important for me? Sex with Joyce is good. She's not inhibited, and she's never said no in all these years. She has multiples, for Christ's sake! Well...not for *his* sake. I'm getting thought disordered now, stinking crazy. ...But it's not the sex! It really isn't. It's the love! I'm not even sexually attracted to Jack...but I could be. Why does this idiot kid inside me have to have the moon? Then he wants the sun and the stars! He just sits there and pounds on his high chair to get whatever he wants. This idiot within! But what does my brain serve? Me? My body? Society? Most people don't give a damn if you're alive or dead! Am I not my body? Am I my body's keeper? I'm going crazy again. Oh, Jesus, I don't even know what I'm doing! All these years of college education, postgraduate education, university professorships, and I'm here in this damned tent in a forest in Kentucky with a man beside me in his underwear, and I don't know what the hell I'm doing! Maybe there's a government publication for people who don't know what the fuck they're doing. I can see it now—a public service announcement—sweet old Helen Hayes saying, "If you don't know what the fuck you're doing, just write Washington, 25, D.C.!" They'd be sold out all the time if there were. ...Physician, heal thyself! Sure! Why do I want to touch Jack, to know him? *Why is touch so damned important?* I'm not a blind person, I can see! ...But maybe I *am* blind. Oedipus, digging his eye-balls out of his head with his own bloody fingers! Oh God! ...Maybe I've been blinding myself all my goddamned life! Just learn not to be yourself, then you, too, can be a normal, respected member of the community—a com-munity that doesn't really care if you're alive or dead. ...Why do these thoughts cause such a rush of emotion in me? God, *the incredible power of these feel-ings!* What's happening? I want to touch Jack! I do, don't I? ...Yes, I do! ...I really do!

Just then, Jack said, "Denny? I know you're awake. It's lonely over here. Come on over here. I want to give you a hug good-night."

My heart was pounding to the beat of a frantic, spastic drummer. We groped awkwardly for each other in the cool darkness. When I found him, his warmth was shocking. He put his powerful arms fully around me and pressed me to his firm, muscular chest. He whispered, "I never imagined it would be this wonderful, Denny. I feel like I've known you forever. Yet, we've just begun to know! I'm so happy inside." He was whispering into my ear, and I suddenly remembered the very first time ...when Keith whispered into my ear, "You've never done this before?"

We lay there holding each other, just thinking and feeling. I remembered Joyce and I holding each other like this. Suddenly, it all seemed humorous; he was so massive, firm, and flat-chested, not like Joyce at all. Thank God for humor, the divine safety valve. I tried to suppress a laugh but couldn't. "What's so funny, Denny?" Jack asked, seeming slightly put off.

I said, "This is weird! Where are your soft big tits? Did you have a double radical mastectomy, Jackie? And your whiskers are like a wire brush! Doesn't it feel strange after all these years with a woman, Jack? Doesn't it?"

"Shit," he said, "look who's talking! You're more flat-chested than I am. You aren't even ready for a training bra! ...Yeah, it does feel different, and you sure don't feel like a woman to me, but I like the way it feels—close, comfortable, masculine. I don't feel so lonely now."

"Neither do I."

"Are you still having conflicts, Den?"

"Yeah."

"Take your time. Relax. We don't have to go anywhere. Just be your-self. Be human," he said. Such wisdom.

I held him and felt him holding me, and I was aware of cleansing waves of happiness surging through me. The warm life of his skin contrasted with the coldness of the night air. Life is warmth, I thought. That isn't profound, I thought, not even true, sort of dumb; why did I think that? Warmth? Heat? Hot? We were lying on our sides facing one another, and I noticed that Jack had kept his hips and legs away from my body. I wanted to be fully in touch with him, so I moved closer, only to be shocked by my graphic awareness of the massive, rock-hardness inside his shorts. I wasn't even slightly erect. I didn't dare move, but I felt it there, pressed against me, hard and hot. What am I doing in bed with an aroused man, I thought. After a time, not wanting to sexualize our relationship, I moved back and cautiously put my hand on Jack's face, tenderly, with affection. It was like a dream; I was actually touching his face! Neither of us dared to move. Jack, sensing my hesitation, rolled over on his stomach and was silent. I thought about the pressure of his weight on his erection. I ran my fingers through his thick, wavy hair and felt my hand sensing him, absorbing him, knowing him. My emotions were singing like a choir of angels in heat! To be in touch! Yes, yes, yes! I wanted to etch forever into my memory the knowledge that was flowing through my hands into my consciousness—and I did. I was touching a miracle, that from which we create the images of our gods. I knew exactly what he was feeling as I touched him. I carefully explored his neck and shoulders, his arms and hands, and his muscular back, and I heard the sounds of his groans of understanding and pleasure. I knew every sensation he was feeling. And when, at last, I reached the elastic band of his boxer shorts, I hesitated, then lifted my hand and slowly lowered it to the cloth covering the naked, massive power of his firm buttocks; Jack moaned from the pleasure of this intimacy. I moved my hand back to the elastic waistband and rested my fingers on his warm skin. I wanted to put my hand under his shorts and feel his naked ass, but I was anxious, and hesitated.

I became aware of the sounds of spring crickets in the distance and a great old bullfrog croaking in the river. This was my moment of truth, and I knew it. This moment had always been there, in the shadows. My world was wobbling on its axis, but I still had a choice. It was as if I were standing on the tips of my toes on the very edge of the Grand Canyon, and I had to leap to the other side—an heroic leap of faith. Fear and trembling, life or painful death! I'd never felt more awake or alive than I did at that moment. I felt his smooth warm skin and the elastic band—the barrier, the entrance to...to what, I wondered. Eternal life? Death in a mental hospital? A prison? What could guide me? My intelligence was like a muttering, old, confounded fool. Clichés, not wisdom; rules, not reasons. I thought, George Kelly, my old mentor, where are you now that I need you? Rotting in your coffin! What would he think if he could see me at this moment, I wondered. Would he be shocked or would he laugh his ass off at my predicament? How would he advise me? Professor Kelly, should I feel Jack's ass now, or shouldn't I? He'd say, man is like a scientist; our behavior is the way we pose questions to reality. Life is experience—change! The purpose of life, he'd said, "is to be on with it!" ...To be on with it! To be...on with it! To be! I was at an irreversible fork in the road of my life; and, no matter which path I chose, the consequences would be forever. I said to myself, you pay for each leaf you pluck from the tree of knowledge with your whole life. Each path leads to different structures of meaning. Choose life. Choose your bliss!

Then I remembered that line from the novel *Victory* by Joseph Conrad—that strange line that had popped into my mind at odd times ever since I was 20: "Ah, Davidson, woe to the man whose heart has not learned while young to hope, to love—and to put its trust in life!" Yes, to put my trust in what I am! To dare to be real. To be...me! To let my life be! I suddenly understood.

I slipped my informing fingers slightly beneath the waistband of Jack's shorts and raised the cloth away from his body. I hesitated for an existential moment at the very brink of being...to reconsider. Then, in the most significant single gesture of my life—the rebirth and affirmation of my life, I plunged my seeking hand down hard onto his smooth, warm, firm, naked, muscular ass. He exploded with passion, ripping his clothes off and mine, and then it was all nakedness and trembling and groans and hands and gasps and quivering muscles and movement and feet and teeth and buttocks and tongues and lips and skin and saliva and positions and hair and sweat and nipples and arm pits and thighs and tightening testicles and jetting penises and lungs like bellows convulsing with each orgasm and the warm slipperiness and musky man-smell of spent semen everywhere! Then the gasping for air and the full-chested panting, our rhythms slowing, and the breathing becoming more peaceful again, then quietness...and the awed silence. Some, the willfully ignorant, will see only sex, but they are pathetically blind and do not know it.

Sixteen long years had passed since I'd last known this passion of love, this holiest communion. Surely something would have diminished in the faithful abstinence of those many long years. As I lay there listening to the sounds of a spring night with Jack, warm, beside me, I knew I was a transfigured being, for during that night I had known a far, far greater intensity of love and life than I had ever been, or felt, before. There, beside the springtime waters of the Green River, I felt the mystical passion of the gods, and I became real and whole and alive again after a long, restless, troubled sleep of 16 years.

Our repressions tend to lift only after the successful resolution of our conflicts. As I listened to Jack's peaceful breathing while he slept, I wept with complete gratitude for him. This woke him, but he understood. He just held me in his arms as I continued to cry, because I was finally experiencing the terrible loneliness of all those long years. I didn't know then that the amused gods of Olympus had only just begun to teach me their divine and painful lesson.

The next morning, I woke to the touch of Jack's lips on my forehead. He was dressed and had made coffee, scrambled eggs and sausages for our breakfast. It was the happiest morning of our lives. On the drive back to Ohio, I asked Jack if he'd thought about what he would do if our wives objected to our relationship. "Sure I have!" he said. "We'll just have to go behind their backs if that happens. It would be easy to do. I've worked out some of the details already. No one can end this relationship except us, Denny. No one!" I was relieved.

I wanted to tell Joyce about Jack as soon as possible, but it was very important for me that she meet him first; I thought that then she would be more understanding. We invited Jack to dinner at our home a day or two later. His wife, an unsociable person, had no interest in meeting us or any of Jack's friends. The dinner was dramatic and comical. Sitting to my left was my lover, Jack, and to my right, my lover, Joyce. Jack unnerved me from time to time by discretely winking at me. Once, when Joyce went to the kitchen, Jack playfully reached over and grabbed my crotch. He couldn't stop laughing at my facial expression of pleasure and terror, even when Joyce returned. She looked confused and suspicious. I believed Joyce was unaware that Jack and I had been lovers; Jack didn't know Joyce was becoming strongly physically attracted to him, and I didn't know that Joyce already suspected Jack and I were lovers.

Jack was charming, Joyce was gracious, and I was tense and possessive of them both, especially when Jack asked Joyce to dance with him to some Tim Weisberg records he said he'd just happened to bring along. Jack was a superbly expressive dancer; he hadn't told me he'd been a professional dance instructor. Joyce, who loved dancing, was captivated by Jack's erotic style, and Jack enjoyed watching my silent jealousy of them both as they danced. Dancing, for me, had always been frustrating foreplay at best, or the antic gestures of retarded mutes at worst. This was a great disappointment for Joyce. When she became tired and sat beside me, Jack really began to show his stuff. Joyce and I sat stunned and aroused by his incredible, flowing sensuality. He knew the effect he was having, and he loved it.

As we were driving to dinner at a friend's house the next evening, Joyce and I talked about Jack. Carefully, she asked if he and I had been lovers. I pulled the car to the side of the road and told her everything, then we sat through the long dinner at our friend's, looking at each other questioningly. Joyce initially felt some insecurity and hurt, but she was reassured by my openness. I loved her and was not dissatisfied with our marriage. She knew that I truly believed I was not homosexual, although I'd acted on a bisexual potential, feelings she had also experienced. Neither of us believed that my relationship with a male could be a threat to us. Besides, she liked Jack, and he liked her. Our sex life became more intense, because I felt more known by Joyce than I'd ever been. In months that followed, I was amazed that I would come home and make passionate love with Joyce even after having just been in bed with Jack. I loved them both. I didn't understand that the sex with her was passionate precisely because I had just been to bed with Jack. The sexual experiences were different, however—oranges and apples or, perhaps, popular and classical music—well, to be frank, it was like that for only a few months, then it became more like Kool-Aid in a paper cup and vintage champagne in Baccarat crystal. Maybe it had always been that way, but I couldn't admit it. I wanted to love her.

Jack told his wife about us. She had no objections as long as he was not sexual with Joyce. She wasn't much into sex herself. I suppose I provided a vacation for her, or so Jack said. The four of us began to socialize. One time, at their home, a friend of theirs arranged a series of stoned versus unstoned experiences for us with some of his best Colombian grass. Joyce and I had no desire to use drugs, having seen the damage done to too many of my graduate and undergraduate students. On that evening, however, we were completely stoned. I was having religious experiences of profound beauty. Jack, quite stoned himself, came over to me and held my hands as we both looked into our transforming faces. We were flooded with such feelings of love for one another that we both began to cry. Suddenly, his face seemed to turn ashen-white, and I saw an expression of unbearable sadness as the vivid outlines of his beautiful face began to blur and smear like wet paint running down a canvas. It was shocking, but with horror, I knew I had just anticipated the end of our relationship.

Jack had never been to Canada, and I longed to take him there; so we planned a two-week canoe trip into the wilderness at the end of August. At the beginning of summer, Joyce and I and the boys went to Canada, but every day I was there, I ached for Jack and could hardly wait to get back to him. One night, to drown my loneliness for him, I drank Beefeaters gin until I passed out. The next day, Joyce told me I'd become irrational and had frightened the family. In the middle of the night, I'd awakened, screamed at her to get out of our double sleeping bag, and insisted Nathan sleep beside me. I didn't remember any of it.

The summer passed quickly, and Jack and I counted the hours until we would be free together. The week before we left for our vacation, Jack had a raging battle with his wife. She'd suddenly changed her mind about our trip and had threatened to divorce him if he went. (I can't remember her name although I knew it quite well; but then, I have good reason not to remember.) He told her to divorce him if she must, but nothing, absolutely nothing, was going to stop him from being with me for those two weeks. She knew he meant exactly what he said, so she dropped the issue. Joyce, in contrast, helped us pack, made food for us, and was as excited about the trip as if she were going herself—well, at least, she acted that way. We loaded the car with the twin, square-stern canoes and two six-horsepower outboard motors. We were going far into the wilderness and needed to carry two weeks of supplies. As we pulled out of the driveway, Joyce and the three boys stood waving good-bye until we drove out of sight. I'll never forget that scene. I was leaving my family. This would be the longest time I'd ever been away from Joyce. Jack and I talked of our sadness about leaving our families behind; but, by the time we'd left the Ohio border, we were kids again, off together into the adventures of the wilds.

Jack and I were raised in the unquestioned tradition of the patronizing sexism of our era. As I was riding with Jack on the same highway to Canada that Joyce and I had taken several months earlier, I recognized again the traditional roles of inequality that Joyce and I had assumed with each other in our marriage. It would never have occurred to Jack and me to assume anything but equality in our brotherhood, the equality conferred by our male status, but not necessarily by equal competence.

Jack and I talked at great length about these issues, often comparing our experiences and feelings together with those of being with our wives. We could be open, dependent, fearful, vulnerable and weak with one another and display with pride our raw, uninhibited love of sexual lust without guilt, shame, apology...or foreplay. But best of all, we were united with our own kind again after too many years away in a foreign land, blood brothers—rejoined. "Gentlemen, gentlemen, off on a spree"—this time going from here to eternity!

After we loaded our canoes, Jack and I started the outboards and headed deep into the uninhabited wilderness. We arrived at our first campsite late in the afternoon. After pitching the tent, Jack and I went for a naked swim in the clear waters; afterwards, we made love for the first time in the openness and grandeur of the natural world—and again that evening to the plaintive call of a Canadian Loon. Jack was used to having sex with his wife once a week or less; his bisexual image of himself was becoming threatened by the frequency and passion of our lovemaking. He said we should try to hold it down to a couple of times a week; I told him twice a day, or I was packing up and leaving. We talked about his fears and eventually reached a reasonable compromise of two times a day, which seemed fair to me. After awhile, as he relaxed about his self-image, we made love whenever either of us felt like it.

I can't describe all that we experienced and learned during our two weeks together in the majesty of that vast wilderness, but neither of us will ever forget. We were boys again. We fished, hiked, climbed, portaged, and shot great, roaring white-water rapids and lived to tell of them. We were at one with the world and ourselves. We were the songs of love fulfilled, sung in harmony with nature under the accepting eyes of the sun and stars in the magical, golden days of a summertime regained.

One day, Jack said he wanted to teach me something that would be of great value to me. We often did psychotherapy exercises with one another, so I was excited to learn what he had in mind. He'd been playing with my arm, hand, and fingers and had noticed that, when he moved them, I would always return them to the position I wanted them to be in rather than the position he'd put them in. He said he knew my parents had given me little emotional support; as a consequence, I was reluctant to depend on others and believed that I always needed to be in control. He explained that for the next 12 hours, I would be totally dependent on him for everything; I would be completely under his control whether I wanted to be or not. He pointed out that he was physically more powerful than I. Of course I didn't agree to this, but he just smiled knowingly and told me I had no choice for the next 12 hours or until I learned what he wanted to teach. Every cell in my body rebelled at this, so I jumped up and ran toward the canoes. I'd leave this island, and he'd never find me until I wanted him to, because I knew this wilderness, he didn't. He wouldn't be able to find his way back to the main camp; and even if he did, I had the keys to the car. I'd show him who was going to control whom. I believed I could easily outwit him, but I heard him laughing, and he made no effort to stop me. When I got to the canoes, I saw why. The gas tanks and paddles were missing.

For hours, I tried every strategy and tactic I could think of, but physical power was on his side. I tried compliance to buy time to think and eventually trick him, but he wouldn't be fooled or easily satisfied. This was no longer a game; I was becoming desperate. I wanted a weapon, but he'd hidden our ax and knives. I saw the circle of stones around our campfire and slowly edged toward them. When I grabbed one, Jack just laughed and walked over to me casually, daring me to hurt him. He knew I wouldn't, so I dropped the stone, but enough was enough; I lunged at him, knocking him to the ground. In one powerful movement, he grabbed my leg and toppled me. Complete rage exploded in me, and I wanted to fight him to the death; I would never be controlled. I thought I had him a time or two, but I began to tire, then he dominated me completely. He sat on my chest and pinned my hands to the ground above my head. He held me this way until I stopped struggling and was completely quiet for a very long time. Then he said, "I control you now. You're totally dependent on me and my will, and we both know it. You have no choice. Now you can learn what I want to teach you. Even though you're helpless and dependent now—and this is one of your greatest fears, I want you to know this...." Jack's voice broke with emotion. He paused for a moment and then looked into my eyes and said with great feeling, "I will never harm you, because I love you, Denny. You have no need to fear me...ever. Life won't harm you just because you don't have control. No one controls life."

He released my arms, and I looked up into Jack's loving face, now smiling. It was the Buddha face of infinite compassion. Behind him were the dancing, brilliant lights of the sun through the moving leaves of the trees. I felt tears forming as I became overwhelmed by what I was learning—Jack and the world were one! No one controls life. His face became larger, then it completely filled my vision as he slowly bent down and kissed me. He gently wiped my tears away with his fingers, then stood and helped me up. For hours, I gazed at the world with astonishment and reverence, for Jack had just changed the status of my universe. The world had always seemed somewhat hostile and indifferent to me before—like my father, but then it was gentle, harmonious, and kind, and I was part of it, as was Jack, sitting beside me, holding me. We were the world. Life lives us. I could be receptive. I could love life, and trust it, and put my faith in it. As I sat there holding him, I realized that paradise was happening then. It always had been, but I couldn't see that, because I'd always felt alone in a hostile universe.

We sat around the campfire late that night, talking about all that had happened. The heavens were magnificent and ripe with star clusters; Jack and I paddled our canoe out onto the still waters to see the full view. There we were, the two of us in that canoe, floating on quiet, dark waters, together in the middle of this universe. And then I saw it just beginning. Over there! The northern lights, the aurora borealis! Jack had never seen them before. Soon they became great shimmering sheets of changing colors parading across vast regions of the night sky.

"My God, Denny, they're unbelievable!" he said. "The size of them!" We were lucky, I said, because it was one of the best displays I'd ever seen. "It's like an omen!" he said.

"It's the coming of the gods, Jack! It is! At least, that's what the Indians up here believe it is."

He said, "I know it's subatomic particles from the sun ionizing gases in the ionosphere, forming a plasma influenced by magnetic fields...but it would be very easy to believe the Indians! Why would the gods be coming, Denny?"

"Because of us, Jack. To greet us and to show themselves before we go, so that we'll always remember what was revealed here. This is our last night, you know—the very last one."

"Don't remind me, I'm depressed enough about it already," he said.

We watched until the lights of the gods had disappeared and darkness was everywhere; then, back in the warmth of our tent, knowing it was our last night, Jack and I made love with a tenderness and compassion that we hadn't known before in our lives. Jack wept. ...Perhaps he knew even then that we would never make love again.

As we broke camp the next morning, neither of us spoke, because we understood the depression of the other. Neither did we talk during the long hours on the two-lane highway winding through the tall pine forests of Canada, but shortly after crossing the U.S. border, Jack broke down. "I can't stand it, Denny! I can't stand returning home, back to the way I was living, but I have to. I have no choice." He began to yell in anger and then just sobbed helplessly. We talked about his getting a divorce, but he was deeply worried about the welfare of his children. I told him he and his kids could live with us. What a dreamer I was. Jack developed a migraine headache of such intensity that we had to stop to get medication. His agony frightened me.

Jack didn't see me for six weeks after we returned; I suspected his wife. He planned to visit me on a Friday evening. Joyce was away at a conference for that weekend. I changed the sheets on our bed, sprinkled cologne on the pillows, and looked at my wristwatch so often that I couldn't stand the sight of it, then I heard the familiar sound of his car coming up the driveway. I knew something was wrong as soon as I saw him. He'd gained weight and was depressed. He smiled only faintly when I hugged him; there was no joy in him. He said he could only stay for less than an hour; he'd promised his wife. He came to see me, he said, to tell me in person that he could never see me again. He wanted our relationship to end. "My God, Jack! Why? Why, Jack? I love you!" I said.

He said, "I know you do, Denny, and I love you. I've never been so happy as I've been with you, but it must end. I've been seeing my wife's psychiatrist. I told him about us. He said homosexuality is pathological and a crime. He wants me to stop it."

"Is that what you think, Jack?" I asked, my world wobbling on its axis.

"Of course not, Denny. That's just crap! He's as much of a pathetic fool as most of the psychiatrists I've known. I've got my reasons, though. They're nothing personal about you. I just don't want to talk about them now, and I'm not going to, so don't try to make me. Maybe sometime later I can tell you, but not now. Who knows, maybe someday we can be friends again—I don't know. But that would be a long time from now, if ever."

I told Jack I wanted us to make love one last time, but he said he couldn't. He loved me, and he didn't mean to hurt me, he said, but he just couldn't. He said he felt guilty and ashamed about ending our friendship, and he was surprised that I would still want to make love with him. I begged him to. I actually begged; I was surprised I did that. I could hardly stop begging, but he said no. Then it was time for him to go.

We stood at the front door. As we held each other for the last time, I felt a single sob break from him, then he pulled away and began to walk through the doorway. I realized I was seeing his beautiful head for the last time. I called him back. He stopped and just stared in shame and depression at the ground as I spoke: "Jack, thank you for coming here to tell me in person; that was very kind. I know it was difficult for you. This is the last time we will ever see one another. You and I will never forget this moment—not ever! Jack, listen to me now! Remember what I say for the rest of your life. Listen! I want you to remember always that I loved you." He looked up at me and smiled in sad appreciation. He looked so sad.

I never saw Jack again. The last thing I said to him were the exact words Keith had said to me 23 years earlier. So now it had come full-circle. What I said to Jack was true, but part of me, the hurt and angry part, wanted Jack to carry the same burden of betrayal and guilt that I had carried all those years. Afterwards, I was ashamed of myself, but the deed was done, and Jack was gone.

With the closing of that circle, the gods, not yet satisfied that I had learned their divine lesson, began to teach me humility. I had been warned years before by their messenger Mercury—disguised as Alex, the handsome student in my high school Latin class—that one cannot run from the gods.

I called Joyce at her conference to tell her about Jack. She was concerned about me and came home immediately. I was amazed that I didn't feel depressed. Could I be that well-integrated, I wondered. I didn't realize that I was in a state of denial. Part of me still hoped to hear from Jack. The weeks rolled into months and my pleading letters to him remained unanswered as I began the steady descent into hell, where I was to weep beyond all weeping for more than a year. I must be brief, because it is with much suffering that I now recall that most appalling time of my life.

I felt like a condemned man, condemned for no crime, who must descend into a dark, terrifying realm of horrors in the bowels of the earth and there to weep alone forever. Of necessity, I became a detached spectator of my descent. I watched the incessant growth of indifference, meaninglessness and the anguish of my wife and children. I tried all the methods I knew as a psychologist to ease what I mistakenly thought was my grieving for Jack, but nothing stopped this descent into hell. In final desperation, I tried the sacred images of Keith, but they had no power anymore—none. So I let go and just waited and watched as I tried to ride the depression out. I had no past and no future, just the meaningless present. I reached such a depth of indifference that it was no longer safe for me to drive a car, because I was unable to care where it went. I wasn't suicidal or homicidal. I just didn't care what happened. To commit suicide, you have to at least want to end your pain, but I was beyond that. I had passed the stage in which the soul still longs to leave the body. I watched my own children playing in the living room and realized that if one of them became seriously injured, I would continue to sit and stare into space. I didn't care about anything. And I didn't care that I didn't care. This stage of depression is beyond pain and feeling. It is nothingness—the living death. Reality had become mere patterns of light.

After some months, Joyce wrote to Jack and told him about the seriousness of my condition. She had to drive me to school. I could barely teach my classes. When I came home, I just went to bed, but I had insomnia. I hardly ate. I talked with no one. She begged him to write to me and explain why he'd ended the relationship. I remember the day she brought his letter. I just held it in my hands and stared at it. The long handwritten letter was filled with his many kindnesses. I ran my fingertips over the letters where his fingers had recently been. He explained that he'd been too ashamed to tell me the truth when he'd last seen me. His wife had given him an ultimatum, and he'd completely caved in to her. He was never to see me again nor contact me in any way, or she would divorce him and prevent him from seeing his children by exposing his homosexuality. If he contacted me, she said she would expose me to the faculty at the university to prevent my being granted tenure. He wanted to protect me. His plan was to lie low, go through medical school, encourage her to complete her nursing degree and get a job, wait until his children were old enough to choose which parent they wanted to live with and then divorce her. Because of her unstable mental health, he would do anything to spare his children from the danger of her sole care. He thanked me for our relationship and said it had been a time of the greatest happiness for him and had restored his faith in himself and life again. He hoped that someday, in the distant future, we might be able to be friends again. He said he wouldn't write again because thinking about me was so painful for him.

I started drinking after that. My family became frightened of me, as well they had reason to be. The worst part of it all for me was at night. I often woke up screaming in terror from my dreams. I slept with a night light on, because I couldn't tolerate darkness, emptiness, nothingness. My poor wife was living with a madman; she had no husband, and my sons had no father—only a strange madman who lived with them.

I didn't have dreams; I lived them. That was the terror of my nights—to have to undergo the torture of trial by the reality of dreams. Have you ever been forced to eat your own flesh, to taste and chew and choke on your own organs, to swallow your packed intestines, and then to drink a chalice of your own warm blood, and then to throw up and be forced to drink your rancid vomit? I have. Craziness? Not at all. After surviving each night's interrogation with the Grand Inquisitor of Darkness, I would try to understand the messages of my dreams. Dreams are visual construing, pictorialized thinking, the relevant motion-picture Rorschach cards of our spiritual life, and they have much to teach us about what we are. For me, my self-cannibalizing dream symbolically portrayed how I felt at that time about what churches had done and would continue to do to me. In an evil travesty of the sacred, I was made to be a human sacrifice for them. They mocked God by forcing me to have holy communion using my own flesh and blood. Their actions were a monstrous crime against nature—a crime against my human nature.

In another dream, I saw from a balcony a large religious procession coming toward me. There were thousands of peasants shuffling along a dusty road. They carried tattered religious banners and venerated old wooden statues. As they came nearer, I saw that their faces looked lifeless and dead, but they were marching on. In the center of the procession, I saw them carrying three heavy black wooden coffins. The lids of the coffins were open, and I could see the black-skirted bodies of a trio of dead priests, one young, one middle-aged, and one who looked ancient. What horrified me was that, from time to time, one or another of these dead, vacant-eyed, passionless priests would rise up and, with the motions of a robot, make the sign of the cross and bless the spectators. Just as mechanically, he would lie down again in his coffin. This was the procession of the dead, of people hopelessly trapped in the myths and ideology of a different tribe, one that had lived and died in an ancient era. Weird? Just look around you. I also recognized the lifeless genuflections of the dead priests in myself, of beliefs that had not originated from my own vital experience, of the unexamined, hollow motions of my own conformity and spiritual deadness...caused by fear.

There were many painful lessons for me to learn in this night school of the gods, this classroom of the unconscious. There were lessons of such suffering and horror that I still, many years later, can't endure the memory of them. Joyce and I did seek the advice of several professional colleagues of ours. She begged me to see others; but I knew this trial by truth could only end if I, myself, met my desires and fears alone and suffered them through to victory or insanity. I had to face myself, my worst and most feared enemy. There is no greater knowledge than that of what you are. There is no sweeter victory in life than to change yourself and to become fully human—to become real, to be what you most inwardly are without fear. The greatest tragedy in human life is to die and never know who you are, to never live a day in which you are real, to be a mere human *doing*...and not a human *being*. This is the fate of countless millions of people whose lives are not their own, but merely those of other people. There is a tombstone in Scotland which reads "Here lies Sandy McTavish, born a man, died a grocer."

Toward the last, in my darkest hours of combat with myself, I did use antidepressant medication and told Joyce how to have me hospitalized if need be. I promised to tell her if I thought I was becoming suicidal. After about two weeks, the medication caused side effects; so I abruptly stopped taking it. I couldn't stand the false body cues I was getting. I was being chemically unplugged from the information from my body, painful though it was, and this increased my confusion.

Weeks later, as I was sitting in bed wondering why I was taking so long to grieve the loss of Jack, I realized that I hadn't been grieving for Jack; I'd been grieving for me! I was the one who had died—like the dead priests of my dream! I realized at that moment, for the first time, that, very deep within me and well beyond my awareness, I had always hoped to love again someday as I had with Keith. I finally understood that I had been living for that all along—all those long decades!

What is it that is fundamentally true about me right now, I asked myself. And the answer came: I am lonely beyond all endurance. But I have a devoted, loving wife who would give her very life for me, I thought. She is the mother of my three fine young sons. My God, can I never be satisfied, I asked. And again the truth came: I am lonely beyond all endurance. But look at what Joyce has suffered through with you for a year now, I said to myself. Not once has she complained. You have responded to none of her needs, yet she is there for you, in sickness and in health, for better or for worse. My God, how she has suffered! And I am the cause, I said. God, have mercy on me, forgive me! And again the startling truth came: I am lonely beyond all endurance! My loneliness is cosmic! *My Keith is dead!*

That night, even though I was exhausted, I was more terrified of closing my eyes than ever before. Joyce held me for a long time as I rocked in fear at the familiar entrance to darkness. Something had come to life in me. I sensed this night would be the worst trial of my long ordeal, but I had to journey to the very center of darkness, the realm of my deepest fears. I kissed Joyce as if saying good-bye to her forever—and in a sense it was so; then, in terror, I forced my eyes to close and entered the dream realm of my demons. The dream I had, of ultimate fear and love, changed my life forever. Jack and I had toured the Mammoth Caves in Kentucky on our trip to the Green River; significantly, the setting of this life-giving dream was very much like that place. Many people never remember having such complex and vivid dreams, but these dreams have been a valued part of my life since age 18, when I studied psychoanalysis and kept written records of them.

On this fear-filled journey through long dark tunnels to the center of hell, I was naked, exposed, and many strange things happened along the way. Eventually, I became more committed and confident, even proud and defiant. Then suddenly, I was at the center place where I knew all would be won or lost forever. This center place was a huge, cold, black chamber, a cave with many passageways running from it. It had been carved into a vast core of solid coal—an endless source of fuel for fire, heat and light. I looked around and saw weapons here and there on the coal floor; but, as I reached for each one of them, they disappeared. I was to have only my naked self. I waited, then I heard from deep within the tunnels the low droning and humming of a threatening chorus of deep male voices. The voices were announcing and praising an unknown life-form. It was coming! It knew I was there! I heard its heavy, clopping footsteps thundering and echoing through the black passageways as it approached to destroy me! In a rush of fear greater than any I'd ever known, I realized that I was about to confront ultimate evil itself! I was to be a sacrifice to it! The chorus became shatteringly loud, then, suddenly...echoing silence. It was here! It would show itself! I waited. Then I saw the thing blazing with brilliant colors as if lit by carbon arc lights! That huge thing stood there before me, heavy on its massive four legs. It looked like a gigantic cloisonné pig with beautiful, vivid colors of every kind covering its appallingly grotesque body, except for its tiny head. It had the head of a dark-bearded man. It didn't look at me for awhile, and I hoped, if I didn't move, it wouldn't notice me. Then slowly this monstrous thing began to turn its terrifying human head toward me. It knew I was there to challenge it! When I saw it looking at me, I realized I was utterly helpless before its incredible power, because it was a being of unlimited, supernatural intelligence, but what made it completely terrifying was that it was not human; it was inhuman! It was not capable of feeling human compassion. My reality was of absolutely no interest or value to this inhuman creature of absolute evil. Its eyes looked at me with cosmic indifference as it completely read my trembling, naked soul. I had seen a look like that before...in the eyes of my own father...when I was six...when he took me down to the coal cellar and flogged me. That thing was looking at me like that as I stood naked before it and waited for its dreadful judgment and horrible wrath. The male chorus began a steady, throbbing drone. Then this being of ultimate evil looked through me in a way which conveyed its final judgment, a judgment of absolute indifference to my existence or non-existence. Then it turned and lumbered awkwardly out of that evil place! I was dumbfounded! Then I understood this life-giving lesson of the gods! *Indifference is the nature of a being of evil!* I imagined what the existence of such a pathetic creature must be like, to be so *indifferent*...as my father had been, as my society was, as I had been, and I felt compassion for it, because it was not yet human.

I stood there trapped in the center of this massive, cold, dark core of fuel. But with this new insight, my fear left, and I became strangely calm and resolved. Then, abruptly, the scene changed. I was swept upwards through the earth and into the blazing sunlight of the sky. Great choruses of angels were singing the most beautiful music I'd ever heard. Then I saw it. It was a portrait of a young man of the Renaissance, except he was vibrantly alive! The entire background surrounding him was of deep green, the green leaves of the tree of life, and I remembered the line from a poem by Dylan Thomas: "Time holds me green and dying." The face of the youth was the most supremely beautiful thing I've ever seen. He was the perfectly compassionate being, the perfection of human life. He was fully aware, and he was allowing me to know him. I have never felt such intense, aching love for anything as I did for him at that moment. I knew I was looking at the face of a God, of my metaphor for that complex idea—that projection of our human energies, and I realized again that humanness is the sacred ground of our life. We are human in proportion to our abilities to passionately love and to deeply care. Our humanity comes from being awake. It is the pain, the grief, and the joy of being truly alive—the burning point of life in which we are willingly purified for the holy sacrifice.

The next day I felt rested for the first time in over a year. The revelations of this particular dark night of my soul changed my life forever. I went into the living room to see again the troubling *Portrait of a Youth* I'd bought in Washington so many years before. I couldn't believe what I saw! It wasn't the same youth! It was as if the picture had been repainted. I knew it was the same; I must have been the one who changed, but it didn't seem that way. I looked at this amazing new youth for hours, and he looked back at me with tenderness and compassion. Through him, I came to understand that the cloisonné demon pig and the perfectly compassionate youth symbolized opposite aspects of my conflict, ultimate fear and love. I realized that my own indifference, my spiritual deadness, my own demon pig, was caused by my early self-betrayal, out of social conformity and fear, of my true need and ability to love; that is to say, of my betrayal of my natural ability to love a male. I understood then that I had been irritated for so many years with this *Portrait of a Youth*, this projected conscience of mine; because, at some level, I sensed that this wise and ideal youth had known all along that I was betraying what I am. I wouldn't admit to myself that I loved him, but he knew that from the first moment I saw him. He had always known that I was a lover of men.

It's not easy for a committed married man with children and a wife he loves to know and live with such a truth, a truth he has feared throughout his life. It seemed unthinkable, yet there it was, but I remained immobilized with this truth month after month. A gay graduate student of mine, Eli Coleman, knew of my suffering. He was a caring friend. He took my hand one evening and said, "Denny, it's a lot easier once you're on the other side." I wanted to believe him, but I was still afraid.

I've often wondered what my life would have been like if I hadn't met Jack, or if Joyce had insisted I not see him. I would have stopped if she'd asked me, but I doubt I would have wanted to continue to live, not after what I understood. If by chance I did live, it would have only been out of obligation to her and our children, out of their need for me. If I hadn't met Jack, then I would have continued to limp along in the deadening rut of my career and lonely daily life, living with a vague hope that something of interest might just happen someday...before I died. Perhaps a vacation, or maybe a natural catastrophe. It was like watching a grade C movie on TV in the middle of the night when you're very tired and all alone. You know it's a completely rotten and boring movie—like life, but you keep watching in the unlikely chance that there just might be one good scene before the end. Many people live like that, some only hope for a good scene after the end of life.

But then there was a most extraordinary occurrence of amazing grace. Joyce, like the Kuan-yin of Infinite Compassion, demonstrated a selfless love beyond the capacity of most of us. Because of her act of love, I am alive today and you are reading this book. She came to me and said, "Denny, enough of this. You can't go on living without relating to a man. I want you to start relating to a man."

I said, "Joyce, I can't! That's impossible! Do you know what you're asking of me?"

"Yes, I do.. You can't be happy without loving a man!"

"For God's sake, Joyce, do you understand what that would mean? Do you? It would mean the end of our marriage; I couldn't stand that! What about our children?"

"Denny, listen to me! I would rather have you gay than dead. Your sons would rather have a gay father than none at all. Now don't argue with me! I've invited a very nice young man who works at the Counseling Center with me over here on Friday evening. You're going to relate to him no matter what!"

"I won't! No way! Forget it!"

"You will, besides, he's already accepted the invitation."

She wouldn't budge. I told her I was too depressed to see him for a whole evening and said he'd have to leave after an hour, or I'd throw him out myself. "Who is he?" I asked.

"Gary Goodman."

Gary was a graduate student in our doctoral clinical psychology program, with just his doctoral dissertation to do. I didn't know him on a personal level. "Why him?" I asked.

"Because he's the kind of person I think you would like. I like him very much, so do the other people at the Counseling Center. We've become good friends. He's very kind and gentle. He's sensitive and considerate."

"Is he gay?" I asked.

"I think so, but I'm not sure if he knows that yet. He has a very attractive girlfriend. She desperately wants to marry him, but he sometimes talks to me about a friend of his in Boston, Joel, and the look he gets when he talks about him ... well, I just know. He's never said anything, but I know."

I told her I couldn't relate to a graduate student, because I was on the faculty. "Oh, for heaven's sake, Denny!" she said. "He's a responsible adult! He's more than capable of making his own decisions. He's passed all his exams; he has only the dissertation left. Just talk to him for an hour or so, that's all. You haven't related to anyone socially in...I don't even remember the last time."

"Okay, but just this one time, just for an hour, then you've got to make him go. Don't tell him about my depression, or Jack. I don't want people to talk any more than they already are."

Gary Goodman was tall and broad-shouldered. He was a femininely handsome man, fair and blue-eyed, of English, German and Yugoslavian background. With his striking, youthful good looks, he could easily have passed for a high school athlete, although he was actually 26, 12 years younger than I. He'd been raised with a strict Catholic upbringing and education in Wisconsin. He was a recovering Catholic who had assimilated the best of the Franciscan tradition while gladly unburdening himself of the guilt, authoritarianism and irrationality of Catholicism. He was also a person of great compassion, depth and sensitivity. To support himself during undergraduate school, he'd worked in a psychiatric hospital taking care of abandoned, psychotic, severely retarded elderly men. He said the shock of this experience humbled him and taught him compassion. He actually enjoyed caring for them and wept when one would die. He had studied concert piano for 13 years and loved music and the arts. In his senior year in high school, he'd been elected president of his school. He'd been an altar boy who had lusted after the handsome young priests he served.

I wasn't sexually attracted to Gary, although entirely too many people found him irresistible. I was still quite depressed, so sex held no interest. When he visited us, he was shy, approval oriented, reserved and gentle. I had trouble reading him, but Joyce understood him intuitively because of her own need for approval. He visited us regularly, and I eventually looked forward to seeing him. I wouldn't talk about my depression, Jack or my sexual conflict, but I was open about other areas of my life and showed a sincere and growing interest in him. He and Joyce had a good friendship; he admired her. He used to say that she was the kindest, nicest person he'd ever met. Many people saw her that way. Joyce and I agreed not to discuss my depression with him or my fear about losing my marriage if I related to a male, so he had no way to understand my reticence about becoming close. The weeks became months, and almost six months had gone by when I became quite confused about his behavior one evening and talked to Joyce about it after he left. "You mean you really don't understand, Denny?" she asked. "It's so obvious to me. He's in love with you! Can't you see that?"

I hadn't. I probably didn't want to, because my issue was being able to love, not being loved. A few nights later, on March 26th of 1974—a clear, cold Tuesday evening—Gary came by, and we talked as usual; but he seemed to be on edge and irritated. I asked him about this. He demanded to know when I was going to stop spinning around. I asked what he meant.

"For months, Denny, all you've been doing is spinning around in circles about relating to me. I'm fed up with it! Either you want to relate to me, or you don't! Now, which is it going to be?"

"Well, I want to relate to you, but I don't know. There are things I'm not sure of. I need time."

"That's not good enough! Is it yes or no? Make up your mind."

"Look, I know I've been spinning around, but just give me time. There are important issues we haven't talked about."

"I'll give you exactly five minutes. If I don't have an answer, I'm leaving, and I won't be coming back." I knew he meant what he said.

I went into the kitchen to be alone to think. I checked my watch, five minutes! Five minutes to choose my destiny! Think clearly, I reminded myself, my life depends on it. My God, just five minutes! This is the most important decision of my life, I thought. All my professional training comes down to this one moment. I looked out the window at the night sky and saw a shooting star; I wanted it to be a good omen. Do I really trust my knowledge of Gary and myself enough to make this decision, I asked myself. Then my brain began to race like this: I don't love him, but I could in time. I don't feel any physical attraction. He's tall; his face is beautiful. But I don't feel attraction toward anybody these days; it's the depression. What about Joyce and the boys? Better gay than dead, she said. Am I really gay, or just bisexual? Bisexual is safer, but a lie; I know what I prefer. How can a person not have at least some preference? Does it matter? I am feeling better now that he's been coming over to see me. He's not Jack, but Joyce was right to make me see him. Comparisons don't help love. She has no doubt that he loves me. How can she understand him so easily? I envy that. I don't want just an affair; I couldn't stand that; I couldn't survive it. Why do I hesitate? He's only 26, and I'm 38, almost 40, for God's sake! He's not bothered by the age difference; I am. So admit it! I'm worried I'll get old, and he'll want to leave me! Well, that was honest, at least. So what shall I do? I wish I could just flip a coin. Here, I've got a quarter. Heads is yes. And if it's tails? ...I'd flip again! So now I know, don't I, I said to myself. My whole life rests on my trusting this intuition. So be it! Let life be, I whispered to myself and went back into the living room.

When I returned, I think he already knew; he was smiling. I said, "Yes, Gary, I do want a relationship with you, and I have stopped spinning around. My God, Gary, do you realize all that we've begun this night? Do you understand the enormity of it? Do you?"

Neither of us did, of course, but the next Saturday, with Joyce's blessing, I spent the day at Gary's house. We talked about everything except what was really on our minds. We were both nervous and waited for the other to initiate. We talked all day and into the evening. Gary claims that he never really thought about it, but he cleaned the house, took a shower, dumped cologne all over his smooth body and put clean, fresh sheets on his bed that morning before I came over. By nighttime, both of us were so keyed up by the indirection and suspense that we could hardly look at one another. I couldn't stand it any longer, so I decided to take indirect action: instead of telling him what I wanted, I said, "Gary, be honest with me. What do you really want from me right now?"—as if I didn't know. He became noticeably more anxious and stared at the floor. He found his courage and, with a shy, embarrassed expression, said, "I want you to go to bed with me." Later, he told me he'd never been so bluntly honest before in his life.

Still indirect but pleased, I asked, "What took you so long?" I had to be certain about him.

"Well, you're married and have children." His shy smile indicated that he was pleased with my reply.

"So what?" I said. "What's that got to do with us? I've been waiting all day for you! Joyce knows I'll be staying overnight, that's why she invited you for breakfast tomorrow."

"Well, I was waiting for you!"

We hesitated for a moment, still waiting for the other. My brain rattled on like this: Well, it's his house; he's supposed to be the host; but he's probably waiting for me, because I'm older. I'm nervous; so is he. I wonder if I can be sexual with him. I've never done it with a guy taller than me. Real men aren't supposed to sleep with guys. What am I worried about? I'm married; I've got three kids; they're all boys, too. You don't lose your masculinity just because you sleep with a guy. Gary has no hang-ups in that department. He does what he wants and doesn't care whether it's masculine or feminine. He's got more balls than I do about that. This is silly; we both want the same thing; he's sitting there picking lint off the cushion, waiting for me; I'm cooling out my cortex. The purpose of life is to be on with it.

"So let's be on with it, Gary. Is that your bedroom?"

We felt uncomfortable about the prospect of undressing. Fortunately, Gary had to go to the bathroom, so I quickly undressed and jumped under the sheets. When he returned still dressed, he saw my clothes piled on the floor, making him even more nervous; the way I had my eyes locked on him didn't help either. He took off his shoes and socks, then slowly unbuttoned his shirt, glancing self-consciously at me from time to time. His skin was smooth. He unbuttoned his Levi's and pulled them off. He stood there facing me in his Jockey Classic shorts. We both knew the moment of truth had come. He paused and looked very embarrassed and nervous. Then he quickly bent and stepped out of his shorts. He stood there in a self-conscious, but beautiful, shy pose, his head turned questioningly to one side as I looked at him. I was stunned by what I saw and felt inadequacy and a tinge of fear. I'd never seen a penis that large. It seemed to have an existence of its own, living symbiotically on his body, having obviously outgrown its nest of pubic hair.

Gary turned out the bedroom light and lay down beside me on the twin bed. We talked briefly, nervously, then I began to touch him on his arms, chest and face. He was lying on his back. It would take some time before I would have the courage to touch that other being living down there. I knew quickly that Gary was not very sexually experienced, but he was affectionate; he often said he valued that more than sex; I certainly didn't. I thought briefly about Jack and my depression and reminded myself that reality is only in the present. I let go of the past then and focused on being with Gary in the reality of here and now. When I did, it was as if a high-voltage switch had suddenly been turned on. My need and desire for him exploded, and I held on to him like a drowning man clinging to a life raft.

I'd never had so many orgasms or felt greater passion; I just couldn't stop. He and I made love until we were bathed in full sunlight, the light of a new reality, and I wept in his arms with gratitude for his very existence—and, at long last, for mine. Later, he confessed that he had been awed and over-whelmed by our insatiable sexuality and his realization that he had just made love with a married man, a father of three children, his professor, and his dissertation chairman. This beautiful young Christ of Love Incarnate raised me, like Lazarus, from the living dead to life. Ever since that night of holiest communion, I have always believed that Gary was, indeed, the gift of God in my life, and through him and because of him I live in a state of amazing grace—not too shabby for an agnostic secular humanist.

. . .

Love must be incarnate. Mere imaginings and intentions will never do. Even today, to watch Gary put on a shirt is visual poetry for me. And when I put my hands on his outstretched, naked beautiful body, I touch a most sacred holy altar, like a priest. I have known such ecstasy making love with Gary that it became unbearable, like a madness, a divine madness—the mystical passion of the gods. I still cry in gratitude for him after we make love. I did last night. And tonight I hope I'll be a total basket case!

The best part of my story is that Gary and I have been living together as soul mates in complete faithfulness to one another for 25 blessed years. Our gay friends tell us this period of gay fidelity should be in the Book of World Records. We've had some great fantasies, of course, and several close calls, and some bitchy lovers' spats; but we shared them in truth, as we do every aspect of our lives. Our security is our total intimacy; we don't tolerate non-communication or loneliness. We have no secrets—well, maybe just one or two *teeny-weeny* ones. And where are we living? Where else! Out West, of course! Near San Francisco. We are two who have become one during our quarter century of vibrant happiness. We both know that we shall remain as one...until death do us part.

This long tale of oppression, betrayal, and grief is now resolved. It was Keith whose love so many years ago first gave birth to my soul; but, because of fear, it took nearly three decades and the love of many people before I could become real. But once you are made real and alive through love, you can never be made unreal again! I am a man who loves a man, and I thank reality, human nature, the gods and Gary for that every day of my life.

. . .

Joyce, Gary, the boys and I moved to California and lived together for three years. It was wonderful to be with the man and woman I loved, and I felt whole and complete. We were three psychologists who loved one another; but, as even we knew, trios rarely work. It made good sense for each of us to try. Joyce stayed with me too long, because she loved me, and I loved her. I believe we both still do, but we never speak of that anymore.

I became unable to be away from Gary for even a night to be with Joyce, and soon she was sleeping alone. I'd always prided myself on being a reasonable and rational person, but for the first time in my life, I knew what it was to feel both homicidal and suicidal fits of rage, jealousy and possessiveness. I never knew it was possible to love with the mad ecstasy I feel with Gary. A single frown on Gary's face can turn me into a trembling mass inside. Never have I felt such love or such raw hate! I would happily give my life for Gary at any time, and if a person should ever harm him, I would hunt that person down...and murder him, slowly and painfully. This would be the ultimate violation of my deepest human values, ethics and rationality, but such is the power of my love for him.

Gary and I raised the three boys. After 20 good years of marriage, it made sense for Joyce and me to divorce. Joyce initially allowed my affair with Jack, because it seemed to be no threat. We believed I was merely bisexual, and it added excitement to our relationship. As it became more emotionally serious, she decided to ride it out in the knowledge that most men eventually end their affairs if their wives allow full communication about them and aren't totally rejecting. When Joyce finally admitted that I was gay, always had been and always would be, it made sense for her to try to save me, and the marriage, by including Gary. After all, he was a person she deeply cared for as well, and he cared for her. Never once did he attempt to interfere with our marriage. He never said a word against it, although it caused him pain to share me. Joyce happily remarried one month after our divorce became final. The youngest and the oldest sons elected to live with Gary and me full time while the middle son lived with us half time. We moved near Joyce, so the boys could come and go as they wished. Of the difficulties of that period of time in which she suffered greatly, Joyce has said, "All's well that ends well." She says her new husband is far more emotionally supportive and understanding of her than I was—a view I doubt, but one I very much hope is true for her.

Joyce, who had never had a weight problem, was startlingly beautiful on the day she remarried, but within several years, she gained well over one hundred pounds. I hardly recognized her. Emotionally, at the level of her brain stem, she felt abandoned and betrayed by me, although her intellect knew the truth: we were both victims of the institutionalized homophobia of our society. She became hardened and withdrew socially. She is obsessed and preoccupied now with ornamental plants that can be eaten. It is the central focus of her life, but we have remained friends. Occasionally, I see in her flashes of the Joyce I used to know, that warm, beautiful woman I loved...who loved me, but who is no more.

Love endureth all things; love abideth forever. The pain of my knowledge of Joyce's suffering, the sorrow of my sons, and my own loss will be with me forever. Not one jot of this sad truth can be erased. Would I do it again, knowing now what I know? Yes, instantly. The great tragedy of our human condition is that such choices have to be made, but they do. I chose life—my authentic life.

Gary and I live in a beautiful home with two Burmese cats and two Shetland Sheepdogs, Nickey and Mikey. Our home is filled with art from our many travels around the world. The boys moved away to go to college and are now in their 30's. I admit publicly that each is a self-confessed, practicing heterosexual. They each were even married in public. But we still regard them as being our sons, and if they're happy that way—even though we wouldn't want that for ourselves, considering how unnatural it seems to us, we will always accept and love them, no matter what. After all, they didn't choose to be that way. The benefit of their odd sexuality is that I am now a grateful grandfather.

The boys were 8, 9, and 11 when I decided to tell them about Gary and me. We were still living with Joyce. The family assembled, and I began a nervous, rambling discourse on God, Man and the Universe. It's not easy for a father to tell his sons that he's gay, especially when they've heard antigay remarks every day at school for years from both students and teachers. Brendan, the middle son, interrupted: "Are you trying to tell us something?"

"Well, yes—in a manner of speaking, I am," I said.

"You seem to be beating around the bush," he said. "Are you trying to tell us you're gay?"

"Aaa, well, you see...yes! Exactly!"

And he said, "I knew that! We could hear you come out of your room and go into Gary's room upstairs!"

Nathan, the oldest, was smiling knowingly. Brett, being the youngest, however, looked totally confused and asked what gay meant. He knew only that it was a bad name used for people who were hated. Nathan leaned over and whispered into his ear for awhile explaining, then Brett laughed uncontrollably. This went on until I began to worry that he was really crying, but each time I tried to get him to explain, he only laughed harder. When he did collect his wits, he explained, "I was thinking, wouldn't it be funny if one of you guys got pregnant!" Everybody cracked up then; the tension was gone, and we could talk.

The boys had no difficulty with our relationship. I believe they benefited by the example of two males being loving, cooperative and caring. The relationship among the boys is exceptionally loving and caring; people often comment favorably about that. They were harmed, however, by the vicious, antigay remarks they heard daily for years from homophobic teachers and students. Having a gay father put them in a closet. When I asked each of the boys after they graduated from high school what they'd learned from school, each said he had learned to hate. Even the book they used in their health class said that gays were probably mentally ill and warned high school boys to beware, because gay males were child molesters, it claimed. The book was written by a medical doctor. It showed a picture of an evil-looking man in a trench coat lurking near a school playground. My sons knew these were political right-wing lies, but they were still hurt, especially when they protested to their teachers who, as one would expect, did nothing.

To know a person well is to know their dualities, contradictions. When I told my father that I was gay and that Joyce and I were getting a divorce because of this, he grabbed my hand and said, "My God, Denny, how you must have suffered in your life!" I couldn't believe what I was hearing; such compassion from my father! But a week or so later, I received a letter from my parents totally disinheriting me—a very substantial sum of money—unless I gave up Gary. My mother had warned me when I was 12 about the consequences of being a pervert. I never saw them again, and that was many years ago. They never saw their three grandsons after that time either, because each of my sons refused to relate to them. Although I forgave my parents, for my sake, and tried to reconcile, they've remained true to character and never did. Dr. Samuels had been perceptive and wise concerning them; he had warned me years before.

The institution of the family is an abstraction, a set of rules, social practices, rights and responsibilities. I often ask my clients who are in conflict with their parents if they would want to spend time with them if their parents were just neighbors, not relatives. They quickly see the point. The solution to a problem often consists in not making the problem in the first place. But within me, there will always be a quiet place of love and grieving for my mother and father, a place I will not often visit, for there is no way to end my loss. My sister told me my father slowly died of Alzheimer's disease in an institution. He was tied in a chair for the last two years of his life because he had become violent. He had intended to commit suicide before his disease progressed too far, but he had waited too long. He was psychotic and constantly overwhelmed with emotions. He had no memory or contact with reality. I had always hoped that someday he might let me know him... in spite of everything, I loved him. My mother joined a Bible group to assure a place for herself on the outgoing bus to her heaven. She was killed in a car accident at age 84 shortly after my father died.

My sister, Judy, who didn't have much of a part in my early life, lives in the Bay Area, too, and we became close as adults. She is an astonishingly beautiful and intelligent woman, but she never married or lived with a man. She's not gay. She vividly remembers Keith and his golden curly hair.

. . .

My 25 years of grace and joy with Gary are filled with beloved memories of our many friends, adventures, travels around this precious planet, and laughter and tears—enough to fill a book or two, but these particular memories from a trip to Indonesia are a fitting end to my story:

Some years ago in the spring, Gary, my son Brendan and I went to central Java to see Borabudur, the largest Buddhist monument in the world, built in the eighth century. Nearby is a recently uncovered, perfectly preserved, seventh century Hindu temple. Two handsome, Islamic Indonesian men in their early 20's were sitting on the steps of that temple watching us. Indonesian males particularly noticed Gary, since he is tall, handsome and blond. Earlier, at the Hindu temple complex at Prambanan, a group of Indonesian Moslem high school boys noticed us, and one was so taken with Gary's appearance that he said in perfect English to Gary, as a sincere compliment to him, "You're beautiful! I love you!" His classmates, understanding him, nodded their agreement.

I watched the two young men sitting on the temple steps as they talked with one another. I knew immediately that they loved one another and that each was the joy and life of the other. With astonishment and a feeling of gratitude, I watched one of them stand and reach out his hand to help his beloved friend, and then they casually walked away holding hands the way lovers do. For them, in their culture, this was the most natural of things to do; they were not self-conscious. There they were, two handsome young men expressing their love in the open sunlight. There were tears in my eyes, for we cannot yet do that in America, this land of the free, without fear for our lives.

There is a beautiful artists' village in the lush mountains of the enchanted, volcanic island of Bali. In this village of Ubud, Gary and I stayed in a native cottage overlooking the tropical green canyon of the Campuhan River. Throughout mystical Bali, we were moved by the graceful and natural ways that males related to one another with love and affection. One day, I talked to our houseboy, Ngurah Adnyana, about the relationships of Balinese men. "I notice that males here in Bali express great affection for one another, openly," I said. "Do they also make love with one another?"

He smiled warmly. "Yes, of course!"

"Do many of them do that?" I asked.

"Certainly! Many young men in Bali make love with one another before they are married—with their best friends, of course. Some continue that with their friends even after they are happily married and have children; sometimes for many, many years."

I asked, "How do people here feel about men who make love together?"

"In Bali, love is a natural thing between people. And when we are in love, we want to show that. It doesn't matter if the one you love is a man or a woman. It is best when people love one another, is it not? In Bali, we believe that, in the peak of the act of lovemaking, the lovers are visited by the gods! We believe that. Do you believe that?"

I told him, "For too many years, I didn't. I tried to run from the gods, but now...yes, I do believe that!"

. . .

It was night, and Gary and I were scuba diving in the Banda Sea of the Moluccas near the Spice Islands of Banda-Naria in Indonesia. We went down together deep into the complete darkness of that warm sea to search out with our diving lights the caves in a colorful coral wall where huge white-tipped sharks rest at night, and we found them. One of them, blinded by my light, came from the cave entrance toward me, and it came so close to me that I had to push its massive head away with my flippers.

The beauty and mystery of the tropical undersea world of a coral reef at night is without equal anywhere on this earth, and we knew the photographs from our underwater camera could only hint at what we were experiencing in that magnificent, watery kingdom. Our glowing diving gauges reminded us that the time had come for us to ascend. We turned off the diving lights for a few moments and felt the total disorientation of complete darkness and weightlessness. We could only tell which way was up by feeling the direction of our rising bubbles. We made rapid movements in the water with our hands to watch the bioluminescence this caused. The points and streaks of light against the blackness of the sea were like stars and meteors against the night sky. Then slowly, Gary and I ascended, as if becoming awake. Suddenly, we crossed the barrier between water and air. We inflated our buoyancy vests, signaled our far-distant ship with our lights, and waited for a boat to be launched to pick us up. The underwater current had been very strong; it would be quite some time before the boat would reach us, but that was fine with us. We turned off our lights and held on to one another, bobbing gently there in the tropical warmth of the Banda sea; and we remembered the extravagant, silent splendor living beneath us. Everywhere around us was blackness and distance, and above us, covering to the far circle of the horizon like a vast, vaulted cathedral dome, were the countless stars and galaxies of this universe. And Gary and I, clinging to one another, were floating at the very center of it—like the jelly fish—and with no more real understanding of this ineffable grandeur than they. And that didn't matter at all, because I was so profoundly happy; and I knew at last that I could now die with no regrets about not having lived. I was holding the one I loved who loved me, there in the center of the blackness and grandeur of the universe; and I knew we were a part of this whole— a manifestation of it, and it is eternal. It is us. It is paradise, and I know that now.

The author at 18; photo
by his friend David Rose

Dr. Dennis Hinkle is in private practice in Santa Clara, California. His e-mail address is DNH1@EARTHLINK.NET